MORDECAI

MORDECAI

AN EARLY AMERICAN FAMILY

EMILY BINGHAM

HILL AND WANG

A division of Farrar, Straus and Giroux

New York

Hill and Wang
A division of Farrar, Straus and Giroux
19 Union Square West, New York 10003

Printed in the United States of America
Published in 2003 by Hill and Wang
First paperback edition, 2004

Family tree by Jeffrey L. Ward
Map by Kim Kolarik

The Library of Congress has cataloged the hardcover edition as follows:
Bingham, Emily.
    Mordecai : an early American family / by Emily Bingham.— 1st ed.
    p.   cm.
    Includes bibliographical references.
    ISBN 0-8090-2756-9 (hc : alk. paper)
    1. Mordecai family. 2. Jews—Genealogy. 3. Jews—United States—
Genealogy. I. Title.

CS71.M8345 2003
929'.2'0973—dc21

                                                              2002027488

Paperback ISBN 0-8090-7016-2
EAN 978-0-8090-7016-9

Designed by Abby Kagan

www.fsgbooks.com

1   3   5   7   9   10   8   6   4   2

For Stephen, Cason, Henrietta,

and the family we make

Say not of me that weakly I declined
The labours of my sires, and fled the sea,
The towers we founded and the lamps we lit,
To play at home with paper like a child.
But rather say: *In the afternoon of time*
A strenuous family dusted from its hands
The sand of granite, and beholding far
Along the sounding coast its pyramids
And tall memorials catch the dying sun,
Smiled well content, and to this childish task
Around the fire addressed its evening hours.

—Robert Louis Stevenson,
from *Underwoods*

CONTENTS

PART TWO: LOVE AND MARRIAGE

PART THREE: WILMINGTON

PART FOUR: A NEW HEAVEN AND A NEW EARTH

The Mordecais' America

Maine

Vermont

New Hampshire

Massachusetts

Troy • *Boston*

Wisconsin

New York

Rhode Island

Connecticut

Michigan

Pennsylvania

Philadelphia •

New Jersey

Illinois

Indiana

Ohio

Maryland

Delaware

Virginia

Patriot •

W. Virginia

Richmond •
Petersburg •

Missouri

Warrenton
Raleigh

Kentucky

North Carolina

Tennessee

Wilmington •

Arkansas

La Grange •

South Carolina

Charleston •

Mississippi

Alabama

Georgia

Mobile

Florida

Louisiana

While primarily settled in and around Warrenton, North Carolina, in the years between the American Revolution and the Civil War, the three generations of Mordecais in this volume lived as far north as Boston, Massachusetts, as far west as La Grange, Tennessee, and as far south as Mobile, Alabama.

MORDECAI FAMILY TREE

MYER MYERS
1723–1795
m. (1) Elkaleh Myers-Cohen c. 1753
m. (2) Joyce Mears c. 1767
12 children, including

---

(1)
SAMUEL (Samy)
1755–1836
m. Judith Hays
7 children

(1)
JUDITH
b. May 8, 1762, New York
d. Jan. 9, 1796, Warrenton
m. Jacob Mordecai
6 children

(2)
RICHEA
1769–1837
m. Joseph Marx
9 children

MOSES MEARS
1771–1860
m. Sally Hays
3 children

(2)
REBECCA MEARS
b. April 26, 1776, Norwalk
d. Oct. 1, 1863, Richmond
m. Jacob Mordecai
7 children

---

(1)
MOSES
b. April 4, 1785, New York
d. Sept. 1, 1824, Virginia
m. (1) Margaret Lane 1817
m. (2) Ann (Nancy) Willis Lane 1824

(1)
RACHEL
b. July 1, 1788, Virginia
d. June 23, 1838, Petersburg
m. Aaron Lazarus 1821
(he had 7 children)

(1)
SOLOMON
b. Oct 10, 1792, Petersburg
d. May 7, 1869, Mobile
m. Caroline Waller 1824
8 children

(1)
CAROLINE
b. Aug. 27, 1794, Warrenton
d. Apr. 20, 1862, Raleigh (insane)
m. Achilles Plunkett 1820
(he had 3 children)
3 children, died young

(1)
SAMUEL
b. July 24, 1786, New York
d. April 9, 1865, Raleigh

(1)
ELLEN
b. Nov 10, 1790, Richmond
d. Oct. 6, 1884, Hampton, Virginia

---

(1)
HENRY
1819–1875
m. Martha Hinton 1845
3 children

(1)
ELLEN II
1820–1916
m. Samuel Fox Mordecai
1850 (Sol's son)
2 children

(1)
JACOB
1821–1867

(2)
MARGARET LANE
1824–1910
m. John Devereux 1842
8 children

MARX EDGEWORTH
b. Feb. 6, 1822
d. 1895, Alabama
m. Mary Laurie 1854

ELLEN
b. July 13, 1825
d. 1917, Long Island (?)
m. John Allen 1848
m. Walter Shutt 1862
8 children

Source: Based on Malcolm H. Stern, *First American Jewish Families: 600 Genealogies, 1654–1977* (Cincinnati: American Jewish Archives, 1978), and archival sources.

MOSES MORDECAI
b. 1707, Bonn, Germany
d. May 28, 1781, Philadelphia
m. Elizabeth (Esther) Whitlock *1744–1804*
   (She later married Jacob I. Cohen)

JACOB
b. Apr. 11, 1762, Philadelphia
d. Sept. 4, 1838, Richmond
m. (1) Judith (Judy) Myers
   June 16, 1784, New York
m. (2) Rebecca (Becky) Mears Myers,
   March 21, 1798

JOSEPH
b. Nov. 18, 1764, Philadelphia
d. July 10, 1839
m. Esther Marache
7 children

ISAAC
b. April 11, 1766
m. Zipporah Russell
3 children

(2)
JULIA
b. Aug. 27, 1799, Warrenton
d. Mar. 15, 1852, Richmond

(2)
ALFRED
b. Jan. 3, 1804, Warrenton
d. Oct. 23, 1887, Philadelphia
m. Sara Hays *1836*
6 children

(2)
ELIZA KENNON
b. Aug. 10, 1809, Warrenton
d. Nov. 8, 1861, Richmond
m. Samuel Hays Myers
   (son of Samuel Myers) 1828

(2)
LAURA
b. Apr. 23, 1818, Warrenton
d. July 4, 1839, Richmond
   *(engaged to
   John Brooke Young,
   brother of Rosina)*

(2)
GEORGE WASHINGTON
b. April 27, 1801, Warrenton
d. Feb. 19, 1871, Raleigh
m. Margaret Cameron *1853*

(2)
AUGUSTUS
b. Oct. 5, 1806, Warrenton
d. July 25, 1847, Richmond
m. Rosina Young *1835*
4 children

(2)
EMMA
b. Oct. 6, 1812, Warrenton
d. Apr. 8, 1906, Brevard, N.C.
Unmarried

MARY CATHERINE
b. Sept. 12, 1828
d. July 5, 1850, Mobile
m. Drury Thompson *1848*

JULIA
b. Oct. 9, 1830
d. Apr. 15, 1873
m. D. D. Smith *1856*

EDMUND TROWBRIDGE DANA
1830–1905
m. Frances Colquehoun Trigg *1856*
3 children

CAROLINE
b. Dec. 5, 1844, Richmond
d. Dec 11, 1928, Washington, D.C.
m. Edward Cohen *1865*

MORDECAI

INTRODUCTION

One evening in 1846 in a New York City boardinghouse, a young woman confided her life story to a stranger. She spoke of her father and mother, both dead, and went on to describe her mother's kin, whom she had left behind in Virginia and North Carolina. The Mordecais were a respected and "wealthy family" of Jewish heritage, the listener later wrote, a family composed, it seemed, "of the most wonderful people the world has ever seen."[1]

They were not famous people, although an early Mordecai home stands today as a historic site in Raleigh, North Carolina. Nor, for many years, were most of them particularly well-to-do. Indeed, the Mordecais who populate this book harbored considerable anxieties about whether they as a group or as individuals would ever be truly wealthy or wonderful or, as it happened, even Jewish. Had these things come easily to them, they probably would not have left the thousands of vibrant letters and papers that make it possible to tell their story today. Their real wonder lies in the wholehearted, energetic manner in which they lived—embedded in their times, shaped by them, yet determined not to be entirely controlled by them. In this they capture something quintessentially American.

Encompassing the revolution that formed the nation and the civil war that tore it apart, this book tells the story of three generations of an American Jewish family. It is inescapably, therefore, a history of religious expression, doubt, and searching. But to view the early history of the Mordecais solely in that light is to forget that each Mordecai was as bewildered about what it meant to be a good American in a rapidly changing nation as about what it meant to be a good Jew. Assimilation was a litmus test for each generation of Mordecais. But to see assimilation as only shorthand for a religious conundrum is to miss the real value of their story.[2] Finding a meaningful and appropriate expression of Judaism in the context of their lives was just one of myriad problems the Mordecais faced. They were also attempting to assimilate as patriots and as southerners. Perhaps most fundamentally, they were trying to assimilate as middle-class whites. Being Jewish compounded every aspect of these efforts, but to reduce our understanding of these efforts to their being Jewish is to do the Mordecais—and ourselves—a gross disservice. In the fierce intensity with which the Mordecais set about becoming middle-class Americans, struggling to achieve economic ease and, perhaps more important, mutually admiring relationships with other respectable Americans, can be seen the origins of the American middle class as a class.

The Mordecais needed to define themselves lest others do it for them, and their project began in earnest when young Jacob Mordecai and his wife, Judy, broke from the established Jewish communities of New York and Philadelphia, where they had grown up, and settled first in Virginia and later in North Carolina. Eschewing narrow religious categories, the couple claimed to love "virtue in whatever garb it appeared."[3] Drawing on Enlightenment ideals of religious liberty and a broad fellowship with all who recognized an overarching God, the Mordecais viewed their nation as a promised land, a "happy country," as one daughter wrote, "where religious distinctions are scarcely known."[4]

The Mordecais escaped the severe prejudice and ghettoization that oppressed so many generations of European Jews. Like American Jews then and now, they rejoiced in no longer being forced to inhabit separate ethnic and religious enclaves. Nevertheless, theirs was an overwhelmingly Christian nation, and the assertion that religious affiliation "scarcely" mattered reveals the wishfulness of any American plagued by a sense of difference. Telling themselves that "character and talents" alone would secure "advancement" and community respect, the Mordecais trained their impressive energies on diligent self-improvement via education and an adherence to stringent moral standards.[5]

The Mordecais' patriotism held that integrity and ability would eventually win them a place of eminence, and to nurture these qualities they developed a familial school of thought, feeling, and action that I have called enlightened domesticity. This family whose difference was proclaimed in their name determined to become, as one Mordecai said, a "little faithful band of love and duty," guided by affection, responsibility, and a deep respect for learning.[6] They pledged to stick by one another through thick and thin, to recognize their God but always tolerate others, and to improve themselves and the world around them. In the crucible of their yearning for security, prosperity, and acceptance in a new region, the Mordecais seized upon a protective covenant fusing bourgeois domesticity, intellectual cultivation, and religious liberalism.

Whether one thinks of the family as a lion's den or a haven from a heartless world, it cannot be understood by examining men and women in isolation. The shifting choices and limitations members of both sexes and various generations faced and the ways they affected one another and society cannot be fully disentangled. In their covenant, the Mordecais embraced a set of principles that, while not peculiar to them, have yet to be framed in historical terms. These principles serve to reunite men and women in the often-segregated mansion of domestic and family history.

The logic of domestic enlightenment rested on the liberal concept that reason produced virtue and that virtue produced greater individual happiness as well as social harmony. Even more liberally, enlightened domesticity claimed for women the same capacity for reason and virtue accorded to men. The ideal depended on men and women working closely together to construct a cultivated and cultivating domestic life that promised a supportive, loving family capable of worldly accomplishments. Home became a site of self-improvement through excellence in labor, learning, moral exertion, and teaching, for the ideal was affirmed through its infusion into the hearts of another generation. As a place that lay within the family's power to define, the home could, it seemed, form a productive, cooperative, emotionally and intellectually fulfilling world unto itself, a microcosm of an ideal nation.[7]

Religious and ethnic persecution was rarely visited upon Jews in the early United States. Rather, the Mordecais noted "small slights and neglect," treatment that sometimes wounded family members deeply.[8] Lingering prejudices could explain social snubs from genteel southern-ers; that fellow Jews often dismissed the Mordecais was harder to bear. Their low status in Jewish circles derived from the fact that Jacob was, as one historian termed it, that "rara avis, an unsuccessful Jew."[9] In an irony difficult for the Mordecais to accept or overcome, it was from fel-low Jews that they felt—or perceived—the most stinging anti-Semitic stereotyping.

The Mordecais were different, at least in their being not as success-ful, not as accepted, not as established as their Jewish or middle-class counterparts. Yet they turned their disadvantages into a source of strength. Perhaps they were outside the golden circle of success. No matter. They told themselves over and over that their educated cultiva-tion, not their religion, was the chief factor setting them apart from most Christians they knew. Likewise they told themselves that their sensitive manners and greater intellectual attainments explained the strain they often felt with the Jews they knew. For their part, they would nurture true virtue, which would bring true respect and real ac-complishments, in contrast to what one second-generation Mordecai called "the fluttering, unthinking herd" who sought the fleeting "plea-sures" of wealth, beauty, and popularity.[10] In setting themselves apart, the Mordecais became, in their own eyes, chosen.

It did matter, of course, that the Mordecais were Jews. Being Jewish meant belonging to God's chosen people. But being Jewish raised the bar on their already challenging agenda, and clearing the bar meant at some level ignoring their Jewishness as a source of difficulty. So, when plagued by feelings of alienation "between ourselves and the generality of those with whom we associate," the Mordecais did not blame religious differences or prejudices arising therefrom.[11] Rather, they located the source of their sense of difference in what most family members took to be secular virtues—diligence in work, intellectual accomplishment, and family intimacy.

Getting inside the Mordecai family means getting inside an always dynamic web of ideas and experiences where individuals never operate in a vacuum or as if frozen in time, where gender roles are never entirely clear, where power cannot be divided from affection, where religion cannot be reduced either to pure spiritual experience or to abstract cultural pressures, where parents are shaped by their children as much as they shape them, where North and South are not the polarized regions of many history books, and where myth and desire, sometimes as much as material circumstances, influence the perception of reality. To reconstruct the web is to see history in constant formation.

The Mordecais' three-generation struggle to achieve independence and belonging by infusing the difference announced in their very name with success reflects a recurrent myth about American identity. Becoming American, in particular a successful middle-class American, was a rite of passage available to the virtuous, the diligent, the patriotic. The Mordecais married this myth to their own circumstances and talents, adhering to its assumptions even in the face of its contradictions and often uncertain rewards. Being white, they could do so. As southern lower-middle-class Jews in the years after the American Revolution, they needed to. They relied on the myth of inclusive American identity and opportunity to offset social slights, economic reversals, religious doubts, and eventually a civil war that challenged the very meaning of patriotism. That the Mordecais' faith in that myth was challenged from within the family fold as frequently as from without is perhaps also quintessentially American.

By concerning themselves with domestic enlightenment, strong Mordecai women, with the support of Mordecai men, assumed a central, and broadly secular, role in the protective family covenant. Such roles and possibilities for cooperation clarify the appeal of domesticity to women in both Europe and America in the early nineteenth century.

The ultimate aims of the covenant—to belong, to succeed, and to achieve middle-class success in a period of opening political and economic opportunity—help explain why the same ideals of domestic enlightenment can be found among German Jewish intellectuals during the period of emancipation. Still, the Mordecais were concerned less with the fate of the Jews than with their sense of themselves as citizens of a new nation of great promise and as members of a family that deserved to succeed. Their covenant provided a safe harbor where family members could feel superior to a sometimes tolerant, sometimes hostile, sometimes indifferent, but rarely reliable outside world.

The Mordecais had no corner on precariousness in the first decades of the new nation's history. National and international politics, class lines, a boom-bust economy, geographic expansion, and war all contributed to a general sense of instability. Many Americans did not achieve middle-class status, and given the turbulent economic conditions in the period from 1780 to 1865, many who did could not sustain it. Yet the Mordecais found a way to mark themselves as destined for success and a means to fortify themselves until it came. The individual characters and dramatic results of this family's aspirations are, as one would expect, unique to the Mordecais; but the ingredients that produced those results are woven into the fabric of American families of their times and our own.

PART ONE

THIS LITTLE FAITHFUL

BAND OF LOVE

AND DUTY

A solitary blessing few can find;
Our joys with those we love are intertwined;
And he whose wakeful tenderness removes
Th' obstructing thorn that wounds the friend he loves,
Smooths not another's rugged path alone,
But scatters roses to adorn his own . . .

Small slights, contempt, neglect, unmix'd with hate
Make up in number what they want in weight.
These and a thousand griefs minute as these,
Corrode our comfort and destroy our peace.

—RACHEL MORDECAI'S TRANSCRIPTION OF LINES
FROM HANNAH MORE'S "SENSIBILITY"

1

ROOTS

It took Jacob Mordecai five days to ride by horseback from Philadelphia to Richmond in 1783. Cold and wet, fording flooded rivers, sometimes losing his way on muddy unmarked roads, he was on the move like so many others after Yorktown. The last redcoats had boarded vessels to carry them back across the Atlantic, and everywhere Americans, liberated from the restriction, stagnation, and uncertainty of an eight-year war, set out like Jacob to make new lives or resume those interrupted by the conflict. Possessing few means of his own, the twenty-one-year-old Mordecai had received a boost from his stepfather, Jacob I. Cohen; he was now junior partner in the Richmond mercantile and investment firm Cohen, Isaacs, and Mordecai.[1] Prospects were good for young Jacob, and not only in business, for he had transcended the hardships of his sodden journey by thinking about Judy Myers.

Indeed, his "heart" was so "fraught with affection and esteem" for Judy that as soon as he settled into his quarters at the tavern Jacob unburdened himself in an eleven-page letter to her in Philadelphia. "I feel sensations too great for the narrow limits of expression," Jacob wrote, "[sensations] which my heart has long told me must continue until vast eternity shall terminate an existence you alone can render happy." Judy's hazel eyes and smooth features seemed to dance before him; her lively but tender manner made his "heart beat with pleasure and delight." Jacob concluded the love letter with a plea and a proposal: "Endeavor my dearest girl to render mutual an affection which I have no doubt will tend to make life's tedious length with pleasure roll."[2]

Swept up by handsome young Mordecai and his passionate way with words, Judy soon granted Jacob his "most fervent wish." But in the dark months that Jacob worked and saved in Richmond, Judy waited impatiently for their plan to come to fruition. In the spring of 1784 he was ready and, flush with success, spurred his mount northward to New York, to which Judy and her family had returned after the British withdrawal. There, on June 16, the marriage contract was signed and a ring slipped on Judy's finger; the synagogue's reader consecrated the union, saying, "Blessed art Thou, O Lord, who makest the bridegroom to rejoice with the bride."[3]

It was to prove an alloyed joy.

On the eve of the wedding, in a blow that altered Jacob's career and dampened his confidence for years to come, Judy's father forbade a move to any such godforsaken backwater as Richmond, Virginia. Richmond, he declared, was no place for a Jew and especially no place for a Jewish family. Caution required Jews to stick together, assist one another, and sustain the religious community. He was willing to give Judy up to the enthusiastic young man she adored, but only if the couple remained nearby. A dutiful daughter in every way, Judy could not oppose her father's injunction, and Jacob acquiesced.[4]

Jacob and Judy inhabited the world of colonial-era American Jews, whose population did not exceed two or three thousand.[5] In so tiny a community, Jacob could not afford to anger elders as important as his stepfather and his father-in-law. What should have been the happiest day of his life consequently became one of the most strained. Leaving his bride, Jacob journeyed south to dissolve the partnership with Cohen and Isaacs. Settling accounts proved difficult and then unpleasant. Receiving less than he believed he was due, Jacob returned to New York resenting his father-in-law, feeling betrayed by his mother, and seething in fury at his stepfather.[6]

Part of Jacob's uneasiness arose from the awkward circumstances surrounding his mother, Esther. When Mrs. Cohen met her first husband, Jacob's father, Moses Mordecai, she was a teenager and he was in his fifties. And her name was not Esther. Elizabeth Whitlock, born in England to Gentile parents, embraced her husband's faith and assumed a Jewish name. The means for an orthodox conversion—had she sought one—were unavailable in colonial America, which had no rabbis. Many Jews would look askance at Esther; converts were rare, and without rabbinic supervision of the ritual process the Sephardic synagogue did not recognize their legitimacy.[7]

Moses Mordecai had his own troubling past. At the age of fifty-one, he had crossed from England to America as a convict, one of hundreds of such Jews whom British authorities transported to the colonies to work off their sentences as indentured servants. He completed his sentence, purchased a kit of small items—buttons, buckles, and sewing needles—and set off as a peddler. Somewhere in his travels, Moses met Elizabeth Whitlock.[8] They settled in Philadelphia, where Moses rose from peddling to small-time brokering, but he never achieved prominence as a merchant.[9] An aura of insecurity, deriving from his mother's Gentile origins and his father's shadowy past and marginal career, made for a difficult coming of age, and Jacob's first job threatened to make matters worse.

Early in the Revolutionary War, Moses Mordecai removed Jacob from a highly regarded school despite his talent as a student and set him to work as a clerk for his well-to-do friend David Franks of Philadelphia. Along with Moses Mordecai, Franks had signed the 1765 Non-importation Agreement protesting British taxes. Franks, who had made his fortune in the fur trade and by purveying to the British army during the French and Indian War, was (owing to close family and business contacts with England) in an ideal position when the Revolutionary Continental Congress needed someone to provide food and shelter for British prisoners of war. Franks's bills were to be submitted to the enemy. It could not have taken the young Jacob long to see that his employer was no American patriot; Franks fawned over the English officers in his care and dealt gently with their government. Jacob might not have blamed him. Witnessing Lord Cornwallis's entry into Philadelphia in 1777 "at the head of the British and Hessian Grenadiers, the flower of the British Army," fifteen-year-old Jacob had to admit that they looked invincible. Most of Philadelphia's Jews supported the Revolution, and fled in droves before the advancing British. David Franks and his family, however, remained, as did the Mordecais. Perhaps at seventy Moses Mordecai was too feeble to travel; perhaps he and Esther did not want Jacob to risk his promising job; perhaps their loyalties to those seeking American independence were more tenuous than his signature on the boycott lists suggests.[10]

Franks also exposed Jacob to a family that gave every evidence of attempting to shed its Jewish identity. In business matters, Franks retained strong links to many Jews, but his sister married a British general, and Franks himself married a woman from a prominent Gentile family. Their children were reared in the mother's faith and stood aloof from Jewish religious and social life. Franks's religious and political loyalties were in doubt, and when American forces regained the city, his appointment, and with it Jacob's clerkship, teetered on the brink. In October 1778 it toppled, an unpatriotic letter having been intercepted with Franks's mail. Arrested and jailed, Franks lost his commission and his fortune.[11] Jacob lost his job and, soon after, his father.

Moses Mordecai died on May 28, 1781. If Jacob was present, he, as the eldest son, would have closed his father's eyes and mouth. The mirrors would have been turned to the wall or covered. The family (Jacob had two younger brothers) would watch over Moses's body until it was laid to rest in the Jews Burial Ground. No will was found, but Moses was not poor. The inventory of his estate showed ready cash and real property amounting to £588 as well as notes and bonds worth £2,762. The cash soon ran out, however, and most of Moses's notes could not be redeemed. Rather than join together to meet the hardship, Moses Mordecai's family began going their separate ways, with Jacob sailing to the West Indies, perhaps in an attempt to collect money due the estate or to supervise cargo sales and purchases for import. On returning to Philadelphia in 1782, Jacob met Judy Myers, a refugee from British-occupied New York. The two young people, perhaps while discovering their shared interest in books, fell in love.[12]

While Jacob found love, his mother faced destitution. Jacob could do little to assist her. The account of her husband's estate that Esther submitted to the register of wills showed a paper value of more than two thousand pounds, but that money seemed unlikely ever to materialize. Although she had moved to cheaper quarters, Esther could not pay the rent. Two days after submitting the account, "Widow Mordecai" appealed to Congregation Mikveh Israel for charity and received nine pounds.[13]

Other resources waited in the wings. The same 1782 meeting of the synagogue's board that granted Esther charity also received an application for membership from Jacob I. Cohen of Virginia. At the outset of the Revolution, Cohen joined a company of volunteers in Charleston, South Carolina, but he was soon captured by the British and imprisoned. As a condition of release, Cohen could not return to Charleston, so he went briefly to Philadelphia in 1781, soon after Moses Mordecai's death. Thirty-six and never married, he was ready for an entirely new venture and for a wife. No wonder, then, that as Cohen established his business in Richmond, Virginia (where no marriageable Jewish women resided) that fall and winter, his thoughts returned to the widow in Philadelphia.[14]

Cohen rescued Esther Mordecai from penury, promising aid to her children as well. But their wedding took place over the objections of Philadelphia's Jewish leaders, for Esther Mordecai had once been Elizabeth Whitlock, and as a member of a priestly line, Cohen by law could not marry a convert. In years past, Philadelphia's synagogue Mikveh Israel might not have been so punctilious. But in 1782 the congregation had plans for a new house of worship; it had collected fifteen hundred pounds and, inspired perhaps by hopes for a strong religious presence in the newly independent nation, acquired a renewed emphasis on religious orthodoxy. The synagogue's *adjunta* (council of elders) deliberated for six weeks before ordering its hazan (lay leader) not to perform the ceremony. "Neither are you to be present at the wedding, and are hereby strictly forbid [*sic*] to mention said Cohen or his wife's name in

any respect whatsoever in the synagogue." Any member of Mikveh Israel who participated in the wedding was "subject to censure or punishment," the nearest thing to expulsion. The decision made the
Mordecai boys painfully aware that, though they considered themselves Jews and were perceived as such by the non-Jewish world, when
it came to other Jews, the Mordecais were not quite authentic.[15]

A handful of friends defied the council's order and came to the
couple's side. Haym Salomon, a respected broker and commission
merchant, signed Cohen's ketubah (marriage contract). The elders
dared not retaliate against Salomon, who had pledged to finance
one-third of Mikveh Israel's building costs. As for the marriage ceremony, Cohen himself, by virtue of his priestly heritage, may have performed it.[16]

Jacob hated being drawn into the mire. He tried hard to please and
had, according to his limited means, given generously to Mikveh Israel's building campaign.[17] On account of his mother's wedding, he
now faced rebuke, even ostracism, from the congregation. On the
other hand, his stepfather promised to make him his partner in Richmond. Falling in love with Judy seemed, at first, only to complicate
matters further.

The heterodoxy Esther Mordecai and Jacob I. Cohen exhibited in
1782 troubled Jews who were committed to preserving religious law
and ethnic tradition. One of these was the formidable father of Jacob
Mordecai's beloved. Myer Myers had been a highly sought and successful colonial silversmith in New York City.[18] Revolution interrupted this
comfortable renown. In 1776, as the British advanced on the city, Myers
abandoned his home and business and fled with his family to Connecticut. In 1782, the family moved to American-held Philadelphia,
where his wife had relatives who could shelter them. When British
troops finally abandoned New York, Myers returned "from exile," pro-
claiming loyalty to "a Constitution wisely framed to preserve the ines-
timable blessings of civil and religious liberty."[19] But Myers was wise
enough to realize that tolerance carried its own dangers. To survive as
God's chosen people, to keep their faith, Jews must live together and in
accordance with the law. Collaborating in business, establishing and
maintaining houses of worship, assisting the needy in their midst, and

social life itself—all these both sustained and depended on the culture and faith that set Jews apart from the majority of Americans. The smallness of their numbers made these matters particularly pressing. In this context it made sense that most Jews grouped in New York, Philadelphia, or Charleston, South Carolina.

When Jacob Mordecai called on Myer Myers to ask for his daughter's hand, the young man was not in a position of strength. Esther Mordecai's marriage to Jacob I. Cohen was fresh in Myer Myers's mind; he knew all the members of the Philadelphia *adjunta* and almost certainly approved their ruling against the wedding.[20] By taint of his mother, Jacob was a suspect Jew. Myers also recalled the embarrassment brought on the Jewish community by Jacob's former employer, the British sympathizer David Franks, now a fugitive living in England.[21] Further, in taking a position with Cohen, Isaacs, and Mordecai, Jacob demonstrated more pluck than promise, seeking success in hinterland Virginia rather than in an established Jewish community (so far as one existed in the new nation) such as Philadelphia or New York. Of course, this apparently bright young man could not be entirely blamed for his unfortunate associations; but by standing by his mother's marriage and accepting Cohen's assistance, Jacob had taken a road his future father-in-law found troubling at best. Myer Myers's conditional blessing on Jacob and Judy's marriage was tantamount to a conditional acceptance of the young husband-to-be's merits as a Jew, an American, and a merchant.

THEIR OWN VINE AND FIG TREE

I t galled Jacob to start again from scratch. But he had Judy. Her
companionship banished much of his gloom. Jacob duly joined
his in-laws' New York congregation, Shearith Israel, and a few
weeks before the wedding his luck turned just as Judy assured him it
would.[1]

Myer Myers may have grumbled when Haym Salomon—the rich
and respected broker who defied the Philadelphia *adjunta* by signing
the ketubah for Jacob Cohen and Esther Mordecai—proposed opening
a New York office that Jacob would operate. But Salomon was a man of
character whose religious and political loyalties were beyond reproach.
He had extended credit to—and refused repayment from—Revolutionary leaders, including James Madison, and after Cornwallis surrendered, Salomon helped stabilize the United States' currency. So reliable
was Salomon in all his dealings that, according to the chronicles
of early Philadelphia Jews, "his endorsement on a note made it 'un-
deniable.' "[2]

Jacob Mordecai would manage auctions for Salomon, along with the usual loans, currency exchange, and wholesale commodity brokerage.[3] But, in a pattern that would repeat over the years, Jacob, in hopes of enhancing his income, took risks beyond those required by his position with Salomon. One such risk resulted in a ship's cargo being confiscated and another's stolen.[4] Judy soothed her husband's "grief and disappointment" and never scolded him for the losses, which yet greater troubles soon overshadowed. Eight months after forming the partnership with Jacob, Haym Salomon died. Where could Jacob turn now? By early 1785, commerce had become almost hopeless. The closing of British West Indian ports to American trade led to a collapse in prices; American paper currency depreciated against foreign standards; everywhere financial confusion reigned. The resulting depression—one of several that would plague Jacob Mordecai and his growing family—lasted most of the decade.[5]

Just over nine months after her wedding, Judy Mordecai delivered the first of seven children. The couple named him Moses after his paternal grandfather. Fifteen months later, in July 1786, a second child, Sam, arrived and was circumcised under his grandfather's approving eye.[6] The ceremony symbolized God's covenant with the Jews that they would inherit the promised land of Zion; it also reaffirmed Jacob's bond to his religious heritage. Diligently holding to his side of the bargain with his father-in-law, Jacob took an active part in Jewish communal life, and yet his standing among other Jews, and in the wider social world of the nation's emerging middle class, was increasingly dubious. His New York career was faltering badly.[7] He kept thinking of Virginia.

Jacob wasn't alone in looking to Virginia. Judy's brother Samy and his partner were anxious to recoup their fortune in the wake of their recent bankruptcy. Judy adored her brother and pressed him to include Jacob in their plans, for she held dear the idea of their all living together. It was not to be. A quarrel with Jacob over an outstanding obligation, and perhaps a fear of overextending themselves, led the two men to forge ahead alone. They leased a storefront in Norfolk, Virginia, selling an array of items, "very good and cheap!" The venture lacked the glamour of their prior transatlantic trade, but business flourished, and the partners restored their damaged mercantile reputations.[8]

Jacob was indignant. In 1784 Judy and Samy's father had forbidden him to settle in Virginia. By obeying that injunction, Jacob seemed to have missed the boat.[9] Three years later, in consideration of the lack of opportunity in New York and his son Samy's relocation to Norfolk, the silversmith relented. Jacob and Judy migrated south.

But they went not to Norfolk, nor even to Richmond, but to Goochland County, northwest of the capital, where (perhaps with a loan from his stepfather's booming firm) Jacob opened a country store. The move from wholesale to retail trade marked a step down in status; the move from New York to a rude, unnamed crossing of paths in the wilderness marked not just a step down but a step away—away from partnerships that had always served Jacob ill, away from parents and stepparents, in-laws and siblings, and away from the network of Jews in which Jacob and Judy grew up. Despite her close attachments to her family, Judy did not complain about the isolation. She set to making her own little family's home as cheerful as possible. In the heat of their first summer in the South, Judy gave birth to their daughter Rachel.[10]

The Mordecais' wanderings had not come to an end, however. Goochland County was outside the plantation district, and business proved poor. Before two years passed, they gave up the store and moved into Richmond.[11]

Jacob cast about for opportunities. He could not blame friends and relations for hesitating to open their purses or offer him recommendations. The more generous of these decided that Jacob's ill fortune wasn't really his fault, though in granting him reprieve from his failings as a merchant, they called further into question his heritage as a Jew. Their generosity extended to concluding that "his native business instinct . . . [had] been dulled through having a mother of Gentile blood." Under the stereotype of Jewish mercantile acumen, Jacob was dismissed by his own people as a half-breed.[12]

Judy, who had lost her home more than once during the American Revolution, refused to be discouraged. But with the arrival of their fourth child, her sunny outlook began to dim. After delivering Ellen, Judy was stricken with "an inflammation of the womb . . . attended with very painful and debilitating symptoms." The crisis shocked Jacob into action. He sent seven-year-old Moses to live with his Myers grandparents in New York and transferred Judy and the younger children to Petersburg, Virginia. In Petersburg they lived near Judy's brother Samy Myers, who, with two teenage brothers fresh from New York, had moved to the city considered "*the* tobacco market" of the day. Judy's reunion with Samy compensated in part for Jacob's frequent absences as he scouted a location for yet another country store.[13]

Jacob's determination to get the family peacefully settled and comfortably provided for escalated again when the birth of yet another child brought Judy's symptoms back "with redoubled violence." She couldn't nurse baby Solomon for months and rarely left her room. Though writing made her tremble with dizziness, Judy found strength enough to press her parents not to spoil their grandchild Moses and thereby "undermine the structure I have endeavored to raise since his infancy." It was a structure experienced by all the Mordecai boys and girls and one that met Jacob's hearty approval, for Jacob and Judy shared, along with their affection, a commitment to education and a strong belief in the potential for rational self-improvement.[14]

Affection, education, and improvement were of little value without good health, and despite the climate's ill effect on Judy more Myerses came south. Judy's younger sister Richea arrived to take over the household management, supervising not only the baby but the feeding and care of Sam (six), Rachel (three), and Ellen (barely two) as well. The doctors predicted that Judy would recover as long as she did not become pregnant again, yet there were days when she feared death might overtake her before she and Jacob were reunited. While Judy remained behind with the children in Petersburg, Jacob marshaled his efforts for yet another business venture a hundred miles to the south.[15]

The Mordecais' years of wandering ended in a small county seat in the middle of North Carolina's plantation country. Warrenton was far more isolated than Richmond or Petersburg or even Goochland

County in Virginia; there were no "connexions"—Jewish or otherwise. Indeed, Warrenton was precisely the wilderness Myer Myers had feared. Yet it was the backdrop against which the family defined the myth that would shape not only the living Mordecais but many who came after.[16]

As newcomers and as Warrenton's first Jews, the Mordecais were constantly in the public eye. Established only fifteen years earlier and now inhabited by some two hundred souls, half of whom were enslaved, Warrenton was a village where everyone knew everyone. It was imperative that Jacob's store become a trading place both pleasant and fair. Jacob's customers would ideally regard the store as a gathering site for political debate, gossip, and games of backgammon. When the county court was in session, people from all around would come to litigate, trade, and socialize. Court days would also mean amusements: cockfighting, horse racing, and liquor, all making for a busy time at the shop. Farmers came in to buy salt and molasses and luxuries such as ribbons or books, most paid for by tobacco, the region's chief commodity. Small producers covered purchases by promising next year's crop, which some farmers entrusted Jacob to sell for them. In short, because tobacco served as the local medium of exchange, the Mordecais became as dependent as any planter on the leaf's fluctuating market.[17]

Jacob readied for the day Samy Myers would escort Judy, Richea, and the children to Warrenton. Through the winter of 1792–1793, as President George Washington laid the cornerstones for the White House and the Capitol in the new District of Columbia, Jacob lived alone, laying his own foundations—stocking and manning the store and overseeing improvements to the house next door. Following Judy's directions, he smoked enough beef and laid in enough soap and candles to last the year.[18] Separation, meanwhile, had underscored his affection for his wife: "Think me not enthusiastick in any thing but love for thee," he wrote on a springlike day in February as their reunion drew near. His wife's health, his greatest "treasure," his "means of happiness," must not be further risked. She must once again "be a hearty woman."[19]

Their new "country" life pleased Judy. She set out to make a home where their children would grow up safe and happy, a home whose order and affectionate relations would satisfy her craving for community and security. Her siblings had supplied intimacy and stability to Judy in a household ruled by the rather authoritarian Myer Myers and uprooted by war. Samy was her "best brother." Richea she prized, and she always carefully sent love in her letters home to the babies of the family, Becky and Benjamin. Accomplishing this level of intimacy and mutual support required care, particularly in rearing and educating offspring. Her children deserved no less. But they must first be together, and to this end Judy called Moses back from New York.[20]

In the spring of 1794 the Mordecais showed signs of fast becoming the kind of family Judy had worked and wished for. Moses's return coincided with Richea's departure; she was to marry Joseph Marx of Richmond. Richea would be severely missed, both as a beloved relative and as a substantial contributor to the household. To compensate for this loss, Jacob contracted with a neighbor for the hire of a female slave "to superintend family affairs"—an indication of his improved business success, solvency, and position.[21]

Then Judy was pregnant again. She and Jacob recognized the danger; the pregnancy contradicted the advice of every doctor they had consulted as well as her own stated desires. Miraculously, the birth brought about none of Judy's former agonies. She recovered well, and she and Jacob must have rejoiced in their blessings.[22]

The blessings were many. They named the baby Caroline after the state where they had finally united comfort, health, and happiness. Jacob breathed more easily. Judy was strong, and the house was filled with promising, delightful children. Warrenton had welcomed the store, and Jacob expected the profits soon to erase his unpleasant debt to his stepfather's firm. Indeed, he had never felt so at ease: people deferred to his education and metropolitan background; he joined the Masonic lodge.[23]

The children advanced wonderfully. Moses and Sam attended the town's classical academy. The girls stayed home with Judy, whose skills as a teacher Jacob suspected surpassed those of the celebrated local schoolmaster. Judy gave six-year-old Sam a patch of garden to lay out and plant for himself. Rachel and Ellen learned to read and write at such early ages that they "excite[d] the admiration of strangers"; instructed in needlework, Rachel and Ellen, at five or six years old, performed a significant portion of the household sewing. Using techniques derived from the most advanced pedagogy of the time, Judy offered praise in place of "pecuniary rewards." From their mother, these children learned that happiness could always best be found at one's own fireside and in the service and society of one's own family.[24] This keen sense of the power of domesticity would preoccupy middle-class women and families for most of the following century. Ironically, having abandoned urban New York for Virginia's wilderness, Jacob and Judy had forged a life as authentic, as true to their dream of belonging within the new nation, as they could have hoped for.

In early 1796, however, it grew difficult for the Mordecais to praise and thank "the Father of Mercy" as Judy daily had them do. On New Year's Day another sibling was born, fifteen months after Caroline. Judy appeared strong in the months before delivery, but the experience was too much for the infant, who quickly died—and for its mother, too. The Sabbath afternoon of January 9, Judy's brother Joseph and several Warrenton neighbors joined Jacob at her bedside. With "tear swoln [sic]" eyes, they heard Judy's traditional prayer for forgiveness: "May my present sufferings be atonement for all my transgressions." Near midnight, crying, "I shall die, I shall die!" she did so as Jacob held her in his arms.[25]

Joseph Myers fulfilled his sister's deathbed request that he read the funeral service. At this remove from the American Jewish enclave of her father's New York, Judy's concerns for appearances and acceptance had taken a practical turn. She had asked Joseph to "omit such parts 'as from their novelty will make my Mordecai appear ridiculous.'" Judy, who held primary responsibility for shaping the family's religious life in Warrenton, pointed out that they lived "among people unaccustomed to our religious rites"; she did not want to arouse attention.[26]

Jacob himself was frantic with grief. More than two weeks later, he confessed to his Masonic brethren that, much as he tried to acknowledge God's will, "I find there is no reasoning down our feelings when the heart is corroded by affliction." He was unable to compose himself. Three months after Judy's death, he repeated the same thing to his mother: "To reason down the feelings of the afflicted heart is impossible." He said that his life had no value, except as it might "promote the happiness of my little orphans."[27]

That summer, Jacob composed for the six children a long letter delineating Judy's life and describing her death. The letter amounted to a covenant, setting forth the precepts that would keep Judy's influence alive among them. The manuscript pointed a way out of the confusion they faced in light of their loss, but also as Jews and as newcomers to the South and as Americans in a free society. The letter became for the Mordecais a road map to virtue.

The document constituted the legacy of Jacob and Judy's union, for in 1796 there was little to show in the way of worldly goods or success. However, in his portrait of Judy's life Jacob consecrated the founding of a family that was different, chosen, and not simply because they were Jews. Religious duties received but passing acknowledgment in Jacob's letter to his and Judy's children. The spirit of the covenant was emancipated, and reverently so. What Jacob consecrated in this document was the family's commitment to aim for the highest levels of intellectual cultivation, family solidarity, and dedication to useful work. The implication was that these qualities would raise the Mordecais above others, nourishing their spirits and encouraging them to earn respect and recognition—not so much as Jewish Americans but as Americans who happened to be Jewish.

The covenant required that Jacob use reason when governing the children and never lose his self-control. He was to be "their best friend to whom they may with confidence unbosom themselves." Theirs was to be a loving family, sensitive to feelings, yet also a rational family that valued education, ideas, and books, and a liberal family that tolerated people of all faiths, embracing "virtue in whatever garb it" might appear.[28]

The demands on the children were broad, almost elastic, but stringent nonetheless. They were to "fulfill [their] duties in life." They were to improve themselves and the world around them yet remain modest at all times. They must keep faith by giving glory and thanks to God in some way every day, although this need never interfere with their work or play. Finally, the Mordecais must "foster and protect each other."[29]

CAST DOWN AT THE FEET
OF FORTUNE

As John Adams succeeded George Washington as president and hostilities flared in Europe, Americans wondered how the fragile young nation would weather the transfer of power. No doubt, national and international politics was the stuff of Warrenton gossip, but the Mordecais could be excused for their focus on matters closer to home. Judy's death had brought its own anxious season in the Mordecai household. Jacob's 1796 covenant with Moses, Sam, Rachel, Ellen, Sol, and Caroline was a valiant effort to stabilize the family while recognizing their terrible loss. As memories of their mother faded, the covenant became a carapace supplying the shelter they required, both as orphans and as outsiders seeking to establish their identity as enlightened and respectable Americans. Growing up, each of the Mordecai children made the father's inspiring words his or her own, but tensions surrounding the fulfillment of the ideal became apparent almost immediately.

For instance, the domestic rearrangements and geographic separations in the months following Judy's death seemed like salt in the wound. Another slave was hired to keep house and care for the toddler Sol. Moses (eleven) and Sam (ten) would remain in Warrenton to continue their schooling. But, in what might have been read as a violation of the covenant to foster and protect his children, Jacob sent the girls away. Caroline (almost two) went to her aunt and uncle, Richea and Joseph Marx. The elder daughters, Rachel (seven) and Ellen (six), accompanied by Uncle Samy, went to live in New York with their Myers grandmother, the old silversmith having died the year before. Shortly thereafter Samy married the wealthy Judith Hays of Boston, and with Rachel and Ellen in tow, the newlyweds arrived in Richmond to make their new home. Enrolled at Mr. Hodgson's School for Young Ladies (which advertised classes in "Reading, writing, cyphering and all kinds of knowledge, needlework and female accomplishments") and among near relatives, the girls nevertheless missed Warrenton keenly. Home seemed frighteningly far away.[1]

Father and daughters kept in touch by letter. The pleasures of correspondence depended on the girls' obedience to Jacob's "desires" —desires he promised would always be reasonable. A primary expectation was that they perform well in school. Their studying hard would gratify him, he told them. More important, he said, the knowledge they gained would bring countless "pleasures" and "advantages." (And education did not end with school. Jacob quizzed anyone who finished a book as to what new things she had learned from it.) Once it was clear that Rachel and Ellen were succeeding in the classroom, the topic of schoolwork fell from the letters, and matters of comportment took precedence. In this department, the girls struggled to make their father happy or, as he made clear, to "merit" his love. They must rise early, "avoid every species of sullenness," and be always neat and clean. Kisses often followed fast upon injunctions—perhaps in response to bruised feelings. Yet over and over Jacob signaled that his love depended on their success. He relied on such standards—and on the carrot and stick of his affections—both to prove his parental competence and to ease any doubt as to his family's respectability.[2]

Three years passed. After such a long separation, Rachel and Ellen wanted more than anything to resume the intimate and protective family life their mother had taught them to value and Jacob had vowed to foster. Resumption, however, was impossible, for the Mordecai family of 1799 was not the one Rachel and Ellen had left. It had a crucial new member. Jacob had determined that to raise his family properly and recapture some portion of life's happiness he should remarry. In 1798 he proposed to mild-tempered Becky Myers, Judy's baby sister.

When six and seven years old in New York, Becky had known Jacob as her newlywed sister's husband. Fifteen years later she again met her brother-in-law and agreed to join him in Warrenton as his wife.[3] Never as forceful or resourceful as her sister, aware that Jacob did not love her as he had Judy, unskilled at soothing his wounded feelings, and easily hurt when he did not seek her counsel, Becky struggled to gain a purchase as Mrs. Mordecai. Introducing a new person into the family circle, even an aunt, was uncomfortable and hinted at the difficulties the Mordecais would later have assimilating in-laws. Not surprising, one way Becky and Jacob eased the strain was to delay the return of the three girls. Long months passed. Caroline, a tractable four-year-old, came home early in 1799. Rachel and Ellen's return was put off until that summer. By this time Becky's status as "Mama" had been secured in fact if not in feeling; there was not only a new mother but a new sister to meet—Julia Judith, born May 17, 1799.[4]

The girls continued to view their father as a benevolent and affectionate patriarch; any animus at their long exile was directed elsewhere. When Jacob retrieved his daughters from Richmond, he left his son Sam in the city to learn the merchant's trade. Sam went to work in the countinghouse of his uncle and namesake, Samuel (Samy) Myers, learning a trade if not earning a living. Jacob objected to Sam's taking wages because he was provided room and board in the Myers household and training at no cost. Moses stayed in Warrenton, assisting at his father's store. Enterprisingly, the brothers soon started a business, as Sam recalled, "on the smallest scale imaginable," in which Sam purchased and sent from Richmond to Warrenton India rubber, candies, nuts, and notebooks for Moses to sell to the students at Warrenton's male academy.[5]

The children from Jacob's first marriage were old enough not to require their stepmother's constant care but young enough to require some sort of supervision. A girls' school, opened in 1802 by an English couple, the Falkeners, proved a boon. With their school situated conveniently on Warrenton's Main Street, the Falkeners taught Ellen, Caroline, and Sol, who attended there briefly before moving over to the male academy. Central to the curriculum were decorum, penmanship, and needlework.[6] Rachel remembered this period as a carefree, if uninteresting, time. Her stepmother made few demands. Rachel honed her sarcastic voice in correspondence with Sam, mocking the building boom in their drab little village—a well, a market, a few two-story houses. The dreariness of Warrenton was relieved for Rachel by visits to the plantation homes of school friends and prolonged stays with relatives in Richmond.[7]

Except during these occasional visits by his sister, Sam was miserable. He had not been working long in Richmond before he made the surprising and unpleasant discovery that his mother's beloved brother Samy possessed, as Sam phrased it, "a passionate temper not soon appeased." The months in the countinghouse crawled by. He escaped by reading whatever book came into his hands and studiously behaved within the boundaries of respectable society. Patience, hard work, and mentoring from a more benevolent uncle, Samson Myers, kept him focused on advancement. In the summer of 1802, Sam "attended to the books and most of the business" at Uncle Samy's firm, and he was awarded a salary of $150 per annum. He saw little of it, however. His first earnings were needed back in Warrenton.[8]

Jacob's persistent debts added urgency to the Mordecai children's commitment to overcome the obstacles that had plagued their father's career and to carry forward the vision of family happiness and success that they read in the 1796 covenant. Moses, Sam, Rachel, Ellen, Sol, and Caroline distinguished themselves through their attention to education, domestic affection, familial solidarity, and, particularly among the boys, honest enterprise.[9]

The role of religion, and its relative importance within the covenant, were less clear. Each Mordecai struggled individually with the tension between reason and received belief, between romance and religious restrictions, and between personal autonomy and family identity. But for the first decade and a half of the nineteenth century there were no marriages to divide them, and the covenant supplied sufficient wiggle room to prevent conflict over its interpretation. By virtue of his presence in Richmond and his association with the Jewish community there, Sam supplied the family's links to orthodoxy. In 1805 he provided dates for the holidays—Rosh Hashanah, Yom Kippur, and Sukkoth. Their strict observance would have caught all Warrenton's attention. The store would have been closed. The children would have missed several days of school. But close religious observance was not compulsory for Jacob, his immediate family, or his Myers in-laws in Richmond. As a justice of the peace, Jacob spent many Saturdays occupying his seat on the county court; he may also have kept the store open on the Sabbath. But then, he did not face congregational fines or even excommunication as Jews in New York or Philadelphia did. The charter of Richmond's Congregation Beth Shalome (the community had no house of worship until 1821) contained no such regulations. Besides, Judy herself had made a point of bending religious practice to suit their lives in Warrenton.¹⁰

Just where Jacob and his family fit—either in Warrenton, where they partook, sometimes uneasily and sometimes comfortably, in local social life, or among other Jews—remained uncertain. On Yom Kippur in 1805, Jacob found his attempts to expiate his sins, forgive others, and adjust himself to God's will difficult. His mother's death the previous year reopened old wounds. The tiny Richmond congregation refused her a place in the Jewish burial ground, and Esther was interred in the cemetery of St. John's Church. Even after more than forty years of living as a Jew, his mother (and by extension Jacob himself) remained illegitimate in their eyes.¹¹

Jacob found a target for bitterness even closer to home. He began to feel that Warrenton was turning on him. When Robert Johnson, the son of a prominent Warren County planter who also acted as court clerk, opened a mercantile establishment in town, Jacob panicked. Absent Judy's calming influence, his fears mushroomed until he grew convinced that Johnson was circulating malicious rumors to drive away his customers. In a fit of pique, Jacob filed suit against Johnson alleging libel and seeking damages.¹²

A deep gloom settled over him. Becky felt helpless to alleviate her husband's mounting cares, and Jacob resisted bringing her into his confidence as he waited for action in his case. None came. In March 1806 he went to Richmond to retrieve Rachel from her winter sojourn and in hopes of securing badly needed capital for his business. There Jacob celebrated Passover, perhaps praying for deliverance from his troubles. At night, he tossed and turned. Anxiety and depression weakened his judgment, and in an effort to recover his business Jacob recklessly invested in a large load of tobacco.[13]

All shipping had become exceedingly risky because of hostilities between the United States and Great Britain—tension that would prompt President Thomas Jefferson to impose a complete trade embargo. The value of Jacob's tobacco plummeted, and, as Rachel wrote, he "found himself a ruined man." Rachel's description suggests how powerfully this turn of events impressed his children. "Everything was immediately given up to the creditors," she continued, and Jacob, father of ten, "found himself reduced . . . to absolute poverty." For a time he could hardly function.[14]

Lacking good options that summer, Jacob accepted a friendly offer from the trustees of Warrenton's male academy: he would, Rachel explained, "fill the place of steward at the [school], obtaining a house, rent free, and boarding the students." It was a great change—certainly a step down. It meant selling their house and, for the older children, ending childhood itself. It meant leaving the garden where Sam had grown vegetables, the piazza where they played on rainy days, the home where their "tender mother" had taught Rachel and Ellen to read and sew and pray—"and where she breathed her last." All this was to be exchanged for the steward's house, one of the town's improvements that only recently had been the butt of Rachel's sarcasm.[15]

Hardship forced the Mordecais to draw more heavily than ever on their greatest resource: the enlightened domestic life they had embraced as a model since Judy died. As they performed the melancholy task of packing and prepared to meet the household needs of a herd of unruly schoolboys, the Mordecais affirmed their faith in themselves as chosen people. Their talents might be overlooked by outsiders, but under the elder children's influence they began to perceive themselves as a family different from other families, better than other families. As they circled the wagons, modesty sometimes took a back seat.

Eighteen-year-old Rachel and her elder brother Sam made a pact to correspond regularly, not only to convey family news but also to enter into each other's thoughts, troubles, hopes, and dreams. The exercise opened a world for Rachel: with Sam she overcame the embarrassment she sometimes felt in expressing her views and perfected her already marked skill as a correspondent. She pushed herself to improve and drove Sam to do so as well, subjecting his letters to thorough criticism and requesting the same in return. Sometimes she drove too hard, berating him so much for one "unfortunate epistle" that he almost regretted sending it. But if he had not sent it, he would have been accused of emotional neglect.[16] The letters mattered so much because they testified to the affection and intellect that allowed the Mordecais to transcend their fallen status.

At this nadir of their fortunes the Mordecais made a most astonishing and cheering discovery: congenial neighbors. The Kennons were drawn to Warrenton by its male academy, headed by Marcus George, a graduate of Trinity College, Dublin. Elizabeth Kennon, the recent widow of a Virginia planter and politician, enrolled three sons and settled into rented quarters with her daughter, Sally. There had never been any people in Warrenton whose company—charming, warm, and intellectual at once—appealed so much to the Mordecais, who generally showed more interest than most Warrentonians in books and the art of conversation. Rigorous reasoning, wide knowledge, sharp humor, and Romantic feeling were all prized. For once it seemed they had found real sympathy, and from outsiders they judged to be of similar enlightened aspirations and merits.[17]

The Kennons eased the Mordecais' transition to Oakley Cottage, the steward's house that took its name from the tall trees shading the academy grounds. Among its inmates was the sought-after instructor Marcus George. Rachel related to Sam how the schoolmaster's "excessive bashfulness" took several weeks to "wear off" enough that he could "speak to be understood, play with the children, and now and then pass a few words with us."[18] At the same time, the new drawing and music teacher at the Falkeners' girls' school, Alexander Calizance Miller, impressed the family. Reputedly "a very handsome man and an excellent companion," Miller claimed to have fled France in 1797 after fighting in Napoleon's German campaigns. Rachel, generally slow to praise, was smitten. Ellen began secretly to fall in love.[19] Enrollment at the academy was up—good news since the Mordecais' income came directly from the boarding scholars—and Jacob busied himself hiring and supervising the slaves who cooked, cleaned, and did laundry for the students.[20]

Amid the relative calm, the Mordecai children progressed within the spheres open to them, each according to his or her own talents and ambitions. Moses set his sights on a legal career. For a Jew to engage in retail or wholesale trade was predictable, indeed almost expected; the law, however, was not a profession associated with Moses's forebears, because most judicial systems excluded Jews from the bar. Having obtained his license to practice, Moses moved to Petersburg and worked under an established attorney, earning $450 per annum with free room, board, and medical care. He expected to have enough cash left at the end of the year to buy his own law books. This did not satisfy Moses, however, who complained to Sam, "I could do no better."[21]

Solomon, whom the family called Solly and who called himself Sol, spent his time wringing a superior education from the male academy. At fifteen he was versed in Virgil and embarked upon the study of Greek. His learning far exceeded that of Rachel and Ellen—the classics, higher math, and chemistry being outside the realm of female education. If Moses was to be their first lawyer, the family, in keeping with its commitment to upward mobility, expected Sol to be the first Mordecai to attend college.[22]

Given the circumscribed opportunities for self-improvement open to them, the Mordecai women flourished, and one, Rachel, excelled. Rachel, like her parents—Jacob courted Judy with Goethe's *Sorrows of Young Werther*—and almost all her siblings, loved books and ideas. According to Ellen, Rachel had the kind of mind that simply absorbed knowledge. She seemed to learn without studying or the guidance of any teacher and, even when a child, read whatever was in the house.[23]

Ellen did not display her older sister's aptitudes. But she had more fun than Rachel when it came to socializing.[24] Their characters were vastly different. Super-rational, even-tempered Rachel always seemed perfect in her manners. Ellen's moodiness made her playful and lighthearted one moment, then sulky and depressed the next.[25] Next to Rachel, Ellen felt inadequate. While a new schoolmaster, William Crawford, who had assumed the helm at the male academy, bored Ellen ("his conversation is so philosophical that no one can comprehend it but Rachel"), he fascinated the elder sister.[26]

Whatever Crawford's charms—or lack of them—the Mordecais now depended on him for their meager livelihood. Marcus George had surprised all Warrenton when, after years of contented bachelorhood, he suddenly married. His new preoccupations had a deleterious effect on the school, and by the end of Jacob's first year as steward the academy had steeply declined. The public examinations (traditionally held at term's end to demonstrate the students' progress) proved a fiasco.[27] Throughout the Christmas break, the Mordecais waited for news of George's replacement and felt grateful when Crawford was induced to take the job. The Mordecais continued at Oakley Cottage, albeit a little uncertainly. Marcus George's departure wasn't the only cloud threatening the school. Congress had recently voted to halt all foreign trade, cutting directly into the livelihood of tobacco planters whose children made up the academy's roll.[28]

Ironically, the confusion and decline in Warrenton's schools ultimately worked to the Mordecais' benefit. Their friend Alexander Calizance Miller spent many evenings at the Mordecai fireside complaining that the Falkeners' girls' school, where he taught music and drawing, was "very badly conducted and falling into disrepute." He was tempted to leave town for a better situation. In their turn, the Mordecais groaned about their "unpleasant and humiliating" position and the "ill fortune" they were suffering due to the male academy's declining student body. Miller threw out an idea. Familiar as they now were with the operation of a boarding school, why didn't Jacob and his family open a girls' academy of their own? Miller would join its faculty, and he predicted that the Falkener students would flock to such a school.[29]

Miller's proposal took them aback. Jacob was in no position to resume mercantile trade, but he had never envisioned himself at the head of a school. It was not something American Jews had attempted, and the Mordecais' relatives in Richmond would probably laugh. On the other hand, the thought of playing the schoolmaster flattered Jacob. When he consulted other friends in Warrenton, they seemed enthusiastic; they had noted his penchant for learning. But religious revivalism, which had erupted in Kentucky in 1800, was spreading through the country. Would Christian parents send their daughters to a school run by a man with what Rachel termed the "diffident name" Mordecai? Had liberalism rooted itself that deeply in the new nation? Apparently, Jacob, who marched down the main street with the town elders on the Fourth of July to hear the reading of the Declaration of Independence, thought it had. He would open a female academy.[30]

The three years since Jacob's bankruptcy had been harrowing. Scarred, the elder children responded by dedicating themselves, each in his or her own way, to the realization of the security and respectability their mother's ideal promised. Their successes, achieved in the shadow of economic failure, were remarkable: while the elder sons initiated promising careers, the children as a group had comforted their father and raised his spirits in a thousand ways; they had fashioned a family in which they felt superior to most outsiders and from which they derived intellectual cultivation and considerable emotional security. Jacob hardly realized how rich a resource he had in this family—or that it would become the key to his school's success. Nor did the children see this. What was increasingly apparent, however, was Jacob's need of their aid. Whatever else the wider world might think of their family name, the individual Mordecais knew it to connote exceptional abilities and high moral character. In this spirit, and despite their father's poor business record, they jointly agreed to put Jacob's plan into effect with the hope that in ten years the school would earn enough for him to retire from active labor. Profits, if invested well, could then sustain him and Becky into old age.[31]

KEEPING SCHOOL

In order to attract families willing to spend hundreds of dollars a year to educate their girls, Jacob Mordecai needed to assure the public that his academy met the highest standards of pedagogical excellence and moral respectability. Therefore, that fall, when Rachel was invited by an old friend to her home near Petersburg, Jacob pressed his daughter to go even though the family could ill afford luxuries like travel. Rachel would enjoy the change of scene, of course, but Jacob justified the journey on other grounds: Who could better promote the Mordecai academy than his accomplished daughter?

At Petersburg's horse races and parties, and then in Richmond, where she would visit aunts, uncles, and cousins, poised and sensible Rachel would communicate the academy's educational ideal—as well as the family's respectability. Rachel was a walking advertisement, proof of Jacob Mordecai's ability to shape female character and intellect in the girls who attended his school.[1]

As she had from childhood, Rachel thrilled at the opportunity to "oblige the best of fathers." She obliged him now not as a child displaying simple obedience and devotion but as a twenty-year-old woman whose very person made him proud. Rachel felt the compliment keenly. Ever since the demise of Jacob's store, she "wish[ed] that I had been a son, that like my brothers I might at least relieve him by doing something for my own support." Tutoring her young half siblings, maintaining her father's spirits during the years at Oakley Cottage, and helping with the family sewing were, in Rachel's mind, simply not enough. But in 1808, as Jacob worked out the details of his plan, he made the most flattering, most wonderful proposal: He said he could imagine no one better suited than his Rachel to assist him at the school. Would she become his partner? Of course she would! How better to fulfill her most "ardent wishes" to help her father, aid in the recovery of his finances, and thereby make him happy again. Jacob's eyes filled with tears. His arms went around her. "Your dear Mother told me you would be a blessing to me," Jacob said, "and so you are."[2] Rachel could receive no better tribute.

Still, anxiety mixed with Rachel's joy. The post had drawbacks. Genteel women did not, as a rule, take on paid work. Rachel understood further that while female education was gaining support across the land, so-called learned women risked being seen as asexual and unfeminine. In committing to teach, Rachel certainly would postpone, and possibly even forfeit, her chance to marry.[3] Years later, Ellen recalled a dream Rachel told her of: "She had taken her seat for the first time . . . behind her little table. But no sooner had she done so, than she turned into an old woman, her forehead all wrinkled, her hair all gray—cap, spectacles and checked apron on. She tried to extend her hand for a book, but it was so stiff and painful she could not move it."[4] Rachel could not help fearing that coming to her father's aid would render her, at the age of twenty, a crone.

Stronger than her fears, however, was the knowledge that she was needed and the prospect of contributing materially to the family's welfare. Indeed, concern over her abilities to meet her new responsibilities plagued her the most. Rachel worried whether she could "command the respect which my station would require." Moreover, she knew full well her "own deficiencies as to regular education"—composed of a few years' indifferent instruction in Richmond—and turned to sixteen-year-old Sol for impromptu preparation. This reassured her only slightly; Rachel felt "almost sick" to think of the "thousand faults" she possessed—and which, she was sure, her students would soon point out.[5]

Yet in relieving Jacob "of part of his burden," Rachel found herself strengthened. She came to shoulder the burden with skill and even with pleasure, for she thrived as a teacher.[6] One effusive pupil remembered her as "my angelic and beloved preceptress." She would not win all her students' hearts, but she got results. At term's end, townspeople along with the pupils' parents were welcomed to the public examination showcasing the girls' achievements. The performance astonished the audience. "I actually wept for joy," Rachel wrote, for "to receive the commendations of all around me and to have the assurances of my own heart that they were not unmerited was happiness far greater than I had ever before enjoyed or even hoped for."[7] Thus Rachel firmly took her place at the center of the educating and educated family, becoming a pillar of the Mordecai myth that their family was more intense and intelligent than any they had ever met.

Rachel had reason to be proud. Though she would not have liked anyone to say it, she effectively headed what became the Mordecai family's business. For all public purposes, however, it was vital to have a man at the helm of an educational institution, and people called the academy "Mr. Mordecai's school." At first, Jacob and Rachel divided teaching duties, but the father never achieved his daughter's confidence in the classroom. Increasingly, Jacob turned to Rachel for her opinion on school matters and was nearly always, as Ellen wrote, "directed by it."[8] In thus serving each other's deepest needs—his for affection and guidance, hers for approval and authority—father and daughter became a productive unit without disrupting the lines of patriarchal power.

The decision to place Rachel at the school's core was perhaps the most brilliant business move of Jacob Mordecai's career. Her hunger to please him, her intellectual ambition, and her patient good temper and rational outlook made Rachel perfect for the job.[9] Other matches were not so lucky, other jobs not so rewarding. Despite early expectations of her active involvement, Becky, who gave birth to her fifth child (Eliza) when the school opened, was consumed by repeated pregnancies and the care of young children. Becky's indisposition affected school matters very little in the end, because Ellen ultimately assumed her role as domestic superintendent.[10]

Ellen, as emotional and "full of life" as Rachel was rational, wanted something different. She was not supposed to work at the school at all. Perhaps Jacob had hoped to spare her or thought she was more likely than Rachel to marry. Rachel later implied that Ellen lacked the maturity teaching required. Whatever the case, while Rachel represented the family at the Petersburg races, seventeen-year-old Ellen was riven with frustration and self-loathing. If Rachel was her father's "blessing," she, Ellen, must be his curse. "I almost envy her," Ellen confided to Sam, for she felt so very inferior, so humiliated at "being of *no use.*"[11] At times she wished she had never been born. But with the opening of the school, the depression passed. Crucial tasks required her attention once the pregnant Becky's lying-in approached, and soon there wasn't time to complain. Ellen became the dormitory manager for dozens of little girls.

Regulating the domestic lives of nearly fifty children was exhausting and largely menial work. But no one could claim Ellen did not greatly contribute to the family's good. At times Ellen seemed to derive satisfaction from the knowledge that when it came to the family enterprise, she did more for her father than Becky, who increasingly became the target of her stepchildren's frustrations.[12] Ellen devoted herself not to intellectual enlightenment but to its underpinning—order—in which punishing an elderly house slave for being slow ranked at the same level as washing up the china.[13]

Ellen's day began about five each morning. While the students dressed and attended their first class, she oversaw the preparation of the enormous breakfast, which was served at "a long table," with "Miss Ellen" (assisted perhaps by one or another sibling) as proctor. After the meal, lessons recommenced, and Ellen directed the slaves in cleaning the dormitory rooms. Next, dinner (the day's largest meal, taken in mid-afternoon) had to be prepared and supervised. Once the dishes were cleaned and put away, Ellen's workday was done. But there were also weekly chores, including supervising the slave who combed, brushed, and rearranged each student's hair and overseeing the colossal loads of laundry.[14]

The strenuous pace of their days left the Mordecais little time for one another—for conversation, reading, correspondence, needlework, exercise, or games. But hard work distilled family members' feelings into an ever more potent intimacy. Letters grew more affectionate, and what time there was for shared leisure assumed an almost religious aspect. Rachel longed for winter break. Then the school's daily grind would give way, and Sam would visit from Richmond. Sam, who missed his family desperately, wished "some violent concussion of the earth would throw Warrenton and Richmond a little nearer each other." They saw less of Moses, who took over the Franklin and Northampton County practice of North Carolina's newly appointed attorney general, necessitating long periods away from home. Engrossed in his final term at the male academy, Sol boarded out and visited only twice a week. Yet each night, after completing his lessons, he wrote Ellen, his favorite, "a little note" or "poetic epistle," carefully folded and sealed and sent over to the school, probably in the hand of a slave. On days when Ellen wished she'd never been born, it did immeasurable good to read the tender lines signed by her dashing brother Sol.[15]

During the school's first session, the family debated fifteen-year-old Sol's future. Jacob nursed hopes of sending his son to Princeton. Though Sol was undoubtedly qualified, he urged his father to give up the idea.[16] With many more students attending their academy than they had expected that first term, and even greater numbers anticipated in response to the public examination, the school badly needed additional faculty. Sam counseled against hiring an outsider; operating costs would soar, eradicating the high profit margin family labor made possible. In any case, decent instructors were rarer than hens' teeth. In a move that disappointed his father and went against his own professional interests, Sol determined to fill the gap. Nothing could have done more to enhance the school's reputation. With the understanding that teaching was merely a temporary "detour" in his career, Sol became, as Rachel wrote, "a partner in our toils" at the beginning of the second term.[17]

Sol eventually took over most of his father's remaining classes. The teaching duties were heavy, extending well beyond class time, and Jacob, distrusting his abilities, spent evenings painstakingly preparing for the next day. Also there were the "cards," the Mordecais' labor-intensive system for monitoring pupils' academic progress and general deportment—and for shaming those who fell short. Each Thursday, class performance records and Ellen's "Neat List" of infractions—dishevelment, untruthfulness, or carelessness for losing a key or a glove—were assembled; on that "curs'd day," Rachel or Sol or both wrote out a card for each student. The chore sometimes ran well into the small hours. At Friday afternoon assembly, the cards were read aloud. The next day, after classes, students wrote home, and on Sunday an instructor checked the letters for grammar and content and folded them together with the matching cards, all ready for Monday's mail.[18]

With the exception of Moses, who as an ambitious attorney was already well along a lifelong path that was increasingly autonomous, the elder Mordecai children—Rachel, Ellen, Sol, and Sam—contributed to the school, and consequently to the immediate family, in some way. Indeed, they grounded their identity on, and found their place in the world through, service to the family. Personal ambitions, time, and even the opinion of others were, to varying degrees, subordinated to the greater family good. As a teacher, Sol might be considered less manly and certainly less promising than Moses, who spent these years steadily and profitably ascending to the top of North Carolina's legal profession.[19] Their work rendered both Rachel and Ellen less appealing to suitors. Rachel, totally immersed in her profession, wrote "business" letters, the antithesis of ladylike correspondence, keeping Sam informed of the plans for the school's expansion, hiring of staff, and scheduling of examinations and interim breaks. Sam contributed to the family operation by providing not only management advice but, free of charge, his services as a commission merchant, filling hundreds of orders for supplies: ribbons and medals for student awards, atlases, slates, grammar texts, India ink, violin strings, and toothbrushes.[20] In exchange for their assistance, the siblings won the gratitude and affection of "the best of fathers."[21]

Yet the young Mordecais began to have their doubts. Jacob did not conceal what he called his "aversion to trade," and his "dislike for the details of business" did not inspire confidence, even in his own off-spring—perhaps especially in his own offspring.[22] In the school's first years, Jacob often failed to collect tuition. Seeing their labor unre-warded as well as unpaid led to grumbling. Was Jacob careless, they wondered, or overly generous when he avoided fulfilling his financial responsibilities?[23] Either case required action.

Sol once again became the solution. By taking charge of the bulk of the academy's accounts—which he kept, Rachel emphasized, "with the utmost correctness and regularity"—he very possibly saved the family business. More parents paid in advance, and less tuition came in the form of depreciated paper notes from state banks.[24]

There were practical benefits to the second generation of adult Mordecais' committing their time and talents to their father, the family enterprise, and consequently their collective good name. With the markets in continual disarray due to President Madison's lifting and then reimposing the trade embargo with Europe, Jacob's shift from a mercantile to a pedagogical enterprise proved sage, regardless of who shouldered the day-to-day burden of the business.

There were personal benefits, too. The success of the Mordecai School in some measure spoke to the success of the Mordecais, to their bonds of fealty and love as well as to their talents and abilities. If only a small portion of the wider world was beginning to value the Morde-cai name, the Mordecais sought and now increasingly saw evidence of their worth among themselves. Whatever their doubts as to Jacob's qualities as a businessman, they saw in each other reasons for pride and hope.

5

A SERIOUS DEPORTMENT

One side of Jacob—his charm, sweetness, intellectual tendencies, and desire to please—called forth his children's striking
devotion. And while these qualities often unsuited him for
management, they could serve him well in relations with his patrons.[1]
Jacob's other side—his flashes of temper, his history of acting rashly in
commerce, the chip on his shoulder about his shaky status as a middle-
class American and a respectable Jew—upset the household and confused the children who loved him. Irrational outbursts were not
uncommon, as when Jacob angrily reproached Ellen in the morning
for indulging the slaves but by evening had begged her to forgive him
because it made him too sad to see her feelings hurt.[2] In another instance, he berated his nine-year-old daughter, Eliza, calling her "Stupid
girl" for being unable to find a way to sweep a stray coal back into the
fire. Her feelings wounded, Eliza protested to Rachel. But Rachel refused to find fault with their father and told Eliza "it is the duty of a
child to submit . . . to the blame or punishment which a parent thinks

proper to inflict." Reason and rational parenting, hallmarks of the family covenant, were subordinated, for girls at least, to the father's will.[3]

Other times Jacob was unnervingly benevolent. His mild response when a slave attacked him left the family alarmed and perplexed. Early one morning, Jacob went in search of Frank, who was engaged in constructing several buildings for the school. Finding Frank "by the fire preparing a dram," as Rachel explained in a letter to Sam, Jacob ordered the man to work. Frank cursed in reply. Jacob went to "strike" the slave, upon which Frank grabbed an ax and "aimed a blow with the butt" at his master's head. Jacob's cheek was grazed and Frank landed in jail, where he evinced no remorse. Ellen surmised that Frank was drunk and would have murdered Jacob if he could. Jacob disagreed (or perhaps knew of a motive for Frank's assault beyond what he told the family) and refused to sell Frank out of state as the children thought he must.[4]

Only such extraordinary incidents provoked mention of slaves in the Mordecais' letters. Slaves performed vital, often intimate labor in the Mordecai household, yet they apparently never penetrated the emotional borders of the little faithful band. Slavery seemed to ruffle no one, perhaps in part because the Mordecais settled in the South at a time when slavery was not only a southern institution. The silversmith Myer Myers employed slaves, and enslaved Africans were not uncommon in colonial Philadelphia. In Warrenton, the family owned or hired between three and five bond servants. Later, in the 1820s, eighteen adult slaves would labor on the Mordecais' farm outside Richmond.[5] That interlude was brief, however, and most were hired out or sold when the family moved to Richmond in 1832. The small town, small farm, and urban settings most Mordecais shared with these captives belie the typical image of gang labor on large plantations growing staple crops.

In these more domestic settings slaveholding played a role particularly central to the lives of the Mordecai women. Domestic slavery preserved white women from the dirtiest and most onerous toil, leaving them free to undertake tasks more highly valued by an emerging middle class. An enlightened domestic life was a central expression of the family's covenant, and domestic slavery helped the Mordecai women gain direct access to, and authority within, that ideal. It left them free to write the hundreds of letters by which the Mordecais maintained family bonds and identity—and without which this white family's story could not be told. It left them free to perform needlework, often done in company with other family members while someone read a book aloud. It left time to read or draw or play a musical instrument. And it permitted teaching—one's own children, younger siblings, and even paying pupils. In short, household slaves were central to the fulfillment of the Mordecais' aspiration to bourgeois cultivation.[6] And while domestic slavery buttressed the Mordecais' unique understanding of themselves, it also played a critical part in their efforts to establish their membership among the southern bourgeoisie.

Jacob never doubted his right to that membership, regardless of his occasional economic straits and the odd social slight. A child of the American Revolution, he celebrated self-determination and the democratic principles that suggested quality will win out, and he disdained force even when he could not control his own temper. But when matters of religion captivated Warrenton, these principles, combined with his desire to fit in and his need to please, spelled trouble.

As the fall term of 1810 began, the newly opened hotel at Shocco Springs near Warrenton attracted travelers and provided Jacob with the opportunity to publicize his academy. A "party of Methodists," perhaps a conference of ministers, expressed a wish to visit the school. After touring the buildings, they accepted Jacob's invitation to breakfast. If they asked how, as a Jew, Jacob Mordecai undertook the religious education of the pupils in his care, he would have replied that in such matters he always followed the directions of the parents. Each Sunday, Mordecai family members accompanied students to worship services (though Warrenton, nicknamed by Evangelicals the "Gomorrah . . . of Carolina," was hardly known for its organized religion). Jacob's presence in church proved his willingness to fulfill his duties to the girls in his charge; it also evinced the family's liberal respect for "virtue in whatever garb it appeared." Ellen reported that the Methodists "went away very well pleased."[7]

But in 1810 the family discovered that religious tolerance did not necessarily diminish religion's importance. Some Methodists stayed on, gathering nightly to pray for Warrenton's awakening. Local citizens, Ellen reported, were "turning religious as fast as they can conveniently fall, without hurting, one another." A group of Baptists began to meet as well. A revival seemed to be taking hold. What textbooks blandly call the Second Great Awakening, the wave of religious fervor that broke across antebellum America, had come to town.[8]

Three weeks later, the less holy citizens were laying bets: Had Jacob embraced Christ as his savior or had he not? Rachel laughed off the idea a little nervously, but Jacob had attended evening gatherings, and not in his role as proxy parent. The laughing lessened when Sam encountered Warrenton's pious innkeeper in Richmond and received "the plain unequivocal assertion" that "papa has become one of the elect." Years before, the Mordecais and the Kennons attended a nearby revival, principally to gawk at the assembly and ridicule the preachers, but this time was different. His father's religious loyalties had become, most unpleasantly, the subject of public speculation.[9] Among Jews, apostates were shunned, and even speculation about such a matter besmirched the Mordecai name.

Mixed ancestry, insolvency, and geographic isolation set Jacob and his family on the margins of the Jewish community. But in practicing Judaism somewhat haphazardly, the Mordecais had plenty of company in Richmond. And it did not mean they were unobservant. References to "matzohs," "commemorative crackers," and "the bread of affliction" appear in springtime correspondence, marking the observance of (or attempt to observe) Passover.[10] References to other Jewish holidays— Rosh Hashanah, Yom Kippur, Sukkoth—occasionally appear in their letters, and travel plans might change to conform to their observance. Or they might not.[11] As for the Sabbath, Ellen spent Saturdays supervising the students' grooming and sorting laundry; classes (from which a few orthodox Jewish pupils were exempt) were held; grading and letter writing filled the hours designated for prayer and rest. Tellingly, Jacob's children poked fun at the "kosha ones," boarding students whose families insisted they observe dietary restrictions.[12]

This flexible, nondogmatic approach to religion—the approach Judy outlined on her deathbed—eased daily life, life passed almost exclusively among Christians. It in no way signaled a rejection of Judaism itself. Apostasy—as Jacob, Becky, and all the children well knew—was something else entirely. Spotty religious observance might provoke criticism; converts were shunned.

What, then, did Jacob's presence at the 1810 revival meetings mean? He later wrote that he had grown "estranged from his brethren in faith" and met the earnest invitations of friendly Christians "with a mind little trammeled by the Religion in which he was born." Approached by those who wanted to spread the joy of their own conversions, Jacob "avoided . . . every kind of opposition to their sentiments."[13] The question remained: How much of his avoidance stemmed from politeness, the desire not to offend, and how much from some spiritual uncertainty of his own?

The suspense continued for more than two months. Finally, in a letter to Sam that amounted to an open statement to Richmond's Jews, Jacob "spoke in a way too plain to be misunderstood." He no longer attended Christian gatherings and had adopted "a serious deportment not very natural" to him that "had been noticed by many."[14] Since coming to Warrenton in 1793, Jacob had sought to fit in. When, as with his suit against Robert Johnson, he felt rejected by the community, he grew prickly and defensive. Some mixture of "liberalism," curiosity, politeness, and spiritual uncertainty led him to reach out to proselytizing Christians, and he had been burned. Precipitously, they had claimed him as their own. Now he mourned the distance stretching between Warrenton and his fellow Jews. It seemed that in honoring faith and "virtue in whatever garb it appeared," in assuring his children that Judaism need not interfere with work or play, he had perhaps done himself and his family a disservice.[15]

Jacob's curiosity about, if not flirtation with, Christianity and his subsequent public disavowal of its appeal to him presaged struggles to come. In penning his open letter to Richmond Jewry, and consequently the larger American Jewish community, Jacob consciously or not chronicled the distance traveled by both himself and the nation. The Jacob who once clerked for the closet loyalist and almost assimilated Jew David Franks was not the Jacob who, at least on paper and in public, ran a burgeoning school for the education of North Carolina's elite daughters. While hardly at the center of regional Jewish affairs, he was no longer at the periphery. Just as Jacob's life hadn't stood still, the country's hadn't either. The world of Revolutionary patriotism and nation-building politics was giving way to the reassertion of individual, class, and political aspiration. Further, a nation defined in its founding documents as being based on the separation of church and state was being stirred by religious revivals. Regardless, the means of belonging to middle-class America were becoming more numerous while also becoming more demanding and murky. Religious belief and practice became critical ways of expressing respectability.[16] The Mordecais' relative success meant that appeals to their participation in America's emerging economic middle class in all its cultural forms would likely increase, even as their attitudes toward those appeals would vary.

They had now to prepare for earnest appeals—from converted friends and strangers—that they attend to the salvation of their souls. No wonder, then, that in the years that followed, Jacob devoted himself to studying Jewish defenses and Christian tracts. He met with evangelical ministers and opened a correspondence with a zealous and ambitious young Episcopal priest who, hearing of Jacob's case, implored him to take the step contemplated in 1810 and offer his soul to Jesus. The efforts of the Reverend Adam Empie and others seemed only to strengthen Jacob's commitment to Judaism.[17] Books of theology ordered from friends and relatives in New York and Richmond began to fill his library as he honed his positions on religious questions, and copies of his written responses to Empie were kept as a reference for his children.[18] It was quite a change, and eventually all of Jacob's children would be required to determine the part Judaism would play in their adult lives.

6

SMALL SLIGHTS AND CONTEMPT

The path before the Mordecais would have been smoother had relations with their extended family been more pleasant. Because they were not, Jacob's awkward involvement in the Warrenton revival made Sam especially uneasy.

For twelve unhappy years, Sam worked in Uncle Samy Myers's commission merchant's counting room, supposedly living as "a member of his family" in the grand house built after Samy married the well-to-do Judith Hays. Sam found his uncle to be an inconsiderate and unpleasant employer, and relations between the two men were perpetually strained. But Jacob respected Samuel Myers, and Judy had cherished him. Moreover, Uncle Samy's affluence and willingness to train his nephew rendered complaints ungrateful and unwise. Sam must work hard and wait. "In due time," everyone predicted, Sam would rise from Uncle Samy's clerk to his partner.[1]

Still, after a decade of service, Sam received only his board and a small allowance, which he spent primarily on clothing and books. (Reading would ever remain a central, and consoling, element in his

life.) In 1809 he proposed that his uncle's firm begin trading in tobacco. He would manage the purchase and sale of the leaf in exchange
for one-quarter of the profits. Uncle Samy agreed to the plan, conced-
ing that his nephew also deserved some regular compensation. Sam's
salary was set at $450, less than the Mordecais paid the school music
teacher in Warrenton. Nevertheless, Sam was thrilled. At twenty-three,
he finally had a share in the business and a chance to prove his mercantile acumen—and redeem the credit lost to the family name by his
father's failures.[2]

Sam's tobacco speculations succeeded beyond his greatest expectations. In the spring of 1811, he triumphantly presented his uncle with a
sixteen-thousand-dollar profit. His joy was short-lived. First, Uncle
Samy deducted from Sam's quarter share the twelve hundred dollars
Jacob Mordecai owed him. A bit taken aback, Sam consented, willing
to assist his father financially. That left twenty-eight hundred dollars,
almost certainly more money than Sam had ever possessed. But his
uncle disputed Sam's calculations. Sam could not expect that the capital he used to purchase the tobacco carried no cost. Interest was due.
Finally, Uncle Samy claimed that Sam's quarter share applied only to
domestic transactions, not foreign shipments, and confiscated another
twelve hundred dollars of proceeds from a cargo Sam sold in Rotter-
dam. Hard work (on top of his regular duties) combined with the best
possible fortune had added so much to his uncle's well-packed coffers
and so comparatively little to his own that Sam refused to continue his
tobacco trade. Freshly stung and convinced that Uncle Samy wanted to
keep him in peonage, Sam fled Richmond for a few days' visit to Warrenton, where he hoped to relate his disappointment and consult his
siblings on how to handle his position at Samuel Myers and Co., for it
inevitably affected them all.[3]

Sam's dilemma faded instantly, however, because during his stay
"catastrophe" befell the Mordecais. On a soft April evening, he bade his
sisters and parents good night and, with Sol and Alexander Calizance
Miller, headed to his lodgings. Looking up, they saw flames in the upper story of the house where seventy boarding students slept. The
alarm went out; they rushed upstairs and evacuated the girls. A roll call
confirmed that none of their wards was missing. A squadron of stu-

dents from the male academy saved a good deal of furniture, but the house, which Jacob had erected to accommodate the bulging enrollment and which had been occupied only a few weeks, burned to the ground.[4]

The carefully constructed and quite profitable enterprise of the Mordecai School threatened to break apart. The trauma of the fire and its effect on public confidence (rumors of negligence and arson inevitably began to circulate) frightened all the Mordecais—well acquainted as they were with calamity. Sam spent the next day moving students' beds and trunks and salvaging what remained of the family's possessions. He and Sol retired that night "fatigued and . . . distressed," only to be shaken awake by a slave. Jacob was ill. Rushing to his bedside, they found their father writhing, Sam wrote, "under a most violent attack of the gout in his stomach."[5] It seemed too much; the school ravaged by fire, then his father's frame in the throes of "exquisite and lively pain."[6]

Sam returned to Richmond determined not to sell himself short. His father and family needed him too much to waste more time earning so little. Sam confronted his uncle directly. Courtesy quickly devolved to feelings of ill-usage matched by charges of ingratitude. Sam quit. Announcing the break to Rachel, he sounded calm, claiming the split to have been "amicable." As he wrote home for the last time from the desk he had occupied for nearly half his life, Sam tried to be cheerful. Their Aunt Richea's husband, Joseph Marx, took him in, providing "an elegant chamber spread with a Brussels carpet [and a] curtain suspended from gilt cornices, ornamented with convex mirrors. In short," he reported to Rachel in Warrenton, "I repose in princely magnificence."[7]

Sam's situation was anything but princely when it came to his own fortunes. For a few months he traded independently. President Madison's erratic attempts to punish warring Britain and France for violations against American shippers depressed the mercantile climate, and in May 1812 Sam's business languished under congressional restrictions on trade. The outbreak of war between the United States and Britain presented new opportunities. Forsaking his independence, Sam accepted a risky commission from his uncle Joseph Marx to take a cargo of flour to Cádiz on the southern coast of Spain.[8]

With all the hostilities on the high seas, Sam's voyage yielded more adventure than profit. The sailing was smooth until a British man-of-war captured his uncle's frigate, the *Henry*, and ordered it to Gibraltar, where its Yankee crew, including Sam, was taken into custody. Released a few days later, they returned to the vessel and set sail for Cádiz. But the fearful winds that plague the Straits of Gibraltar caught up the *Henry*, broke its masts, and cast it adrift. At sunrise the ship lay on its side near the Spanish town of Algeciras. Split wine casks from a nearby vessel (one of more than a hundred that wrecked that night) colored the water red. Fortunately, Sam was able to sell the flour in Algeciras at a reasonable profit. The hulk of the *Henry* he dumped for nineteen hundred dollars.[9]

Soon he was counting his blessings. In Cádiz, weakening French forces lifted their siege, and the price of flour plummeted. The wreck in Algeciras had preserved him from much greater losses. Landing in Gloucester, Massachusetts, with other former British captives, Sam enjoyed a hero's welcome.[10]

Not all of Sam's relatives applauded his luck. Two years had passed since Sam had left Uncle Samy's office, a break that released the floodgates on what had been only a trickle of recrimination between the two families. According to family correspondence, the Myerses treated the Mordecais with an admixture of arrogance and abuse, such that Ellen declared it did "violence to [her] inclinations" to spend a week at Uncle Samy's while on an extended stay in Richmond. Although no explicit falling-out marred relations between the Mordecais and Uncle Joseph Marx's family, various Mordecai children felt the brunt of their haughtiness as well.[11] Forcing some reconciliation fell to the British.

The War of 1812 had gone poorly for the young nation. In August 1814 the White House was burning, and the enemy seemed poised to strike Richmond. Seeking refuge, the Myerses and Marxes flew to Warrenton. For once, they were the guests, the Mordecais the muchneeded hosts. Rachel and Sol surrendered their rooms to relatives and expressed their sorrow that the house could not accommodate all the refugees.[12] Seeing the Mordecais in their own sphere forced the Marxes and Myerses to adjust their preconceptions. Mr. Marx's sister, Henrietta, declared "she never knew us before." The weight of "prejudice" seemed to lift, Sol noted, and the titles "Aunt" and "Cousin" came pleasantly to his lips.[13]

Sam spent the hot summer months with the militia. Sent to the Virginia tidewater presumably to block a British advance inland, his company, the Light Infantry Blues, commanded by Thomas Jefferson's son-in-law, never saw action. This was fortunate, because the officers were inexperienced and the deployment of troops incompetent, to Sam's mind at least. After a few uncomfortable weeks in the woods, the Blues marched home, "tired of waiting for [the enemy] and feeding mosquitoes." Within a few months the war was concluded by the Treaty of Ghent, signed weeks before the dramatic and unnecessary American victory at the Battle of New Orleans. Nevertheless, Sam had fulfilled his patriotic duty to what Jacob reverently called "the land of your birth." If Sam's service fell short of heroic, it did allow him to return to Richmond to his relatives' gushing reports of the Mordecais' "accomplishments."[14]

But the Mordecais' popularity with their relations faded quickly. Sometimes it seemed to Jacob's children that their name itself was cursed, and their remarks suggest how difficult it sometimes was to sustain the confidence their covenant presumed in America as a promised land where success and the respect of others could be earned by integrity and ability alone.

Rachel and all the other Mordecais were keenly aware that their name was "marked" as belonging to "the tribe," that "Mordecai" rang uneasily in the ears of Christians and could excite "the universal prejudice against our unfortunate sect."[15] It hurt even more when people with whom they expected to feel most at ease looked down on them. As they entered their twenties and grew anxious about marriage, Jacob and Judy's children felt each slight acutely.

The strain grew palpable in 1816, when Sam Mordecai proposed to his first cousin Louisa Marx. Her refusal came swiftly. She objected, she said, to the Mordecai "name" and to thirty-year-old Sam's not yet being "settled in business." Soon thereafter, the ill-treatment his sister Julia suffered from relatives while visiting Richmond further provoked Sam's sense of affliction. Perhaps "when you are very rich and very fashionable and your name is not Mordecai, those whose eyes always look above themselves will see you," he wrote bitterly to Ellen in Warrenton. He warned her to expect no parties in her honor and to fear the moment of introduction, when "your name will be mumbled unintelligibly, and if you are drawn into notice or conversation, it will be by the politeness of strangers." Rachel conceded, "The name is not, I allow, the one I would select from all others." But she quickly returned to the pride in their sense of difference, of being almost everywhere outsiders. The name, Rachel told Sam, as if drumming the truth into him, "is borne . . . by our revered father with so much respectability, a respectability [to] which his sons have rather added." Even in protesting injustice, Rachel suggested that it fell to Jacob's children to enhance (or perhaps secure) the honor of the name of Mordecai.[16]

Around their dread of bearing an insurmountable inheritance Jacob Mordecai's children erected little fortresses.[17] Yet as they moved toward adulthood, the Mordecais elaborated their defenses against the despair and isolation they often experienced. When hurt or frightened, they need look only to one another for comfort.

Recalling (and perhaps idealizing) their mother's vaunted cheerfulness, which neither misfortune nor debility seemed to have diminished, Rachel rallied her siblings to her own interpretation of their mother's legacy, a stoic "philosophy" that promised to shield them from the slings and arrows of others. Strict yet understanding, harder on herself than she ever was on others, Rachel had, according to Sam, "a head and a heart an angel might envy—if angels could be envious."[18]

When Sam lost patience with his unfeeling relatives for their treatment of his sister Julia, Rachel outlined a "criterion" of conduct that would fix the Mordecais above the pettiness of others and prove beyond all question the honor of the family name. Rachel called for rigorous emotional control—the quality that apparently failed their father at crucial times. Feelings belonged "under the guidance of reason and duty." Again and again, she made clear, the Mordecais would have to turn the other cheek, but Rachel claimed it worked. "I have always found," she said, "that to pursue the straight course," despite the cruel "eccentricities of others," brought the greatest satisfaction. Justice would follow virtue; reason would conquer prejudice whether expressed by Christians or by other Jews.[19]

Rachel's stoic creed had shortcomings. When Louisa Marx announced her engagement to another Jewish suitor only weeks after refusing Sam, whose attentions she had encouraged for years, everyone in the family agreed that she had acted abominably. Yet Rachel, seeking to console and advise her heartsick brother, urged him to act toward the Marxes "as if nothing had ever happened." Sam must not dodge the wedding by retreating to Warrenton or arranging business to demand his presence elsewhere. If he must express his anguish, let him do so in a way that would preserve his good character. "We are most of us subject to fits," she once wrote, and for a "fit of passion" one should "walk out in the open air; you may speak your mind to the winds without hurting anyone." Sam teased that for plain old sympathy he must rely on Ellen's "tender heart and the more tender heart of Sol and the most tender heart of Caroline" rather than on the "obdurate heart of Rachel." All the same, he did as she would wish and attended the wedding party.[20]

Perhaps her more obdurate heart shielded Rachel from her relatives' disdain. In fact, her creed was based on her overriding faith in humanity's reasoning powers. While Rachel did not live exposed as Sam did to their stinging comments, she assessed the Myerses and Marxes coolly, not as Jews or blood relations, but simply as people who failed to meet the standard of true "friends." True friends took a real interest in one another's welfare. True friends shared the Mordecai bent for intelligent companionship. Such friends were rare; they were also, in her experience, Gentiles. Jacob's string of failures and the family's uncertain fortunes, intellectualism, and odd religious "persuasion" did not fluster the Kennons, Miller, or Oliver Fitts (who rescued the fire-damaged school by lending the family his large house).[21] To them the Mordecais were interesting. But the Mordecais were always, first and foremost, interesting to one another. A consensus formed among Jacob's children: just as they must define themselves as a family lest others do it for them, they must nourish one another when the wider world would not.

One night in 1815, Rachel, Ellen, Sol, and Caroline (who by then had joined the family business as a teacher) retreated to Sol's quarters, a six-foot-square outbuilding and a "sanctorum" from the academy's constant bustle. Drawing themselves into "a little circle round the office fire side," the siblings spoke of "the world, of people in general, of individuals . . . and at last," Ellen wrote only half facetiously, "modestly concluded that [their own] 'amiable family' was superior" to or at least as good as any they had ever known.[22] Perhaps "the fluttering, unthinking herd" would always pity the Mordecais. Nevertheless, it was the Mordecais who were more truly chosen. Hard lessons learned early had granted them the greater wisdom. It seemed increasingly obvious that the secret of family happiness lay within the family itself. In a formulation that took Judy's ideal of affection and duty and fireside delights to a radical new extreme, these Mordecai children asserted that family could—indeed must—supply all their wants.[23]

7

REASON COMBINED WITH VIRTUE AND NOURISHED
BY EDUCATION

No doubt the Mordecai siblings often resented their reliance on one another and wished to be more like other people. They strove for stoicism in their dealings with others because it protected them by proving they could transcend the common herd. In this way they erected a fortress around their difference—a creation they would spend years embellishing. The struggle to bring honor to their father and his name was borne by all the Mordecai children. Smitten by not infrequent social slights, the Mordecais sought financial security and respect as Americans and members of a broader community than the one they inhabited day to day. They aspired to join the cultivated, genteel, transatlantic middle class.

While Jacob's sons committed themselves to promising careers—in law, business, medicine, and the military—his daughters, by working for the school, helped make their brothers' professional advancement possible. Women, as ever, stood at the center of the family covenant. And no one achieved more or found more meaning in this project of self- and family improvement than Rachel.

Rachel Mordecai looked to Enlightenment culture and ideology, which saw knowledge and reason as agents of social transformation and liberation, to develop her almost sacred approach to education as the family's lifeblood. Teaching also evoked memories of Judy, Rachel's first and most important instructor. The Mordecais' emphasis on learning echoed a Jewish scholarly tradition, and perhaps Judy sought to communicate that value, but it is important to recall how absolutely the rabbinic tradition and Talmudic studies excluded women. Still, if Rachel taught and wrote without reference to specifically Jewish inspiration, such ideas may have lain beneath the surface, melding easily with the emancipationist ideals of human progress through human enlightenment. Most important of all, perhaps, was the way that Rachel, in establishing herself at the heart of an educated and educating family, enhanced her authority as a woman and as an architect of enlightened domesticity and republican virtue in the broadest sense: by improving young minds, she played a direct role in improving the world. Whatever the sources of her inspiration, they energized her labors well beyond the classroom.

Teaching school had brought the family badly needed income. But Rachel believed that instructing family members at home, besides being more respectable, would promote prosperity and, more important, secure for the Mordecais the moral virtue and domestic happiness they had sought since Judy's death.

Pursuing such lofty goals was bound to prove difficult, and the day came when even Rachel confessed she "hardly had the spirits to pursue my ordinary vocations."[1] Among all the tasks she had undertaken, only the work of homeschooling her younger half sister Eliza Kennon Mordecai could discourage her so thoroughly. For Rachel, educating Eliza became the symbol of her aspirations of family fulfillment.

Eliza was born just as the Mordecais' school opened. At first Rachel did not welcome the child, whom she dubbed Jacob's "eleventh wonder."[2] Becky's pregnancies occurred about every three years, and Eliza was passed willingly into Rachel's hands upon the birth of Emma in 1812. Perhaps Rachel was flattered. Her talents as a teacher and guide to children had earned Jacob's gratitude and public recognition. What might have seemed yet another family duty indeed became a delight.

Rachel plunged into the task and applied pedagogical methods culled from her reading and lessons learned from her years in the classroom. The journal she kept to record Eliza's progress eventually ran to two volumes. Rachel's excitement increased as she saw that Eliza was indeed a "wonder" whose "early and strong intellect" seemed to glimmer through her childish expressions.[3]

Eliza had private lessons before, between, and after the scheduled classes Rachel taught. The dozens of girls who paid tuition and whose report cards Rachel sent out each week gradually faded from their teacher's interest. It dawned on Rachel when Eliza was only five years old that "when I ... speak of Education, I do not mean our extensive plan [the academy], I confine my thoughts to our family, perhaps I ought to say to one member of it, my little Eliza." Her other pupils were marred by imperfections, flaws that parents had allowed to take root in their early years. Such children might never truly learn. Eliza would be different. She represented a blank slate, a promising testing ground for her sister's talents and nearly utopian faith in the Enlightenment theory that with proper cultivation a child would blossom morally and intellectually into a happy and wise citizen.[4]

Thus "little Eliza" became not only Rachel's favorite but also her hope, which nothing must spoil. Accordingly, Eliza required constant oversight, and Rachel vowed to "destroy each canker that would enter [her] bosom." This meant rigorous quarantine from corrupting influences. Rachel insisted that Eliza not join the paying students in classes, though the child begged to "learn her lessons ... as other children did." Rachel monitored Eliza's amusements as well. Eliza sat out the schoolyard game of "corners," since its premise rested on doing the opposite of what one was told. Playtime and playthings must all conform to the general plan of mental and moral improvement. Because Rachel expected Eliza to "value things according to their usefulness," Sam was forbidden to bring her any fancy toys from his travels abroad.[5]

Rachel's restrictions were not easy for Eliza to accept or to understand; they deprived her of peers. On the other hand, Rachel stressed that for Eliza education need never be laborious, repetitive, or dull, something she could not promise the girls she taught in class. To a certain degree at least, Eliza did enjoy the things her instructor hoped to instill: knowledge; responsibility and cooperation; the desire to please others and thereby secure her family's affection, just as Rachel had done as a girl. "Mamma, I have a great many pleasures," six-year-old Eliza told Becky one day. "I will count them." She "reckoned eighteen," Rachel recorded in one journal entry, among them "saying her different lessons, reading for her own amusement, taking her music lesson, watering her garden, doing little regular offices of *assistance* for her brother [Solomon], being a good girl, etc." Indeed, in the first two years, Eliza rarely disappointed her exacting instructor.[6]

Eliza was not always good, of course, and Rachel scrupulously recorded her pupil's weaknesses as well as her strengths. Eliza promised to correct her habit of "lolling about on the sopha," but increasingly she resisted admitting her shortcomings.[7] A point came in the winter of 1817 when Rachel feared all was for naught. Eliza had demonstrated several instances of deceitfulness—a fault so profound that it must, Rachel believed, reflect some tragic error in her stewardship.

Seven-year-old Eliza studied independently, meeting with her teacher to recapitulate what she had learned and to advance in a new subject or skill, and though Eliza claimed to have worked on the multiplication table, daily saying it forward and backward, she had not. She told Rachel she had reviewed and memorized several children's poems, to keep them fresh in her mind. Instead, she forgot them.[8]

"Get up out of my lap," Rachel commanded. Mortified, Eliza listened as Rachel listed her lies. That night she received no good-night kiss from her teacher, and the next morning Eliza read in the book Rachel used to outline her lessons for the day, "God does not love people who tell *lies,* nor will any one have confidence in them." Eliza's lack of truthfulness polluted the sacred community, in this case the family. Eliza learned that until further notice, she must find an adult to vouch that she had done each of her lessons, for Rachel could not "believe what *you* say."[9]

The Mordecais monitored seven-year-old Eliza, but she soon stumbled again. Eliza was entrusted with the care of a plant, which on warm days she set in the sun, and then brought in for the night. One morning Sol discovered the plant, frostbitten, on the stoop. Eliza was to inform Rachel of her oversight. That night, when she tucked Eliza into bed, Rachel asked, "Have you been a good girl?" "Yes," Eliza replied, not wanting to face her sister's disappointment. Of course, Rachel found out, and the following day Eliza stood accused of "heedlessness and deceit." Without replying, Eliza crossed the room, climbed into a chair, and opened a volume. Ashamed, angry perhaps, trapped by others' expectations, she did what she could to endure the moment. To Rachel, her behavior appeared as indifference. After years of the most careful cultivation, Eliza seemed as frostbitten as her plant.[10]

Rachel convinced herself that with better teachers, her prized pupil would bloom brilliantly. She imagined not just any teachers but particular ones whom she knew solely from the closely printed pages of their books. Rachel declared without exaggeration, "To me, the authors of *Practical Education* appear almost as individual friends." They did not know it, but the celebrated Richard Lovell Edgeworth and his even more celebrated daughter Maria, far across the ocean in County Longford, Ireland, performed the offices of true friendship in Rachel Mordecai's life.[11]

It was a family she tried in every way to emulate, for the Irish Edgeworths seemed to embody the enlightened domestic life central to the Mordecais' identity, particularly as Rachel attempted to live it. The Edgeworths' large clan (there were sixteen children) spent hours on end together in the library, where the eldest sister, Maria, and the parents guided the youngest in their lessons. Mr. Edgeworth, whose interests ranged from engineering to philosophy, mathematics, and pedagogy, was personally acquainted with Jean-Jacques Rousseau, and his friends were among England's most prominent minds: Erasmus Darwin, Joseph Priestley, Josiah Wedgwood, and Thomas Day. But Richard Lovell Edgeworth tended to focus his energies on matters close to home: his children's education and the rational management of his estate. Moving between the busy library table and her little desk in a corner of the room, Maria, his brilliant daughter and collaborator in *Practical Education* (1798), assisted him. She maintained the estate's accounts and instructed her younger siblings, while composing widely read and praised novels and some of the earliest and most successful tales written expressly for young readers.[12]

A handbook for parents teaching young children at home, *Practical Education* drew its lessons from the Edgeworths' extensive experiments and experience. But to its reader in Warrenton, the book meant much more. The Edgeworths' cooperative family-based educational work, combined with their literary and scientific accomplishments, bathed them in a golden light. And the close partnership between Maria Edgeworth and her father inspired Rachel: Did she not help Jacob in similar ways? Truth to tell, Rachel not only dreamed of what the Edgeworths might make of Eliza; she sometimes entertained the "delightful chimera" of fancying herself among them, their companion in the library. Impossible, of course; meanwhile, she did all in her power to enable the American Mordecais one day to shine as brilliantly as the Irish Edgeworths.[13]

The Edgeworths' writings produced in Rachel an array of emotions: they inspired, scintillated, and comforted her. When she felt most inept, Rachel "re-perused" *Practical Education* and found friendly counsel there.[14] When Sam discovered a new work by the Edgeworths, *Readings on Poetry* (1816), he sent it to Rachel with a note: it "shows that your system and theirs is the same and gives your own practice in their words."[15] Her sense of mutuality might appear strange, given that the Edgeworths lived wholly unaware of Rachel's existence. But even that distance was about to be bridged.

Maria Edgeworth could have had no more avid enthusiast than Rachel Mordecai. But in one instance Maria aroused in Rachel feelings—of pain, anger, betrayal—familiar to all the Mordecais and ones to which even stoic Rachel could not reconcile herself. Those feelings struck her as she read Edgeworth's 1812 novel *The Absentee*, part of the series *Tales of Fashionable Life*. The plot exposes moral corruption among Irish landowners living in London and squandering their wealth on jewels and card games or the latest equipage while their estates fall into neglect and their tenants sink helplessly into want. An admirable theme, surely. But moving fawningly among the story's idle rich, deftly sucking off their wealth through loans bearing exorbitant interest, is Mr. Mordicai, a London coach maker.

Thus it was that Rachel's father's name—the name she heard spoken by schoolgirls and Warrenton folks of all types fifty times a day, the name she hotly defended to Sam when he pointed out the low esteem in which it was held by the Jews of Richmond—blurred sickeningly in her mind with the image of the fictional Mordicai. Maria Edgeworth's villain, an extortionist who torments his debtors even on their death-beds, owes his fortune to his moral bankruptcy, and wears his corruption on the features of his "dark wooden face," which move "not by the will of a living creature, or from the impulse of a rational soul."[16]

When Sam sailed to Europe in 1815, he took with him a letter from Rachel addressed to Maria Edgeworth. She had hesitated a long time before writing it. The celebrated Miss Edgeworth received many unsolicited communications, and Rachel's might be viewed as yet another intrusion. But Rachel had something particular to say to Maria Edgeworth; the forces of reason, pride, and duty to family made her say it.[17]

"How can it be that [Maria Edgeworth], who on all other subjects shows such justice and liberality, should on one alone appear biased by prejudice?" Rachel implored. Even worse, Edgeworth, an educator sensitive to the dangers of false associations, had, by publishing *The Absentee*, instilled "that prejudice into the minds of youth!"[18] The Enlightenment principles on which not only the Edgeworths and Rachel based their lives would be worse than useless if they permitted a great teacher like Maria to propagate cruel and unreasonable smears on an entire class of people.

Perhaps where Maria lived, where Jews "are oppressed and made continually the subject of scorn and derision," ill-treatment gave rise to figures like Mordicai the coach maker. But "in this happy country," Rachel, sounding a note of patriotism, informed Maria Edgeworth, "where religious distinctions are scarcely known, where character and talents are all sufficient to attain advancement, we find the Jews to form a respectable part of the community." In fact, Rachel knew few Jews in America or elsewhere. But, extrapolating from her family, she told Edgeworth that most of them were "liberally educated." Many eschewed lending money altogether and were "following the honourable professions of the Law, and Physick, with credit and ability." Rachel suspected that if she looked a little harder, Maria would find Jewish people of sterling character.[19]

More than a year passed and Rachel heard nothing from Edgeworthstown. Americans celebrated the stunning victory of the outnumbered militiamen and regulars under Major General Andrew Jackson over eight thousand British troops in New Orleans. Napoleon, defeated by England at Waterloo, abdicated and was banished to St. Helena. And the world's first steam-driven warship, the *Fulton I*, was launched in New York harbor. Life for the Mordecais rolled along; most of them knew nothing of the letter to Ireland, anyway. No answer, it seemed, would come. It made Rachel sorry. She had hoped for more from Maria Edgeworth. Rachel decided to show a copy of her letter to Jacob. He "seemed pleased," Rachel said, to know that she had defended his name and the position of Jews in the United States.[20] Without a response from Ireland, Rachel tried to satisfy herself in having done right by Jacob and by her own convictions.

8

MORDECAI A HANDSOME NAME?

As they gathered around the table on an otherwise normal fall day at the Mordecai School, Rachel, Ellen, Solomon, Julia, Caroline, Jacob, and Becky could barely eat. Happiness drove their appetites away; "tears of pleasure" sprang to their eyes; joyous words echoed through the rooms. The younger members of the family wondered what was the matter. The day's mail had brought not one but two letters to Rachel—from Edgeworthstown. It was, she said, the most perfectly "agreeable" thing that had ever happened to her.[1]

Rachel had not misjudged Maria after all. In one letter, Richard Lovell Edgeworth, inventor and pioneering educator, warmly praised Miss Mordecai's "generous mind" and her "understanding and feelings" and requested, "pray, make us better acquainted with your real self." There was more. Maria would soon publish a new work, one her father hoped Rachel would especially appreciate.[2] Rachel's "polite, benevolent and touching letter has given me much pleasure, and much pain," the great author herself began. "As to the pain I hope you will sometime see that it has excited me to make all the atonement and reparation in my power." Rachel had convinced Maria of her wrong and given "the very best evidence" against prejudice. Rachel had not only argued well; she had set an example all should follow. "The candor and spirit of tolerance . . . you shew," Maria concluded, "you have a right to expect from others."[3] Rachel was vindicated.

A year later, traveling home from a restorative summer at Saratoga Springs and Ballston Spa, Sol Mordecai entered a New York bookshop. There he found Maria Edgeworth's *Harrington* (1817), the novel the Mordecais had been waiting for. Opening the volume, Sol was "lifted above the world." In a brief preface, Richard Lovell Edgeworth credited his daughter's inspiration to "an extremely well-written letter . . . from a Jewish Lady, complaining of the illiberality with which the Jewish nation has been treated in some of Miss Edgeworth's works." For perhaps the first time in his life, Sol saw his heritage as something other than a burden. "At that moment," he confided to Sam in Richmond, "I could have felt pride in saying, 'I am a Jew.' "[4]

Sol devoured the first chapter while standing in the bookseller's. When Harrington, the young child of a wealthy London family, refuses to come inside one day, his nurse threatens to tell the Jewish ragpicker to stuff the boy in his sack of old clothes and carry him away. From that day on, Harrington goes to bed each night in terror. Speaking through Harrington, Maria reproves herself for including such bogeymen in her fiction—the prejudice of *The Absentee* contradicted the rationalism of the Edgeworths' handbook for parents, *Practical Education*. Harrington warns the reader that ideas, including unjust ones, "early influence the imagination, and afterwards become strong habits, prejudices, and passions."[5]

Maria Edgeworth's contrition was not the best of it. Reading further, "an ecstatic feeling . . . thrilled through [Sol's] soul," for the heroine who overcomes Harrington's bigotry is an American Jew named Berenice Montenero who had grown up "in a happy part of that country, where religious distinctions are scarcely known—where character and talents are all sufficient to attain advancement." They were Rachel's own words, published for the world to see. Alongside Berenice and her rich and genteel father, the novel introduces educated and attractive Jews, all belying young Harrington's "foolish prejudice."

Rachel's appeal, her image of the United States as a virtual promised land, was being deployed by Maria to press England toward like tolerance.[6]

Rachel quickly won Sam's applause for so "admirably gaining [her] point." Rachel did not want her role in the book's conception to be spoken of in public, however. It violated the domestic creed for ladies to bring upon themselves the attention of strangers. But such exciting news could not be contained. Sol shared it with his uncle Joseph Marx, and he in turn told everyone he saw. Jews in New York and Philadelphia heard about Jacob Mordecai's daughter. They congratulated Sol for having "such a sister," and Sol took to calling Rachel "Berenice." The unwanted celebrity only slightly dampened Rachel's thrill. Sam predicted that Rachel's association with Maria would "not stop here. You must admire and love each other." He told her that only "seldom do such minds meet and it seems almost providential that you should have formed an acquaintance across the Atlantic." Without courting fame, Rachel Mordecai had gained wide respect for herself and her family.[7]

The difficulty came when the Mordecais and other Jews actually read the novel. Either Sol did not finish *Harrington* before he reached home, or it did not matter to him that the heroine proves to be, as Sam bluntly expressed it, "but nominally a Jewess." Indeed, when Harrington falls in love with Berenice Montenero, his parents' anti-Semitic opposition to the match evaporates, for although Berenice respects her father's religion, she does not practice it. Berenice is the child of intermarriage, and when her Christian mother dies, Mr. Montenero raises Berenice as a Protestant. Edgeworth had marred "the very purpose" of her novel, Sam complained, for Berenice's virtues belong to "one who was but apparently of that condemned faith."[8]

Rachel agreed with Sam about Berenice. It was impossible to view her as a representative of the people *Harrington* proposed to vindicate. One might even suspect Maria Edgeworth's motives, for if all Jews behaved as Mr. Montenero does, Jews would soon disappear.

None other than her own father stepped forward to relieve Rachel regarding Maria's intent. Very probably, Jacob suggested, Maria had Berenice grow up a Christian as "an additional proof of the united liberality and firmness of Mr. Montenero." Putting the father at the center of the drama enabled Jacob to imagine a man who "married a lady of different religious persuasion, without being inclined to swerve in the least from his own." Montenero rears his daughter "in the belief of her mother, but with an equal regard for both religions," proving, Jacob suggested, that "the modes of faith and forms of worship are immaterial; all equally acceptable" to God.[9]

Such a stance, while confusing coming from the patriarch of a Jewish family, fit comfortably with Rachel's approach to family identity; virtue and reason knew no religion. Jacob's calm, enlightened "liberality of sentiment" endeared him even more to Rachel. When shortly thereafter Richard Lovell Edgeworth died, Rachel keenly mourned Maria's loss. Her own profound love for Jacob made her acutely sympathetic. Rachel thrived on her father's affection and approval. She worked in his school without pay. She defended his religion and his name. Through him, she kept alive her mother's vision of a cultivated family marked by domestic affection. Her fervent words of condolence to Maria suggest that Rachel harbored a fantasy that Jacob was in fact a patriarch as brilliant—or able to sire offspring as brilliant—as Mr. Edgeworth himself. Perhaps in the end, despite his false starts, Jacob Mordecai would be recognized by outsiders for his superior talent and virtue.[10]

Immersed as they were in the transformative project of education, Jacob's offspring undertook to fashion a grand image for their father, and Richard Lovell Edgeworth presented an irresistible model. Once they helped Jacob leave behind his long train of financial reversals, once the name "Mordecai" attained the stature they thought it deserved, then the accomplished, liberal, sweet-natured patriarch they adored no doubt could flourish. The often depressed and sometimes rash man they knew would recede. Meanwhile, they protected Jacob from maligning outsiders, shielded him as much as possible from their own sorrows, blamed only Becky for bringing so many little Mordecais into the world, and promoted Jacob to the public as a benevolent head of household and a competent man of business even as they ran his school.[11]

The father's battle to succeed and find a comfortable place in

America became the children's battle as well. They acted for him—and for themselves. Even while Rachel was involved in her momentous transatlantic correspondence, the Mordecais were putting older demons to rest. By the end of 1816, school keeping in Warrenton, the "wild scheme" their relatives in Richmond once dismissed, had enabled Jacob to repay his debts and accumulate more than fifteen thousand dollars—a small fortune in that time. Sam's investments of those profits would, they felt certain, add thousands more. For the first time since dissolving the partnership with his stepfather just after the American Revolution, Jacob stood unencumbered by obligations. What is more, he was the head of a business returning some seventy-five hundred dollars every year.[12]

The family seemed to have defeated its greatest foe—debt. Though their plan had projected ten years of teaching, revenues made it possible to consider selling out sooner. As early as the summer of 1815, Jacob had announced to the elder children that their labors' end was in sight. In short, *Harrington*'s publication and Rachel's resulting fame joined a happy concatenation of events, all of which seemed to justify the years of toil and the observance of the dictates of the family covenant.[13]

So it was that Rachel's sunny description to Maria Edgeworth of the Jewish experience in America, "where character and talents are all sufficient to attain advancement," could seem accurate as well as rosy. Scores of parents who wanted their daughters to attend the Mordecai School were being turned away for lack of openings. A member of their own family had inspired a best-selling author to write a novel peopled with admirable Jews. The Mordecais pinched themselves. Was it true? "Don't you begin," Caroline asked Ellen, "to find Mordecai a hansome [sic] name?"[14]

But even as they neared the end of their labors, the day they could sell the school, the shadow of sickness fell across the Mordecais' success. When Sol collapsed in March 1817, the family feared the worst—tuberculosis—and briefly reconsidered selling the academy. Instead, they pressed on, sending an almost spectral Sol away to recover his health. Ellen, whose chest pains also suggested tuberculosis, spent the summer of 1817 under medical treatment. Like most female consumptives, she stayed home. The doctor bled and blistered her and pre-scribed large doses of purgative mercury and nauseating foxglove. She remained weak, and the family's days were edged with excruciating un-certainty.[15]

The same institution that knit them together, rescued Jacob's for-tune, and added luster to their name had unleashed forces that could tear the Mordecais apart. It was then commonly held that teaching, like other sedentary professions, created conditions ripe for consump-tion. Before Sol's collapse, Sam had begged his brother to reduce his class load. Sol could never regain his health, Sam said, "cooped up with a hundred children." But Sol would not hear of it—there was too much to do—until he literally could not perform his duties. To take up the slack, seventeen-year-old George Washington Mordecai taught Sol's writing, geology, and mythology classes and oversaw the school's ac-counts. Even Jacob reentered the classroom. Similarly, when she fell ill, Ellen shrank from "being a useless member of so industrious" a family and resisted giving up her responsibilities for the students' Neat Lists, laundry, and mealtimes.[16]

The Mordecai School held its final public examinations in Novem-ber 1818. Two weeks before the tests, the students assembled before Ja-cob for a lecture on the family watchword, "duty": the last stack of report cards had been one of the worst in the school's history, and the Mordecais could not allow their career's crowning moment to become a crowning embarrassment. Rachel told Sam that in response to Ja-cob's exhortations the girls promised "to do well," and they did. In-deed, it was the best examination ever; some in the audience were moved to tears. The Mordecais received thanks and praise; one parent after another called the family irreplaceable. Yet replacements were at hand. Two Philadelphia teachers, along with the school's longtime mu-sic and drawing instructor, Achilles Plunkett, had already purchased the school for ten thousand dollars.[17]

During the decade they operated the female academy in Warren-ton, the Mordecais affirmed the family covenant that sustained them as they applied their character and talents to overcome ill fortune and win a place of honor as citizens in the tolerant promised land of the new United States. Indeed, the covenant had already brought financial success—and a sign from across the Atlantic that they were interesting to illustrious outsiders as well as to one another. An axiom of the family myth held that by sticking to their values of moral and intellectual excellence and by fostering and protecting one another, they would survive the anxieties their difference from others necessarily produced—a difference that they preferred to ascribe to their cultivation rather than to their religion. In proving their merit in a nation that was itself a testing ground for the most progressive ideals of the era, the Mordecais demonstrated how revolutionary the United States was. They would define themselves—as genteel, virtuous, industrious, and, ultimately, eminent. Such self-determination and the myth the Mordecais built to support it, however, obscured the threats inherent in their efforts, threats to their identity as Jews and to their freedom to act as individuals outside the close-knit family fold.

PART TWO

LOVE AND MARRIAGE

I told them that the liberality of sentiment on points of religion in which our father had educated his children constituted them Jews but by name.

—SOLOMON MORDECAI TO ELLEN MORDECAI,
JULY 28, 1821

There is no one thing I have felt more sensibly than the peculiarly disagreeable and unfortunate situation of our sisters . . . They are either obliged to lead a life of seclusion and celibacy, marry a man whom they cannot admire or esteem . . . or they must incur the certain and lasting displeasure of their parents by marrying out of the pale of their religion.

—GEORGE MORDECAI TO SAMUEL MORDECAI,
JANUARY 15, 1834

RELIGIOUS SCRUPLES ASIDE

For years Moses, Jacob and Judy's eldest child, had been too busy for love. The importance of avoiding his father's financial failures impressed itself on Moses, who plied the county courts as a circuit lawyer year after year with, as he said, single-minded "alacrity." The first Jew to join the state bar, Moses slept beneath a single blanket in freezing rooms in small towns, survived recurrent malarial fevers, and gradually built a practice and reputation that dispelled the fear of poverty and disgrace that had laced his youth. Moses was the first in the family to attain such prosperity, and in terms of power and wealth his was the greatest of any of his siblings.[1]

For a Mordecai, Moses possessed a singularly unsentimental character. At the ripe age of thirty-one, however, he was transformed into a "romantic." Moses now had wealth, but "ragged footed celibacy" plagued him as he sang the rhapsodies of "love and matrimony."[2] In 1816 Mary Long, a Raleigh girl with money and a good family, became the object of his affection and hope.

His siblings knew her to be "sensible, pleasing in her manners," and so they rooted for the match. Sam dryly remarked that they must all rely on Moses to improve their standing "in the fashionable world," and indeed his brother's courtship of an accomplished young lady indicated a social position that seemed far beyond Sam's reach in Richmond. As it happened, beyond Moses's, too, for Mary refused him when he proposed. Several months later, after a dinner of bear's meat with the chief justice of North Carolina's Supreme Court, Moses determined that he must "fall desperately in love again."[3]

Moses met rejection twice more before he found a wife. During the same years Sam, less intrepid and less ready to transfer his affections from one woman to another, despaired of ever finding a companion as talented and charming as his sisters.

In the fall of 1817, just as Maria Edgeworth's novel *Harrington* appeared, Moses became engaged to Margaret Lane, granddaughter of an early Raleigh settler and Revolutionary War patriot. Margaret's parents died when she was a child, leaving her and three sisters dozens of slaves and lands that covered much of the present-day city. In a hasty note to Sam, Moses announced his engagement and an approximate wedding date, appending a list of necessary household items suggesting the high style in which the couple would live together: a sideboard; a dining table; two card tables; a sofa, bedsteads, and toilet tables, "such as I saw at [their uncle] Mr. Marx's"; a dozen chairs; a set of twenty-four knives, forks, dessert knives and forks, and teaspoons; along with table china, decanters, two dozen tumblers and wine glasses, a silver chafing dish, and candlesticks. Sam was glad to assist with procuring these items. But when he passed his brother's news on to Warrenton, Jacob wrote back saying his "pillow was wet with his tears." Having just confronted the complexity of Jewish intermarriage and assimilation in the case of Edgeworth's fictional Monteneros, the Mordecais found themselves facing in real life the same uneasy questions.[4]

Jacob's children were at first surprised, then alarmed. Why was Papa so upset? Was it because Moses had not told him first? Was it because, as he claimed, the engagement seemed sudden? Or was it because Margaret was a Christian who expressed no intention of converting to Judaism as Jacob's mother, Esther, had done when she married the elder Moses Mordecai? Would his firstborn be tossing away his religious legacy? Jacob himself may not have known the reason, but in his distress he entreated Moses to break the engagement, invoking his full patriarchal authority to bid his son not to "be a stranger to my wishes."[5]

If Moses thought his father seemed unreasonable, he probably thought his sister Rachel seemed excessively critical. Rachel questioned his wisdom in selecting Margaret Lane as his life's partner. From all Rachel knew, Miss Lane and her family were not sufficiently educated to meet the Mordecai standard, and she doubted Margaret was "capable of comprehending your sentiments, appreciating your worth." Concerned that marrying Margaret would consign Moses to a household unblessed by the enlightened domesticity she prized, Rachel quizzed him further: "Can she converse with you, be your friend and companion, as well as your housekeeper, be the guide and directress as well as the mother of your children," as their own mother, Judy, had been? Moses might not want "a learned lady," Rachel conceded, but he must "want a sensible, not an ignorant one."[6]

Rachel's commentary reflected her misjudgment of Moses. Of course he would not want an ignorant woman as his wife. On the other hand, having quite early gained his ease, he was less invested in the family covenant and its attendant ideal of intimate and educated domestic life. Moses refused to defend Margaret against his siblings' aspersions. Their disapproval stung, but not enough to deter him. Given his long quest for a wife, Moses had no intention of abandoning his wedding plans. He informed his family that he, not they, was marrying Miss Lane; they might therefore refrain from, as Sol said, measuring his "happiness by any other standard than his own."[7]

Jacob's opposition posed a more delicate problem. Rachel wrote that their father was "bowed down with grief." Moses must somehow assuage his concern. He caught the stage to Warrenton and, amid the bustle of the school week, set about reconciling his father to the match. In the "interview" that followed, the proudly independent son explained himself with all the deference he could muster. Already lackadaisical in his adherence to Judaism, Moses admitted having, as Sol put it, "taken religious scruples aside" in his choice of mate. Had he suspected, he said, that "it would occasion [Jacob] one pang," he would never have asked for Margaret's hand. The interview ended inconclusively. Seeking perhaps to appease, Moses promised to reconsider. Seven weeks later, in an act that represented his partial secession from the mythically unified clan, Moses was married without Jacob's blessing.[8]

Jacob and Becky planned to conceal Moses's marriage from Becky's mother, the venerable and orthodox Grandmama Myers, now a resident of Richmond. On the wedding day Jacob remained at home while a notably small contingent of Mordecais (Rachel and Sol) celebrated with the couple in Raleigh.

It was the timing of Moses's wedding and the family crisis it provoked that more than anything else distressed his sister Ellen, for it spoiled her reunion with "my happiness, my everything," the brother she loved more than anyone on earth.[9]

That brother was Sol. Months earlier he had left Warrenton seeking health and strength by taking the waters at the northern spas. After bidding him farewell, Ellen went to his room, knelt at the foot of his bed, and wept. The following night, Jacob spent hours pacing the length of the hallway with his arm around an inconsolable Ellen. Writing to Sol in New York, she vowed it would be "the last time I ever will consent to be separated from you, the very last!"[10]

Three months had passed. Waylaid in Norfolk by a storm on his journey homeward, Sol declared that he, too, could "no longer consent to be separated." And yet he lingered, enjoying the company of several young ladies. When Sol finally arrived in Richmond, where Ellen was recuperating from her own illness, the news of Moses's engagement and Jacob's distress came between them. Sol sped home to Warrenton, hoping to comfort their parent and help mend the rupture. Ellen, stranded at the Marxes', did not see Sol again for seven weeks. "When I cannot think as I ought I must try not to think at all," Ellen wailed; "poor me." No one understood.[11]

Everyone understood this at least: since their late-teenage years, Sol and Ellen had been intimately linked. There were little notes passed before bedtime, shared journals no one else was allowed to read, and a special garden, jointly tended to, around the office where Sol lived.

Their closeness also yielded occasional spats and, as when Sol went north in 1817, a very morose Ellen.[12]

The attachment began at a time when Ellen saw herself running a distant second in affection and accomplishments to Rachel, whom Jacob had selected as a teacher in the school. Rachel possessed genius and an even temper; Ellen described herself as "teasing, ill natured, serious, wild, boisterous." Rachel was admired; Ellen had, well, moods.[13] Subscribing to the European spirit of the age, Ellen and Sol shared the Romantic appreciation of emotion for its own sake, a sensibility that set them apart from Rachel and Moses, who charted their lives more along the lines of reason.

Sol had not always been alone in Ellen's stronger affections. Alexander Calizance Miller, the handsome music teacher, had captured her interest. During the school's first term eighteen-year-old Ellen took piano instruction from him, and one day she snatched and placed in her scrapbook a sketch Miller had made of a crab-apple blossom. Secretly she began to dream of marriage. Ellen's crush became sufficiently obvious that Rachel issued solemn orders about appropriate conduct.[14]

Miller himself rendered Rachel's heavy hand unnecessary. That winter he proposed to a young lady whose planter father had been a state senator. It was a magnificent match for a music teacher.[15] It seemed that despite Miller's attentions to her, Ellen never had much chance. Some weeks after the wedding she could contain her sorrow no more and confessed it all to Sol, the only person to whom she felt able to say that she wished it had been her wedding. Tears came to his eyes, but he urged her to view the situation dispassionately. Had Miller really behaved generously, even honorably toward her? No. Was he a man of feeling? No. He had followed the scent of money and "never was worthy of the hand of my Ellen."[16]

Sol did more than soothe Ellen's sore heart. He opened up his own. Sol was secretly and nervously awaiting word from the girl he called his "nymph." His religion seemed not to deter Sally Sawyer, and yet she told him their marriage could never be. When he asked why, she refused to explain. In fact, Sol was rebuffed because Sally had fallen in love with her uncle. They soon conceived a child and eloped, with only

Ellen knowing how bitterly Sol mourned Sally's fall. Brother and sister seemed similarly star-crossed, ill-fated in matters of the heart.[17]

Ellen and Sol's romance centered on the tiny office where he lived and the garden that surrounded it. With Sally Sawyer's fall from grace still fresh, Sol planted three "little firs" and dedicated them to Ellen. He called the spot "Bachelor's Bower" and over time graced its landscape with shrubs, each of which bore meaning in the flower language then gaining popularity: ecstatic jasmine, humble broom, and hopeful hawthorn. Magnolia and crab apple arched above its yard. Beneath them, lucky clover formed a cool bed. Ellen trained lilac up the cedars' trunks and branches as an emblem of her embrace and implored Sol to "support your parasitical little vine."[18] Inside the "sanctorum" that was his dwelling place Sol would lie, his head on Ellen's lap, the fire soothing them. Sometimes they conversed for hours. Ellen decorated the room so that everything reminded him of her. In turn, Sol had notes delivered to her in the main house, bidding her to come spend the evening with "one that truly loves you." Sometimes as he prepared for bed, she waited outside the door until he signaled that he was beneath the covers. Then she would go to him, "take his pillow and warm it and double it over, and run with it from the fireplace to his bed for fear it should get cold before his dear cheek rested on it."[19]

A breaking point came in 1814. Sol spent the school's winter vacation in Richmond, where Sam said he "excited" notice among the ladies. Upon his return to Warrenton, he turned on Ellen suddenly, icily, accusing her of being "too communicative." She must "alter," or else, he threatened, he would change his "opinion, feelings, actions" toward her. He shunned her company until finally, with pen and paper, Ellen begged for mercy. "Tell me how I am to act, speak to me as you would a child . . . leave nothing for me to imagine for I never was so completely lost." He replied that she must think of him less. This Ellen could not do, not without stamping out her every thought.[20]

Did Sol not understand her love? It differed from the feelings she had for the other brothers and sisters. "There is something in your manners, disposition, and situation," she told him, "which excite in the bosom of too fond Ellen a deep, a particular interest." There. She had said it. Ellen loved her brother "as she should love the man she married."[21]

Sol did not seem surprised by this revelation; very likely he knew the depth of Ellen's ardor all along. Such an attraction seems understandable given the way the Mordecais confronted an often unaccepting world. What simpler solution than to turn to one another for affection and admiration? As for Sol's coldness, he told Ellen it was in fact benevolence. He said he did not mind her "entering so deeply, so entirely into my feelings." But he claimed that he was cutting her out of his emotions in order to prevent her descent into his own depressed state of mind. Very likely he was also trying to set some bounds to their entanglement. Yet even for Sol those boundaries were elastic; after chastising Ellen, he told her to "fly to my arms and in them once more be embraced as the invaluable treasure of your own" dear brother. Perhaps Ellen flew before she read the final dedication of the letter: "from a heart of Feeling, not of Romance."[22]

A truce of sorts developed. No longer hidden, their desires for others and for each other formed a complex bond. The asymmetry of their affection grew starker over time, however. While Sol would turn to Ellen in times of need throughout his life, he was her beloved, and she dwelled morbidly on her fear of losing him. Sol might leave her, die, or, as he had once threatened, stop caring, so she labored to deserve and keep him.[23]

Between 1817 and 1824, Jacob's eldest children passed from their teens and early twenties into their late twenties and early thirties. Pressure mounted. They became, as Rachel once wrote, a pack of aging "hopefuls." Sometimes it seemed they would remain single yet together always, "a queer, old fashioned, stiff set." But Jacob's children did love and marry outside the family, often over one another's and their parents' objections; meanwhile, the unity that sustained them through hardship and isolation cracked but did not crumble.[24] In obvious ways, they were moving out into a wider world. In their own marriages and households, or even under Jacob and Becky's roof, the circumstances that had wrought the covenant of their youth no longer existed. The culture and values surrounding them were shifting as well—becoming more individualistic, less rewarding of cooperation and duty. The children of Jacob, Judy, and Becky Mordecai responded in their own ways to the opportunities, challenges, and burdens of adulthood. Yet it was still jarring to Jacob's offspring sometimes to find themselves unprepared for life on the outside—or, worse, out of step with the family they held so dear and whose members were pledged to "foster and protect each other." The idealized unity that they believed would bring happiness and eventual glory to their name remained powerful, but it grew more obviously theoretical as family members left home and the sense of belonging, to one another if to nothing else, was thwarted by varying levels of success, a growing network of kin relationships via in-laws, and new religious experiences.

10

THE CHILDREN OF DISAPPOINTMENT

In 1815, when the Mordecais first began rolling the word "retirement" around their tongues, they were too focused on their mission to imagine that in gaining release from school keeping they would compromise what Rachel hailed as "family union."[1] No one liked to think of separation. So in 1818 Jacob began searching for a place where the family could resettle without dramatically altering the household. Richmond seemed the most appealing destination. Sam was there. Becky could be near her Myers siblings. Richmond's commercial strengths dwarfed Warrenton's, and there was talk of Sam's opening a hardware store with one of Jacob's younger sons, Sol or George, as junior partner. Sam objected that the city did not need such a shop, but he did arrange an apprenticeship for George. The work took George far from home, to Kentucky, where Sam was buying and processing large amounts of tobacco.[2]

It was hoped that Alfred, the next youngest son after George, would soon leave as well. He applied for admission to the United States Military Academy at West Point, a bold bid for a Jew. The New York school had slots for only two students from each state. After a long wait, he was accepted as a cadet. For Jacob, the honor of having a son ready to advance himself in the nation's service outweighed his wish to have Alfred nearby.[3]

Jacob's daughters had no distinct prospects in the family's evolving plans. Rachel, thirty, Ellen, twenty-eight, and Caroline, twenty-four, had passed the usual age for marriage while the academy was paying off their father's debts and earning his future security.[4] After many years with little leisure, the Mordecai women might look forward to a life of reading, studying, walking, riding, and visiting family and friends. Whether or not genteel spinsterhood held any appeal, that prospect greatly increased with the sale of the Mordecai School. With close to twenty thousand dollars invested and with the expectation of a steady flow of cash from payments on the school, the Mordecais' trials were at an end.[5] The question, however, remained: Where would they live?

After several months of searching, Jacob found a four-hundred-acre farm in Henrico County, north of Richmond, that caught his fancy. Four miles from the city, it boasted an attractive four-room house with kitchen and outbuildings, several barns, and a large garden. The soil was poor, but Jacob expected that with improvements it could sustain crops and livestock. They took the plunge, and in the spring of 1819 the blooming apple trees and the surrounding acreage at what the Mordecais would call Spring Farm belonged to Jacob and Becky at the cost of $11,700.[6]

The Mordecais left Warrenton in 1819 from the very house Jacob had stocked with soap and candles and cured meat in anticipation of Judy and their children's arrival from Petersburg more than a quarter century before. (They had rented the old home after the school's new owners took possession of that property.) Poignant as this was, the move struck the family's human chattel most dramatically. Some slaves were bought, some sold, and others sent into Richmond to be hired out. Much of the family's furniture went up for auction. The rest they packed onto wagons.[7]

Sol and Caroline stayed behind to oversee the disinterring of their mother's remains for reburial in Richmond's Hebrew Cemetery. Finding that her coffin had disintegrated, Sol gingerly gathered the bones from the sodden spring ground, placed them in a small case padded with cotton, and carried them on the stagecoach heading north. Approaching the family's new home, Sol and Caroline drove by a picturesque millpond, turned down a little lane, passed the barns on either side of the gate leading to the house, and walked up to the door on a path lined with sweet-smelling Scotch broom. Everything seemed in place.[8]

Instead, everything came apart. Julia, Becky and Jacob's first child, was twenty when she looked around the farm and decided "everything was going wrong, everything was going to destruction." She almost certainly included herself in this estimation. The smell of food made her ill. Doctors bled her and treated her for malaria, and when these measures failed, she was connected to the local museum's "electrifying machine." One moment Julia was "mild, gentle, interesting, affectionate," the next "violent, positive, almost ungovernable." She seemed to be going mad.[9] As if disaster were a virus, Julia seemed struck by only one strain of a spreading disease. Discord rent family seams wherever they were weak. Ellen charged that Becky was useless—"neither the mistress of her house, the mother of her children, nor the companion of her husband"—and wished Jacob had never remarried.[10] As if escaping from a sinking ship, Alfred and Sol soon departed to study in faraway places. Perhaps of greatest long-term concern, farming suited Jacob Mordecai no better than trade.

Social life was a source of sometimes excruciating disappointment for those at Spring Farm. Caroline concluded that their uncle Joseph Marx, for whom they had always had warm feelings, "would rather give us [$]500 en charité than . . . invite us to one of his grand dinners." The neighbors were kind but offered poor company to a family that was, as Sol said, "fond of literature." Rachel, who had hoped for more sophistication in Richmond, found its society superficial, and ever since their "rustication," as Sam called their life at the farm, even Jacob had complained of feeling "no attachment" to the people in town.[11] Without friends, and with fewer family members, the Mordecais found Spring Farm an increasingly comfortless place.

To the want of familial concord and of friends was soon added a want of money. Sam's tobacco speculations had at first proceeded brilliantly; in partnership with Joseph Marx and an agent in Kentucky, Sam shipped some $230,000 worth of processed tobacco from Louisville to New Orleans and onward to England. Using capital from Mr. Marx and from the Mordecais' savings, he invested liberally, confident of being able to repay them with considerable interest. This was his labor of love, for Sam managed the family's finances and oversaw their expenses, down to Sol's tuition and the ham for the larder. But by the summer of 1820 he could hardly bring himself to journey a few miles to see his family.[12]

In 1819 mercantile markets shuddered. Banks that had offered easy credit in previous years were forced to call in their loans. Hundreds of smaller state banks and commercial firms failed as property and commodity prices fell sharply, slashing the value of the tobacco and western lands in which Sam had speculated. The 1820 payment to Jacob from the school's purchasers went directly to Mr. Marx to help cover part of Sam's enormous debt. Repaying the savings of his father and siblings necessarily came second. "If you knew how painful my visits [to Spring Farm] are," Sam confided to Ellen, "you would not blame me if they are seldom made." Jacob, at the age of fifty, and his dependents once more faced financial distress.[13]

Only slowly did the family realize the extent of their loss—that Sam was all but ruined. Such a blow could scarcely be mentioned, yet they wondered how Sam could have left them so dangerously exposed. They cherished Sam and were at pains not to add to his remorse. It was easier, in some ways, to question their father's judgment in entrusting so much to his hands. Had the bulk of their savings been placed in bank stock, Ellen argued, they could now assist Sam; instead, as they had with Jacob in earlier times, "we all sunk at once powerless when we thought our life of comfort . . . just about to commence." It seemed doubtful whether Sam could ever "refund what was so hardly earned."[14]

There was an appearance of prosperity. The Mordecais owned eighteen adult slaves and their children. Luxuriant clover grew in the fields. New wool was sheared from their flock of sheep. They maintained an extensive garden yielding produce for sale in town. And their swift phaeton was ready to carry family members into Richmond. But Spring Farm in 1820 was beset by worry and contention. The lone male at home (Alfred was at West Point, George and Augustus were working in Raleigh), Jacob proceeded to cut expenses. He fired the overseer, and the farm hobbled along under his own management. It was, as Ellen said, "painful indeed" to see their savings "wasting gradually in supporting the negroes and improving the land."[15]

Again, something had to be done. Almost since arriving in Virginia, the idea of returning to school keeping hovered as a threat, a fantasy, a final resort. The three eldest sisters proposed that the farm be sold or rented out and the family move to town. In Richmond, they would open a school, with Jacob installed as its nominal headmaster. In exchange, they would give up to Jacob their "claim" on profits from Warrenton (he had earlier promised but never conveyed to them eight hundred dollars apiece). Most important, Ellen explained, all the profits of the Richmond academy would be "independently ours, Rachel's, Caroline's, and mine."[16]

The sisters' plan would sting—their father and Sam especially. The farm venture would be declared a loss, and the women's return to work would expose the Mordecai men's failure to provide even modest support. While the brothers broke off to pursue their professions, Rachel, Ellen, and Caroline felt shackled to perpetual dependence, including, it seemed, barely genteel poverty.[17] Although their planned educational venture won Jacob's and Sam's reluctant approval, it never went into effect. Within a year, both Rachel and Caroline left home to marry.

11

TWO WEDDINGS

Caroline looked forward to teaching school again only because she could not have what she truly desired, a life shared with Achilles Plunkett, who had taught French, drawing, music, and dancing at the Mordecai School. She had wanted it for so long she could not remember a time when it did not define her world. Years had passed since Caroline (then nineteen) had fallen in love. He, a gray-headed widower with three children, had been forty-two. From the outset, the Mordecais declared the match unsuitable. An inappropriate union that might drag the family down economically or threaten the carefully cultivated values of their covenant was plainly worse than no marriage at all.

For his part, Achilles Plunkett returned Caroline's love with all his heart. As the affair gained momentum, the scolding commenced. Late nights in his office, Sol tried to argue his sister out of her attachment. Caroline argued back, and neither budged. Sam was called upon to bring Caroline to her senses. She agreed to give up her French lessons with Achilles, and with them hours of his companionship, but continued to pray in vain that her family would come around. Although once possessed of substantial holdings in Santo Domingo (today's Dominican Republic), Achilles fled in 1809, when Haiti's revolutionary forces invaded, and had arrived penniless in the United States. This background made little impression on Caroline's family. They found Achilles far too old and pointed out that he was not rising in his profession. Further, his three children might make Caroline's life miserable. Notably, if his Roman Catholic roots constituted a mark against him, the Mordecais did not mention it in their correspondence. When Achilles proposed in 1814, Caroline bent to pressure applied by her father, Rachel, and her brothers and replied with "a positive rejection." Having done her duty to those whose sole interest was her well-being, she could not, Rachel mistakenly concluded, "be otherwise than . . . happy."[1]

Caroline had stoically tried to take satisfaction in doing what her family wished. In the souring mood of Spring Farm, she could not do so any longer. Instead, she felt betrayed, for this certainly was not the happy domestic circle her loved ones had been promising her for so many years. She longed for escape and snapped up a chance to visit Moses's family in Raleigh (and pass through Warrenton and see Achilles on her journey). Yet in Raleigh Caroline's mood continued to blacken, and she returned to Spring Farm more despondent than ever. Caroline could find few reasons to live.[2]

Twelve months passed in this way until one afternoon, as Caroline lay on her bed "lost to us and the world," Rachel and Ellen entered and asked her, "Caroline, do you wish to be happy?"

"Yes, to be sure," came the weak reply.

"Then be so," Rachel said, "for Papa has given his consent."

"To what?"

"To your marrying Mr. P[lunkett]."

Caroline did not believe her ears. Rachel and Ellen repeated the phrase until she leaped up, rushed to Jacob, covered him with kisses, and blessed him for his mercy.[3]

"I would do anything . . . that would conduce to your happiness," Jacob once told his children. But in this case he had yielded neither to happiness (as he saw it) nor to reason but "to necessity." Family members grew concerned that Caroline's depression might lead her to suicide. Such mercy as Jacob displayed may also have been easier to grant when he considered her alternative—supporting herself by teaching school in Richmond. Yet Caroline's happiness brought her parent pain and embarrassment. Jacob told Rachel that this second intermarriage meant that should any more of his offspring choose spouses beyond "the pale," he would be unable to "oppose their wishes." Nevertheless, he would not permit a ceremony repugnant to his "religious principles" to take place in or near Richmond. These principles were growing stronger every year; indeed, Jacob was poised to take a leading role in the Richmond synagogue. If Moses would host the wedding in Raleigh, so be it. Jacob would not attend.[4]

Incredibly, Moses, who had received Caroline's warmest sympathy during the family conflict over his engagement to Margaret Lane, urged his sister to break her engagement to Achilles Plunkett. Jacob became flustered and, perhaps thinking Moses had damaging information about Achilles, revoked his assent to the union. Such indecisiveness left Rachel and Ellen, along with Caroline, "thunderstruck." Their combined effort managed to overturn his reversal, and Caroline fled to Warrenton, where the family's old friend Judge Oliver Fitts united the couple. No Mordecais were present.[5]

Even in the moment of her greatest happiness, when Ellen and Rachel burst into her room gleefully announcing that she could wed her beloved, Caroline envied the elder sister who did everything right. Rachel, too, was to marry, and her engagement gave her father joy, not pain.[6]

Just a few months after Caroline and Achilles' quiet wedding in Warrenton, Jacob presided proudly as Richmond's Jewish families, the Kennons, and other friends gathered at the house at Spring Farm. The Richmond congregation's hazan, Isaac Judah, conducted the traditional ceremony. Sol made the journey home from Philadelphia, his first visit since leaving the farm a year and a half before, and Moses urged the newlyweds to stop over in Raleigh. The circumstances of the sisters' weddings contrasted too sharply for Caroline to make an appearance at Rachel's, but Ellen filled her in: "We played and sung, talked and laughed, partook of refreshments."[7]

The happiest member of the wedding party—with the possible exception of Ellen, who had Sol at her side—was the groom, "short and stout" Aaron Lazarus. He had waited a long time to call Rachel Mordecai his own. Aaron had grown up in Charleston (then the country's largest Jewish community) and in 1803 had married Esther Cohen, the daughter of his father's business partner. Neither the elder Mr. Lazarus nor Mr. Cohen was very prosperous, but both men played important roles in Charleston's Jewish community. Like Jacob, Aaron left family behind and moved to a less developed market. In Wilmington, North Carolina, he opened what would eventually grow into a substantial shipping business with the West Indies. Before long other businessmen elected Aaron a director of the Bank of Cape Fear, and he purchased waterfront property for warehouses. He could buy his wife fine jewelry, and they had begun construction on an imposing Federal-style mansion overlooking the town when Esther died in 1816 at age thirty-two.[8]

Left with seven children, Aaron sent his eldest daughter, Phila, to the Mordecais' academy. Another daughter followed her the next year. The girls spoke enthusiastically about the Mordecais, including their teacher Rachel. Aaron, curious and eager to remarry, stopped in Warrenton en route to New York in 1817. Rachel predicted that despite his recent bereavement, not much time would "pass without a honeymoon" for forty-year-old Mr. Lazarus.[9] Her otherwise notable powers of observation failed her, however. The idea of *sharing* a honeymoon with Aaron seems never to have entered her mind.[10]

Just as the Mordecais handed their school to its new owners, a letter came from Aaron asking for Rachel's hand in marriage. She could not have been more surprised. Her decided views about the requirements for an enlightened domestic life meant that the proposal was readily answered. Financial ease Aaron seemed to have. But from all she could tell, he lacked education, cultivation, and a harmonious, virtuous home. "I of course endeavored to render his disappointment as little mortifying as possible," Rachel told Sam, who might have felt a pang at the thought, since by then he had a collection of letters like the one Rachel had just written to Aaron. But Aaron thanked her for "the flattering manner" in which he had been refused and hoped that, with the school sold, she would gain the happiness she deserved.[11] Of course, that was not to be.

Perhaps Aaron Lazarus heard of Sam's (and thus the family's) financial reversals in 1819 and sensed an opportunity. Possibly, he simply could not forget the accomplished green-eyed woman who, in the face of Maria Edgeworth's prejudice, had defended her people's honor. Whatever the reason, in August 1820 Aaron drove up the lane to Spring Farm. He passed a few pleasant hours with the Mordecais that evening, went into Richmond for the night, and the next day drove to the farm again for dinner. Afterward he "renewed his addresses" to Rachel.[12] He had business in New York and had journeyed by land rather than water in order to see her. Would she reconsider? A year and a half had passed, and this time Rachel's decision was not so easy. The enlightened domesticity she looked forward to living out so fully at Spring Farm was proving more elusive than it had when they all worked so hard in Warrenton. The sweetness of their family circle had soured. Aaron Lazarus went away having extracted one promise at least; upon his return south, Rachel would give him her answer.

Rachel hesitated on several accounts. Stepmotherhood was one. Another was the poverty threatening the Mordecais. The national depression showed no sign of lifting, and, on the one hand, Rachel saw her marriage as a chance to lighten the burden on her family. But would Aaron expect a dowry? Like so many heroines in nineteenth-century novels, Rachel found herself uneasily contemplating the role money concerns could play in such a momentous choice as this. Her chief reservation centered on Aaron himself. To be sure, he had positive qualities, but she did not pretend to find this modest merchant irresistible. "He is not the man my youthful fancy would have portrayed" as a husband, she confided to Sol in Philadelphia. Such fancies died hard, and Aaron, unlike some of her brothers, for example, in no way resembled that "engaging person [of] a superior understanding enriched by cultivation [and] a love of study exceeding and capable of guiding my own."[13]

When Aaron arrived for his answer, Rachel stood frozen for several minutes before descending the staircase to greet him. She sighed al-

most audibly when he steered their conversation to "general subjects"—the weather, her father's health, his journey—long enough for
her to collect her wits. Then Aaron asked for her decision. She did not
speak. Instead, she handed him a sheet of paper and left the room. He
read a carefully enumerated list of concerns. Perhaps he smiled. Re-
entering the parlor, Rachel looked into his face and found it calm.
They discussed the items on her inventory one by one. The education
of his children would remain utterly apart from her duties as his wife,
Aaron said, except that he would seek her advice. He remarked that her
complete "want of fortune" changed nothing, giving him the chance to
prove he valued her for herself alone. As she grew more calm and the
learned partner of her dreams retreated, Rachel saw a man of flesh and
blood, full of what she called "friendship and tenderness," standing before her. "I yield," she told Solomon, "and care is no longer an inmate
of my bosom." Aaron rejoiced.[14]

12

RELIGION, FAMILY, FORTUNE

On his return to Philadelphia after Rachel's nuptials, Sol began a yearlong clinical internship at the Philadelphia Almshouse, where a select group of top medical students were permitted to treat indigent patients. Not long into his internship, Sol fell ill with fever.[1] The illness initiated an attachment that tested the boundary between intermarriage and something more radical—total assimilation.

His surgery professor, Dr. Joseph Parrish, encouraged Sol to recuperate at his family's summer lodgings in Long Branch, New Jersey. At the beach, amid fashionable society, Sol encountered something far "more interesting than the dashing waves," a "sweet amiable girl," not pretty but, more important, able, he told Ellen, to "converse." Born in Calcutta to British missionaries, Anna Tennant resided in Philadelphia with her childless aunt and uncle. Within days, Sol was courting her. He introduced himself to her guardians, supplying, as he told Ellen, all important facts pertaining to his "religion, family, and fortune."[2]

What Sol told them led Anna to believe not only that he was prepared to unite with her as a Christian but that he wished to do so from conviction that Christ was indeed the Messiah. Writing to Ellen, Sol explained his religious position somewhat differently. He had told Anna's family that "the liberality . . . on points of religion in which our father . . . educated his children constituted them Jews but by name."[3] That Sol could state this so baldly and with apparent conviction eloquently bespeaks the protean nature of the family's evolving covenant with themselves and the wider worlds in which they increasingly moved. It also bespeaks the differences, sometimes stark, that could keep company within the ambit of the 1796 covenant and Rachel's elaboration of ideal enlightened domesticity. Reason was trusted to lead routinely to rational choices, whether regarding one's investments, one's soul, or one's heart. Finally, it bespeaks the vast distance that was beginning to open up between Jacob's religious views and some of his children's.

Sol was in love. Anna was smitten. As the summer moved toward fall, they met as often as possible. Sol wrote home for "a slip of jessamine"—jasmine was his favorite flower—so that he could press it into her hands. Anna began a correspondence with Ellen, whom she acknowledged as her suitor's "favorite companion," and sought instruction on how best to return Sol's love. The two women shared the same birthday, an apparent sign of cosmic alignment. Anna told her correspondent in Virginia that she dreamed of a day when she, Sol, and "our Ellen" would share a happy home.[4]

Six weeks after his seaside encounter with Anna, Sol addressed a letter to her parents presenting himself and his wishes to their attention. Anna's aunt and uncle had welcomed him in their home, and his suit looked to bid fair.[5] But as Sol waited for word from India, Ellen plagued him with questions and accusations. That he had fallen in love with and hoped to marry a Christian did not surprise her. Sol might, moreover, be forgiven if he deferred to his wife in the religious upbringing of their children. She granted, too, that she, like Sol, would not have chosen to be born into a faith that carried with it so many "difficulties." Certainly, he wanted to allay the prejudices of Anna's evangelical parents. But his offer of apostasy went too far. It subverted, she told him, "the proper pride and independence for which we [Mordecais] have ever been respected." Convictionless conversion was, in Ellen's estimation, base conduct—even for her beloved Sol.[6]

To Sol's dismay, the readiness to convert that Ellen found so odious ultimately proved his undoing with Anna Tennant. "All is at an end," Anna told him. He at first assumed she meant that her parents had rejected his proposal because of his Jewish origin, but Anna was at pains to explain her real reason. Her aunt had observed that to be happy, a couple must stand united in their "religious views." So Anna had thought they were. But as she listened to Sol more closely, she recognized that when it came to what she considered "this greatest of all our duties," he had very different ideas. As he himself wrote, religion for Sol was a matter of "peace of mind" and a means to secure "the good opinion of society." Such were his convictions. He would embrace her Savior not because he believed in him but because he believed in so little.[7]

Anna was miserable. She released a man she loved. She felt ashamed that because she had misjudged his views, Sol was now suffering. For a few months Sol clung to the hope that by sincerely finding his way to Christ, he might win Anna back. She discouraged him. He retreated to the solitary misery his honest unbelief seemed to have brought upon him. Not, as he said, "an Israelite" or a Christian, Sol struggled to discover what, and who, he was.[8]

Needing love, Sol gravitated back to Ellen, who pardoned all. In the year following his tumultuous affair with Anna Tennant, Sol passed his medical examinations and began considering where to open his medical practice. Ellen waited patiently, looking forward "to the period which will fix us together forever and ever in this world."[9]

But again Sol's choices placed him out of Ellen's reach. His profession was overcrowded; no place near Richmond offered the opportunity Sol sought. His bitterness and confusion regarding his Jewish roots no doubt contributed to his anxieties. Though he talked of it as a temporary move, Sol, in selecting Mobile, Alabama, as his destination, took himself farther than any Mordecai had from the band of love and duty, to a place where who he was and what "Mordecai" meant would be his concerns alone.[10]

Alabama had joined the Union as a slave state only three years earlier, in 1819. Andrew Jackson's defeat of the Creek Indians had opened the area to rapid white settlement. But Alabama remained "distant" and "wild" to the Mordecais. In 1822 Mobile had fewer than three thousand residents (Richmond had five times that many), and violence plagued the surrounding region. Native Americans resisted, sometimes violently, as a booming cotton economy led to constant encroachment on their lands. For whites, Indian removal was the most pressing political issue.[11]

Not only did Sol move to Mobile, but, after a residence of eighteen months, he stood together with Caroline Waller as the Reverend J. B. Warren, a Methodist, presided over their marriage. Sol's letter announcing his engagement reached Richmond after the wedding. The Mordecais had but a glancing description of Caroline: "sweet tempered, amiable . . . and well informed." That she was not a Jew he did not need to say. He did make the point, however, that Caroline was not rich and asked Moses to help finance his partnership with another physician in the town.[12]

Hasty as the marriage appeared, Ellen could not pretend to be shocked. As a bachelor doctor, Sol had been at a disadvantage. Families, and especially ladies, overlooked him, calling instead on his married colleague. He did not say whether they overlooked him because of his Jewishness as well. During this trying time, Sol met Caroline Waller, "a pretty girl with a most poetical name." In the abstract, Sol's marriage did not nullify his intention to live with his sister. But even Ellen realized how unlikely that outcome would be.[13] Indeed, the previous year Ellen, for the first time she could remember, seriously looked at another man.

Ellen's affections had found an attraction closer to home, in familiar Warrenton. John D. Plunkett, Achilles' eldest son from his first marriage, had always been a favorite, especially of Rachel's. He had assisted his father in the art department at the Mordecai School and continued this work after Achilles became part owner of the institution in 1819. His real love was science. He collected insects and built kaleidoscopes. In 1823, John's stepmother (and Ellen's sister), Caroline, was recovering from the birth of her second child, and Ellen came to help her with the household and teach some of her classes. When John declared himself to Ellen, she was surprised and flattered. Most surprising of all, she began dreaming of a future with a man she had known for years, though never intimately. Interested in literature, accomplished in conversation, John offered the enlightened companionship the Mordecais thought ideal in a marriage. It was a standard few men could meet.

Notwithstanding John's attractions, they were not worth alienating her family. Having witnessed the chilling effect of Caroline's marriage to Achilles on her relationships with Jacob, Moses, Sol, and Sam, Ellen swore *she* would never unite herself with anyone of whom her family did not unanimously approve. And she saw little reason John Plunkett would find acceptance where his father had not. Returning to Spring Farm, Ellen said she hoped that John would "overcome" his feelings for her, retract his proposal, and thereby spare them both. Instead, John begged permission to court her formally. Ellen decided to throw the matter completely to Jacob, whose response astonished her.[14]

For Ellen to marry outside the Jewish community did not, Jacob said, entail "a sacrifice of religious sentiments on my part, for I know my children to be morally good and leave them in that particular to the guidance of their own good sense and feelings." But no wedding would take place, he added shrewdly, until the Plunketts fully paid what they owed the Mordecais for the Warrenton school. Even Ellen had more severe conditions than this. Because John planned to attend medical school in Philadelphia, he could not support her for several more years. Five years might elapse before he received a medical degree and opened a practice; Ellen would be nearly forty. Perhaps it would be better to marry quickly and live simply in Warrenton with Caroline and Achilles while John pursued his studies. If children came, however, he might have to halt his training. Jacob seemed unable to render a judgment on—or take much interest in—these matters. Ellen was almost hurt. For the right price, Jacob appeared prepared to let her go.[15]

Ellen begged Sol to tell her what to do. He, too, declined to make her decision for her. Confusingly as ever, he reminded her of their pledge to grow old together, but, he said, "to see you happily married and comfortably situated would be a thousand times more delightful." When Moses registered "his cool uninfluenced judgment" that John

Plunkett, a schoolteacher with dreams of a medical career, was simply too poor for Ellen to marry, she gave in.[16]

Ellen remained alone, therefore, while Sol took a wife. He had told his fiancée's family that with some assistance from his brother, the distinguished Raleigh lawyer, he could join forces with another doctor. Business would rapidly expand. Another brother, the tobacco merchant, would purchase new furniture, china, and silverware for the couple. And he outlined his scheme to buy a nice lot in town and build a house with room enough to hold children and, should she ever wish to come, his sister Ellen.[17]

Almost two months after the wedding, the mail brought word from Moses in Raleigh. In reply to Sol's request for a several-thousand-dollar loan, Moses accused him of having lost his wits. Indeed, Moses said Sol could and must not marry yet, and he should expect no credit as a reward for foolishness.[18] Sol's siblings had reacted coolly to his marrying Caroline Waller. His father had charged him with violating filial duty by marrying without first seeking a paternal blessing, but, considering Moses's experience, Sol can hardly be blamed for proceeding with the wedding before circulating news of his engagement.[19] But Moses's scolding and accusations of bad judgment and sloth galled him the most. After all, Sol had labored without pay for ten years as an "abcdarian [sic]" in Warrenton while Moses established a legal career, saving each penny he earned. It seemed profoundly unfair, and not at all in line with the mutual support the Mordecais were pledged to give one another, that Moses now denied assistance. Moses, meanwhile, had just added much to his own coffers when, his first wife having died, he married her elder sister, Ann (Nancy) Willis Lane. Entering upon what would prove a difficult and not particularly joyful marriage, Sol gritted his teeth and announced, "I shall in strict observance to duty . . . live . . . frugally and economically." His relations must expect no visit from the newlyweds. Travel was beyond his means—and very likely his inclination. Sol never visited Spring Farm again.[20]

Jacob mourned the rift between his sons. Yet Moses soon occasioned his father sorrow of the keenest sort. At the time he was dispensing his austere advice to Sol in Mobile, Moses was too weak from malaria to work. Years of practice in the plantation region's circuit courts had ruined his health, and he could ingest only crackers, tea, and buttermilk. That summer, Jacob's brothers-in-law Samy Myers and Joseph Marx rode out to Spring Farm with the news that his eldest son was gone. Death, it seems, was stalking the family. That same year, cruelly on the heels of the loss of two of their children, Caroline's Achilles died.[21]

As Jacob and Judy's offspring struggled to define themselves, they often rendered their loves, marriages, and intermarriages the battlefields in the contest to control the manner of their own assimilation and acculturation. Each clash left scars; events had driven wedges between parent and child, brother and sister. Seeking succor and a way to account for what was taking place in his family, Jacob turned to God. Thirty years earlier, he and Judy had come to the South to forge a life outside the narrow communities of their youth. He now found himself deeply involved in the erection of Richmond's first Jewish house of worship. In the graceful brick building down the hill from the Jeffersonian State Capitol, Jacob's faith at last stood in full public view. In this house of peace, he had found another home.

Thus it was Jacob Mordecai, who spent so many years far from his fellow Jews, who mounted the pulpit at Beth Shalome on the occasion of the synagogue's consecration. He used the opportunity to do what he had not done in all the years before, what he had not done for his own children. Jacob exhorted the scattered flock of Israel to return to God. True happiness was not in worldly things; it came only with obedience to the Almighty and his laws. "Settled in a land flowing with milk and honey," the Jews of Virginia had too often, Jacob said, "sinned against the Lord." They ignored his commandments, abused the Sabbath, forgot the festivals. The purpose of these laws, he declared, "was to keep [the Jews] distinct from other nations by whom they were surrounded, and with whom it was not intended they should commune." A return to Jehovah was necessary to ensure the separation of Jews and Gentiles.[22]

It was a surprising, if not alarming, stance to the children Jacob reared in Warrenton. Jacob now said that the family's cautious, understated approach to religion, which omitted aspects of Jewish practice that might be awkward or might offend Gentile neighbors, violated God's intent. For some in the second generation, the gap between Warrenton days and the orthodoxy now practiced and preached at Spring Farm would dominate their relations with their father.

As Jacob formulated this new approach to community and faith, Sol and Ellen negotiated their paths, defining themselves as members of an emerging American middle class and in relation to their father's family. A single Jewish woman such as Ellen had few prospects that would not jeopardize her class position (as marriage to John Plunkett might) or alienate her from her father. She rededicated herself to her duty to Jacob and her devotion to Sol, no matter that he fell outside her geographic compass. A man with superior professional training, Sol had ready access to the respectability and security (if not affluence) of the American bourgeoisie. Having never experienced its benefits, he felt little loss in letting his Jewishness go. Given Jacob's intensifying orthodoxy, Sol judged well in moving toward such complete assimilation far from home.

13

SOUTH AND NORTH

The rooms of Dr. Solomon Mordecai's home in Mobile, Alabama, echoed with his three sons' shouts and laughter. Five years had passed since his marriage to Caroline Waller. It had been eight years since Sol left Spring Farm—or saw his sister Ellen.

At first she had written him every Friday, though he responded once to every four or five letters received, and eventually Ellen curtailed her correspondence. Occasionally he raised the prospect of her coming to Mobile. Ellen sometimes balked, fearful of how she might be received by Sol's new family; then she would complain if he didn't press her. She continued to hope that Sol would move back to Virginia, or at least bring his family for a visit. But he always claimed that he could not spare the interruption in his practice, and Ellen began to doubt they would ever meet again.[1]

Logistical challenges and emotional obstacles made her chances of reaching Mobile seem remote indeed. "A lady cannot travel alone," she reminded Sol in one letter, "and a poor lady cannot travel [at all]." Ellen hated this restraint on her freedom, this emblem of her dependence. In

1830, however, Sol seemed resolved. She *must* come for a long stay, perhaps of several years. Friends of his were planning to spend the summer months in the North, and, their vacation finished, they could escort Ellen to Mobile in the fall. He dreamed, he said, "of enfolding you in my arms, with wife and children to witness and sympathise in the transports we shall feel." Ellen might have wished for fewer witnesses, but she imagined sitting together with his beautiful head in her lap and telling him "all."[2]

Not money, not distance, but Jacob presented the greatest barrier to the fulfillment of Ellen's dearest wish. Merely the thought of Ellen's going to Mobile distressed her father. One evening, he drew her into his room and stated his opposition to her traveling "by water, and with strangers." Ellen objected that thousands made the passage down the Mississippi every year and that her escorts would be Sol's friends, hardly "strangers." Perhaps her answers failed to satisfy Jacob because a deeper fear danced before him. Once in Mobile, Ellen might never return. So many of his children had moved beyond his reach; they were dead, or distant, or half severed from his heart for not upholding the religious heritage that now absorbed him. Jacob did not have to spell out what Ellen already knew. As an unmarried woman, she owed her first duty to her father. Reading his countenance, however, Ellen recognized something more. He seemed to want her there because, as she explained to Sol, should difficulties arise, he could depend on her to help him in a way no other member of the household could—not his wife, his son Augustus, or his daughter Julia. To be so needed gave Ellen pause. Jacob had once leaned on Rachel in such a way—how jealous Ellen had been then! She would, she told Sol, submit to their father and repress every "sigh of regret."[3]

In typical fashion, Jacob changed his mind two days later. When Rachel included a line in a letter expressing her hope that Ellen would soon visit Sol, Jacob declared, "Well Ellen, two against one . . . are too much and I retract my veto." Ellen tried to smile, but her father's fickleness was unnerving. Did he not need her after all? Might not his veto be as easily reinstated as retracted? In the following months, Jacob never inquired about her Mobile plans.[4]

Ellen had missed the chance to travel with Sol's Mobile connections, but Sam stepped forward to escort her. It was agreed. Accompanied by her brother, she would follow her heart's fondest wish and make the journey south. But in making the trip, brother and sister not only followed Ellen's heart; they joined the current of a nation in motion. Riding in the stagecoach through western Virginia's mountains, Ellen and Sam passed a whole family moving west and watched as the children, traveling on foot, collapsed, exhausted, behind the wagon. At the rain-swollen Jackson River near White Sulphur Springs, the party waited to ford and passed the day with a family and its cows in a log cabin, partaking of a feast of "grilled venison, poached eggs, maple molasses, fried bacon, biscuit, coffee and milk." At the Kanawha they boarded a steamboat pointing northwest to the Ohio River, and in Louisville, Ellen and Sam's steamer chugged around the falls through the new Portland Canal. From there the way was smooth and clear for the slow ride down the Mississippi.[5]

At New Orleans, they took the morning packet boat to Mobile. When a passenger said, "Mobile is in sight," Ellen blanched. Asked by a fellow traveler if she felt ill, Ellen shook her head. It wasn't that. She reached the boat's deck as the vessel cut toward the wharf. The crew tied off the lines while she examined every face on shore, praying not to see Sol's. She had begged him to wait for her at home, fearing that the emotions of their meeting might overwhelm her. Sol had obeyed her wishes and sent Caroline's father to greet the travelers. Mr. Waller led Ellen and Sam through the streets of Mobile and at last pointed and said, "That is the house." Ellen ran to the porch, where a door flung open. He stood before her. "Is it possible?" he asked as they embraced. Age had changed nothing. He was to her "the same, same— same."[6]

That same year, 1831, two other Mordecai siblings journeyed together, but this time in a northerly direction. Moses's eldest child, Henry Mordecai, was to enroll in a New England boarding school, and in June he set out from Raleigh with his uncle George. In Washington, D.C., they met Alfred Mordecai and proceeded toward Northampton, Massachusetts, and the experimental Round Hill School.[7]

Henry's attendance at Round Hill signified a Mordecai victory in the debate with their in-laws over Moses's children. Indeed, the Lanes had very different ideas about rearing children. They considered the Mordecais overbearing when it came to learning; fresh air and affection were at least as important as regular study, and Moses's orphans were encouraged to spend long hours exploring the plantation surrounding the imposing Greek Revival house, which the Mordecais dubbed "Moses Manor." This lightly supervised upbringing and the children's constant companionship with "little house darkies" shocked the Mordecais. The children's characters and mental development, the Mordecais believed, could only suffer.[8]

The Mordecai triumph in the tug-of-war over educational principles became the occasion for a reunion of George Washington Mordecai and his younger brother Alfred. The offspring of Jacob's second marriage, the two had hardly seen each other in the decade since Alfred enrolled at West Point. Coming of age just as Sam's losses in the panic of 1819 threatened the family with want, George and Alfred pursued their careers single-mindedly, hoping soon to be able to offer assistance to their parents.[9] Their dedication had begun to pay off handsomely.

George had studied law in Raleigh under his eldest brother. After Moses's death, George remained as the head of his half brother's household, serving as guardian and trustee for the four children—Henry, Ellen, Jacob, and Margaret—who were beneficiaries of an extensive estate. George himself inherited much of Moses's practice. He hesitated to say something so egotistic, but at the age of twenty-nine he took comfort in informing his family, "I am possessed of a competency." In 1831 he reported earnings exceeding ten thousand dollars.[10]

Alfred, who had studied at the Mordecai School and been tutored by Sol, early impressed his instructors at West Point. Four years later he graduated first in his class and was commissioned second lieutenant in the Army Corps of Engineers. For two years he served at West Point as assistant professor. After this, Alfred helped construct two forts near Norfolk, Virginia, and at the age of twenty-four he was detailed for duty as assistant in the Washington office of General Alexander Macomb, the head of the War Office's Engineering Department. These were plum appointments for any young officer, and the Mordecais greeted each with joy. Long absence, however, made for awkward homecomings, and Alfred complained of feeling detached from his parents and siblings—excepting Rachel, whom he adored almost as a mother. Living in the nation's capital, attending parties, Alfred nevertheless worried about his future under Andrew Jackson's administration. He alternately feared sinking unnoticed into the mass of other young men or being found to lack the talents ascribed to him.[11]

The pleasure of traveling with his brother alleviated such bleak reflections. It was a "delightful" journey. In New York they bought tickets to a freak show featuring a live anaconda and eight-year-old Deborah Tripp, who weighed 180 pounds. Steaming along the Connecticut River to Norwalk, they admired New England's trim, productive appearance. In New Haven the Mordecais paid their respects to U.S. senator James Hillhouse and complimented his magisterial elm plantings throughout the town. A few miles on, they stopped for the night at Hartford and, as Alfred would recall, "heard the first low mutterings of a storm which, thirty years later, swept and desolated the land." Seeing a notice for an abolition meeting and having nothing else to do, George, Alfred, and Henry joined a small audience to hear an address by William Lloyd Garrison, publisher of the still-obscure *Liberator*.[12]

To the southern travelers, twenty-six-year-old Garrison appeared mad. He lambasted the venerable American Colonization Society, the established national voice of antislavery that had arranged passage to Africa for some fifteen thousand freed slaves. Garrison alleged that in shipping the former slaves off the continent, colonization advocates revealed their prejudice against black people. Worse, their snail-paced program ignored the daily tragedy slavery represented for more than two million souls. In a better nation, Garrison said, black and white people would share equally in the promise of American democracy. "I *will be* as harsh as truth and as uncompromising as justice," Garrison vowed, and said he was prepared to "die a martyr" for the cause of immediate abolition of slavery. The Mordecais shifted uneasily in their seats. Young Henry's share of Moses's estate would bring him human chattel worth more than ten thousand dollars. Alfred tried to brush off the evening as mere spectacle, but it was provoking in ways the obese Miss Tripp was not. He told Ellen he had "seldom seen George so much vexed."[13]

Within months many more southerners would be vexed with Garrison, blaming him for bloodshed in Southampton County, Virginia. George had just returned to Raleigh from New England when the alarm sounded throughout the white South. On a hot August night, Nat Turner led a band of fellow slaves in a rebellion that left fifty-five white people dead. Seventeen African-Americans were subsequently executed and hundreds more reportedly murdered by whites in revenge. Garrison's rhetoric still rang in George's ears (the reformer had once spoken in support of a Wilmington-born free black man's call to revolt). George believed slaveholders must halt the "unwarrantable indulgences" permitted so many bond servants; slaves, he said, should "submit quietly to their unfortunate condition." Other family members downplayed the events and the general hysteria that followed. Petersburg (along with cities throughout the region) went on alert, and Sam, who had moved his tobacco-trading office there, performed his share of patrol duty. But he told Ellen not to believe any newspaper accounts she and Sol's family read in Mobile—everything was overblown.[14]

When an alleged slave conspiracy was discovered in Wilmington several weeks after the Virginia revolt, the Lazaruses stayed home while many of the city's white people crowded into the bank and the churches for protection. Rachel expressed her desire to leave the slaveholding state, but not because she rejected the slave system. Rather, she declared it "deplorable in the extreme" to live where "soon or late we or our descendents will become the certain victims of a band of lawless wretches who will deem murder and outrage just retribution" for their enslavement.[15]

The panic cost Aaron a good deal in valuable property. Three of his slaves, probably stevedores working at his warehouses, were among the twenty-three blacks imprisoned for conspiracy, although they were not among the "*ringleaders*" reported by the *Cape Fear Recorder* to have been lynched "by the PEOPLE." In a grotesque warning to all black people, the heads of those lynched were taken from the corpses and "placed on poles in conspicuous places."[16]

Washington Lazarus, Aaron's twenty-three-year-old son who had just gained admittance to the bar, defended his father's slaves Billy and

Adam in court, but without success. Convicted, the slaves died by firing squad and hanging; Aaron was compensated by the state for a portion of their value. Slavery grew harsher in Wilmington and across the South, with curfews, badges for free blacks, and the tightening or elimination of laws on manumission.[17]

Aaron, Rachel, and the Mordecais resisted the "horror-stricken" mood that gripped many slaveholders in 1831.[18] But the advent of Garrison and such overt resistance to the slave system as Nat Turner had organized made unavoidable a new, more regional consciousness. During the coming decades, American politics became enmeshed in questions of slavery's territorial expansion, and a strengthening abolitionist movement strained the slaveholding Mordecais' nationalistic outlook. Sam, Aaron, and George threw in their lots with the Whig Party, which sought to keep the slavery issue from controlling the political agenda. As the Whigs slowly crumbled, with sectional tensions giving way to more acrimonious debate, Jacob found solace elsewhere—in recollections of a fonder past and hopes for a greater, eternal future.

14

RECEIVED LIKE A PROPHET
IN ISRAEL

till experiencing the aftershocks of Nat Turner's revolt, the Petersburg militia stood on the alert in September 1831, when Sam Mordecai and his father departed for Philadelphia. Traveling with Ellen to Mobile that spring and now accompanying Jacob to his birthplace, Sam decided that escorting loved ones offered greater rewards than his last several years of tobacco trading—a period during which his debt to the family hovered at around twenty-five thousand dollars. There seemed little prospect of his ever meeting this greatest of obligations. Over the past decade, Sam had looked on as Spring Farm limped along. Alfred voiced the shame he felt at seeing his "aged parents struggling with misfortune." George shared the concern and, beginning in 1828, set about convincing his father to give up the place. Depressed, Jacob relented. Spring Farm was for sale.[1]

It was still on the market as Jacob journeyed to Philadelphia in 1831. An auction just before his departure produced no sale. Why should anyone till such worn-out soil when there was rich land in Illinois and Mississippi? So the fields were put to grass. The family would remain, and the large market garden would continue, but nearly all the slaves and livestock must go.[2]

The trip to Philadelphia came, therefore, as a welcome distraction. All along the route, Jacob felt like Rip van Winkle. He recalled every watering place between Richmond and Philadelphia from the times he had made the journey in his youth, but most of them had vanished. More than forty years had passed since Jacob walked the streets of his childhood. It thrilled him to show Sam and Alfred, who joined them from Washington, his former home and the site of old Captain Stiles's school, whose cadets had paraded the nation's Founding Fathers into the city. At Mikveh Israel the congregation had replaced the modest building whose construction Jacob long ago helped finance with a grand neo-Egyptian structure. Jacob called on the hazan, Isaac Leeser, Jacob's protégé and a former Richmond resident, who was boldly revitalizing Philadelphia's Jewry.[3]

Jacob's warm reception among Philadelphia's prominent and well-to-do Jews was especially rewarding. He was no longer Jacob I. Cohen's poor stepson dragging a trail of business failure and debt. At the age of sixty-nine, Jacob was not rich, but he had established an acclaimed girls' academy and retired respectably. He had become, in the words of one Philadelphia Jewish lady, "a venerable gentleman." Moreover, Jews who took their religion seriously admired his scholarship. His wavering in Warrenton twenty years earlier had helped transform him into a devout and active member of his community, one who was convinced, as he told Rachel, "of the reasonableness of our laws, of their truth and excellence," and determined to reject "every thing that mistaken men have written to weaken our belief in the perfect Unity of God."[4]

Although Jacob never published his religious writings, he had established a reputation as a font of Jewish knowledge, as a defender of orthodoxy against proselytizing from the outside and reform from within, and as a mentor to young Jews trying to sustain ancient traditions in the modern, and sometimes hostile and prejudiced, world. Jacob corresponded with Christians directly about Judaism and protested the anti-Semitism inherent in most Christian missions. He led the Richmond congregation and had spoken at the dedication of its sanctuary. Over the course of two decades, he compiled a commentary on each book of the New Testament, drawing attention to passages where Christ's life did not accord with Jewish prophecies, and a lengthy critique of efforts to liberalize the form of worship at Charleston's Beth Elohim. For these efforts, Alfred said, Jews in his hometown hailed Jacob as "a Prophet in Israel."[5]

A retired Jewish merchant and recent member of the Philadelphia City Council led Jacob on a tour of urban improvements—the water system, canals, and wharves. Jacob spent many hours annotating a tattered book listing the circumcisions performed by Pennsylvania's eighteenth-century mohel Barnard Jacobs; no living soul knew as much as Jacob about Philadelphia's early Jews. He also called on Rebecca Gratz, the most prominent American Jewish woman of her day, who was rumored to be Sir Walter Scott's model for Rebecca in *Ivanhoe*. Deeply committed to her faith, Gratz never married, and she adapted the benevolent work of middle-class urban women to Jewish causes. She founded her city's first Jewish women's charitable organization and the first Sunday school for Jewish youth. Jacob Mordecai's "patriarchal manner" and wise conversation delighted Gratz; his knowledge of Hebrew impressed her, because so few Jews, including herself, understood the ancient language that expressed their identity as a people. Gratz also applauded Jacob's religious studies and writings. It pleased her to note his modesty; Jacob wrote not to satisfy any personal ambition, Gratz felt, but to help his people resist assimilation. His researches would, he hoped, "make his own children and grand children well acquainted with the religion they profess."[6]

Gratz and many others in Philadelphia felt obliged to Jacob for Isaac Leeser. Mikveh Israel's new hazan, whom Jacob called "a shining light" to his people, was probably the most significant Jewish religious figure of the antebellum period. Nineteenth-century American Jews, unable to attract trained rabbis to their shores, expanded the role of the hazan (cantor) to encompass the duties of a rabbi or a Protestant minister. Jacob was a lay leader in Richmond's congregation when eighteen-year-old Leeser arrived there from Germany in 1824. Leeser worked in his uncle's dry-goods store, studied English, and, when he could, met with Jacob Mordecai. He was for Jacob a fascinating companion and a resource. In an incident that marked the beginning of

Leeser's career, the two men discussed an essay in the *London Quarterly Review* in which an apostate labeled Jews "vermin" and prayed that they come to their senses and convert. With Jacob's encouragement, Leeser registered his protest. The *Richmond Whig* ran his response, in which he contended that Judaism was not only *not* false but "historically and spiritually superior to Christianity."[7]

In one sense, then, Isaac Leeser was the orthodox son Jacob Mordecai did not have but, particularly as he aged, must have longed for. Leeser's talents ensured that Jacob would not long enjoy the young man's company. Soon after his defense of Judaism appeared in the *Whig*, Jews from elsewhere began making inquiries. Mikveh Israel needed a hazan, and Jacob recommended Leeser on all counts. Leeser hesitated. He liked Richmond; he did well by his work at the store and at night had time to write his first book, *The Jews and the Mosaic Law*. Realizing what his protégé could do for American Jews, Jacob helped coax Leeser into accepting Mikveh Israel's offer. Yet Leeser struggled through his first years in Philadelphia. His newfangled English sermons edified some but irritated others, and the hazan chafed when the congregation refused to back a Jewish school. Months of conflict with Mikveh Israel's leadership over his salary and contract must have made his reunion with his old friend and mentor as sweet for Leeser as it was for Jacob.[8]

While Jacob was enjoying the companionship of Jewish leaders in his childhood home, a prospective buyer visited Spring Farm. Torrential rains poured down that day, but the Mordecai women made up for the foul weather with charm. Thomas Lawson's offer of $4,000 surpassed previous ones but fell painfully below the $11,700 Jacob and Becky paid in 1819. And that number did not include their improvements. Regardless, a decision was made: they would sell. No definite plan had been formed for where the family would move next. Sam argued for Petersburg, while George pressed for Raleigh. The Spring Farm contingent finally turned them both down. Richmond it would be, despite exposing the remaining family to "cold, heartless" treatment from "odious" relatives. But Jacob likely drove the decision. He was president of Congregation Beth Shalome and often officiated at weddings and funerals and on holy days. He and Becky, at least, now felt attached to the place. They could, Augustus reckoned, live comfortably in town by renting in a fashionable neighborhood. The news cheered few.[9]

The words of the man Philadelphia Jews welcomed as a "prophet" were not always attended to within his own family. During this same period, Caroline Mordecai Plunkett took steps that amounted to an outright rejection of Jacob's religious teachings. Her intermarriage had given Jacob pain, but nothing could compare with the shock he was about to receive.

No Mordecai married more happily than Caroline—or so tragically. Between 1823 and 1825 she had lost Achilles and each of their three small sons. After this bereavement Caroline refused, despite the pleadings of her siblings, to return home. Warrenton was the site of all her past joy, and Caroline would not abandon her stepchildren. For the next five years, she taught school and—to the extent the Lane aunts would permit—kept Moses's three elder orphans with her as boarding pupils. She had lost three children of her own; perhaps she could rebuild a family with the remnants of her dead brother's.[10]

It did not work out that way. The Lanes removed her nephews and niece from her care, and depression stalked Caroline as her stepchildren slowly slipped away as well. Ellen's former suitor, John Plunkett, eventually practiced medicine in Virginia, taking a younger brother, Achilles junior, to live with him. Louisa Plunkett remained with Caroline and earned a modest salary by teaching music at the Warrenton school. But Caroline began to doubt the school would ever flourish. Warrenton's economy had declined, neighbors had left for Tennessee and Alabama, and she faced increased competition from other academies. George totaled her accounts and judged she cleared no more than $250 in 1830 despite working herself nearly to death. Caroline was shaken as she regarded the increasingly desperate situation that threatened to compromise her independence. Visiting her family, she thought she saw reproach in every look and heard "distaste" when anyone addressed her.[11]

The world seemed to be closing in, and eventually Caroline took refuge near Rachel in Wilmington, launching one more school. "Mrs. Plunkett's Seminary for Young Ladies" began promisingly. When her pupils' parents prepared to spend the summer at the seashore, some of Caroline's new friends put her up there and supplied a classroom. In this way, her establishment continued through the hot months with thirty-five scholars. Caroline's teaching duties may have remained steady, but her life did not go on as before: she announced her conversion to Christianity, and she fell in love.[12]

Caroline's conversion did not come suddenly. While its details and development are not clear, she had studied the question for more than a year. However, Caroline never consulted Jacob before taking a step that her Christian acquaintances in Wilmington (who included a former Mordecai School student and friend of Rachel's) must have celebrated. Her announcement met with a different reaction in Richmond. Jacob railed at her for giving him no opportunity to "orally . . . encounter your doubts and meet your arguments." He denounced his daughter in such harsh terms—calling her foolish, inconsiderate, disobedient, and weak for being swayed by false friends—that Caroline felt incapable of responding. She had, he said, dealt him "a pang . . . which time can never remove." Caroline held fast, refusing to give her father any hope of reversing her action and apparently willing to forfeit his love if it came to that. "If I ever become convinced I am in error I will tell our dear parent immediately," she told Ellen, "but you know I cannot say I disbelieve what I believe."[13]

This was not the convictionless act Sol once contemplated during his courtship of Anna Tennant. It was not the abnegation of Jewish filial duties Sol opted for when he married Caroline Waller in Mobile. Caroline had taken a step that rested on belief. It would not be the last such crossing of the increasingly murky boundary that separated the Mordecais from their Gentile friends.

Despite the bravado, Caroline feared losing them all. She distracted herself with teaching, work she always took strength from and enjoyed. She tried to fill her leisure time with activity and began taking botany lessons from a tutor in the household where she held her summer classes. The Massachusetts-born Moses Ashley Curtis had read widely and in several languages, though he was only twenty-four. At some point, their mutual love of books and ideas spurred him to make a bid for her affections. Curtis stunned Caroline by proposing marriage. He had no money and probably never would, since he planned to enter the Episcopal ministry. Did this trouble her? Caroline's heart leaped for the first time in years. Could this remarkable youth love a thirty-eight-year-old widow? She doubted it and, enamored though she was, refused Curtis's offer.[14]

Caroline bitterly regretted her decision. The following winter, Curtis became engaged to the twenty-year-old daughter of one of Rachel's Wilmington friends. Lovelorn, Caroline brooded more than ever on her father's curses. Just when she most needed support, her conversion froze her out. She longed to "quit this mortal scene," even as she recognized that such a wish was wrong. "Resignation, Submission, Contentment, Endeavor, these ought to be my watchwords," she wrote to Ellen. After a year of misery, Caroline exiled herself to LaGrange, Tennessee, seeking refuge with old Warrenton friends who had opened a female academy. Even though she considered herself banished, perhaps with the work she loved and a welcoming family of her choosing her wounds could heal.[15]

Jacob may have been relieved when Caroline quit the scene. Her conversion—"a subject I cannot dwell upon with patience or charity"—pricked Jacob's conscience at its sorest spot: what he regarded as his derelict conduct as a Jewish parent. "Worldly concerns were suffered to engross too much of our time and thoughts in Warrenton," Becky told Caroline in 1834, "and the eternal welfare of our dear ones were [sic] left too much to chance." Jacob and Becky could therefore read Caroline's embrace of Christianity as their own agonizing but predictable (and perhaps deserved) punishment. Some Jewish fathers treated a child's apostasy as a death by rending their shirts and wearing mourning clothes, and apostates were shunned by the community. Jacob's shame festered into anger as he tried to pin blame on others for leading her astray: Caroline herself, cunning Christians, and his daughter-in-law, Moses's widow, Nancy Lane Mordecai.[16]

The powerlessness and bitterness Jacob felt over Caroline's defection from Judaism recurred when three of his grandchildren—Moses's orphans—received baptism. As if to underscore that religion was but one (and for most family members not the primary) realm by which the Mordecais defined themselves, Jacob was compelled to hold his tongue when Nancy brought his Christian grandchildren to Richmond the following month. After much persuasion, she had agreed to let the Mordecais educate Henry, Ellen, and Jake. Education was the one thing needful, implied George, who had negotiated the arrangement. But the plans would quickly unravel if Nancy thought Jacob blamed her for Caroline's conversion or criticized her for leading Moses's children to the baptismal font.[17]

Privately, in a sign of the widening gap between the ways family members incorporated Judaism into their identities, George approved of the baptisms of his wards. He considered it natural that Nancy wished them to share her religious convictions—just as it was natural that Jacob wished them to share his. More, George told Ellen that he thought the step "desirable." Surely "there is no inducement so far as their *temporal* happiness is to be consulted, for [the children] to profess or be taught to believe in the jewish [sic] religion." For him and, as he assumed, for Ellen, the disadvantages were too familiar to require elaboration.[18]

The household these grandchildren joined wore a grim aspect. Jacob and Becky's maiden daughters Julia (thirty-four) and Emma (twenty) managed the family's domestic arrangements with difficulty, prompting Alfred to urge Ellen's early return from her visit to Sol in Mobile. Since the move into Richmond, Becky had suffered from debilitating arthritis and spent long spells in bed. Nor was she the only invalid. While at the Round Hill School, Henry—Moses's eldest—contracted juvenile rheumatoid arthritis. He would never walk again without a limp. He joined his siblings in Richmond but required intensive nursing, which Ellen, recently returned, provided. Julia and the youngest of Jacob's children, Laura, supervised the instruction of their Raleigh pupils. Jacob, meanwhile, sought refuge from domestic disorder and anxiety about his family's assimilation in faith and religious researches.[19]

15

RECONCILIATION

Twenty-one-year-old Emma Mordecai impatiently awaited the arrival in Richmond of Aunt Nancy and her three recently converted children, for she would return with Nancy to spend the season in Raleigh. There she would have escorts in brothers George and Augustus, and, despite the Lane women's limited intellectual exertions, she would enjoy some semblance of a social life. Augustus, twenty-six, had relinquished his earlier dreams of training racehorses and sold the bloodstock he once kept at Spring Farm; now he acted as a junior partner in George's side project, a dry-goods store called Mordecai and McKimmon. Augustus was not bookish, but he had a winningly genial temper and a kind heart. He was especially fond of Emma, who could "entertain more persons at one time than any lady." He planned to introduce her to his Raleigh acquaintances. Indeed, Emma had blossomed into a pretty and vivacious young woman, whom one young gallant called "the very soul of life."[1]

Emma played a dangerous game that year as she negotiated her way through Raleigh society. On the one hand, she did what her parents asked of her. She wrote home that for Yom Kippur she "kept [her] promise faithfully, eat [*sic*] not a mouthful and read the prayers through, repetitions and all, without interruption." Emma's devotions were solitary ones. Neither George nor Augustus joined the fast or prayers for atonement. But in a scene that hints at the way the Mordecais' religious identity had become both more contested and more expansive, Emma reported that one evening that winter, while George worked in his room and Aunt Nancy and her sister Miss Tempe read "their Bibles" upstairs, Nancy's sister Harriet Lane made Augustus stay in the drawing room and read aloud Isaac Leeser's *The Jews and the Mosaic Law*—sent no doubt by Jacob. "She knows," Emma explained, "he won't do [it] unless he's looked after, at least she says this is the reason, but I believe she is half inclined to the Jewish faith herself."[2]

Once again it was matters of the heart, not articles of faith, that threatened family peace. Rumors reached Rachel in Wilmington that Emma, who two years earlier had almost accepted a proposal from Aaron's brother Benjamin Lazarus, was now engaged to Gavin Hogg, a close friend and associate of George's—and an energetic Episcopalian. In fact, it was not Hogg but William Grimes who had won Emma's affections. Born poor and orphaned young, Grimes had recently settled in Raleigh and opened a store. One year later he had a second outlet in Chapel Hill, and George considered him "very worthy and respectable." He was no genius. But William made Emma feel brilliant, something her family did not. And he wanted to marry her. She asked for time and went, as planned, to visit her sister Rachel in Wilmington. William bore the separation badly, spending every evening at the Mordecai house in Raleigh mourning Emma's absence. Within a fortnight he appeared at the Lazaruses' in Wilmington, but Rachel carefully withheld this news from her letters home for fear of upsetting Jacob.[3]

The affair had reached a critical stage, however, and George undertook the task of mediating what everyone in the family knew would raise trouble at home. In Warrenton days, Jacob's children had learned to shield him from the money matters that flustered and annoyed him. In subsequent years, they tiptoed around his delicate temper. His children's courting often unnerved Jacob, but nothing vexed him more in this period than the apparently constant threats to the family's Jewishness. Conscious as she had become of Jacob's concerns, Emma, like the others, followed her own course.

Emma was not the only young Mordecai in love. Augustus first met Rosina Young when she was a child. The Youngs owned the farm and gristmill next door to Spring Farm, and at age ten Rosina joined the Mordecai household as a paying pupil, learning alongside Laura. Augustus waited a long time to reveal his feelings. By early 1834, the Raleigh dry-goods store had shown a handsome profit, which meant Augustus had money. He rode to Richmond to pay suit to Rosina, then fourteen. And, as he wrote ecstatically to Emma, she had accepted him! Emma could tell no one but Rachel. "Do not mention it in your letters home," he warned. He would inform his parents, but only after careful preparation.[4]

But, as a daughter, Emma had a far harder road to travel than Augustus. George understood this and considered it unjust. Jacob's sons could strike out independently in work and marriage without wholly forfeiting their father's respect and risking the family's support. Moses had regretted that his intermarriage had hurt Jacob, but he had reminded his family he was a grown man, a successful lawyer, and fully competent to choose his mate. Jacob accepted the situation and developed a happy relationship with Moses. Indeed, Jacob once admitted that he half expected his sons "to marry contrary to his religion." Marriage "depended on inclination and taste," he told Ellen, and there were not many Jewish girls "to be had." Such reasoning did not always sustain him, however, and Sol's wedding in Mobile had inaugurated years of coolness between the two men.[5]

Male status and physical distance protected Moses and Sol and ultimately Augustus. Jacob applied a different standard to his daughters. Thus Caroline suffered years of despair before her father allowed her to consummate her wish of eight years: union with Achilles. George denounced the double standard as unjust. "There is no one thing I have felt more sensibly than the peculiarly disagreeable and unfortunate situation of our sisters" with regard to marriage, he complained to Sam. They had three choices, all wretched. Like Julia and Ellen, they could avoid conflict by remaining spinsters, leading what he called "a life of seclusion and celibacy." Or, like Rachel and Eliza (who in 1828 had married her Richmond cousin Samuel Hays Myers), they could marry a Jew the family could not "admire or esteem." (George and Sam agreed that neither Aaron nor Samuel Myers deserved their Mordecai wives.) Or, George concluded, "they must incur the certain and lasting displeasure of their parents by marrying out of the pale of their religion."[6]

The independence and freedom of choice George wished his sisters could enjoy formed part of a gradual and difficult shift away from the deference eighteenth-century parents in genteel families typically expected. Young people of the Jacksonian era considered mutual affection and sufficient financial means, not parental permission, the two things needful for a successful marriage. Abiding by this new sensibility was hard for many parents. During the same period, interfaith couples tended, as Sol and his wife had done, to come to an understanding regarding the religious upbringing of their children. For Jewish-Gentile couples, the decision seems most often to have been to fold the family into Christian practice. To Jacob the implications were clear: the eventual disappearance of the American Jewish population. Consequently, these marriages of assimilation were for Jacob at best uncomfortable and at times excruciating. Having rediscovered Judaism, he increasingly measured his own success and the larger fate of American Jewry by the religious identity of those to whom his children gave their hearts. But Jacob's frustration manifested itself unevenly, with his daughters catching the worst of it. In this, he was not inconsistent with either Jewish tradition or his times, for, even as it advanced the rhetoric of responsible choice, feeling, and affection in courtship and marriage, the new middle class still expected women to submit to the judgment of men.

With George's support, Emma accepted William Grimes's proposal. William's childhood guardian wrote to testify to his good character, family history, and modest but promising "pecuniary affairs." This letter George forwarded with one of his own to Jacob and Becky, presenting the alliance as a fait accompli. Emma was happy. Would her parents rob her of her joy?[7]

It is not clear whether Jacob and Becky consented to the match.

Possibly, they never decided, for hardly had the letter reached them in Richmond before the engagement exploded in a scandal that remains a mystery since it was too mortifying to mention on paper. William did or said something, revealed some fatal flaw or deception that led George to withdraw his support. Under pressure from her erstwhile defender, Emma broke with her lover. Hearing the news, Sam thanked heaven his sister's "happiness for life" had not been "compromised." Emma did not see it quite this way. All her hopes evaporated, and in desperation she unsuccessfully attempted suicide. Augustus escorted his brokenhearted sister back to Richmond, where only one course remained: acceptance of her lot. Emma tried not to resent her parents' relief but still dwelled on her dashed love with what she called "unwholesome constancy." She would never marry.[8]

Alfred Mordecai had long recognized that career military officers like himself could "seldom think of marriage till late in life." In 1832 he still earned a small salary. But at twenty-eight he was also passionately in love. During the summer of that year, he traveled to Detroit as aide to the secretary of war, Lewis Cass, and witnessed the ravages of a cholera epidemic among both soldiers and civilians. His mind, however, wasn't entirely on the misfortune of others. When Alfred returned to Washington to present to Congress legislation he had drafted for Cass, he was also intent on winning the heart of Jeannette Thruston.[9]

Alfred had been a frequent caller at the Thruston household for some time. James Madison had appointed Jeannette's father, a former senator from Kentucky, to the federal circuit court of the District of· Columbia in 1809, and one of Jeannette's brothers was Alfred's fellow officer. The judge liked Alfred, who shared his dismay at the corruption within the Jackson–Van Buren administration.[10]

But Jeannette immediately "declined" Alfred's addresses. She appeared miserable, and her explanation was oblique at best. She could not marry him, she said, because she realized she could never make him happy. Despondent, Alfred declared himself "unworthy of such love as she could bestow. I am fit for a mere drudge" and "should never aspire to anything elevated." Anti-Semitism, at least in the Mordecais' view, seems not to have played a role; indeed, Alfred's disappointment astonished his sisters. Eliza could not imagine anyone rejecting "so noble a suitor." Perhaps it was for the best. Another interfaith marriage would have given Jacob yet more cause for sorrow.[11]

There had been other women: Rebecca Hays Myers, Uncle Samy's daughter, whom Alfred liked but would not court because he would "not desire to be associated with" her father; and Sara Hays of Philadelphia, who possessed more good "qualities" than he usually found "among *our* [Jewish] ladies." But no one had made him feel the way Jeannette did.[12]

Alfred no longer took part in the social life of the city. He went into seclusion in his new quarters at the Washington Arsenal, of which, as a captain of ordnance, he had been appointed commander in the weeks after Jeannette's rejection. His isolation and low spirits continued through 1832, even as his career seemed charmed by success. Writing to Ellen, Alfred described his household and the comforts he would soon be able to offer her. "My pleasantest dreams now," he said, "are to have one of my sisters always with me."[13]

Alfred was not the only Mordecai man pining for a more fully realized and enlightened domestic life, and, in consequence, Ellen was destined to join another brother. The cloud that had hovered over Sam's business affairs since 1819 and his move to Petersburg finally lifted in 1833. His investments looked promising, and he hired an assistant in his countinghouse. Sam lacked but one thing. After a year at a boardinghouse, he swore to live decently. "I am very conscious," he told Ellen, "that I cannot have a comfortable home without" a sister "to superintend it."[14]

Sam was forty-seven. Years ago he had relinquished any hope of marriage. In his early twenties, while apprenticing for Samy Myers in Richmond, Sam had felt unable to pursue Sally Elcan of Buckingham County, Virginia, whose father was Jewish. Their fondness was mutual, but his meager salary made marriage imprudent. Sam watched, wretched, as Sally, under pressure from her father, married a man she did not love. He later courted his cousin Louisa Marx, who objected to his "name" and his not being financially well settled, and a much-liked Norfolk Jewish belle, Adeline Myers. Between those two episodes, he sought the hand of the niece of a prominent Irish family in Richmond. All three attempts left Sam battered. Out of marital options, he turned to his sister for help and the domestic companionship to which he was by nature so well suited. So it was that Ellen became, for the first time in her life, the mistress of a house. Rachel offered encouragement and advice. On the basis of her experience, Rachel predicted that managing slaves would be Ellen's greatest challenge.[15]

There was another family matter in which Rachel took special interest in 1834. She remained her father's pride. Her loyalty to his faith, her healthy family (by this time she had four children), and her unmistakable affection for him all endowed Rachel with uniquely lofty status in Jacob's eyes. Thus, when she asked him to do something excruciating, Jacob listened and obeyed. At her insistence, quite possibly using her own words, Jacob wrote to Caroline Mordecai Plunkett in Tennessee, offering to mend the rift between them. He penned the words as if swallowing a draft of gall. "If my forgiveness can afford you any comfort," Jacob wrote, "it is fully extended." He left her in God's "hands" and would "for ever drop the subject" of her apostasy.[16]

Though she lived in a log cabin nine hundred miles away, Caroline was no longer banished. "I cannot tell you . . . how *emancipated* I feel," she gushed to Ellen after receiving the letter from Jacob. "All nature wears a new aspect."[17]

Rachel's diplomacy had succeeded, but she experienced little of Caroline's exultation. Rachel felt isolated and not at all "emancipated," and she envied Ellen and Sam, snug in their trim Petersburg home. "I never so much wished for an hour's conversation with some of my brothers and sisters," Rachel wrote Ellen sadly. "We are too far apart."[18] Distance had always posed challenges as the Mordecais tried to sustain their identity as a chosen family bound by their covenant. But beneath Rachel's loneliness lay a despair, the results of which deeply shook the Mordecais and their sense of themselves.

PART THREE

WILMINGTON

"My soul thirsteth for God, for the living God, O when shall I come and appear before God?" but why must I add, "my tears have been my food day and night."

—PSALM 42:2–3, QUOTED BY RACHEL MORDECAI LAZARUS
TO CATHERINE DEROSSET, AUGUST 1, 1835

You say[,] my sister, that you wish I could have struggled through when harassed as I was last summer. Alas! Had you seen our father as I did almost a maniac, feeling himself bound by the [Jewish] law to utter curses against his apostate child, while yet his heart yearned toward her . . . lacerated by intolerable anguish[,] you would have found that to kneel in humility . . . was your only resource.

—RACHEL MORDECAI LAZARUS TO ELLEN MORDECAI,
AUGUST 21, 1836

16

SO MUCH TO ADMIRE AND TO LOVE

lthough leaving home and family had been a difficult decision, Rachel had not always felt as far away as she did in the
spring of 1834. During the years that her brothers and sisters navigated the channels of career and marriage that were nearly always complicated by the question of religion, Rachel set out to find her
place as a wife, a mother, and a domestic manager in a new town.
Indeed, to the siblings who had always admired her, Rachel's life—
kind husband, intelligent children, and comfortable home—appeared
nearly idyllic.

Aaron Lazarus was hugely proud of Rachel. Her courageous stand
against anti-Semitism and her success as a teacher were known in the
Jewish circles of Charleston, which the newly married couple visited
on their wedding trip. Charleston in 1821 harbored the largest Jewish
community in the United States, and the Lazaruses' social and commercial life revolved around the observant Jewish families who made
up the congregation of Beth Elohim. How odd it was for Rachel, so accustomed to being a Jew among Christians, to be surrounded by those

purporting to be of her kind. In Charleston, Jews and Gentiles generally did not intermingle, and if Rachel felt a little anxious, no wonder.
She was an outsider all over again.[1]

In Charleston, Rachel entered a synagogue for the first time in her
life. Still, she regretted that Passover observances consumed evenings
she would rather have spent at the local theaters. On the whole, her
husband's hometown life—including its tedious social whirl, innumer-
able visits, and shallow emphasis on fashion—failed to interest her. But
Aaron had chosen her, not another Jewish woman from Charleston,
and Rachel would apply her own values to being a wife, a mother, a
housekeeper, and a Jew. Her worries revolved around whether she
would succeed in establishing the rational, cultivated, and affectionate
home she craved. Her worries did not prevent the new Mrs. Lazarus
from lavishing her devotion on her "chosen friend" and "beloved husband," whose "tenderness" she repeatedly praised. By the time they left
for Wilmington, Rachel had become pregnant.[2]

As their steamer labored noisily up the Cape Fear River past rice
fields and toward Wilmington's wharves, Aaron watched his wife take
in the surroundings. He so hoped she would be happy there. From the
boat, they caught a clear view of the home they would share, a brick
mansion with a lot covering an entire city block. Young trees dotted
the large yard. But Aaron's eye returned to the remains of his waterfront warehouse. While in Charleston, he received news that a fire
had whipped through Wilmington's business district, destroying lumber and naval stores—pitch, rosin, tar, and turpentine—including
Aaron's.[3]

He did not frighten easily. In fact, the fire was only one reversal
among many, yet he had not cut short the honeymoon. Having built a
fortune before (beginning twenty years earlier, when he imported and
auctioned dry goods), Aaron felt sure he could do it again. Aaron and
his partner reentered the naval-stores business, but only as commission merchants servicing other exporters. The new husband and
father-to-be kept his saltworks running as well, and over the next
several years he cleared his debts, recovered much of his fortune, and
began his shipping enterprise anew.[4]

During this difficult period in his career, Aaron rejoiced in Rachel's support and deepening affection. She found ways to reduce domestic expenses even as she strove to make a happy, charming home. He marveled at her energy. In addition to supervising the education of her sister Eliza, who accompanied the newlyweds to Wilmington, Rachel insisted on guiding Aaron's younger daughters' studies even as she directed a household of half a dozen slaves. She proved a tender nurse during the "tormenting" migraines that attacked Aaron in times of stress. More than all of this, he saw his warmest feelings reflected in her countenance. "For my part," Rachel told Ellen, "I find so much to admire and to love in witnessing the strength of mind, integrity, and almost unequalled excellence of my husband's disposition" that she felt honored to be at his side.[5]

The house was delightful, by far the grandest Rachel had ever lived in. Tall, with high windows that let in as much light and air as the season allowed, it boasted spacious rooms and a spiral staircase of deep-brown mahogany. The grand sitting room, running the entire depth of the house, had windows on three sides to keep it bright all day long. There, Rachel arranged a parlor and a dining area. In an approximation of Edgeworthstown House, the children worked their lessons at the dining table while older family members talked, sewed, read, or wrote near the fire. Framed maps of the continents decorated the walls. The house's four bedchambers, fifteen by twenty feet each, easily accommodated visitors and ensured that no one felt cramped. Handsome brick outbuildings, one housing the kitchen, flanked the yard. Rachel set to trimming and transplanting, and soon climbing roses, yellow jasmine, lilac, and althea in red, purple, and white welcomed all who entered their yard with almost perpetual blooms.[6]

Four of Aaron's seven children were home that first spring and summer of the marriage. The two boys, seventeen-year-old Gershon and thirteen-year-old Washington, concerned Rachel less than Aaron's daughters. Male education was not her province. But the three youngest girls would soon return from their long sojourn in Charleston, and Rachel's memories of adjusting to a new mother made her especially fearful of her reception by the Lazarus girls. Far more than penury, the "evil of family discord" was the object of Rachel's dread. It might come at any time, she knew. But she had a good start. "The children do not tell me in words of their affection," she reported to Ellen, "but they evince it in a thousand ways more grateful to my heart: they love to be near me, to assist, to oblige me." Over and over she thanked heaven for giving her courage enough to marry Aaron in spite of them.[7]

Her greatest surprise of all was her husband. Never had she dared to hope for this: truly reciprocal affection and the conviction of being "sincerely loved." Aaron was her "kind and tender partner," "the tenderest of husbands," "the dearest of friends who sympathizes in my hopes, my fears, and wishes." Ellen had long considered Mr. Lazarus uncompelling, a man Rachel would never have married except from necessity. Having now felt his full embrace, Rachel wrote that "unless you *know him* as I do, you cannot know how good, how amiable he is." She promised that the more Ellen saw of Aaron, "the more you will love him."[8]

Aaron himself had not been certain that things would go so well. He had proposed marriage to a dutiful woman who also possessed a sparkling mind. She had rejected him, then relented. He did not know if her heart would respond to his. Seven months after the wedding, Aaron wrote Sol feelingly but economically, "I am blessed with her affection; more I need not boast."[9]

All was not bliss for Rachel, however, and Aaron could not dispel all her anxieties. Establishing domestic order, especially with regard to slaves, proved challenging. The slaves, including the all-important cook, were more assertive than she was accustomed to. Rachel blamed the willfulness on the Wilmington slaveholders who gave "negroes their time," a practice by which slaves hired themselves out and kept half their wages. Even the slaves Aaron owned adopted the attitudes of the hired servants. Rachel repeated orders, chased around the house for help she expected to be at hand, and struggled with frustratingly high turnover rates.[10]

Just how little sympathy existed between this mistress and her slaves is suggested by the story of Sophia, the servant she had hoped would be the most reliable. Rachel's relationship with "Saint Sophia," as Rachel called the cook, became so contentious that Aaron finally sold her. Sophia blamed the troubles on Rachel's Jewishness; "the great difference in our religions [had] made it impossible for her to be contented," an outraged Rachel reported to Ellen. Very possibly Sophia was sincere. She may also have used piety as an excuse for insubordination. In either case she risked a good deal (sale to who knew whom) in stating her desire not to work under a Jew.[11]

Early in her marriage, Rachel confronted a greater stumbling block to happiness—an "evil" consequence, in fact, of the happiness she and Aaron shared. In the fall of 1821 she admitted to Ellen that she was pregnant and "very unhappy." Aaron was confused: Did Rachel not aspire to motherhood? But Rachel was afraid. She could not forget that childbearing ruined her mother's health and finally took her life.[12]

As her term neared, Rachel stayed busy. When Aaron's mother arrived from Charleston to assist at the birth, Rachel had been working in the garden, having beds prepared and sowing seeds. Three days later she gave birth to a boy and was, Aaron said, "as well as can be expected," sorry only that her sister Ellen had not arrived in time. They named the baby Marx after Aaron's father, Marks, altering the spelling slightly. Rachel added Edgeworth, in hopes, no doubt, that he would embody the enlightened ideals the name betokened.[13]

After a few weeks, Rachel described her son as dotingly as any new mother. He was "a fine plump little fellow," she told Caroline, "as fat as a rice bird, does not promise to be fair, has full dark eyes, whether blue, grey, or black, we cannot yet determine, a nose like his aunt Caroline's, a pretty mouth (as I think) and a great deal of dark hair." He was an intrusion, but a darling one. Given Rachel's earlier trepidation, Aaron was struck by her devotion to the baby. She was, he told Jacob, "so much the mother, and so much the wife, that her time is completely engrossed."[14]

17

A PEW AT ST. JAMES

fter Marx Edgeworth Lazarus's birth, Rachel had a great deal less time to keep up with siblings and with friends "of the heart" like Mrs. Kennon from the Mordecais' Warrenton days. This mattered particularly because Wilmington did not offer such companions—at least not yet. During her first week in the city, Rachel moaned about the "dressing, visiting, and receiving company" her arrival generated. Not to take part in such "idle business" was unthinkable; even so, Rachel considered it "the greatest foe to rational employment."[1]

Idle business wasn't Wilmington's sole distraction. Indeed, for years the town had been more taken with religion than with recreation, uplifting or otherwise. Evangelical revivals washed across the nation in the first decades of the nineteenth century in a wave historians have called the Second Great Awakening. Hundreds of Wilmingtonians, including many women and many from the highest social class, had experienced repentance followed by "new birth" in Christ. Some attended Methodist or Baptist services. St. James Episcopal Church, whose congregation nearly expired after the American Revolution and the Anglican disestablishment, also enjoyed strong growth.[2]

The same Adam Empie who had shown concern for Jacob Morde-cai's soul in Warrenton applied evangelical energy to the pulpit of St. James. His success, lamented Ellen, who visited Wilmington in 1818, helped render the town a dour and pious place. She reckoned that half the townspeople attended church twice on Sunday and went to Wednesday evening Bible study too. Nevertheless, Rachel was a little startled to find that some of Empie's most enthusiastic parishioners were also her favorite Wilmingtonians. Amiable and respectable as these acquaintances were, this preoccupation with religious matters was a source of exasperation for Rachel. Writing to Ellen in 1821, Rachel thanked her "for mentioning books. I hardly meet with them here." She supposed that no household in Wilmington except her own could lay claim to three books "beside the prayer book and bible."[3]

Rachel grew familiar with the religious lives of Wilmington's well-to-do. They were her neighbors. But she also worshipped with them, in Aaron Lazarus's pew. In 1811 Aaron had joined other prominent men in raising funds to fill the long-empty pulpit at St. James. Thereafter he made annual contributions and attended services. When the parish be-gan selling pews, he purchased number seventy-eight.[4]

This unorthodox step, Aaron argued, in no way meant he rejected Judaism. He said he "could worship Jehovah in any temple." A handful of poorer, less educated Jews lived in Wilmington at the time, but not enough for a minyan (quorum) and far too few to justify a synagogue. In any case, the Lazaruses did not associate with them. Rather, they as-sociated with the community of better-off Christians, went to church, and observed the Sabbath and high holy days in private. The Lazaruses also disregarded the orthodox practice of all-male, all-Hebrew prayer: the shortage of male readers meant that Rachel and her stepdaughter Phila conducted much of the service for Yom Kippur. The women read English translations, with occasional relief from Aaron. Rachel did not object; her duty was performed, she felt, though she admitted at its conclusion to being "glad . . . it is over." She felt similarly relieved when she could report to Ellen on a Sunday in 1823 that the day's church service was behind her. What mattered to Rachel was the replication of the Mordecai family covenant. Her prayers centered on rearing her little boy. He must be a credit to them all, an enlightened and high-performing member of society. To her mind, the task before her had less to do with religious practice than with moral duty and proper intellectual training.[5]

Not everyone in the Lazarus household found the sermons at St. James as "dry" as Rachel did. They inspired nineteen-year-old Gershon, Aaron's eldest son. He had yet to establish a career, despite an apprenticeship at a mercantile house in Charleston, and he was looking closely at the life his father had carved out for him. Gershon complained of the "want of decency" in the Hebrew service at Charleston's Beth Elohim. St. James felt more like home. He sometimes suspected that his father shared such thoughts. Every Sunday, Aaron listened to the supplications the Reverend Mr. Empie offered the Lord. Gershon noticed that if the family had company at sundown on Friday, the candles were not lit and the Sabbath prayer was not said. To him such acts indicated a degree of disrespect toward Judaism. Perhaps, he thought, the Jews had made a mistake and were just too proud to admit it.[6]

When Gershon asked Rachel why Jews rejected Christ's divinity, she could find no answers to satisfy him. Nor could Aaron. Disconcerted by his constant "questioning," Rachel appealed to her father for aid. Jacob promised to send a copy of the address he delivered at Beth Shalome's consecration. Rachel also requested the old correspondence between Jacob and Adam Empie. Perhaps those letters in which Jacob answered the priest's fervent advocacy of his conversion would allay Gershon's doubts.[7]

Instead, Gershon's doubts multiplied. Possibly he received accounts of Joseph S. C. F. Frey, founder of the American Society for Meliorating the Condition of the Jews, who toured the South that spring raising funds for missions to the Jews of the United States. Frey himself was a German-born convert and the latest agent of a movement with solid organizational roots in England. American Christians swept up by predictions that Christ's millennial reign would be preceded by Jewish conversion donated thousands of dollars to his cause. Speaking as one who came out of the Jewish tradition, Frey tried to make conversion sound not only desirable and reasonable but easy as well.[8]

The struggle in Gershon's soul took a toll on his body. He grew ill and weak. He felt drawn to convert, yet he understood that even though they did not always follow the dictates of their religion, his father and Jewish relations would denounce him as a traitor. It was demeaning to be told by Aaron that he was "too young, and had read too little to form" a firm opinion for himself. Indeed, his stepmother was a source of comfort to Gershon during this trial. After months of struggle, Gershon handed her a letter to Aaron. It contained, Rachel said, "an enthusiastick declaration of his conviction of the truth of the Christian faith and of every article of its creed." Gershon could think no "differently," she told Ellen, and now "hoped his father would not oppose" his impending baptism.[9]

What did Rachel think? Gershon struck her as "sincere," and Rachel predicted that if he adhered to his new belief, he would become a better man. But when Rachel showed the letter to Aaron, he was appalled. Bedridden with a migraine and anxious not to drive Gershon further into the opposing camp by overreacting, Aaron decided to wait before confronting his son.[10]

His father's silence seemed to be the blessing Gershon had so long awaited. He went to St. James and told Mr. Empie that he could now enter Christ's flock.[11] Gershon kneeled. The priest poured water over him, read a prayer, and made the sign of the cross on his forehead. In lifting the Communion wine to Gershon's lips, Empie felt his hopes and spirit also rise; perhaps this was the opening that would, as he thought, permit all the Lazaruses to see the light.

On returning home, Gershon found his father's written response to his declaration. Aaron's letter forbade the very action Gershon had just taken. Aaron promised one thing: if, after studying with Jacob Mordecai, Gershon at age twenty-one remained convinced of the truth of Christianity, he would permit him to follow "the dictates of his conscience." Tragically, Gershon had defied his father's wishes before they were known to him. During the ensuing explosion, Rachel tried to calm both men.[12]

The news spread quickly through the town; soon it would reach Charleston. But Aaron stood his ground. Politely yet firmly, he took Empie on. Writing to Empie's superior, the bishop of Virginia, Aaron surmised that "the glory of having gained such a convert" had been too much for the minister. Otherwise, he would not have urged a child to take "the awful step of abandoning his father's faith" without serious study. Empie defended his actions. According to his understanding of the Talmud, a Jewish boy came of age at thirteen. Moreover, Gershon had led Empie to believe that Aaron did not oppose the baptism. The priest regretted the misunderstanding, but Gershon had made his choice, and Empie hoped that Aaron, who had sat in his church for so many years, would harbor no bitterness.[13]

When Aaron persisted, Empie allowed that Gershon could only benefit from a more "thorough investigation" of the evidence and proofs surrounding the divinity of Jesus Christ. So it was that Gershon Lazarus traveled to Richmond. He read Jewish and Christian arguments under the dual guidance of Jacob Mordecai and Bishop Richard C. Moore. Gershon studied hard for three weeks. Years later, he recalled that in Richmond "the light of reason burst forth" upon him and he recognized his error. It was a relief to Aaron and a triumph for Jacob, who could be said to have saved a soul for Israel in a victory that dramatically enhanced his reputation and authority among his people. Indeed, Jacob's writings and mentoring had worked exactly as he hoped—and as he hoped they would for many other Jews as well. Convinced of the falsehood of Christian claims and with his doubts about Judaism allayed, Gershon wrote to Mr. Empie renouncing the baptism.[14]

18

NOT EXACTLY AS SHE MOST WISHED

Empie and others in Wilmington anticipated that Gershon's zeal for Christ would spread to the entire Lazarus family. His reversal was accepted graciously enough, however, and for this Rachel credited "the example of mildness and moderation set by Mr. L[azarus], who had so much cause of resentment and provocation." Aaron withdrew his support of St. James, and relations with the minister and his family cooled. The Lazaruses' nearer friends did not trouble them with uncomfortable inquiries. Nevertheless, Gershon's brief apostasy was a harbinger of trials to come.[1]

For the most part, Rachel's concerns lay elsewhere in the first years of her marriage. Her commitments to family and self-improvement as the keys to domestic happiness formed the center of her life in Wilmington, as they had in Warrenton and at Spring Farm. For years Rachel had guided and instructed young people, whether paying students (some of whom were now Wilmington matrons and friends), siblings, or stepchildren. With parenthood, her already remarkable sense of duty strengthened. So did her anxiety. "I must be more than ever vigilant in training *myself*," Rachel resolved, now that she was responsible for Marx's development as well. It was a thrill, a challenge, and also a burden, justified only by what Rachel considered the greatness of the task.[2]

The Edgeworths' *Practical Education* had few if any other readers in Wilmington, and no mother there seemed to take quite the pains Rachel did. Yet Rachel seldom doubted that the extra time and attentiveness Marx received from her would produce positive results. When the family visited her friend and former pupil Jane Dickinson at the seaside, Marx was judged much the best child among the little ones. But then, others were not "brought up à la Edgeworth." Of course, because of Eliza, Rachel had practice in this technique—or rather system—of education. Yet Eliza had been five when Rachel undertook her management; with Marx she confronted the task of training an infant and toddler for the first time. Unable to recall how her ailing mother had handled her youngest children, Rachel, avoiding Becky's example, focused on the Edgeworths and on her idealized image of her parents' commitment to education—a commitment tragically interrupted by Judy's death. Adapting to her situation the aspects of the 1796 covenant she had absorbed so fully, Rachel pledged not to view motherhood as tiresome or dirty work and prayed for the strength and wisdom "to form [Marx's] infancy, to guide his childhood, to advise his youth, that in opening manhood he may love and revere his parents as his best of friends." More than ever before, Rachel felt the rush of love and power intertwined.[3]

Rachel's approach to motherhood drew on sources other than the Edgeworths' writings and her mother. It drew on the Jewish tradition that views improving the world as a religious obligation.[4] More consciously, Rachel took hold of a raft of ideas arising from the Enlightenment, ideas that influenced Revolutionary politics in America and France, ideas that, combined with an advancing market economy and industrial development, sparked new gender conventions. Upper- and middle-class Americans grew especially preoccupied with womanhood and motherhood, and in this debate Rachel took a distinctive stance that accorded to women a measure of cultural authority previously denied them.[5]

Caring for very young children commanded little respect in the late-eighteenth- and early-nineteenth-century United States, which helps explain the puzzled reactions of other parents to Judy Mordecai's and Rachel Lazarus's intense involvement with their offspring. Yet Enlightenment philosophers had theorized that the cognitive development of the young human brain was susceptible to great variation and influence. Reason and tolerance would, the argument went, bring forth better governments and greater individual happiness. Rachel, like the Edgeworths, found especially compelling the idea that even very early experience might forever alter an adult's character.[6]

Women like Rachel (who read Mary Wollstonecraft and Hannah More along with Maria Edgeworth) turned these concepts of cognition to their own ends. For such women, the idea that women's rational capacity was equal to men's formed a bedrock—and radical—belief. Since mothers cared for young children, did it not follow that they, more than fathers, controlled the child's development into reasonable adults? The political, social, and religious implications of such thinking were far-reaching. Mothers, it seemed, might be the first and therefore the most critical guardians of social morality and good citizenship. Such views helped justify the rising number of schools for girls in the early-nineteenth-century United States—a trend the Mordecais had exploited in their Warrenton academy.[7]

Rachel carved out as large a space as possible for intellectual achievement within the tenets of her own strenuous expression of the Mordecais' dedication to enlightened domesticity.[8] She wrapped her ambitions (which were potentially unbecoming for a woman) in the mantle of domestic life and claimed that her efforts would improve that very sphere—render it more reasonable, more intimate, happier. The Edgeworths, Irish landed gentry, seemed to have achieved this around their oval library table. The challenge for Rachel was to embed the cultivation of the mind in the life of a home and family, the realm to which respectable American women were largely confined.

For Rachel in Wilmington, teaching within the home helped resolve the tensions between domesticity and intellect. It provided a valued service to the family while exercising Rachel's talent, knowledge, and training. An intellectual acting as a teacher, Rachel constantly pressed herself to understand the world more fully and explain it more clearly. She was acutely aware that her education was never complete. The exercise of her mind improved her, she felt sure, and in holding that faith, she joined liberal philosophers in granting humans a level of control over their destiny that had more traditionally been ascribed to God. Rachel viewed herself as a reformer aspiring toward the loftiest goals: reason and education could free humanity from suffering and oppression; all humans, given the proper intellectual tools, could minimize pain and exploitation.[9]

Caught up as she was in pressing for greater authority for women, Rachel considered it important that her program was in no way specifically feminine. She did not seek to take from men the duty or opportunity to enlighten humanity. Hers was a modest—and rational—proposal that depended on men and women, husbands and wives working together as friends and partners. She wanted to join men in fulfilling that obligation. Ideally, Rachel would have shared her teaching duties with Aaron—as Maria Edgeworth had shared them with her father. His working outside the home (as were growing numbers of American skilled laborers and professionals) prohibited this— had Aaron been inclined to pursue it, and no evidence suggests that he was.

One aspect of enlightened domesticity requires special notice. The watchword of the American Revolution, "independence," had particular meaning in Rachel's world. She rejected the radical individualism that set each human being on his or her own path to freedom. Independence, in the eighteenth-century sense, existed in relationship with others, in the happiness and trust that came with a justly functioning community free from tyranny, the community she and her family tried to establish through their covenant. Members of the family were independent in that they acted according to strictly held principles; that their principles might undermine the family group that gave them strength was too disturbing an idea to contemplate.

With their commitment to reason and self-improvement, the Mordecais—and especially Rachel—also designated a place where family members could cultivate intimacy with one another and a sense of connection to a wider realm. Indeed, their bookishness bolstered their sense of forming their own community. Experienced largely within the family that read together, corresponded frequently, and taught one another, intellectual life for Rachel overlapped with happiness and intimacy. Moreover, in aligning herself with a world of advanced ideas in which few in Warrenton or Wilmington were much interested, Rachel gained a comforting sense that whether or not she was understood or appreciated by her neighbors, she had compatriots around the world committed to the progress of reason. At home, the ties of affection should twine together with the ties of reason, making happiness possible no matter what troubles the world might serve up. A family such as this held parents and children and siblings in loving and mutually enlightening contact. In Marx, Rachel set out to form the ideal companion, one guided by a sympathetic and cultivated mind.

And Rachel's "lively, docile, affectionate" boy augured well for his mother's mission. At the remarkably early age of eighteen months, he spoke in full sentences, declaratory, exclamatory, and interrogative. Rachel tolerated no whining, no tantrums. Writing to her sister Caroline, Rachel boasted of Marx's helpfulness. He carried messages and parcels and every morning came to Rachel for the "poon" (spoons), which he put away in the sideboard after breakfast.[10]

Marx clearly delighted in pleasing his mother. Rachel's unhappiness and his own misbehavior became easily associated in his mind. One day, fourteen-month-old Marx watched the raindrops slipping down the windowpanes. Hearing his mother express disappointment in the weather, Marx addressed to the rain the only rebuke he knew: "Bad boy." Highly verbal, extremely sensitive to others, Marx was certainly an extraordinary child, and the "gradual expansion of his intellect" understandably compelled his mother.[11]

Teaching and education fascinated Rachel, but even the best pupils test their instructors, and Rachel sometimes resented the time and care that the details, large and small, of motherhood involved. "If I never have another [child] I shall account myself most happy," Rachel informed Caroline, herself then pregnant. Rachel began to feel that more children would mean a shriveled mind. Her interests—current events, natural science, philosophy, contemporary European poetry and fiction, letters and memoirs of great men and women, the early flowering of American literature signaled by James Fenimore Cooper and Washington Irving and Catharine Sedgwick—all squeezed into tinier and tinier parcels of Rachel's time. She had never shirked a duty and saw no way to reduce hers, but mental cultivation was not a luxury to Rachel. It was a necessity, the nourishment that fueled her for relationships and everyday affairs. As a wife, mother of one, and stepmother of many, she was angrier than she liked to admit.[12]

Early in 1825 Rachel realized she was again pregnant. Her heart sank. "This you know," she reminded Ellen, "is not exactly as I most wished." Aaron, sounding for all the world like Jacob, appeared "as well pleased as if it were . . . his second, instead of his ninth," making Rachel's dark feelings all the more distressing. Congratulations came in from her dispersed siblings. "You see," Aaron teased upon reading Ellen's and Caroline's reactions, "you cannot get anyone to sympathize with you." After all, Aaron reminded her, she had the same response to her first pregnancy. And look at Marx, the delight of their lives, the luckiest of children "in having," as another sister said, "such a mother."[13]

Rachel's recovery from childbirth in the summer of 1825 stretched over four months. Wilmingtonians who could afford to do so fled the city during the "fever" season, though Aaron and Rachel dismissed the annual exodus to the coast as an expensive and largely unnecessary affectation. Indeed, some summers passed without difficulty, but 1825 was not one of them.[14]

That spring, Marx, Aaron, and his daughter Almira caught the measles, and by July, when Rachel went into labor, both she and Aaron suffered from malaria's debilitating chills, fevers, and sweats. The doctor warned that the baby, so jaundiced and weak she "scarcely whimpers," might not survive. But after six weeks, little Ellen Lazarus was thriving. Rachel, however, remained "thin and weak," downcast, and "much indisposed." Fortunately, this time her sister Ellen was there to nurse her, to supervise Marx, and to oversee the household. Ellen remained through the first frost, when Rachel's illness lifted, and Rachel sadly bade good-bye to the sister whose name her infant bore.[15]

With baby Ellen's health established and her own strength revived,

Rachel turned to Marx. His education worried her more than ever. An outsider would have difficulty seeing why. At four, he read and spelled with startling aptitude, and at four and a half he learned six or seven hard words a day during "dictionary lessons" with his mother. At five, he added and multiplied whole numbers "with ease." Such precocity drew praise from many; still, Rachel demurred. Though Marx's abilities in some areas were extraordinary, he trailed, she said, in "common things." Despite her long experience, Rachel told Ellen she found teaching "as difficult even now as if I were a complete novice."[16]

In managing Marx, Rachel often returned to the work of Maria and Richard Lovell Edgeworth. If only she could "reap half the benefits you have placed within my reach," she told Maria plaintively in 1827, "I should rejoice indeed; but I am often dissatisfied with my own endeavors and wish that you were near, to confirm or advise me."[17]

Maria and Rachel were never near enough for Rachel simply to turn and ask the older woman's advice; that they couldn't easily meet face-to-face saddened them both. Yet during Rachel's early years in Wilmington their friendship assumed an emotional and material dimension that must have surprised them. They not only established a critical dialogue on American, English, and French literature, supplying a "feast of reason" Wilmington generally denied to Rachel.[18] They also gradually shared intimate news of family members and began exchanging gifts—items each thought the other would enjoy. Books, plants, flowers both rare and common, seeds, sketches, needlework, insects, and jewelry crossed the Atlantic addressed to Miss Edgeworth, Edgeworthstown, Ireland, or Mrs. Lazarus, Wilmington, North Carolina. It amounted to a sharing of two worlds separated by an ocean but fondly knit together by thoughts, feelings, and things.

One day in 1824, having closed a letter to Rachel, Maria appended the question "Why should not you come to Edgeworthstown and visit us? *Answer this.*" Almost ten years had passed since Rachel first made contact with the Irish author. The command was the final proof that Rachel really had won a place in Maria Edgeworth's heart. Her letters from North Carolina showed, Maria said, "understanding, plain uprightness of character, and real tenderness of heart which attach me as

**ITEMS EXCHANGED BETWEEN RACHEL MORDECAI LAZARUS
AND MARIA EDGEWORTH, 1821–1827**

RACHEL TO MARIA	MARIA TO RACHEL
Manuscript Indian treaty	Sketch of Edgeworthstown House by
Henry Rowe Schoolcraft, *Narrative*	Sophy Edgeworth
Journal of Travels through the	Maria Edgeworth, *Frank: A Sequel to*
Northwestern Regions of the United	*Frank in Early Lessons,* 3 vols. (1822)
States (1821)	Blake Family [attributed to Mrs. Henry
"Cotton in its several stages"	(Ellen Price) Wood], *Letters from the*
"A small collection of seeds": Venus's-	*Irish Highlands* (1825)
flytrap; lady slipper; clematis; palma	Maria Edgeworth, *Harry and Lucy*
Christi; syringa; Carolina eglantine;	*Concluded,* 4 vols. (1825)
euonymus; yaupon; Cherokee	"Saul," poem by Francis Edgeworth
(nondescript) rose	[Harriet Beaufort], *Dialogues on*
Speech by an Indian	*Botany, for the Use of Young Persons:*
Collection of insects: "doodle"	*Explaining the Structure of Plants,*
(*Formica leo*); katydid; grasshopper	*and the Progress of Vegetation* (1819)
shell and legs; spider; creeping leaf	[Louisa Beaufort], *Dialogues on*
"Ground puppy" (lizard)	*Entomology, in Which the Forms and*
Spanish moss	*Habits of Insects Are Familiarly*
Specimens of nondescript rose and	*Explained* (1819)
yaupon for transplanting	[Mary (Frances Reeve) Kater], *A*
Catharine Maria Sedgwick, *Redwood*	*History of England for Young People*
(1824)	(n.d.)
Branch with Spanish moss attached	*Friendship's Offering; or, The Annual*
Seeds and three potted specimens	*Remembrancer: A Christmas Present*
packed in wire cage: nondescript	*or New Year's Gift for 1825* (1825)
rose, cassine, *Rosa multiflora*	Purple crocus bulbs
Mordecai Noah, Address on Ararat	Lucy Aikin, ed., *Works of Anna Laetitia*
Hummingbird's nest	*Barbauld, with a Memoir,* 2 vols.
Soda apple	(1825)
James Fenimore Cooper, *The Last of*	Samuel Bailey, *Essays on the Formation*
the Mohicans (1826)	*and Publication of Opinions and on*
	Other Subjects (1821, 1826)

Veil made by Rachel ("the most beautiful imitation of lace [Maria Edgeworth] ever saw")	Purple crocuses and flower seeds from Edgeworthtown House garden
Ricebird's wings	Drawing of *Pyrus japonica* bud for
Mockingbird (one of four Rachel shipped to Ireland)	Marx Edgeworth Lazarus by Pakenham Edgeworth
William Ellery Channing, *Remarks on the Life and Character of Napoleon Bonaparte* (1827–1828)	French edition of *Harry and Lucy Concluded*
Catharine Maria Sedgwick, *Hope Leslie* (1827)	*Friendship's Offering: A Literary Album* (1827)
Stuffed mockingbird	

Source: Compiled from Edgar E. MacDonald, ed., *The Education of the Heart: The Correspondence of Rachel Mordecai Lazarus and Maria Edgeworth* (Chapel Hill: University of North Carolina Press, 1977).

much to you as [I] can possibly be to one whom I have not seen and actually known." Maria's question hung in Rachel's mind for days, for it was the wish of a lifetime. Three years earlier a similar invitation came from Ireland, but Rachel was just married and pregnant and Aaron's warehouses lay in ashes, making a voyage to Europe impossible to contemplate. This time, the playful urgency of the query, "Why should not you come?" struck Rachel as even more sorrowful because her answer remained the same. Rachel had just completed Eliza's education and returned her to Becky and Jacob at Spring Farm, and Aaron's business affairs were improving. Nevertheless, he could not leave them unattended, and she could not suspend her instruction of her three younger stepdaughters. A European sojourn was out of the question.[19]

Maria and Rachel's worlds grew closer anyway. In describing her surroundings in Wilmington to her friend, Rachel mentioned the Spanish moss that gave trees "a hoary and to me not uninteresting aspect." The plant had its practical uses as well, Rachel explained. Stripped, dried, and cleaned, it made "excellent mattresses." Of all the exotic and carefully packed items that came to Edgeworthstown from Wilmington, the Spanish moss was judged "the most extraordinary."

What a perfect subject, Maria decided, for a passage in her sequel to the scientific sketches for children she and her father had begun together years before. Would Rachel mind if she referred to the moss in *Harry and Lucy Concluded*?[20]

The literary product of this botanical and pedagogical collaboration was long in making its way to Wilmington, whose eerie oaks inspired it. The wait proved worth it. When Rachel finally received *Harry and Lucy Concluded* and found the passage on the moss, she exclaimed, "Delightful, delightful!" In the story, after Harry and Lucy perform an experiment to prove that the moss is indeed "vegetable" and not, as they first think, horsehair or thread, Lady Digby brings out the letter from the "kind" friend in North Carolina fully explaining the specimens.[21]

19

OUR RELIGIOUS EXERCISES

The Lazaruses read Maria Edgeworth's account of their Spanish moss amid rich and fashionable new interior decorations. Rachel's explanation of the double-valance bed curtains she had made with fabric Aaron selected on a recent trip to New York filled a page and a half of a letter to Ellen. The dining room, with its striking and fragrant new Indian straw mat and tea table, was converted into an informal sitting room with dark-green blinds to bar the summer sun. Framed lithographs of the first five presidents of the United States joined the continents on the walls. Two of the great men, Thomas Jefferson and John Adams, had nearly simultaneously departed this world on Independence Day, 1826, marking the close of the Revolutionary generation. With its blue-and-gilt chairs, card tables, and brass fireplace pieces, the room, Rachel said, looked "grand indeed."[1]

In the place of honor, above the sofa, hung an item Rachel may have prized more than all the contents of the house. Sam had urged their father to sit for a portrait as a gift to his beloved daughter. When the crated painting arrived and Rachel peered in, she was astounded and moved nearly to tears. Marx exclaimed, "Why it is grandpapa!" and little Ellen strained to touch the canvas. Jacob's features seemed so true and expressive, his "venerated lips" so dear, that Rachel actually kissed them.[2]

In the crate beneath the canvas lay two discourses her father had recently delivered before Richmond's Congregation Beth Shalome. The first Rachel enjoyed; the second, titled "Remarks on Harby's Discourse Delivered in Charleston (S.C.) on the 21st of November 1825 before the Reformed Society of Israelites on Their First Anniversary," alarmed her. In his letter Jacob bade Rachel, "Correct anything harsh that I may have said."[3]

This was a problem. Rachel found her father's attack on Isaac Harby, one of the forty-seven men seeking to reform Charleston's Beth Elohim, "harsh" from beginning to end. She knew of Harby's effort; Aaron's younger brother Michael and his brother-in-law Aaron Phillips were among its leading advocates. Two more of Aaron's sisters' husbands signed the 1824 petition calling for changes in the service that was submitted to Aaron's father and the other elders of the ruling council. The news of a possible schism within the Charleston community—and within the Lazarus family—reached Wilmington rapidly. The *adjunta* had refused on procedural grounds to consider the reformers' requests, and it denounced the proposals as heretical. Now Jacob was adding his voice to the council's.[4]

During these early years of her marriage, Rachel had to learn how to manage a large and complicated household. She was striving at the same time to fit her intellectual ideals into her duties as a wife and mother. On another level, she was drawn to examine the question of what it really meant to be a Jewish wife and mother. Her father's once lackadaisical but now engrossing interest in the topic, her husband's orthodox upbringing, her fearful pregnancies, and the responsibility of motherhood all led Rachel to consider the place of God and religion in her world.

In the absence of a communal life or synagogue in Wilmington, the Lazaruses' Jewish religious practice was exclusively domestic. It was an extreme version of female Jewish experience. Women, who were excluded from religious education, Torah study, and full communal participation, infused Jewish life into their households. As a dutiful daughter, wife, and Jew, Rachel kept the Sabbath and festivals. It isn't known if she kept a kosher kitchen, but it seems unlikely. The paucity of references to domestic religious practice suggests that her observances, whatever they were, ranked low in her interest and sense of self. In tackling how to balance her Jewish heritage with the concerns of a covenant she experienced as broadly secular, Rachel sided clearly with a program that tied religion to faith more than to specific practices. Other Jewish women throughout the nineteenth century found the religious aspects of domesticity empowering in ways Rachel apparently did not.

But Rachel did not have the benefit of her mother's upbringing in a closely observant Jewish home with daily ties to a larger Jewish community. Nor did she greatly admire her stepmother, Becky, who enthusiastically supported Jacob's rediscovery of Jewish piety and practices. And in Wilmington, of course, she had no community of Jewish women who might serve as models or offer fellowship in this regard. What she had seen of orthodoxy she did not relish; Rachel had never felt true kinship with the Richmond and Charleston Jews she knew who were strict in their religious observance. Meanwhile, especially in 1820s and 1830s Wilmington, she observed that for the active Christian women in her social circle, faith not only transformed individual lives and mandated spiritual leadership within the home but also justified greater public roles through religious and charitable organizations. Jewish women in urban centers eventually followed suit, but not during Rachel's lifetime.[5]

And yet, especially in the period immediately following Gershon Lazarus's conversion and return to the fold, Rachel reexamined her beliefs. Why, she asked herself, had she accepted as genuine Gershon's conversion, something she later acknowledged as a youth's mistaken infatuation? Why had she so few answers when, months before taking the Christian sacrament, her stepson approached her with his doubts? Her brother Alfred, when pressed into discussing Gershon's crisis, said he felt that the matter of religion "is not of vital importance."[6] Religion seemed to have relatively little to do with Rachel's version of the 1796 covenant, her commitment to an enlightened family life.

But she looked at Marx and Ellen and wondered what kind of mother could so poorly convey the substance of her faith or, worse, had none to convey. Just as Aaron had hoped, Gershon had become "from principle what he was first, from accident," a Jew, and Rachel, ashamed of her ignorance of her religion, resolved to follow his example. In the fall of 1823 she read a chapter of the Pentateuch every day. Once a week, she, Eliza, and the Lazarus girls spent an hour discussing a religious topic. "They as well as myself find the pursuit very interesting," Rachel told Ellen. "I only wonder that I was not sooner incited to the inquiry."[7]

But "inquiry" did more to sharpen Rachel's critique of her religion than deepen her commitment to it. Domestic Judaism simply did not satisfy her. She grew increasingly frustrated with rituals that failed to engage her spirit. She described feeling like the psalmist who sang, "As the hart panteth after the water brooks, so panteth my soul after thee, O God," and wrote to Jacob suggesting he turn his attention to "our religious exercises" and "present form of prayer." Both, she declared, stood in dire need of improvement.[8]

In 1815 Rachel had denounced a famous author's unenlightened anti-Semitism; in 1824 she challenged orthodox Jewish prayer. Just as she had with Edgeworth, Rachel identified the problem with firmness and care, certain that it could be rationally resolved. Jews required "a thorough revision of our english [sic] prayer book by some person of ability and judgment, who would sacrifice ancient form to real utility," Rachel explained to Jacob. Tedious repetition ought to be expunged, and each festival paired with appropriate Scripture and explication. Such a devotional text would be a great step forward, for "if good sense and true piety formed the basis of our publick worship," Rachel surmised, "instead of what I am almost tempted to call Rabbinical jargon—if we were all instructed to understand our religion, we should become more happy, more truly pious and virtuous and . . . more respectable as a sect than in latter days we ever have been."[9]

In her critique, Rachel was not alone among Jews or even alone within her family. While studying in Philadelphia, Sol had attended a Yom Kippur service at Mikveh Israel. He found the prayers incomprehensible and the atmosphere void of "devotion . . . all noise and confusion." Concluding that the Jews were "an ill-fated race," he left the synagogue prepared to renounce his heritage when it burdened his romantic life. In Warrenton in 1796, Judy had feared the impression their rites made on Gentiles. In the 1820s her children expressed uneasiness with the rituals themselves. Surely their religion was amenable to reasonable reform.[10]

Once again, as in her pedagogy, Rachel's ideas placed her at the forefront of contemporary thought. American Jews would spend the next century debating whether and how far to reform the traditional practices—both in the synagogue and at home—that marked them as a distinctive people. Indeed, the debate continues. But in the 1820s, while Rachel strained to infuse her domestic religious exercises with devotion, Charleston Jews inaugurated Reform Judaism in America by publicly expressing dissatisfaction with Beth Elohim.

The Charleston group complained that "defects" in the services had driven "them from the synagogue" and induced "religious apathy and neglect" among countless Jews. Like Rachel, the reformers sought prayer "from the heart," which, Isaac Harby added, "must proceed from the understanding." A shorter, more decorous service was called for, including a "discourse" in English expounding on Scripture or some matter of faith such as Christian ministers delivered on Sundays. The benefits of such alterations seemed overwhelming: Jews, Harby predicted, "would . . . know something of that religion, which at present they so little regard." The reformers wished "not to *abandon* the institutions of Moses, but to *understand and observe them.*" They would then "worship God, not as *slaves of bigotry and priestcraft*, but as the enlightened descendents of" a "chosen race."[11]

Having expressed to her father her objections to the current practice of Jewish worship, Rachel was interested in his opinion of the doings in Charleston. As his discourse she had found packed with the portrait made clear, Jacob did not approve. Indeed, he found the tenor of the Charleston reformers' petition treacherous and predicted that should the reformers succeed, a schism as destructive as the French Revolution would ravage the Jewish nation. To remove Hebrew from the service would sever the tongue linking Israelites across the globe, the tongue that sang of their promised restoration to Zion, the tongue that prevented them from disappearing into what he called the "common mass." Rachel tried to reason with him. Harby and his supporters resembled Martin Luther, not Robespierre, for, Rachel said, they wanted only to dislodge a complacent leadership grown deaf to its people's needs.[12]

Rachel's appeal wasn't the only one to fall on deaf ears. The ruling council at Beth Elohim dismissed the petition. But the reformers persisted. They wrote a constitution, incorporated themselves under state law as the Reformed Society of Israelites, and in 1825 began worshiping with their families at a Masonic hall. Services included hymns sung by a choir, instrumental music, English prayers, and a sermon. Men did not cover their heads during the ceremony, as they did in Beth Elohim. While Rachel wished to attend such a gathering, Jacob wrote to the reformers' correspondence committee upbraiding them for contumacy and willful error. His scholarly denunciations changed no one's mind, however, striking Harby and his followers as yet more rabbinic unreasonableness. Jacob accused Harby himself of "abominable sophistry" and self-serving villainy. The prophets warned of this, of strangers "among the children of Israel."[13]

Only days before Jacob's portrait and his tirade against Isaac Harby arrived in Wilmington, Rachel had opened the latest number of the *North American Review* to find among its contents an article titled "Harby's Discourse on the Synagogue." There in the country's leading journal of literature and politics appeared what Rachel saw to be a complimentary account of Charleston's Jewish reformers, based on the very address by Harby that had incensed her father. The author, a Unitarian minister, enumerated the most "prominent peculiarities" of orthodox worship and applauded the reformers for "imbibing the liberal spirit of the age." Bolstered by the national attention the *North American Review* piece elicited, and convinced that Beth Elohim's leadership would not relent, Aaron's brother Michael and the Reformed Society's officers published an appeal in the Charleston paper for contributions toward the construction of a synagogue. The schism appeared complete.[14]

The *North American Review*'s account of Jewish reform in Charleston had elevated Rachel's hopes for Judaism in America. Her father's condemnation of the reformers therefore cut her personally. Merely reading his discourse, with its insistence on thorough orthodoxy, was difficult for Rachel. She stopped often, perhaps looking up to where his likeness hung on her wall. How could she respond? Jacob had called Harby an atheist. Would he call her one, too?

After consulting with Aaron, Rachel decided not to argue with the man who had already preserved one member of her family from apostasy and whose biblical and religious knowledge so far surpassed her own. Jacob did raise legitimate doubts about Harby. Even if he was sincere, Harby understood the faith less fully than Jacob did. Harby, who did not know Hebrew, dismissed rabbis as "blind expounders and commentators on the Bible." He based this sweeping conclusion, Jacob noted, on hostile Christian texts. Nevertheless, it troubled Rachel that in railing against the perils facing American Jews, Jacob seemed almost to favor the condition of unemancipated Turkish Jews ruled by rabbinic tribunals over life in what Harby called "this happy land" and Rachel herself had called "this happy country." Nevertheless, the manuscript, with a few moderating insertions suggested by Rachel, made its way to Charleston. Aaron's father, with others at Beth Elohim, requested permission to print fifty copies. While the family celebrated Rosh Hashanah that fall, Rachel hoped the following year would bring peace and unity among Jews and her own heart closer to God.[15]

20

CHRISTIAN FRIENDSHIP

The clarity Rachel sought in religious matters did not come. Yielding to her father on Jewish reform (which she did not out of conviction but out of respect for him and his superior learning) did not ease her mind on so contentious a subject. On the matter of religion, she had few resources to draw on once she parted company with her father. Aaron spent long hours at his office, where business had again fallen off, and Rachel's world seemed more separate than ever from her husband's. And her enlightened friendship with Maria Edgeworth did not have many answers for her on these points. Rachel sometimes turned to her sister Ellen, who offered an understanding ear, but more and more she found distraction, support, and comfort elsewhere, amid a circle of Wilmington friends, Christian women who structured their lives around faith.[1]

Even though these women had surrounded Rachel for years, it took an outsider to supply the bridge into their world. Born and reared in Rhode Island, Lucy Ann Lippitt, a thirty-three-year-old spinster, arrived in Wilmington in the winter of 1826 to mediate a family rift. Her

brother, a local merchant, had fallen in love with the daughter of a no-
torious North Carolina Tory, and the Lippitts, whose kinsman had
commanded a Rhode Island regiment in the Revolution, were up in
arms. Lucy met the girl and gave her approval to the match, but the
lovers' relief could hardly have exceeded Rachel's pleasure. In Lucy she
found a friend.

Educated, well-read, and full of vitality, Lucy Ann differed from
most of Rachel's Wilmington acquaintances. They met and talked. It
was exactly the sort of conversation Rachel craved. She felt awakened,
her mind stretched and improved by their exchanges. As Lucy Ann's
visit drew to a close, the two women spent hours together; best of all,
Miss Lippitt promised to return in the fall and spend another winter in
Wilmington.[2]

But Lucy Ann was also religious. And Wilmington was appealing
not only because of her brother and her new friend Rachel but also because of the genteel women who, like Lucy Ann, had been born again
in Christ. The Episcopal revival in Wilmington had originated with the
city's leading men, including Aaron. Adam Empie's success at St. James
showed most clearly, however, in the women who became his most
active congregants. Beginning in 1820 and with increasing success
through the next two decades, the Ladies Working Society of St. James
demonstrated the female members' support for the parish (through
money they contributed directly) and their benevolent aid to the community (through a "charity school"). These activities also seemed to
give their existing relationships and daily lives a higher, transcendent
purpose. When a friend heard of one young woman's religious awakening, she rejoiced in sharing "the sweet but *powerful* tie of Christian
affection" that would offer "sweet counsel . . . as we journey to the
Heavenly Jerusalem."[3]

Enthusiastic believers buoyed by mutual support and anxious that
their friends and family members join them in submitting themselves
to Jesus Christ, these women, like Lucy Ann, knew and admired Rachel
Lazarus. Respect and toleration meant that longtime acquaintances
could press only so far on religious matters, and after the near conversion of Rachel's stepson by their pastor few wanted to broach the topic.
Lucy Ann had no such compunctions. She spoke freely of Jesus' role in

her life—in all life. She questioned Rachel closely. What did God mean to Rachel? Lucy Ann did more than talk. People had quoted Scripture to Rachel before, had recommended books or tracts for her spiritual improvement. It had always seemed wise to handle such situations calmly and politely, so she accepted from her new friend *The Restoration of Israel*, one of many volumes of the time that advocated the conversion of the Jews.[4]

The book absorbed Rachel. It presented a defense of Judaism by Cambridge University's Hebrew scholar Rabbi Joseph Crool against the predations of the well-funded London Society for the Promotion of Christianity among the Jews. Crool's defense was rebutted by the Anglican divine Thomas Scott, whose annotated Bible sold widely in the United States. Rachel was mesmerized by the scriptural arguments and counterarguments over Jesus' status as the Messiah and over the Jews' prophetic role in Christ's Second Coming. She wondered whether Jacob had read it. Unfortunately for the Jewish side, she told Ellen, the "learned rabbi" sounded like a "conceited and superstitious man," and the priest a "good and wise" one.[5]

The following winter, Lucy delighted Rachel with regular visits to the Lazarus house, which was also enlivened by the dashing lieutenant Alfred Mordecai, then between assignments for the Army Corps of Engineers. After entertaining him in Wilmington, Aaron escorted Alfred to Charleston to survey that city's Jewish belles, taking five-year-old Marx along for the trip.[6]

The house was quiet. In that peaceful time Lucy Ann and Rachel grappled with the question of the divinity of Christ. Rachel brought forward her father's argument that Jesus of Nazareth "was not the Messiah promised to the Jews." As Jacob had written, the ancient prophets foretold no "suffering Messiah, but a temporal prince" to assume the throne of David. He would unite all Israel so that "none shall make them afraid." To counter Jacob's claims, Lucy Ann sought the assistance of her spiritual guide, New England's Episcopal bishop, Alexander V. Griswold. He reminded Lucy Ann that sometimes prophecies are "progressive" rather than literal in their fulfillment. The spreading of the Gospel into every land since the crucifixion was, according to his interpretation, evidence of the gradual unification of Israel. It would be complete and Christ would return when Jews stopped, as he said, "refuting their Messiah." Bishop Griswold and Jacob Mordecai used the same passage from Zechariah to support precisely opposite views. The old neutral ground Rachel had occupied—the policy of respecting the beliefs of Christian neighbors and friends—seemed to crumble beneath her. One man, at least, must be in error.[7]

Then, as Lucy Ann prepared to leave again for the North, Rachel's routine of children's lessons, household duties, and social visits ground to a halt. One of her dearest Wilmington friends, Jane Dickinson, was dying of consumption.

Nearly twenty years earlier, Rachel had written Jane's report cards at the Mordecai School in Warrenton. The star pupil and her teacher were amused and delighted to find themselves contemporary newlyweds when Rachel arrived in Wilmington a few months after Jane's marriage to the merchant and mill owner Platt K. Dickinson. In tandem, Jane and Rachel became mothers. Under the guidance of the Reverend Adam Empie of St. James, Jane experienced conversion. Rachel attended the christening of Jane's child in 1822 and felt fortunate that summer when the Dickinsons remained in town rather than going to the seaside. But after a second pregnancy Jane's health faltered.[8]

Nothing prepared Rachel for Jane's death, however. Rachel witnessed something new and affecting. As the end approached, she told Ellen, Jane clasped her husband's hands into her "poor emaciated ones" and said how short and how sweet their union had been. Jane recounted her blessings—"oh how far beyond my poor deserts"—in her mother, sister, husband, children, servants, friends. A few wishes yet remained, and despite her wracked body Jane's voice gained strength. Jane pleaded for the freedom of her slave Flora. She wanted mourning rings made for her "three best friends," Rachel being one. She begged her sister Mary to write to Empie in Virginia, for "she loved him and wished for him" at her death. St. James's new rector administered the last sacrament. Jane turned to her husband. How she hoped he would seek the comfort of the Lord for himself. Then she addressed to Rachel "a few solemn and affecting words" on the subject of Christ's saving grace.[9]

For two more days Jane Dickinson suffered. "I do not know whether I have succeeded in giving you an idea of it," Rachel told Ellen. "To me it was not simply distressing but soothing, edifying. It seemed to me I could bear all previous suffering to die the death of the righteous—as she did." Ellen did not know the other reason mortality hung heavily on her sister's heart. Rachel sensed danger because again she felt a stirring in her womb.[10]

21

THE VALLEY OF THE SHADOW
OF DEATH

Jane Dickinson's death in the spring of 1828 deprived Rachel of an old companion, and when Lucy Ann Lippitt left Wilmington a few weeks later, Rachel felt bereft indeed. The town emptied further as families left for Wrightsville on the sound, and Rachel complained with uncharacteristic bitterness when her slave returned from the post office with no letter from her family. To Ellen, then toiling to supplement the Mordecais' income with a small school at Spring Farm, Rachel's life appeared perfect, happy, fulfilled. But Rachel could not see it that way, and morbid thoughts crowded her mind.[1]

Rachel was pregnant—and ill and angry. Should she survive childbirth, the idea of educating another child rankled her. At forty, she felt her time was "too much occupied to allow almost any portion to be devoted" to reading or her own "improvement." Rachel's aspiration to a domestic life limned with self-improvement and educated and educating family members seemed bound for failure. As the summer wore on, her physical state mirrored her frame of mind. Though she hid the pregnancy from her Mordecai family, Rachel became, she would later admit, "weak and languid," then "full of pain and much debilitated." Aware that Ellen and Caroline had too many duties to nurse her in Wilmington, she did not want them to fret about her condition or the upcoming birth. And it shamed her not to be able to announce what she called her "unwelcome situation" with any gladness.[2]

Rachel played her old role, the stoic, and on September 12, 1828, Aaron announced gleefully that the midwife had delivered her of a daughter, "a fine plump child." A few days after the birth, however, Rachel's condition suddenly took a turn for the worse. The midwife diagnosed "the milk fever," dosed her, and assured Aaron that his wife's symptoms were "entirely nervous." Dr. Armand DeRosset agreed, and, noticing Rachel's uneasiness about the infant—by then the child had become so ill that he feared it might not live—he had the baby removed from Rachel's room and called in a wet nurse. Rachel merely grew more upset. Her fever rose, and chills and sweats coursed through her body so violently that the doctor was again summoned. He confirmed that Rachel was stricken with malaria. Indeed, the "headaches, nausea, dizziness, and lethargy" that had plagued her during the summer represented a recurrence of the same disease that had finally taken her brother Moses's life, and perhaps her mother's as well. Dr. DeRosset prescribed the only known remedy, quinine, and when he reached home he told his wife, Catherine, that her friend was badly off and needed her help.[3]

Catherine DeRosset rushed to the Lazarus house, where she was met by Rachel's friend and Jane Dickinson's sister, Mary Orme. Finding Rachel weak, the women dismissed the midwife and took over the sickroom. Rachel's fever rose with each round of chills, and the drugs produced in her mind "grotesque images" that kept sleep at bay. Catherine called again for her husband, who, Rachel later told Ellen, "ordered cataplasms . . . administered opium pills," and demanded "a darkened room and perfect quietness." Nevertheless, the extent of Rachel's illness was in doubt. When Aaron left the house one morning, Rachel was "as well as could be expected." Upon returning home for dinner, he found her "not able to speak above a whisper and extremely nervous." Such "sudden prostration" alarmed him greatly, but the nurses chased him from Rachel's bedside, and for the next two days he remained sidelined and helpless as his wife's condition further deteriorated.[4]

Mary and Catherine sat with Rachel as the fever reached its peak and, as she later put it, "a single thread" held her to this world. Observing the effect of Mary's anxiety on their patient, Catherine suggested she leave Rachel in her hands. In Rachel, Catherine saw an excellent woman but a wandering spirit. Like Jane Dickinson and Lucy Ann Lippitt, Catherine felt she held the answer. "Religion," she believed, was "the one thing needful."[5]

Catherine insisted that "the *heart* and *affections must* be engaged in the worship of our maker." This touched a chord; Judaism had not engaged Rachel's heart—several years' attempt to find meaning there had failed. And that night with pious, reasonable Catherine at her side, Rachel seemed to sense the spirit that had blessed Jane's deathbed. Despite convulsions and dire signs, she felt "perfectly collected and," she told Ellen, "perfectly resigned to [God's] will." The next morning the doctor took her pulse. It beat more evenly.[6]

What, Rachel wondered, did the night's events signify? Did she share Catherine's faith in Jesus? Perhaps not, but her heart and soul felt bared as never before; she wanted only Catherine or Mary to nurse her. How could Rachel thank them? She believed that they had saved her from death; they had also given her new life. She named the child, then two weeks old, Mary Catherine.[7]

By the time Rachel named the baby, she had come to understand something of what Catherine DeRosset and her circle called "the value of Christian friendship." These women, who had once seemed to Rachel so woefully disinclined to improve themselves through books and study, rose in her estimation. For the first time, she had the sense that she could be part of a beloved community beyond the Mordecai family, a community that could envelop and protect her from the alienation that sometimes darkened her hours and made her question herself. A friend, writing after the death of one of Catherine DeRosset's sons, had told Catherine how well she remembered "when *afflicted, bruised, and broken*, I lay under the rod of the Almighty, with what tenderness you bound up my wounds—and taught me to feel the value of

Christian friendship . . . a love which I believe will be eternal." Such love, expressed in the language of genteel evangelical piety, suffused these women's letters, and in 1828 it began to appear in certain of Rachel's as well.[8]

While Rachel was still dangerously ill, a letter came from Lucy Ann Lippitt imploring her to think of her soul in light of her pregnancy. Too weak to read it herself, Rachel asked Mary Orme to read the letter aloud—over and over again. Lucy Ann loved Rachel as a friend but longed to love her as a Christian as well. Intellectual friendship and mutual support could not, she believed, fill "the void"; only faith could do that. When she was strong enough to reply, Rachel told her northern friend that she had "walked 'through the valley of the shadow of death,' confiding in [God's] mercy for pardon of my sins and transgressions, and wholly submitting myself . . . to his most Holy Will." "You, my beloved friend, wish I could say more," for Rachel realized that Lucy Ann prayed for an open conversion, "but of this we will not speak." Neither mentioning Christ nor defending herself as a Jew, Rachel equivocally acknowledged the spirit and hoped for its guidance in the life "thus graciously preserved."[9]

Aaron knew and admired the women who had come to his wife's assistance. Grateful for their and God's help in delivering Rachel and his tenth child, Aaron concurred with her choice of names. Mary Catherine's birth and Rachel's brush with death left the couple alarmed, and Rachel tried to assure them both by recommitting herself to their domestic life. Writing to Ellen, she drew a happy sketch of her first full day downstairs, "baby, cradle, and all." She dismissed the wet nurse and proudly supplied the infant with her own milk. Rachel called Mary Catherine "this sweet little creature" and declared she loved her more than she had her other children at that age.[10]

During the 1820s and early 1830s Aaron often thought of leaving Wilmington and its limping economy. Nearly every time he opened the local paper, he saw plantations and homes advertised for sale as owners departed for rich new lands to the southwest. Meanwhile, North Carolina dragged its feet in constructing the internal improvements—roads, canals, and railroads—that mercantile men like Aaron felt were crucial to economic growth. Property values sank to their lowest level in fifty years, and with so much invested in real estate (largely in riverside warehouses), Aaron could not afford to liquidate, let alone move.[11] While Rachel welcomed the thought of moving, perhaps to New York, she feared Aaron could never set aside money enough to make the dream come true. Confined to Wilmington, she tried to enjoy the things she had.[12]

A narrower, more painful sense of confinement gripped Rachel, however, when it became clear early in 1830 that "little Mary will be scarcely two years old before" she had another sibling. The panic, anger, and sense of betrayal—whether by man, or God, or her own body—returned more ferociously than ever. Had she not enough children to live for, to rear and instruct? Rachel's first "child," Eliza, had married their Richmond cousin Samuel Hays Myers, a practicing attorney who had attended college at Harvard. Eliza was expecting *her* first baby that summer; it felt perverse at the age of forty-two to give birth in tandem with her former charge. Rachel realized that her bereft sister Caroline Plunkett would "hardly incline to sympathise in my deep regret," yet to her she confided her despair. "I have hoped that each addition to our family might be the last—but this hope I again find is vain." Given such sentiments, it seems possible that Rachel sought aid in preventing her pregnancies, either with the unreliable devices available at the time or by practicing withdrawal or abstinence. If she did, her efforts failed. Perhaps to deflect her anger from her husband or from God for this unhappy "dispensation," Rachel blamed herself for her fecundity.[13]

Childbirth endangered all nineteenth-century American women, of course, but not all women experienced "parental solicitude" (as she called it) to the degree that Rachel did. Marx called her his "key to knowledge," and indeed, having invested herself so fully in her enlightened domesticity, Rachel seemed to believe that her pride and purpose, her earthly value, depended almost wholly on her success in bringing up her children. But in 1830, when she found herself pregnant for the fourth time, she often felt like a failure with regard to the central, cultivating part of the covenant.[14] She found her energies depleted. Despite her best intentions, she had less patience for her stepchildren. Aaron's sons and daughters could not but feel it. Gradually, the stepchildren's ill health, predictable jealousies and rebellions, and perhaps resentment of Rachel's exalted ideals combined with Rachel's own strain to produce real ill will.

Rachel harped on the "expensive habits" and misbehavior that led Aaron to pull Gershon out of college. She complained of the effects of her stepdaughters' visits to Charleston, for they came home filled with "ideas of extravagance, [and] 'must have' and 'cannot do without,' cause me much trouble all around the house." The poor health of several of the girls also plagued her. Anna Lazarus fell gravely ill when she was seventeen, and high doses of mercury so damaged her mouth and tongue that she afterward spoke with a lisp. Maria Lazarus also struggled with sickness, and through the summer of 1830, as Rachel braced herself for the perils of childbirth, another stepdaughter, Rachel, was stricken with the tic douloureux. The elder Rachel leaned for aid on Catherine DeRosset, who assisted in the nursing, and on God: "There do I put my trust."[15]

Thus fortified "from above," Rachel was safely delivered of another daughter, a redhead named after her sister Julia. An intellectual exchange with Ellen the following year revealed just how lost Rachel often felt—and how far her religious views had shifted. While visiting their brother Sol in Mobile, Ellen had used his library to read the essays of Lord Bolingbroke. Ever the inadequate-feeling younger sister, she assumed Rachel knew about his views on religion. But Rachel was not familiar with Bolingbroke's arguments and berated herself for not making "time for reading." A month later, having studied his writings, Rachel recurred to Bolingbroke. She tarred him as a deist and declared to Ellen that when it came to religion, reason could not suffice. Rachel, the once-passionate rationalist, claimed she would not exchange scriptural faith "for all boasted worldly wisdom."[16]

Not that worldly wisdom ceased to matter to her. Self-cultivation and home education defined fulfillment to Rachel in important ways, and their absence distressed her enormously. For years she had approached religion as she had all important ideas. She studied patiently, satisfied her responsibilities, and expected to apply her understanding to her own and her family's improvement. It had not worked out that way. She remained confused about the role of religion in her life, both as an individual and as a mother. While her enlightened approach to education, parenthood, stepmotherhood, and domesticity might have formed a modern expression of Jewish identity in another time and place, it had not yielded up the happiness or sense of belonging she had hoped for in Wilmington. Rachel began to read Christian devotional literature.

If Aaron ever read such volumes, he found nothing to convince him to alter his beliefs. But he never shared Rachel's ambitions and could not appreciate the feeling of hollowness that came from falling short of them. Nor could he realize how thirsty Rachel was for the solace her Christian friends provided, how reassuring it was to find Scripture that resonated with her troubles. Rachel's pinched appearance, the result of depression, dealing with difficult pupils, failing eyesight, and poor health, shocked her sister Julia, who arrived for an extended visit about a year after the birth of her namesake. Rachel spent more and more time praying, which, since she was unable to control the number of children she had and their impact on the shape of her days, brought its own relief. The grace she felt supplied transcendence at least as powerful as the intellectual transcendence she had so long relied on for meaning.[17]

Early in 1833 Rachel found herself uplifted by more worldly things as well. Business for Lazarus and his partner, Richmond Whitmarsh, had never been better. On a single week in January, fourteen of their vessels were busily unloading cargo. Emboldened by the expanding market for finished lumber, Aaron set his sights on building a steam sawmill, the products of which he could then ship to faraway markets. He would need to raise capital in New York; but it would be more than a business trip. This time Rachel, who had never been north of Richmond, would accompany him on an extended tour with stops in Washington, New York, Boston, Canada, and Philadelphia.[18]

DEVOURING FLAMES

The prospect of a journey thrilled Rachel, and she longed for her sisters to accompany her. Ellen would not join the travelers, because she felt bound to care for Moses's son Henry, who still suffered from juvenile arthritis, but Eliza leaped at the chance to see so much of the nation with her sister and former tutor. Jacob and Becky would keep Rachel's children and Eliza's son in Richmond, and so in May 1833 Aaron and the two women set off for Washington, D.C., where Alfred now commanded a military arsenal and could promise them an insiders' tour of the capital city. At Mount Vernon they paid homage to the father of the nation, and on Capitol Hill they saw the leading spokesman for states' rights, South Carolina senator John C. Calhoun, who had butted heads with President Andrew Jackson over his state's nullification of the tariff of 1832. One day, Rachel cornered Alfred and Eliza as the three were riding in a carriage and questioned them about their "want of religion." She had, she said, found new life through Jesus' mercy, and she urged them to seek it, too. Alfred was stunned. He had no idea of the extent of his sister's spiritual investigations and never imagined her a Christian and a pros-elytizer. Alfred could not reconcile Rachel's appeal with what he had always admired, her "sensible and reflecting mind." He was tempted to regard her new posture as an "abandonment of reason."[1]

Eliza found such pressing inquiries from the sister and teacher she revered even more difficult to digest. In Washington, where the women shared a hotel room, Eliza watched Rachel kneel in prayer each morn-ing and night. She learned that Rachel felt prepared to convert to Christianity, and that Aaron strenuously objected. Rachel said she hoped her husband would soften his position with time, and though every day she passed outside the body of Christ's believers pained her, she would be patient. What could Eliza say? Less than two weeks into the journey, Eliza announced that she missed her husband and their three-year-old son too much and abruptly returned to Richmond.[2]

Rachel and Aaron traveled for three more months. In Philadelphia they socialized with the city's leading Jews, who feted Rachel for her defense of Judaism against—and her subsequent friendship with— Maria Edgeworth. The celebrated Rebecca Gratz acknowledged both Rachel's and Jacob's reputation by inviting Rachel to sit beside her in the women's gallery of Mikveh Israel. Aaron sat below with the men. Rachel's ability to move easily through both Jewish and Gentile circles followed her to Philadelphia. One day she bent her ear to Isaac Leeser's Hebrew, and the next she and Aaron heard the Episcopal liturgy she knew so well and now preferred.[3]

In New York, Aaron met with merchants, hoping to interest them in his lumber operation. He and Rachel toured the pretty new neigh-borhood called Haarlem, and downtown they shopped for carpets, curtains, books, and a bookcase—the first large purchases they had ever made together outside Wilmington. With Marx in mind, Rachel visited an Episcopal boarding school in Flushing, Long Island, and on behalf of Maria Edgeworth she obtained a spotless anemone from the leading American botanist, William Prince. In July she wrote to Ellen from Lowell, where the massive textile mills looked "as neat as possi-ble," and from there they went up to Northampton, Massachusetts, where she examined the Round Hill School. Following a short stay in Saratoga Springs, they traveled through the "wild" landscape of New

York State and arrived at Niagara Falls, which she called "this mighty work of an Almighty hand."[4]

Returned to Richmond, the Lazaruses embraced their four children, and Rachel kissed her now ailing father. While there, she received a letter that, in light of her feelings about Judaism and her presence under her father and stepmother's roof, could not have been pleasant to read. It was from Rebecca Gratz's niece Sara Hays, who informed Rachel that "from my earliest years the name of Rachel Mordecai has been to me almost holy. Educated by the most pious of mothers in the strong and ardent love of a persecuted but hallowed faith," Rachel, in standing up to Maria Edgeworth, resembled "the martyrs and champions of old who died for the God they would not forsake." To Sara, Rachel represented the model of American Jewish femininity, combining piety, duty, intellect, and grace. It did violence to Rachel's integrity to receive plaudits under such false pretenses.[5]

Rachel did not then know that Sara Hays would soon be her sister-in-law. In 1835 Alfred was transferred from the Washington Arsenal to the Frankford Arsenal in Philadelphia and began to see a good deal of Sara and her family, in whose affectionate and genteel society he felt warmly welcomed. He had first met Sara seven years earlier, at her sister's Philadelphia wedding. On that occasion he had not only enjoyed the company but noted the impact of intermarriage: few of the young Jewish women in attendance had ever witnessed a Jewish wedding ceremony. In the intervening period Alfred hotly pursued Jeannette Thruston of Washington but was not blind to Sara's charms. When he crossed paths with Sara at a White House gathering in 1830, he remarked on her sincerity, confidence, and good temper.[6]

The connection with the Hayses, an observant and respected old Jewish family, no doubt pleased Alfred's parents. Sara's mother was Rebecca Gratz's sister, and her father had, like Jacob years earlier in New York, begun his career as a clerk for Haym Salomon. Samuel Hays was known for his civic spirit and service to the Jewish community, and though his later success in mercantile affairs outstripped Jacob Mordecai's, Sara came to the marriage without a dowry.[7]

Sam and Emma traveled to Philadelphia for the wedding, presided over by Isaac Leeser, but their letters home said little about Sara.

George said more. Alfred had been too recently in love, George thought (perhaps he referred to Alfred's rejection three years earlier by Jeannette, or possibly there had been another claim on Alfred's affections). In any case, George felt certain Alfred did not marry for love and had unwisely turned to Sara as "a sort of dernier resort." Once more, a wedding became an occasion to express the Mordecai covenant of family superiority. Not surprisingly, therefore, when Alfred brought his bride to meet his parents in Richmond, he did not continue south to other Mordecai seats in Raleigh and Wilmington.[8]

Back in Wilmington in the fall of 1833, Aaron Lazarus had his work cut out for him. Having secured a commitment for twenty thousand dollars from Seymore, Bergen & Co. of New York, and with thirty thousand more of his own, Aaron contracted with a northern iron founder and steam-engine builder to construct the sawmill. Other merchants were experiencing troubles in 1833, but Lazarus and Whitmarsh's commission business nearly matched the record-breaking levels of 1832 as commodity prices soared. At this point Whitmarsh decided to relocate to New York, and Aaron was left to adjust to the loss of his longtime partner. In addition, for the sawmill gamble to pay off, Aaron realized that Wilmington required a better system for transporting both raw lumber and finished goods. To that end, in the spring of 1834 he led the drive for the Whiteville, Waccamaw, and Cape Fear Canal or Railroad Company.[9]

By nature conservative in money matters, Rachel regarded these large developments dubiously. She told Ellen glumly that she hoped the lumber mill would "be profitable in proportion as it has been expensive." When operation commenced in June 1834, Rachel still had trouble mustering any real enthusiasm for her husband's project. "Unenterprizing [sic] as I am," she admitted to Ellen, "I cannot help wishing it had not been thought of."[10]

Rachel had other reasons to be out of humor. She did not feel well, and while not exactly sick, she told Ellen her "spirits were deprest." She felt left behind when her Wilmington friends departed for the annual state convention of the Episcopal Church.[11]

Most of all Rachel worried about where twelve-year-old Marx would continue his education. Her time with him was drawing to a close, and he deserved other teachers—the best teachers the nation could offer. However, having toured several northern institutions, Rachel concluded that the ideal place for him lay almost right at hand: the school the Episcopal Diocese of North Carolina was about to open in Raleigh. Its establishment was one prong of the bishop's strategy for expanding his Church's influence in the state, and Rachel grew especially interested when Bishop Levi S. Ives recruited Joseph G. Cogswell, a celebrated pedagogue who, with George Bancroft, had previously operated the Round Hill School in Massachusetts. Aaron did not share his wife's enthusiasm. He wanted to send Marx to the Jesuit-run Georgetown College, which they had inspected during their 1833 stay in Washington, D.C. After much debate, Aaron overruled Rachel, the woman whose expertise in educational matters he had never before questioned.[12]

Aaron feared the atmosphere in Raleigh, where Moses's widow, Nancy Mordecai, had recently had three of Moses's children baptized. Rachel's brother George, their guardian and a nominal Jew, had condoned the deed. Aaron saw that his wife's long flirtation with Christianity had not abated as he had once felt sure it would, and he began to wonder what she might do—and what the Mordecais in Raleigh might help her do—concerning Marx. The mistrust Aaron's decision reflected wounded Rachel. Her steady, discreet quest for spiritual truth had not brought him round to her views. Rather, it had frustrated him and made her suspect in his sight. The day Aaron enrolled Marx at Georgetown, he profaned the respect that characterized his union with Rachel and befouled the air between them.[13]

The breach over Marx's schooling introduced a new era in Rachel and Aaron's marriage. There were new pains, new possibilities. The religious aspirations Rachel entertained for herself, for Aaron, and for their children were unacceptable to her husband. Apostates were pariahs. The survival of Judaism depended in some degree on Jews' making conversion represent a crossing into another world in which converts would cease to receive the blessings of their previous, Jewish world. Rachel rejected this practice as both cruel and unreasonable; so it was to one whose only Jewish friends were family members. Conversion for her never meant overthrowing her past or the wisdom in Jewish traditions, and it never meant rejecting loved ones who believed differently. Rachel believed with Christian proselytizers that Jesus came so that "all the families of the earth should be blessed" as the Jews had been, by God. When it came to Marx, she told Ellen, she "never knew a child more impressed with religious sentiments." She prayed with him daily, telling him that Christ was the king the ancient prophets heralded. Aaron begged her to stop. What was more, he was prepared to separate Rachel from Marx, Ellen, Mary, and Julia rather than allow his children to be swept from the religion of their fathers. It would be better, he concluded, if all of them went away to school.[14]

To this Rachel could not accede. Marx was ready for more advanced studies than she could supply, but as long as she had strength she would not stand by and watch her daughters receive inferior instruction from others. Faced with Aaron's threat, Rachel again touted the benefits, rather than the strains, of following the Edgeworth home-education plan. Her youngest daughters, Mary and Julia, "acquire no bad habits and some good ones," Rachel told Ellen. "Their dependence on each other increases their mutual attachment," she continued hopefully, "and I have it entirely within my power to form their temper, to instill good principles, to warm their hearts to virtuous and kind affections, and to render them more amiable if not better informed than" any school would. The once-troublesome elder daughter, Ellen, had improved very much and finally read for pleasure, and six-year-old Mary was "tender and intelligent, learns with ease and . . . retains very well." Rachel clung to the role she played in these children's lives; she would remain, as Marx had dubbed her, their "key to knowledge." But, inevitably, Aaron's silent reproof diluted Rachel's pleasure in the children's progress.[15]

By early 1835 Rachel had come desperately to want to practice the Christianity of whose truth she felt fully convinced. She implored God to help her transmit the love of Jesus to her children. And though she had once been able to confide freely in Aaron—indeed, considered it her duty to do so—this was no longer possible. His patience with her was nearly exhausted; it was clear that he rejected outright her most heartfelt wishes. So Rachel swung miserably between despair at being unable to act according to the dictates of her conscience and determination to do her duty as a wife, keep her faith, and trust God to open her way. The household stood in stalemate; on religion, neither side could give way.[16]

Some comfort was to be had in Wilmington's new ladies' reading society, in correspondence from Lucy Ann Lippitt, and in Hannah More's just-published letters, which documented the life of a brilliant Christian woman living out her ideas. Rachel stayed up late at night reading More, but when her husband needed twenty-five suits of work clothes for the slaves at the sawmill, she laid the book aside in order to cut the fabric.[17]

The workers had worn their clothes scarcely a week when a spark from the planing machine flew fifty yards to Aaron's nearby warehouse, igniting eight thousand barrels of turpentine and millions of feet of lumber. Within minutes the mill itself erupted into flame. The workers sounded the alarm and, joined by neighbors, did everything they could to control the fire. It spread to a nearby rice mill before being blown riverward. In an advertisement in the Wilmington paper, Aaron thanked those who had labored to save his property. No lives, at least, were lost. The loss was his: "Thirty Thousand" dollars, as the newspaper reported, of "our enterprising fellow citizen, Aaron Lazarus, Esq.," and twenty thousand more of his New York investors. Aaron held no insurance.[18]

Incredibly, Aaron had even worse news to contend with than the blaze at the mill. Rachel lay suffering from what she could only call an "extreme and almost unaccountable debility." She penned a few lines telling Sam not to worry, but a distressed Aaron broke the seal and contradicted her assurances. Perhaps fearing a recurrence of the dangerous fever that had struck her in 1828, Dr. DeRosset ordered, Aaron said, "a change of air and scene." With the mill's remains still smoldering, Aaron could not leave town. It pained him to watch her depart, escorted by his assistant, for the high ground of the Mordecai house in Raleigh.[19]

There, at George's home, Rachel's carriage circled the drive and stopped at the two-story columned entrance of a cream-colored green-shuttered house. As the servants carried her inside, perhaps Rachel glimpsed the lane reaching to the outbuildings: her brother George's law office, the kitchen, and the slave quarters. Nancy Lane Mordecai, Moses's widow, called for Dr. John Beckwith, who in an attempt to "draw the sickness out" bled, blistered, and purged Rachel. Convulsions racked her body. She could not eat.[20]

For weeks no one knew if she would live. As Ellen traveled from Petersburg, she feared the worst. George rushed home from his circuit and reported to Sam his shock at Rachel's "appearance." For six weeks Rachel remained downstairs, rarely getting out of bed. Ellen nursed her and tried to soothe her distress, for it became apparent that mental anguish matched Rachel's physical ills. All this time Aaron wished Rachel were not in Raleigh—for the same reasons he had not wanted Marx to attend school there. Depressed and sick, fearing death, she might speak of her desire to abandon Judaism, and, who knew, her relatives might call in the bishop. Over and over Aaron urged his wife to leave Raleigh and spend the summer in Richmond, where her dear father could perhaps return her safely to the fold. Rachel preferred Raleigh.[21]

On the Fourth of July, Rachel feasted on juicy berry tarts and smooth, cooling ice cream. Her condition had so improved that she walked in the garden and began enjoying the company of her relatives. Having put aside quinine and pills, she began to feel remiss; she missed the children desperately and ought now to be at home. Two months had passed since she had seen the girls. Aaron vowed to bring them to Raleigh when he could, but so much work remained to be done. The sawmill lots went on the market late in June, and Aaron remained gloomily in Wilmington to respond to inquiries. But he had even more unpleasant duties ahead; he must travel north to consult his creditors. On this difficult journey he stopped at Raleigh to see his wife and deliver Ellen, Julia, and Mary into her waiting arms.[22]

For Rachel the reunion marked "a day of jubilee." Forty-eight hours in the company of her children healed her more than any week in a doctor's care. Shrieks of "loud merriment" filled the yard as Rachel sat writing on a Sunday afternoon. Hearing them fortified Rachel's resolve to resume her duties as teacher, and she began planning lessons for the weeks Aaron would be away. "I cannot live without occupation," she wrote to her stepmother, Becky, with an invalid's determination to recapture what illness took away. "The improvement of my children I find . . . best suited to my taste."[23]

Her life had been spared—again. Once more Rachel felt blessed. But when she attended church in Raleigh, she almost wept at the bar that kept her and her children from the Lord's table. She despaired of ever finding release from the conflicting duty she owed her "Heavenly and my earthly parent" and the husband who shared her father's views. Nothing in the covenant she had inherited from her mother and re-shaped through her own life prepared Rachel for this contradiction be-tween duty to God and duty as daughter and wife.[24]

A possible resolution occurred to Rachel after reading the urgings of her friend and spiritual adviser Catherine DeRosset. In a letter Rachel called "kind, affectionate," Catherine asked how Rachel would now spend the life God had "graciously" preserved. Catherine's ques-tions and scriptural quotations were not new. But they "probed me to the quick," Rachel said, and "fell upon my heart with such a force of conviction" that her plight seemed more cruel than ever. Rachel "wept and prayed." And then the idea came with a resolution that, she said, transported her. "I was strengthened," she told Catherine, "prepared for the effort."[25]

She would appeal to her father, telling him everything, pleading, she said, "freedom of conscience," and "entreating his forgiveness, his indulgence, and his sanction to pursue the course which my feelings and convictions dictate." Indeed, it now seemed her duty to do so. In Caroline's case, hard as it was, Jacob had proven himself capable of for-giveness. Did not the family covenant itself mandate respect and toler-ance for believers of persuasions other than one's own? On that July day in Raleigh, it struck Rachel that to hide her soul from such a father, the man who brought her up to think clearly and cherish honesty, was "concealment almost amounting to duplicity."[26]

Rachel proceeded to write four letters. The first, addressed to Jacob in Richmond, flowed calmly, fervently, and rapidly from her pen. "I felt," she told Catherine, "as if under the influence of the Holy Spirit." Then she wrote to Aaron. This time the words were harder to find. She promised to let him know the outcome of her plea as soon as it came from her father. Rachel's next letter was for Ellen, who had witnessed what Rachel called her "uneasy and anxious state of mind." Ellen ought to know that Rachel had "at length resolved by a bold effort to disclose my sentiments to our d[ear] father," even though she dreaded "being the cause of unhappiness." Last, Rachel took up her pen to tell Catherine DeRosset her news. But Catherine must not celebrate. "Even if this point be gained," Rachel warned, "I still have severe trials in prospect, but my Helper is Almighty." With his aid, Rachel might soon, she said, "cast myself at the foot of the cross, and be washed in the purifying blood of atonement."[27]

It is a testament to a child's ability to trust in a parent that Rachel thought her plea had any chance of being benevolently received by Jacob Mordecai. In fact, the entreaty outraged him. The daughter of his heart stood ready to betray the God he revered. Only now did he fully understand why Rachel pressed him to pardon Caroline just a year before. He had listened to her then and done what felt like torture to his soul. Thus did Rachel prepare the way for her own apostasy. Was he doomed to watch all his children divorce themselves from faith and truth? How could he grant "sanction" to a child who had the temerity to slander the Jewish people, pointing to "the wretched state in which most of the nation calling themselves Israelites . . . lived, without religion of any kind and without God in the world"?[28]

Rachel had misjudged her husband as well. Aaron's reply was brief but "extremely pressing," she told Ellen. He made himself brutally clear. If Rachel was to convert—with or without Jacob's approval—Aaron would exercise his rights and "separate the children from her." Rachel had underestimated her husband's steadfastness as a Jew—or, as she thought, his "prejudice" against Christianity. His threat appalled her, for Rachel would never take a step that would divide her from her children.[29]

Jacob fought to master his temper. Days passed before he could reply, and when he did, anguish infused each line. He asked two things, requests that Rachel, as his dutiful child, would not deny him. She must take no precipitate steps. The baptismal water, the Communion cup, these she must not touch, not, at least, until the fulfillment of his second request. Father and daughter must meet. He would come to Raleigh at once.[30]

In what Rachel later called a "soul-harrowing" scene, Jacob confronted her. From his waistcoat he pulled her letter asking permission to become a Christian. Then, "uttering a malediction on its contents . . . and almost on the writer," he "tore it . . . frantically into a thousand pieces." Never had she seen him storm so fearfully, "almost a maniac, feeling himself bound by the [Jewish] law to utter curses against his apostate child, while yet his heart yearned toward her." It mattered not that he had told his children that every man had the right "to decide for himself on a subject so important as his religious faith." Unable to reason with him, Rachel was willing to do anything to bring the interview to a close. Falling to her knees, she swore "that I would never adopt any faith but that of my fathers, that I will lay aside the writings of men and adhere to my Bible alone." Confirming her vow in a letter to Becky, Rachel asked for mercy from God: "May the Almighty aid his poor, weak, erring creature in the knowledge and understanding of his will and his most holy word."[31]

Jacob was not satisfied. He wanted Rachel explicitly to renounce Christ, but here her brothers George and Augustus stepped forward and begged him to be still. Rachel's pledge was all he could require, they said, and finally Jacob relented. Writing to Becky, Rachel castigated herself: "Blind, wicked, presumptuous, how can I hope for forgiveness?" But she also felt betrayed and angry. When Jacob demanded that she revoke her "inmost thoughts" and beliefs, the product of ten years of "study and mature reflection," he ridiculed her ability to reason and denied her freedom to express her convictions. Did he not reserve that freedom for himself? Yet filial duty prevented further resistance. Anger was impermissible; pain and guilt, however, were not.[32]

Warrenton, North Carolina, as depicted circa 1805, a decade after the Mordecais settled there
(From Manly Wade Wellman, *The County of Warren, North Carolina, 1586–1917*,
Chapel Hill: University of North Carolina Press, 1959)

Jacob I. Cohen (1744–1832) married
Jacob Mordecai's mother, Esther, in 1782
(Courtesy of Beth Ahabah Museum and Archives, Richmond)

FEMALE EDUCATION,
IN WARRENTON.

IN CONFORMITY to the wishes of some respectable patrons in this place and its vicinity, I purpose to open an INSTITUTION ꜰᴏʀ FEMALE improvement, on the first day of January next. The course of instruction intended to be pursued is the result of observation and some experience, and will be adapted, to the varied dispositions and genius of my pupils, not losing sight of systematic arrangement and progression.—My object, not merely to impart words and exhibit things, but chiefly to form the mind to the labor of thinking upon and understanding what is taught. Whether my plan be judicious, a short experience will decide; and by the event I am content to be judged. The domestic arrangement for an efficient accommodation of my Scholars, will be an object of primary concern, and placed under the immediate inspection of Mrs. MORDECAI, believing it to be no small part of the education bestowed on females, to cultivate a *taste* for neatness in their persons and propriety of manners—they will be placed under a superintendance calculated as much as possible to alleviate the solicitude of parents. In my Seminary will be taught the English language, grammatically; Spelling; Reading; Writing; Arithmetic; Composition; History; Geography, and the use of the Globes; the plain and ornamental branches of Needle Work; Drawing; Vocal and Instrumental Music, by an approved master, of distinguished talents and correct deportment.

TERMS.——For board, washing, lodging and tuition, (drawing and music excepted) $105 per annum; an additional charge will be made for necessary Books, Paper, Quills and Ink.

JACOB MORDECAI.

WARRENTON, AUGUST 18, 1808.

N. B.——Parents are requested to furnish a pair of sheets, a blanket, counterpane, and hand-towells: which without inconvenience to them, will render the accommodation of their daughters more easy and comfortable.

An 1808 advertisement announced the opening of the family's female academy
(Mordecai Family Papers, Southern Historical Collection, Wilson Library,
University of North Carolina–Chapel Hill)

Adam Buck's 1787 portrait of the Edgeworth family conveys the enlightened domesticity the Mordecais, and particularly Rachel, admired and strove to emulate
(Reproduction courtesy of the National Gallery of Ireland, Dublin)

"Eliza and Leanna" (c. 1812). Eliza Mordecai (1809–1861), Jacob's eleventh child, grew up in a town where half the population was enslaved, and in a family that owned and leased slaves. The image is unusual for its inclusion of a black figure, as the daily presence of slaves receives little mention in the Mordecai papers
(Virginia Historical Society, Richmond)

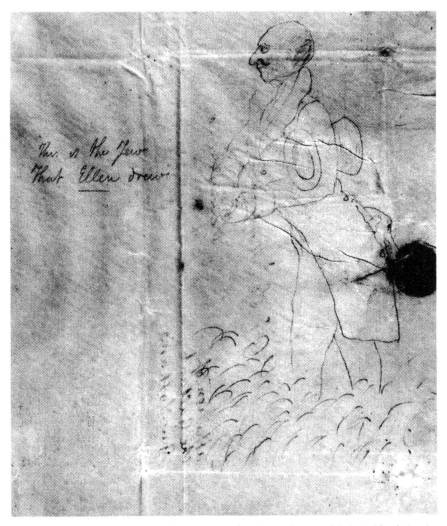

"This is the Jew/That Ellen drew." The tension between the Mordecais and their Jewish relatives is reflected in Ellen Mordecai's sketch of her uncle, Richmond merchant Samuel Myers

(From Ellen Mordecai to Sam Mordecai, September 11, 1826, Jacob Mordecai Papers, Rare Books, Manuscripts, and Special Collections Library, Duke University)

In the months before his death, Moses developed plans for the addition of a Greek Revival block to his eighteenth-century home. The Mordecai house is now a historic site in Raleigh
(Courtesy of the North Carolina Division of Archives and History, Raleigh)

Moses Mordecai, a successful attorney in North Carolina, died at the age of thirty-nine, leaving behind four children under seven years old
(Artist unknown, courtesy of the North Carolina Division of Archives and History, Raleigh)

In 1823 Alfred Mordecai (1804–1887) graduated first in his class from the United States Military Academy at West Point and entered the Army Corps of Engineers
(Portrait by Thomas Sully c. 1830s, courtesy of the Jacob Rader Marcus Center of the American Jewish Archives, Cincinnati)

Isaac Leeser (1806–1868), with Jacob's encouragement, left a mercantile position to lead Philadelphia's Congregation Mikveh Israel. He later published essays by Emma Mordecai in his periodical, The Occident and American Jewish Advocate
(Portrait by Solomon N. Carvhalho c. 1840, courtesy of the Jacob Rader Marcus Center of the American Jewish Archives, Cincinnati)

The Reverend Adam Empie, rector at St. James (Episcopal) Church in Wilmington, North Carolina, sought to convert Jacob Mordecai in Warrenton in 1814. Years later, he became embroiled in a controversy surrounding the apostasy of Gershon Lazarus, a stepson of Jacob's daughter Rachel
(Courtesy of New Hanover County Public Library, Wilmington)

This 1826 portrait of Jacob Mordecai (1762–1838) by John Wesley Jarvis was commissioned by Samuel Mordecai as a gift to his sister, Rachel Mordecai Lazarus
(Courtesy of Southern Historical Collection, Wilson Library, University of North Carolina–Chapel Hill)

"In the midst of life we are in death"

DIED,

In Petersburg, Va. on the 23d, Mrs. RACHEL LAZARUS. Mrs. Lazarus was hastening from Wilmington to Richmond to minister at the couch of a sick father, but was so exhausted by fatigue on her arrival at Petersburg, that she was immediately obliged to retire to that bed whence she was borne to the grave. Truly life is a vain shadow and vanisheth like the mist. The moral, social, and intellectual virtues met together in Mrs. L —the gentler attributes of her own sex were blended with the more masculine of the other, and formed a combination of most rare excellence. Her uncommon mental endowments were improved and enriched by well directed study, which fitted her, alike, to charm and to mend any society. It will be long before we will look upon her like again. Benevolence of character, singleness of purpose, and unaffectedness of manner—' virtues the better for their simpleness'—made her the admiration of her acquaintance and the pride of her friends. A large circle profoundly sympathize with the family, and will not suffer the memory of the dead to perish. Her " remembrance will be richer in our thoughts than on her tomb"—Society will honour in ashes, whom they loved in life. God's peace be with her.

The obituary of Jacob and Judy Mordecai's eldest daughter, Rachel Mordecai Lazarus (1788–1838), was probably composed by her husband, Aaron. It appeared in the June 29, 1838, issue of the Wilmington Advertiser

Rachel and Aaron's eldest child, Marx Edgeworth
Lazarus (1822–1895), became an advocate of
utopian socialism and free love, the topic of his 1852
publication Love vs. Marriage
(Courtesy of Special Collections Library,
University of Michigan)

Hydropathic health reformer, feminist,
and free-love activist Mary Gove Nichols
befriended Marx and his sister Ellen Lazarus
in New York in the late 1840s
(From Nichols' Health Manual: Being Also a
Memorial of the Life and Work
of Mrs. Mary S. Gove Nichols, 1886)

Jacob's eighth child, George Washington
Mordecai (1801–1871), followed his brother
Moses into the law. He also served as
guardian and trustee to many nieces and
nephews
(Ruffin-Roulhac-Hamilton Papers, Southern
Historical Collection, Wilson Library, University of
North Carolina–Chapel Hill)

Solomon Mordecai (1792–1869) taught in the family's school in Warrenton. After graduating from medical school, he opened his practice in Mobile, Alabama
(George Mordecai Papers, Southern Historical Collection, Wilson Library, University of North Carolina–Chapel Hill)

A lifelong merchant who suffered many economic reverses, the next-to-eldest of Jacob's children, Samuel Mordecai (1786–1865), published a memoir, Richmond in By-Gone Days; Being Reminiscences of an Old Citizen *(1856)*
(Courtesy of Valentine Museum/ Richmond History Center)

In 1855 Major Alfred Mordecai traveled with the U.S. Military Commission to the Crimea, one of several prized assignments he undertook during his career in the U.S. Army. From left, Mordecai, unidentified man, Richard Delafield, and George B. McClellan
(Courtesy of U.S. Army Military History Institute)

The twelfth and next-to-youngest of Jacob's children, Emma Mordecai (1812–1906), published writings on Judaism in the decades before the Civil War
(Courtesy of the North Carolina Division of Archives and History, Raleigh)

Ellen Mordecai (1790–1884) is pictured at age ninety-two. She converted to Christianity in 1838 and published the narrative of her conversion, The History of a Heart, *in 1845*
(Southern Historical Collection, Wilson Library, University of North Carolina–Chapel Hill)

Jacob Mordecai's granddaughter, Caroline Myers (1844–1928), married Baltimore native Edward B. Cohen (1835–1888) in 1865
(Cook Collection, Valentine Museum/Richmond History Center)

In 1886 Alfred and Sara Mordecai
celebrated their fiftieth wedding
anniversary at their Philadelphia home
(Courtesy of Mordecai House,
Capital Area Preservation)

23

DUPLICITY

Denied," as she said, "the power" of acting on her own behalf
by the men she most loved, Rachel tried to face the life that
lay ahead of her. It nearly "unhinged" her. Never had she
felt so helpless. Never had she caused so much pain. Of course, the
world did not stop. She must calm herself and write to Aaron, release
him from anxiety. Although she continued to "credit the excellence of
the Christian religion," Rachel told Ellen she now knew it could not be
"for me or mine." Rachel no longer expected "happiness . . . in this
world." Certain that further study would not alter her beliefs, she
looked toward a future in which she would ever stand divided from
and suspect in the eyes of her father and her husband. Her stepchildren might use the episode against her. And, worst of all, as a mother,
Rachel felt condemned to see her children's souls languish in spiritual
ignorance.[1]

Rachel returned to Wilmington resolved to accept her lot. Fortunately, Catherine DeRosset kept secret her foiled conversion. Other
friends, therefore, asked no terrible questions and forced no terrible

lies; they merely welcomed her back and celebrated the restoration of her health.[2] Mary Orme and the members of the Ladies Working Society of St. James reminded Rachel of her promise to act as treasurer for the winter fair they were holding to raise money for the charity school. Rachel did not mention in her letter to Ellen after the event whether Aaron graced the fair or whether his purchases helped fill the society coffers. If he did not attend, he had an excuse aside from his rejection of his wife's religious sentiments. Along with the usual business of loading ships with naval stores and selling salt, molasses, and fine Monongahela whiskey, Aaron had set about the building of a railroad.[3]

No buyer had come forward for the riverfront lots where his planing mill once stood, but a railroad would speed the state's raw materials to Wilmington's mills and thence to distant markets. It would bring new life to the economy and restore the city's property values. Year after year, heeding the majority of its electorate, the legislature in Raleigh had refused to allocate money to railroad corporations, and private funds were insufficient to build the tracks. In consequence, people had begun calling North Carolina the "Rip van Winkle State." But in 1835 the politicians in Raleigh seemed ready to listen to the advocates of internal improvements, and the focus of Aaron's latest efforts, the Wilmington and Raleigh Railroad Company, received a state charter and a promise of $800,000 if the company could raise $300,000 privately. As chairman of the board, Aaron presided over a political coalition—the seed of eastern North Carolina's Whig Party—promising that "the laborer shall find ready employment and receive the reward of his industry; and . . . every class of society shall . . . show forth the smile of contentment."[4]

The newspaper offered weekly updates on Aaron's sales of railroad stock. A month into the drive, subscriptions reached $237,000, and pressure mounted to meet the $300,000 threshold. All was going according to plan. Aaron's shipping trade boomed through the winter, and if he did not look too closely at his family's affairs, he might believe that the bleakness of 1835—the mill fire, his wife's near death and apostasy—had faded for good. What could Rachel do but foster such a view? She had many ways of doing so: she resumed the children's lessons, joined in mourning Aaron's father's death in Charleston, kept the large household in order, and entertained her husband's ship captains at suppers and afternoon tea parties. The coming railroad divided the Mordecais, however.[5]

Raleigh's citizens had snubbed the Wilmington and Raleigh Railroad Company, backing instead the Raleigh and Gaston line that George Mordecai was developing during this same period. Bad feelings erupted when George trumped Aaron by opening negotiations for linkage with the railroad company that Sam was then planning in Petersburg, for both the Wilmington and the Raleigh lines sought connections to Virginia. Aaron, who had only just lost a bid for the presidency of the Wilmington railroad, had to watch as his younger brother-in-law George won the top post at the Raleigh and Gaston line. Rachel ran interference, imploring Ellen to write from Petersburg encouraging Aaron's project "for the sake of my husband," who had set his sights on rebuilding the steam sawmill. Improved railroad transport promised benefits, but this time the investment had to pay.[6]

Rachel sustained herself through the winter of 1835–1836 with help from the twenty-seventh chapter of the Book of Proverbs: "Boast not thyself of tomorrow; for thou knowest not what a day may bring forth." Rachel did not, however, as she had promised Jacob in Raleigh, stick to the Old Testament and forsake all Christian texts. Writing to Ellen, she praised the sermon that the Scottish divine Hugh Blair built upon that verse. At times faith soothed Rachel, restored her hopes, and granted her patience to abide by the Lord's will. But "darkness," anger, and depression returned. Bishop Ives spent a week in Wilmington confirming fourteen new church members at St. James. Kneeling alone in her room (she could not let Aaron see her in the attitude of Christian worship), Rachel could "utter aught but sighs" at what she described to Ellen as the "conflicting duties that forbid me to seek aid, where it might be found"—in baptism, in open Christian fellowship, in liberation from the anguish of a double life.[7]

The need for comfort and support led to duplicity, and the duplicity deepened Rachel's dejection. Stamina and hope sometimes abandoned her. Writing to Ellen in 1836, she confessed to having given up teaching her children: "The task is too much for me." Into this solitary gloom her beloved Ellen introduced cause for envy—and concern.

Rachel read Ellen's latest epistle from Petersburg and, almost in a panic, "destroyed" it. The letter contained stunning and dangerous news: as Ellen later put it, "the Beacon light of heaven, the star of Bethlehem," now shed its beams where Rachel never thought it would—on Ellen. While Rachel strained to keep her word to her father never to convert, Ellen had studied the Bible and the Christian evidences Petersburg's Episcopal priest put into her hands. Then one day, for the first time, forty-six-year-old Ellen said she felt the desire "to pray." She had attended countless church services as an observer; now she went as a worshipper.[8]

A year earlier, Ellen's awakening to Christ would "have filled my soul with pure unmingled joy," Rachel wrote, "and so it ought now, for my views are not changed." Circumstances, however, had changed. "My mind has been torn, my spirit broken," and Rachel could not endure the thought of Ellen's suffering the same "miseries." Ellen must understand that honesty would bring ruin. She must not arouse the slightest suspicion in Jacob or Becky, whose response would "unhinge" her and "rob you of . . . your hopes of salvation." Jesus' Gospel rang in Rachel's ears: "He that loveth father or mother more than me is not worthy of me." Rachel and Ellen were consigned to unworthiness. The alternative of defying their father, and thereby sundering the family bonds that sustained them, was unthinkable.[9]

Fear, logic, and propriety suggested that the sisters' communication end there, but the spiritual companionship Rachel and Ellen shared was too sweet, their predicaments too similar, their need for support too desperate to resist the comforts of further counsel. "Duplicity," as Rachel saw their actions, though "hateful, sinful," eventually grew "unavoidable." Rachel took advantage of Aaron's extended absence on business to communicate freely with Ellen. Ellen observed that "even our thoughts would not be free were it in the power of man to control them." Rachel went further. Did not these men "who would shudder at the Spanish [Inquisition] unwittingly practice the same in kind if not in degree"? To Maria Edgeworth, Rachel had pictured America as a land of religious freedom; to Ellen she now presented her own family members as cruel religious oppressors.[10]

Aaron had given Rachel strict instructions regarding the observance of the Jewish High Holidays. When the Lazarus household gathered for Rosh Hashanah and Yom Kippur, Rachel's heart twisted guiltily in her chest, for she was "repeating prayers of which I cannot admit the efficacy, and keeping festivals which . . . have lost their solemnity." How long could she dissemble so?[11]

In fact, Aaron sensed something awry. He saw so few letters from Ellen that he asked whether all was right in Petersburg. In addition, he found that Rachel had put Christian writings into the children's hands. Julia Lazarus, not yet six, announced to him one day that "Jesus Christ never did any thing wrong, that he did nothing but good all his life." Who told you that? her father asked. "I read it in my little book." Aaron informed Julia, gently but firmly, that "Christ was a man and did as many wrong things as" her own father and "that nobody ought to worship him." Incidents like this made Aaron guard the children more closely than ever. Though he tried not to think of his marriage as a contest over his children's souls, his wife left him little choice.[12]

Aaron did not know the half of it. Rachel could barely control her impulse to lead her children to Jesus, down what she called the "way of truth and righteousness." When thwarted, she experienced a sense of powerlessness even more severe than the lack of control her pregnancies had represented. Rachel fantasized about bringing "my husband to see as I do" and with his support enrolling the children in Sunday school. Together they might all spend Sunday "soberly at church," enjoying the blessings not only of an enlightened but also of a Christian home. If they could believe together, the elusive unity she so long sought through intellect might be established through faith. It nearly broke Rachel's heart when her little Julia reported that Jews "are a great deal wiser and better than Christians" since they did not worship a man like any other. What could Rachel do except say that Julia's "father was mistaken" and instruct her not to talk or think of things she could not yet comprehend?[13]

Through varying degrees of clandestine efforts, Rachel and Ellen strove to convert other family members. Having found Christian faith for themselves, they could not help wanting to share it with loved ones. Rachel imagined how happy Emma would be if she "lay her burden at the foot of the cross . . . then might her wounded spirit rest in peace."

She worried over Eliza, whom she derogated as "an unbeliever in all revelation." Indeed, Eliza, Emma, Sam, George, Sol, and Laura hardly qualified as devout Jews, though none had strayed into apostasy as Caroline, Rachel, and Ellen had. Eliza and Emma begged their elder sisters to leave the question alone, stating that "any change in our religious sentiments would" tear the family apart. Rachel tried to argue that it wasn't so, but what she considered "the mist of error" would not lift.[14]

When nineteen-year-old Laura Mordecai, Jacob's last child, came to Wilmington in 1837, she bestowed on her eldest sister not only the comfort of good company but the unexpected joy of religious sympathy. Aaron had gone away again on railroad business. Rachel's mood brightened as she watched Laura charm her friends and gain the admiration of Wilmington's gentlemen. It pleased Rachel even more to sit with Laura at St. James while Bishop Ives confirmed another crop of new communicants, for she said Laura found the ceremony almost as moving as she did. Though too fearful to speak openly to Laura of religious matters, Rachel considered her "much inclined to believe." For her part, Laura delayed her departure. Her presence dispelled the tension in the house, and on the occasion of Aaron and Rachel's sixteenth anniversary Laura wrote home of her "dear sister" and described Aaron endearingly asleep in his armchair.[15]

Aaron had earned his repose. His planing mill again roared with activity, yielding a warehouse full of fine flooring boards. Construction on the Wilmington railroad was under way, and he had taken a leading role in yet another venture, the Fayetteville and Western line, which would extend his city's commercial reach into the state's midsection. His son Gershon was joining his mercantile business. Having attended Georgetown and a Quaker school in Pennsylvania, Marx was settled closer to home at a classical academy in Hillsborough, North Carolina, preparing for college at Chapel Hill. His and Rachel's daughter Ellen lived safely with her grandfather in Richmond and took her lessons from Aunt Eliza.[16]

While peace reigned in Aaron Lazarus's home that anniversary day, mercantile firms from New York to New Orleans were shaken to their foundations. Panic soon set in. New York banks suspended specie payments, and the domestic items Aaron traded—including the planed lumber from his mill—lost nearly half their value. Amid what the editor of the *Wilmington Advertiser* called economic "desolation," the Wilmington and Raleigh Railroad cars prepared for their maiden trip.[17]

Rachel hoped Aaron and her brother Sam might escape "the general wreck." But conditions seemed to put a Mordecai family gathering, planned for that summer in Richmond, out of the question. Aaron, who had to visit New York in any case, vetoed such economizing. Rachel and Jacob had not met since their "fatal interview" in Raleigh. Would he really receive the daughter who had wounded him so terribly, and would he welcome Caroline, who remained an apostate in his eyes and felt banished from his home? Surprising them all, Jacob urged Caroline to hurry to Richmond, where, he said, "you will be welcome to my heart." The shaky hand in which he penned the invitation bespoke emotion or physical weakness, or both, for Jacob was now often confined to his room.[18]

All Jacob's children crowded into the Richmond house that summer, and many grandchildren besides. The only absentee was Sol. Sam, preoccupied with the fallout from the financial panic, stayed mostly in Petersburg. One of the sisters read aloud to the assembled family each afternoon, they passed the evenings jovially in the parlor, and Rachel hailed her father's remarkable "intellect and benevolence." It was almost like old times.[19]

24

THE POWER OF THE GRAVE

Rachel arrived home from the reunion feeling "buoyant and cheerful . . . capable of fulfilling all my duties." It did not last. After a few months in the Lazarus house, Rachel's spirits fell, and the teaching duties she had approached with "alacrity" hung heavy over her. Shy about committing to paper complaints about her stepchildren, Rachel confessed to Ellen that she turned to God for comfort when "hurt by little incidents" that she could not name or discuss with Aaron. Rachel felt alone, bereft of "sympathy and congeniality," unable to converse with anyone on domestic matters. Worse, the Mordecai rapprochement so recently achieved in Richmond was suddenly threatened as never before.[1]

When word came that Jacob Mordecai was dying, Rachel despaired of reaching his side. Though he wanted to go with her, Aaron was too engaged with business to leave—the national economic chaos now imperiled the railroad. Then another letter came from home saying no time could be spared if Rachel wanted to see her father alive. George and Alfred had held him down as the doctor placed a hundred leeches to his temples to draw off a fever; three pints of blood were thus taken, but when the procedure ended, Laura cried that their father's "mind [was] gone—gone." Two days later, Aaron, Rachel, nine-year-old Mary, and seven-year-old Julia boarded the horse-drawn railroad car and rode forty miles to where the tracks ended. Aaron, who could accompany the party only this far, lifted Rachel down and saw his family safely to the stagecoach that carried them north. Rachel, whose stomach never held up well when traveling by coach, grew nauseated. She ate nothing for the two days it took them to reach the connecting train that would carry them, via Petersburg, to her father's deathbed.[2]

In Petersburg, Sam saw that Rachel could travel no farther. He commanded her to rest at his house and tried to calm his nieces as he called for the doctor and for a friend, Mary Simpson. Rachel needed a nurse, and Sam dispatched another friend to Richmond to bring Ellen from her father's to her sister's side. Ellen thanked heaven for the speed of the railroad cars, which had only weeks before replaced the stage. She found Rachel lying on a couch. They embraced. But Rachel could hardly whisper. The physician had no further remedies to offer. Coffee-colored vomit rose a quart at a time into Rachel's throat, and she recognized that death—not her father's but her own—stood near.[3]

Had Rachel reached that moment anywhere else—in Wilmington or in Richmond or on the train—what followed could not have taken place.

"I believe I have but a short time to live," she told Ellen. "You know what my impressions are and what my wishes have long been." Rachel requested burial in the nearby churchyard. But wouldn't Rachel like to see the minister? Ellen asked. She would, but she must not offend Aaron. Ellen's voice rose. "My dear Rachel," she cried, "you have done your duty to your husband[,] do not now deny yourself the comfort you desire." Rachel asked for Sam, and when he came in, she made of him two requests: that he keep Marx as an assistant for two years after he finished college, and that he bring Petersburg's Episcopal priest to her. Sam nodded twice. He sent for the Reverend Hobart Bartlett, who knew from Ellen of Rachel's religious "difficulties."

Mr. Bartlett asked whether Rachel wished to receive baptism. Initially Rachel demurred. She could not leave "such a thorn" in her husband's "bosom." But after prayers she said in deliberate tones, "Let me die a Christian." Ellen brought water in a china bowl. The priest blessed it. Rachel joined "the ark of Christ's church" in her final act of duty not to any man but to "a Saviour . . . who has died for me." The priest made the sign of the cross over Rachel "in token," as the Book of Common Prayer said, "that hereafter she shall not be ashamed to confess the faith of Christ crucified."

Her hands and head were growing cold. Rachel had one last favor: Ellen should write to Aaron and "not enthusiastically but with solemnity tell him what I have done and that I hope he will forgive me."[4]

George and his niece Ellen Lazarus reached the station in Richmond early that morning. They were following Ellen to Rachel's side. At the depot George was given a letter from Sam. He glanced over its contents while guiding the anxious thirteen-year-old onto the train; but all the way to Petersburg he could not bring himself to tell her that Rachel was no more. The girl flew into Sam's house and "ran frantically into every room . . . screaming 'where is my mother; where is my mother!' " And when she saw the coffin, standing ready for its ride to Blandford Churchyard, she declared she too must die. She begged to "gaze once more upon" her mother's countenance, but Rachel's illness left a ruined corpse, and young Ellen was not permitted to behold what her relations feared "would only shock and distress her more."[5]

"I cannot command my feelings," Aaron wrote five days after hearing the news. Sam's letter to Aaron said nothing of Rachel's baptism, though it reported her last wishes regarding interment in Petersburg. Aaron did not leave for Petersburg; he was unable to bestir himself. Every way he turned, he met, he said, the "void." Nor did he reply to Sam's letter except by forwarding the edition of the *Wilmington Advertiser* containing Rachel's obituary.[6]

Then came Ellen's letter giving "all the particulars" of Rachel's last hours. His "dear, dear ever to be lamented wife" had taken the step he so long had dreaded. To his surprise, Aaron felt no anger. Alfred and Emma met him fearfully at the door when he arrived in Richmond a few days later; but Aaron looked, Emma wrote in her journal, "as if he felt entirely broken up" and said not a word about Rachel's apostasy.[7]

While Rachel lay dying in Petersburg, her father experienced a miraculous recovery. His mind, which all believed had forsaken him, regained its powers. With Jacob largely relieved from pain and happy in the company of Alfred and George, who spent weeks devotedly nursing him, no one could bear to inform him of Rachel's death—and most especially of her baptism. For fear of giving away the secret, the family wore no mourning attire in his presence. And so Jacob lived— his "stupor" came and went—two months more, oblivious to the loss that all around him mourned. The patriarch died at home, surrounded by family. Alfred, who had been called to Watervliet Arsenal near Troy, New York, where he and other members of the Board of Ordnance were testing new weaponry, grieved that he did not "receive his [father's] parting benediction." Aaron lamented that the Jewish "nation has sustained a loss."[8]

When frost came to Virginia in the fall of 1838, two stone slabs capped the new graves of Jacob Mordecai and Rachel Mordecai Lazarus. The distance separating them in death (Jacob's remains rest in Richmond's Hebrew Cemetery, while Rachel's lie on a gentle slope above Petersburg's old Episcopal church) bespeaks their conflict on earth. It places in bold relief the tension between the adaptation and survival of religious tradition and the freedom of self-definition a new world offered. And because Jacob and Rachel presented such stark and opposing examples of the resolution of that tension, the members of their family would be forced to define themselves between these poles.[9]

Words of triumph written in both English and Hebrew mark Jacob's tombstone: "God will redeem my soul from the power of the grave, for he will redeem me." On the day Jacob died, Aaron, then in Philadelphia, selected a design for his wife's memorial, but he deferred to Ellen regarding the inscription. Ellen's Christian beliefs remained concealed; Rachel had burned every incriminating letter, and Ellen had followed her advice not to convert during Jacob's lifetime. In part perhaps for this reason, Ellen's text did not remark on Rachel's spiritual life, but rather celebrated her upholding of the covenant whose standard she had carried for so many years: "Endowed with superior talents / and the most estimable virtues / She was an ornament to Society / and a blessing to her domestic circle." All the while, behind the epitaphs and from beyond the grave, Jacob's and Rachel's religious legacies haunted those they loved.[10]

PART FOUR

A NEW HEAVEN AND

A NEW EARTH

Religion, instead of being a holy ghost, an unembodied spirit, hovering over society and seeking in vain for concrete form and local habitation . . . shall become the breath of life in the reformed institutions of the divine social order, and society shall become the incarnate Christ.

—MARX EDGEWORTH LAZARUS, *THE INCARNATION*

And thus it goes with every generation, changing and passing away, thoughts, feelings, lives, and at last there will be a new heaven and a new earth . . . I have so often wondered why He made the Earth and peopled it with sinning suffering human beings to make war upon each other in all periods and so many ways.

—EMMA MORDECAI TO ELLEN MORDECAI,
SEPTEMBER 25, 1862

25

SOULS

Ellen Mordecai's christening in St. Paul's Church in Petersburg three months after Jacob's death surprised Aaron Lazarus, but it did not surprise the Mordecais. Ellen's brother Sam did not attend the service, but he knew of her intention and received his sister with his usual gentleness. Even Jacob's widow, Becky, reacted to the news less violently than expected; she would hear no defense of this latest blow to the traditions of her fathers, but Ellen was not banished from her sight.[1]

They were, after all, still a family. There was a new generation, Jacob Mordecai's grandchildren, to infuse with the loyalty, hard work, duty, affection, and intellectual cultivation the Mordecais still championed—secular middle-class values that had established them as gifted and worthy of respect. Yet this very same attachment to ideas and commitment to family improvement made it almost as difficult for Ellen, a believing Christian, as for Jacob to leave her loved ones to their own religious devices.

Whereas nearly fifty years earlier Jacob had assured Judith, "Think me not enthusiastick in any thing but love for thee," in Ellen love of family combined with religious conviction to produce an enthusiasm surpassing any feeling she had ever experienced, except her attachment to her brother Sol. And so she crusaded on. Ellen intended nothing less than to try to "pilot" every descendant of Jacob Mordecai to safe harbor in Christ.[2] Nothing since Jacob and Judy migrated south—neither financial crisis nor success, not death, not geographic separation, not intermarriage—divided the family as religion now would. When measured by the family friction they caused, all of these now seemed small troubles indeed. In the sometimes melodramatic struggles that followed, the security of the Mordecais as successful, potentially eminent American citizens was no longer in question. But their security in the 1840s and 1850s had ironic consequences. Whereas Jacob had labored under doubts about his own respectability and his children struggled to determine what becoming respectable required of them, some of his grandchildren questioned whether the respectability Jacob and his children possessed was really worth the bother. Decades of effort placed the Mordecais in a position to make explicit choices—about religion, about middle-class virtues, and, it turned out, about patriotism. During the same period in which many of Jacob's children and grandchildren made these choices, the nation they loved was unraveling before their eyes. Again they would be forced to choose sides.

Ellen's campaign proceeded on several fronts. George, who had expressed his wish to convert, hesitated briefly. His mother was still living, and his defection would break a commandment—and give her great pain. However, by the end of the year, George had joined the ranks of communicants at Christ Church in Raleigh.[3]

Yet another Mordecai tragedy spurred Ellen to press her success. Lovely, vivacious Laura Mordecai inexplicably collapsed in her room on July 4, 1839, as she dressed to attend a parade with the family of the governor of Virginia. Dying when she did, the youngest of Jacob's children avoided the religious decision that might have marred her graceful path through life. But the fact that Laura had *not* come to Christ before her sudden death was for Ellen the crowning misfortune. She vowed to broach the question with each of her siblings, and so, while Eliza and Emma struggled from one day to the next to hold together the melancholy household in Richmond, their sister in Petersburg implored them to consider their souls.[4]

Eliza dreaded an open confrontation about religion, and for weeks she dodged Ellen's invitation to Petersburg. Bowed with grief over the death of her father and two siblings, she had little strength to argue. Eliza's life had proceeded unevenly. For three years, she, her husband, Samuel Hays Myers, and their son had shared the Mordecai house in Richmond. Terrible bouts of gout disabled Samuel for days at a time, compromising his ability to earn a living, an ability the Mordecais regarded dubiously, anyway. And it was not a happy marriage. Though Eliza and her husband had intellectual interests in common, tensions about family and money brought much bickering. The more miserable she became, the more Eliza fell to criticizing herself. The first anniversary of Rachel's death reminded her former pupil "how far different I am from what she wished to make me" and, she observed morosely to Caroline, "in fact how far inferior to a much more ordinary standard."[5]

Nevertheless, Eliza would not let herself be bullied, even if it meant erecting a wall between herself and Ellen on the question of religion. She wrote to her sister, reaching for words "that will not cause you regret." Eliza would not come to Petersburg; her husband was ill and needed her. Now she must be blunt. "I have read and reflected," she told the anxious Ellen, "and I shall continue to read and reflect, but on the subject of religion, let me commune with my own heart, and be still." Eliza declined to enumerate the errors she saw in Christianity; she also declined to present her views, "not because I have a horror of my own opinions but on the contrary because they are sacred, and lie in the depths of my soul." Ellen must "trust the souls as well as the bodies of those you love to the care of the Almighty." But Ellen seemed incapable of this, and the sisters drifted apart.[6]

Emma's position was even more contentious. At the time of Jacob's death, she did not know what she believed. Her mother feared she was inclining toward conversion and, before Emma set off on a visit to relatives in Raleigh in 1839, extracted a promise from her to take no rash steps. Perhaps exhibiting more concern than confidence, Becky wrote to her daughter, "I know I can trust you."[7]

Rachel's death had deprived Emma of the only person with whom she could speak with "entirely confidential confidence" regarding the "sense of unworthiness" that plagued her through these years. Religious faith should have comforted her when her attachment to William Grimes was torn asunder, when her elder sister Julia relapsed into derangement, when Rachel, then her father, then Laura died. But she had none. "God has withdrawn His holy Spirit from me," she told Caroline. In Raleigh, Emma read "pious works," both Jewish and Christian, and visited the daughters of Rachel's evangelical friend Catherine DeRosset, then living in Raleigh. But no voice spoke to her.[8]

Her indecision troubled Emma deeply. She complained that her studies gave little satisfaction; "the investigation," she told Ellen, "takes very much away from the spirit of religions." Following Ellen's instructions, she perused William Beveridge's *Private Thoughts upon Religion* but grew impatient with the volume's tone of stupefied awe; Emma found it impossible to join Beveridge in his ecstasies, and at last she announced that her inquiry was at an end. The result would displease Ellen. Emma herself claimed to be surprised, but all she "read on either side of the question convinces me . . . of my duty to adhere to the religion of my forefathers. My mind is made up," she continued, "and if Judaism were to be publickly professed as Christianity is, I should at once become a member of the Jewish Church."[9]

Having rounded this corner in her life a few days after Yom Kippur in 1839, Emma seized her father's legacy and embarked on an unexpected career as an outspoken and observant Jewish woman. She would hold "fast to the Banner of the Lord of Hosts, in spite of the example of deserters, 'though they be those of my own household.' " "If I am in error as you so surely think me," she concluded in her announcement to Ellen, "still do I hope to be forgiven." On the closing day of Sukkoth, Emma, Julia, and their mother celebrated the Torah in synagogue.[10]

Ellen labored less assiduously for her brothers' souls. Sam, willing to tolerate his sisters' conversions, did not respond to her entreaties. He did not credit the idea that he must choose a side in this contest of religions, and Ellen did not risk their closeness or their home together in Petersburg by pressing him too hard. Alfred, an agnostic who declared that Rachel's conversion was the only act in all her life that disappointed him, was far away in Philadelphia and linked by marriage to an observant Jewish community. Ellen left him alone. Sol, however, was the frequent object of her prayers. They had not corresponded regularly for many years, and Ellen's 1831 visit to Mobile had only confirmed the impossibility of her joining his household. But Sol was not deaf to her spiritual entreaties, fueling Ellen's hope that eternal life in Christ might join them in death even as they had been denied union on earth.[11]

Ellen's evangelical labors among her siblings made relations uncomfortable; pressing the same religious questions on Rachel's minor children came close to severing family ties altogether. That winter, as the Cherokee Nation was driven west on the Trail of Tears, Ellen pledged to honor Rachel's dying wish that Marx, Ellen, Julia, and Mary Lazarus be brought up in the knowledge and love of Christ.

The first blow to Ellen's goal came when Aaron ignored Rachel's deathbed instructions to enroll their three girls in the Petersburg academy operated by Ellen's friend and spiritual confidante Mary Simpson. While in Philadelphia on business, Aaron sought the authoritative advice of Rebecca Gratz. Where, he asked, might he place his girls safely out of the reach of Christian proselytizers? Gratz, outraged, as many Philadelphia Jews were at the news of Rachel's conversion, recommended a small school in Bordentown, New Jersey. There he sent thirteen-year-old Ellen, but Julia (eight) and Mary (ten) were too young. In Wilmington the girls were not safe from what he and Jacob's widow, Becky, called "the baneful influence" of religious zealots. And so, though Aaron hated to part with them, Mary and Julia Lazarus remained in Richmond after their grandfather's death, under the tutelage of Laura and then of Emma. Becky pledged to do all in her power to "keep them right."[12]

Ellen, in Petersburg, remained in close contact with her nieces. Their fate was, in her view, sealed. On Christmas Eve, six months after Rachel's death, she led Julia and Mary to their mother's resting place. The day was bleak and cold. Julia placed on the slab a candy heart whose edge was chipped, upon which Aunt Ellen protested, "Do not put a broken heart on the grave!" Julia took it back, looked up, and replied, "But you know Aunt Ellen it would be something like mother's!" Ellen knew all too well and no doubt became yet more determined. Aaron might watch closely, but Ellen felt sure that "no effort of his will prevent" their coming to "the still waters of redemption" in Jesus Christ.[13]

Difficulties in Wilmington claimed much of Aaron's attention. Early in 1839 his daughter Phila defied him by marrying a Gentile, a local merchant and erstwhile trusted friend. Aaron retaliated by halting all communication with Phila, ordering his other children to do the same, and announcing plans to move to Baltimore.[14]

Aaron never left Wilmington, however. Attempts to sell his steam-driven planing mill and to auction his twelve town lots failed, making the move impossible. His partnership with his son Gershon lasted less than a year, leaving Aaron to supervise his business alone. He continued to support the railroad, though he doubted its prospects even as he joined the celebration of its completion in 1840. The state legislature continued to fund the company's debt, but Democrats loudly blamed Aaron's Whig Party for reckless spending in a deepening economic depression.[15]

Illness, in addition to the rupture with Phila, marred daily life at the Lazarus house. Aaron shuttled his daughters Rachel and Adeline to Philadelphia for medical treatments, trips that did his own health no good. Then, in the fall of 1841 on his way north, Aaron stopped in Petersburg. Too ill to continue his journey, he took refuge at Sam and Ellen Mordecai's home. There, where Rachel drew her last breath, Aaron, aged sixty-four, died of apoplexy. He was buried according to Jewish rites in Richmond's Hebrew Cemetery.[16]

Just as Jacob's passing had allowed Ellen to embrace Christianity, she assumed that Aaron's death cleared the chief obstacle to the conversion of his and Rachel's children. Barriers remained, however. For one, Marx confounded her. He adored his mother, worshipped her almost, yet her furtive pleading about religion had upset him as a youth. Now his aunt aroused in him the terrible feeling that he must choose among his loved ones again. Having reached the age of twenty, Marx detected so many contradictions in religious ideas, so many instances of hypocrisy, that he began to think all religion useless—or worse. "I found the old [*sic*] and New Testaments like the Kilkenny cats," he recalled, "and when the fur had done flying, there were no cats left." Upon receiving his diploma from the University of North Carolina, Marx returned to Wilmington to study medicine. Perhaps intentionally, he saw little of Aunt Ellen.[17]

Ellen's hopes for Rachel's three daughters were more sanguine, yet openly addressing the topic risked new conflicts with the Richmond household. When Emma declared her loyalty to Israel, Ellen not only mourned the loss of her soul but dreaded the Judaism that Mary and Julia would absorb under her care. Ellen's sometimes less than gentle approach to the problem only served further to sour strained family ties.

Sam Mordecai's slide into near bankruptcy forced the issue of Ellen's future relationship with her Jewish kin. Unable to justify keeping house in Petersburg, Sam reluctantly moved to Richmond to share quarters with his immediate family for the first time since leaving Warrenton in 1808. The change was not a happy one, because Sam had to resign himself to the family's increasing dependence on George, whose income as a railroad and bank president withstood the bad economic times. And the Mordecai women returned to working for pay. Emma took on two new pupils.[18]

Ellen's original plan—to come home to Richmond and help the family by teaching Julia and Mary Lazarus—was vetoed by Alfred, who had little taste for her missionary labors. Given the difference in religious sentiments, he advised her not to share a roof with Emma, Eliza, Julia, and Becky. With help from Rachel's friend Lucy Ann Lippitt, Ellen found a position in New York teaching the children of a prominent physician. She became the inmate of a fine home, where she met Julia Ward, then engaged to Samuel Howe, and Lucy Ann introduced her southern friend into her own cultivated literary and religious society. Nevertheless, Ellen, who was never a natural teacher, loathed her work and felt cast out of her home.[19]

Back from New York in the spring of 1843, Ellen split her time between Richmond and Raleigh. George had presented her with a gift of fifteen hundred dollars, and Sam's business had yielded his first profit in years. Ellen no longer had to work. She continued to tread softly around the Lazarus children. Regardless of her concern for their souls, Marx and Ellen, her namesake, soon stood almost wholly outside her influence. Marx would enroll at the University of Pennsylvania's medical college, where Sol had studied some twenty years earlier. And Ellen Lazarus, whose "frantic grief" at Rachel's death left her shy and sad, was plagued by ill health. By the time she turned twenty, she was laboring under chronic back pain and violent bouts of "nervousness." Until 1845 Ellen Lazarus spent little time in Richmond and saw her aunt Ellen only occasionally. In religion, she appeared to lean strongly toward Judaism.[20]

Marx's and Ellen's souls seemingly beyond their aunt's influence, the religious destiny of Rachel's two youngest, Mary and Julia, soon occupied the eye of the gathering storm within the Mordecai family. Mary, sixteen and about to complete her education, was almost an adult. Aunt Ellen, feeling that it would be "sinful to remain silent," took her aside one Saturday morning when Emma and Becky had left to attend services at the synagogue. Spreading Rachel's anguished letters from Wilmington before the girl, Ellen described the progress of Rachel's faith and her "final conviction of the truth as it is in Jesus." To Ellen's surprise and joy, "dear, sweet, quiet, gentle" Mary turned to her with "tearful eyes" and said that "the subject ha[d] occupied her thoughts for a year past, that sometimes when busy in school it would . . . strike upon her bosom," and yet she had not known how to speak of it. Her aunt's intervention seemed providential. Writing confidentially to a cousin in Raleigh, Mary exclaimed, "This has been *God's* work and not the influence of man. He has heard my prayers and sent me the *Holy Spirit*!"[21]

In the following months, Ellen and the Spirit did their work, while Emma enjoyed a holiday in Washington with Alfred, his wife Sara, and their four children, and then in Philadelphia as the guest of Sara's parents. She returned to the quiet household in Richmond feeling "renewed . . . for life." Emma suspected nothing until Ellen sat her down and announced that both Mary and Julia Lazarus stood ready to embrace their mother's religion. Would this alter the Richmond family's feelings for the girls? Ellen wanted to know. If so, George would shelter them in Raleigh. Furious at this betrayal, Emma replied that "it would be much happier . . . if they were not to live here." Eliza agreed. Such coldness shocked Ellen. Did her sisters have so little regard for Rachel, who had done so much for them? It was all Emma could do to hold her tongue at this. Ellen's righteousness appalled her. But she had no stomach to deepen the rift by fighting back.[22]

Three weeks later in Raleigh, on a quiet Sunday afternoon, Mary "arranged [her] hair as plainly as possible" and walked from the grand new house that Nancy Lane Mordecai and her uncle George now occupied to Christ Church to be baptized. That night the memory of Rachel crowded Mary's thoughts. Watching the daylight fade, Mary declared, "Oh *never* did my heart *yearn* for her as it did then." Climbing into bed, she thought how "rejoiced" her mother would have been "to have seen her child kneeling at the altar." The next day Mary wrote to thank the living spirits who had guided her—Aunt Ellen, a school friend, and her teacher—and prayed for her siblings.[23]

George broke the news of Mary's baptism to the family in Richmond. It could not have come as a surprise, but this did not lessen its devastating effect. Emma hoped George would not think less of her because they disagreed on religion. Unable to avoid the cleft in the family, she refused to repeat the arguments "in *our* justification," but she would insist that before Julia Lazarus hurled herself into the Christian fold, she conduct a full and fair investigation. With her aunt Ellen, her teacher Anna Maria Mead, and Emma herself as guides, Julia would study both sides of the question. "I do not wish you to adopt [Judaism] because it is mine," Emma instructed Julia, "or to reject [Christianity] because I do not entertain it. I wish you to examine and judge for yourself." Emma's implication was clear: Mary had not.[24]

Perhaps the bitterness between the sisters had become too upsetting, but whatever the reason, Ellen Mordecai quit Richmond to spend the winter of 1844–1845 with Lucy Ann Lippitt in New York. Perhaps if she removed herself from Julia's decision to convert (something Ellen considered firm), her Jewish relations would not finger her for fomenting rebellion. But the atmosphere at the Mordecais' continued to deteriorate.[25]

Fourteen-year-old Julia Lazarus found herself torn this way and that. She told Ellen that her grandmother questioned her constantly. When Julia asked to be allowed to pray to God to lead her aright, Becky corrected her: "You pray to three Gods." Julia answered no, she prayed to one God through Christ, upon which her grandmother ordered her "not to speak to her thus."[26]

Until Julia's elder sister Ellen arrived in Richmond, Emma and Becky had given up on bringing Julia back to the religion of her father. But the elder sister's reproofs of their aunt Ellen's proselytizing fell on Julia's ears with particular force, and within a month Julia informed the evangelical Mrs. Mead "that she was born a Jewess and a Jewess she must remain." Julia stopped answering Aunt Ellen's letters. Even Mary, who visited Richmond that spring, began to waver when closely questioned by her sister on matters of theology. Hearing this, Ellen Mordecai hastened back from New York.[27]

Mary remained affectionate toward her aunt, but Ellen Lazarus and "her shadow poor little Julia" treated her as coldly as possible. By the end of the summer of 1845 Mary had reaffirmed her baptismal vows and moved back to Raleigh, leaving her sisters behind. Her relationships with them did not survive the rift. Julia meanwhile confirmed her Judaism, cementing ties with her elder sister Ellen.[28]

Unbeknownst to each other, Ellen and Emma Mordecai published religious books at the peak of family discord, in 1845. Ellen had entered the publishing world in 1841, writing under the name of Jacob's Christian-born mother, Esther Whitlock. *Past Days: A Story for Children*, a rambling memoir of growing up in Warrenton and of Rachel's piety, received warm notices in the New York press, although Caroline Plunkett considered such autobiography unbecoming.[29]

Emma's and Ellen's 1845 volumes did not appear under their own names, a bow to the social disapproval female authors still encountered and, perhaps just as important, to the sensitive nature of their subjects among their own relations. Emma scrupulously maintained the anonymity of her work, but in a further opening of the wound surrounding their religious conflict, the Mordecais quickly identified the author of Ellen's book.

Emma's volume arose from her work in Richmond's Jewish community. Well aware of how fragile Jews' ties to religious tradition could be and inspired by Rebecca Gratz's work in Philadelphia, Emma persuaded the hazan at Beth Shalome to open a Hebrew Sunday school. This drew the sympathy and support of Isaac Leeser, who, in addition to his duties as hazan in Philadelphia, published *The Occident and American Jewish Advocate* (the first national Jewish periodical) and other Jewish religious texts. In 1845 Leeser announced the publication of *The Teachers' and Parents' Assistant; or, Thirteen Lessons Conveying to Uninformed Minds the First Ideas of God and His Attributes* by "An American Jewess." Emma's title recalled the Edgeworth text that had shaped her upbringing, and perhaps she felt that a little catechism would have given balance to the broadly secular education she had received from her elder sisters. Many assumed the author to be Rebecca Gratz herself. Emma did not seem to mind the confusion and would have been flattered to know that Alfred's mother-in-law recommended the volume to Sara for use in the bringing up of their children—Jacob Mordecai's grandchildren—as faithful Jews.[30]

Ellen hoped her book would have precisely the opposite effect. In *The History of a Heart* she related her conversion from an uncommitted Jew to a devout Christian. Rachel, though unnamed, appears as the narrator's spiritual model, a believer whose deathbed baptism represented "a triumph of faith." Jacob Mordecai inevitably enters into the narrative as well, as a Jewish patriarch who denounced Christianity as "erroneous" and forbade his children from following the path he had once explored but elected not to take. Ellen's christening becomes a flight "to the bosom of my Saviour and my God!" even though she recognized that conversion would "pain . . . those I dearly love." *The History of a Heart* seemed certain to do exactly that. Perhaps fortunately, sales were not brisk. After two years the Raleigh bookseller had copies on hand from the first printing.[31]

If Ellen's converts among Mordecai family members were fewer than she liked, her slaves supplied a handful of souls over which she held much greater sway. Since her conversion, Ellen had sought to balance her powers as a slave owner with her responsibilities as a Christian. Abby, born into slavery in Warrenton to the Mordecais' cook, was for years Ellen's maid. When Abby became a mother in her own right, Ellen took charge of the children's spiritual cultivation. That duty led her into the sharpening national debate over slavery and briefly into the company of abolitionists.[32]

Abby proved a disappointment to her pious mistress. Her first child was born out of wedlock, her third the result of a relationship with Sam Mordecai's former clerk, a white man. Abby's church in Petersburg expelled her, her African-American husband spurned her, and Ellen considered selling her as punishment. Yet the clerk's role in the affair outraged Ellen; she persuaded Sam to confront him and, on her behalf, threaten him with public exposure unless he turned over a sizable sum for the support of his child. Money was required because Ellen wanted the baby freed.[33]

But manumitted slaves were no longer permitted to remain in Virginia. Ellen began inquiring where she might send the baby. Perhaps on advice from Lucy Ann Lippitt, a Rhode Island native, Ellen wrote to the superintendent of the Children's Home in Providence and secured a place for the "emancipated child." In June 1840 she and Sam put the fourteen-month-old girl into the hands of Miss Harriet Ware. If she passed for white, the girl could stay with Ware; if not, she would be placed at the city's shelter for colored children.[34]

Disappointment in Abby prompted Ellen to redouble her efforts to rear the bondwoman's two remaining daughters to believe in Jesus and live morally, eventually as free people. The eldest, Jenny, attended church with her mistress each Sunday, and in violation of state law Ellen taught her to read. Worried by the effect Abby had on her daughters, Ellen, in an act of dubious charity, sold her in 1842 for $550.[35]

When Ellen, anxious to support herself and perhaps to escape tensions within her family, began looking for a position as a governess, she found that no northern family would accommodate Jenny. Jenny would have to remain behind, but Ellen planned to emancipate the two-year-old, Alice, and leave the child in Philadelphia on her way to her new teaching job in New York. Philadelphia's Shelter for Colored Children had too many needy clients nearby to accept inmates from out of town, but one of its supporters agreed to keep Alice long enough to qualify her as a resident of Philadelphia.[36]

In August 1842, as Ellen prepared to leave for New York, race riots broke out in Philadelphia. A white mob attacked African-Americans participating in a temperance parade and within hours assaulted black citizens, broke into their homes, and destroyed a meeting hall and house of worship. Violence continued into the following day, forcing the mayor to call out the militia. Long opposed to his sister's plans for Abby's children, Sam told Ellen that the hostility of working-class whites toward free blacks in Philadelphia rendered their condition worse than that of "slaves with us." Swayed, Ellen deferred her plans and left both Jenny and Alice in Emma's care in Richmond.[37]

Ellen's six-month residence in New York altered Jenny's and Alice's fates. Ellen had never conceived of such poverty and degradation as she regularly met with and heard of in the metropolis. Her employer, Dr. John Wakefield Francis, said that abolitionists waylaid southern slaves visiting the city with their masters with promises to help them run away and settle in the North as free people. The slaves would then receive food and shelter as long as their owners remained in New York but, once they departed, were "turned adrift without a cent, or a shelter," to join the ranks of the destitute. Relieved to have "looked before I leaped," Ellen vowed to a niece that she would keep Jenny and Alice safe—by keeping them in bondage. Her determination meant years of close scrutiny and discipline for her slaves. Compelled to learn weekly "Bible verses" assigned by Ellen, the girls were punished when they failed to do so. Emma reported from Richmond that Jenny came "along about as well as you expected and no better," having undergone "two whippings, several dry-breads, and one being-kept-upstairs-all-day."[38]

Ellen's family tried to discourage her aspirations for her slaves; Emma said she was willfully blind to their faults. "They are neither truthful nor honest nor in the least trustworthy," Emma judged, and in 1847 she advised Ellen to sell Jenny before the girl caused her mistress the same "vexation" Abby had by succumbing to immoral sexual liaisons. Stripped of the hope of freedom, Jenny and Alice had less reason than ever to adhere to their mistress's principles of purity, piety, and obedience—the same principles with which middle-class men and women in American cities of the 1840s sought to infuse the impoverished and dependent in their midst. Full of hope for the power of Christ to reform lives, Ellen taught Jenny and Alice to read so that they would have "a resource" in the Bible. It is doubtful that the slaves appreciated Ellen's efforts to prepare them "for more good than evil in this life."[39]

26

ESCAPE FROM CONSTRAINT

Ellen Mordecai's slaves Jenny and Alice did not achieve emancipation in the North. Marx Edgeworth Lazarus and his sister Ellen in many ways did. As participants at the most experimental edge of an upsurge in American social reform during the 1840s and 1850s, Rachel's eldest children, intent on benefiting all mankind, pursued spiritual, psychological, and sexual liberation.

In some respects, their activities can be seen as outgrowths of their mother's Enlightenment-based belief in education as the tool of social progress and her experience of personal spiritual transformation. While their attraction to communal living captured millennial qualities of the bourgeois ideal of reforming society through the family and domestic sphere, it violated the middle-class sensibilities and business interests of their aunts, uncles, and cousins. The bourgeois respectability of their southern relations was cast off in favor of expressions of selfhood that transcended boundaries of sectarian religion, social class, and sex. As they dipped into Fourierist socialism, alternative health therapies, feminism, free love, abolition, and transcendentalism, Marx and Ellen appeared to the Mordecais to be the victims of unsavory if not immoral fads whose quackish proponents would soon relieve the young Lazaruses of their inheritances.[1]

While such disapproval stung Ellen and Marx, it did not deter them. The world should and must change, for surely God did not intend his children to inhabit the artificial, unequal, emotionally contorted, spiritually rigid, and physically diseased society that was mid-nineteenth-century America.

Once Aaron's will was probated and his property assessed, his ten surviving children learned that they could expect a legacy of about five thousand dollars in cash each, plus annual rent and stock dividends— a handsome but not staggering sum. Given the bad economic times, it is remarkable he had this much to leave them. As minors, Rachel and Aaron's offspring needed an administrator for these monies, and Uncle George stepped forward, a natural choice because of his many years' experience in administering Moses's estate for the benefit of his four children in Raleigh.[2]

George took his fiduciary role seriously, especially with regard to Marx, whose stability he doubted. Of course, as an attorney, George recognized Marx's right to his inheritance, but it became almost an expression of love for George to keep Marx from it—an expression Marx understandably resented. Their increasingly tense, and terse, correspondence continued as Marx pursued his medical training, occasionally visiting Richmond to charm some of his relatives with his "peculiar genius." George, however, remained wary, unimpressed by his nephew's radical ideas and companions. The work of the French utopian socialist Charles Fourier (whom Karl Marx credited as an inspiration to his own social theory) convinced Marx Edgeworth Lazarus that individual and social perfection could be achieved through a complex system of cooperative living. Relations between nephew and uncle dropped to a chill. Their differences of opinion took on the concrete form of minimal, even no, contact for long stretches of time. Under pressure from his sister Ellen, Marx stiffly notified George that he had received his medical diploma and planned to practice homeopathic medicine in New York during the coming year. In explaining his long silence, Marx pointed out that his uncle never seemed interested in "my sphere of thoughts."[3]

Rachel had instilled in her son a great faith in the value of ideas, and Marx did not hesitate to share his. He derogated "all the existing forces of civilized society" as "utterly false." So-called civilization, Marx told his uncle, the president of a bank and a railroad, "generates every form of narrow selfishness" and "makes it a ruin, in our commerce, to do our neighbor as we would have him do us." Showing his Fourierist colors, Marx indicted "the isolated household" as inefficient and repressive, a hypocritical sphere "where to keep us from scratching each other's eyes out, the mannerism of politeness and etiquette is substituted for . . . earnest kindliness." Sam, who claimed some familiarity with the new ideas coming from figures like Ralph Waldo Emerson, dismissed this provoking lecture; Marx, he admitted to George, had moved "so far beyond ordinary transcendentalism that he soars above my comprehension." George concurred. What a pity, he thought, that Marx, so full of promise as a child, now squandered his time with "such a moonstruck set of philosophers." It would be more than a pity, however—it would be wholly unacceptable—to introduce a young lady, such as his sister Ellen, into this heterodox society.[4]

In the fall of 1845 twenty-year-old Ellen Lazarus, who earlier that year frustrated her aunt Ellen's hopes for Julia Lazarus's conversion, fled the Mordecai house in Richmond. While the contest raged over her sisters' souls, Ellen suffered "almost incessant pain," consisting of terrific headaches and backaches, as if her spine "was all in splinters." Blisters and ointments provided no relief, while medical bills ate up her allowance. She did not think she was "crazy," Ellen explained to Uncle George, but said she might "become so" if her misery continued. Marx diagnosed her illness as neuralgia and urged her to seek the services of a homeopath in Providence, Rhode Island. Ellen petitioned George to invade the principal of her inheritance to cover the cost. Finally obtaining his permission, she was escorted to New York by Aaron's former partner Richmond Whitmarsh. There she relapsed. A New York doctor found her seized with hysteria and diagnosed a nervous disorder of the worst sort. The following day Marx appeared to take his sister to Rhode Island.[5]

After two weeks in Providence, Ellen's symptoms abated. Neverthe-less, she delayed returning south. Marx left to resume medical lectures at New York University, where he took his degree, and Ellen joined her widowed half sister Phila Lazarus Calder and her children, who were then in Boston visiting relatives. Instead of coming home for the win-ter as the Mordecais expected her to do, Ellen secured rooms in Provi-dence with Phila; Ellen would be near her physician and proposed supporting herself by teaching in one of the city's public schools. Her relatives in Virginia and North Carolina were shocked. Despite the family's pedagogical tradition, Uncle George spoke for them all when he told her that no lady far from home should labor in a charity school among street urchins. Ellen, growing more determined, as she always did when she felt unjustly opposed, protested. She wanted to work, for she felt convinced "that if I had some active and important duty de-pending on me . . . I should forget my malady."[6]

Ellen never taught school in Providence—possibly out of respect for her family's scruples, but more likely because she could not find a position or because ill health prevented her from taking one. Her life seemed purposeless, her body hopeless, and apathy overtook her. In March 1846 she arrived "weak and sick" in Manhattan. Marx vowed to see her cured.[7]

Marx's specialty was homeopathy, a much-debated but fast-growing approach to healing employing drugs in minuscule doses that emerged from Europe in the late eighteenth century. Since moving to New York, Marx had also taken an interest in another unorthodox medical practice and had been a regular visitor at the water-cure boardinghouse of Dr. Joel Shew and his wife, Marie Louise. Beginning with only a handful of followers in the early 1840s, water-cure "houses" or "institutes" offering hydropathic treatments opened across the country and attracted thousands of patients in the following decades. Historians have suggested that many middle-class women (including prominent ones like Harriet Beecher Stowe) found in these establish-ments a temporary haven from family expectations and perhaps sexual release through some of the procedures. Water cure and homeopathy provoked much interest during the period as traditional medicine—with its harsh, debilitating drugs that often failed to cure the underlying ailment—came under growing criticism. In contrast, hydropathy approached the body as a system containing the remedy to its own ailments. According to its principles, water supplied the natural agent for purifying the body of diseases of all kinds. Cold baths, vigorous "douches" or showers, wraps in wet sheets, a bland vegetarian diet, exercise, and close physician supervision constituted the typical regimen. Although Marx did not live at the Shews', he took meatless meals there and recommended the boardinghouse to his sister when she sought medical treatment in the North.[8]

Marie Louise Shew regarded the young Marx as a curious but endearing "dreamer . . . over head and ears in Fourier." His long black hair, which he had constantly to push away from glittering "doves' eyes of the brightest jet," and the fact that he had the money to pay his bills added to his attractions. Mrs. Shew introduced her pet "mystic" to Mary Gove, a lecturer in women's health and a hydropathic physician.[9]

Gove, whom the Mordecais would soon regard as a most "dangerous person," befriended Marx, though she found his ideas laughably incomprehensible. Her own ideas hardly conformed to social norms, however. In 1845 she had declared that "marriage without love is sin, is prostitution," and called for liberalizing divorce laws. The two struck up a friendship built on iconoclastic beliefs and Marx's generosity toward Gove, a single mother living under general opprobrium for abandoning her oppressive marriage. If romance lay behind Marx's kindness, the petite black-eyed woman ten years his senior did not encourage it; rather, she treated Marx like a lost puppy. Something deeper happened, however, in the spring of 1846 when he brought Mary Gove to meet his ailing sister.[10]

Ellen Lazarus seemed to Gove "the prettiest young girl" on earth, and the older woman "loved her dearly in five minutes." In Ellen, Mary Gove discovered her disciple; in Gove, Ellen Lazarus found a second mother and a model.[11]

27

A HOUSE ON TENTH STREET

Marx had anticipated the women's affinity. He and Ellen, both having rejected "home" in the South, longed for a domestic life that stimulated and comforted them. Accordingly, he devised a plan by which he and Ellen "should become inmates of [Mrs. Gove's] family," a family of their own choosing rather than one of blood. With this plan, Marx intended simultaneously to effect a cure for Ellen and to provide a launching pad for Gove's career as a speaker and hydropathic doctor.[1]

In March 1846 Marx secured a large house with room enough for Gove's "Lectures to Ladies, on Anatomy and Physiology," the latest hot and cold baths for her water-cure practice, and rent-free apartments for Gove and her daughter.[2] It was an offer too good for Mary Gove to refuse, though the living arrangements violated standards of gentility by mixing together, without the supervision of a married couple, single people of both sexes. No matter. The paying housemates who stepped forward to join them shared this disregard for convention. They also made a highly interesting set.

One resident, Anna Blackwell (whose sister Elizabeth was the first woman to matriculate in an orthodox American medical school), came to the Tenth Street house via Fourierist circles. Anna spent part of 1845 at Brook Farm, where she became enamored of Fourier's chief American "apostle," Albert Brisbane, whom she followed to New York. Osborne Macdaniel—Brisbane's right-hand man and the editor of the Fourierist newspaper *The Harbinger*—who grew up in Washington, D.C., and considered himself, like the Lazaruses, a southerner, also shared the Tenth Street residence. Finally, the Gove-Lazarus house sheltered Charles Wilkins Webber, a writer of some success who published in major circulars like *The American Review*. The Kentucky native had a checkered and intemperate past, which he pledged to overcome.[3]

George Mordecai unhesitatingly vetoed his niece's intention of lodging at the Tenth Street house, despite pleas from Ellen and Mrs. Gove herself. The anonymity of a fast-growing metropolis stirred the anxieties of middle-class Americans like George, who saw everywhere the possibility of deception and danger to young females. Ellen "submitted" to her uncle and lived elsewhere but passed most of her waking hours at her brother's anyway. While Mary Gove supervised therapeutic showers and a careful diet for Ellen, and Marx's mentor, New York's preeminent homeopath, prescribed remedies, George wondered if his niece's illness were not "imaginary." But Ellen turned twenty-one that summer, and whatever her physical debility, she strengthened markedly in spirit while marveling at Gove's medical skill and personal fortitude.[4]

Ellen Lazarus, having already rebelled against the constraints of southern womanhood and having been captivated by new social theories, became radicalized as a feminist. The story of how Mary's marriage in 1831 to a Massachusetts Quaker twenty years her senior had nearly ruined her life made a profound impression on young Ellen. Hiram Gove ignored Mary's pleas to limit their intercourse, and she gave birth to one child and suffered four miscarriages. Emotionally shaken and doubting her religious faith, Mary had then opened a school for girls. Her husband confiscated the profits to pay his business debts—as was his legal right under the laws of coverture. Mary began lecturing and writing on physiology and women's health, and although the marriage deteriorated further, Hiram Gove refused to grant Mary the divorce she asked for. At last she stole away with their daughter, leaving scandal in her wake.[5]

Such a tale would lead some women to back the effort then gathering support among early feminists like Susan B. Anthony to pass married women's property acts and perhaps to call for more liberal divorce and child-custody statutes, and Gove indeed supported such political changes. But her response to her marriage, for which she blamed her ruined health, led Mary to an even more fundamental critique of marital relations. Long interested in health and medicine, she was inspired to write lectures on women's physiology (including discussions of sexual organs and their mode of functioning, which Mary considered vital but much of society regarded as obscene). She delivered her talks to packed rooms and halls throughout the Northeast, using mannequins for illustration. But her message was also about power. Each woman, Gove declared, must determine "whom she will admit to her embraces, and when." She theorized that unwanted unions manifested themselves physically in women's reproductive diseases and excruciating childbirths. It was clear to Mary that women deserved at least an equal (if not the ultimate) say in whether and when to bear children. Unwanted sexual contact produced, she said, "a no-marriage."[6]

Ellen applauded her mentor and, in so doing, appalled her southern uncle George. Had Rachel been alive, Ellen would have shocked her mother, too, with her declaration (one part Elizabeth Cady Stanton and one part Henry David Thoreau) that women must not submit "to be made mere machines and automatons," that they deserved equal and "independent footing" with men. The Mordecai ideal of achievement and acceptance supported by an enlightened domestic setting was designed to operate within a patriarchy, albeit an approving and affectionate one. Ellen wanted to change the ground rules.[7]

While Ellen showered and bathed and ate simple foods under Mary Gove's gentle and inspiring guidance, Marx held out "little hope" of recapturing his own health. Perhaps the world itself was poison to Marx. Increasingly, his interest in medicine lost ground to his interest in

Fourier and social reform. Fourierist Associationism was at the peak of its popularity in 1846, and dozens of utopian settlements (though small and unstable) dotted the landscape from Brook Farm in West Roxbury, Massachusetts, to Ceresco in Wisconsin. Fourierist clubs existed throughout the Northeast and the Old West. Thousands of immigrants, many of them refugees from the Irish potato famine, were arriving every month, and Marx and his associates believed Fourier's ideal communal social arrangement could erase the desolation inflicted by industrializing capitalism. In one of his first articles for *The Harbinger*, Marx surveyed the "foul ulcer" of "abject misery and desperation" among New York City's poor, and he condemned the "squinting sophism" with which the better-off dismissed such conditions. But writing for the cause of Associationism paid nearly nothing, and even his sympathetic sister Ellen predicted that Marx would never establish a career until all his inheritance was spent and necessity forced him to earn his keep.[8]

Whatever her concerns, Ellen had little reason to impede Marx's uneven course. She enjoyed the life at Tenth Street as much as, if not more than, he did. She found the progressive ideas and bohemian characters she encountered there uplifting. Her decision in Richmond to hold fast to Judaism did not in itself fulfill Ellen's craving for meaning, as it did for her aunt Emma during this period. In New York, Ellen encountered men and women who appeared consumed with purpose—either as radical social reformers or as creative artists. On Saturday evenings, writers, performers, journalists, and intellectuals gathered at the Tenth Street house for conversation, music, and dancing. Edgar Allan Poe, a former Richmonder celebrated for his new poem, "The Raven," and Herman Melville, whose exotic novel of the South Seas, *Typee*, came out that year, sometimes joined the soirees. The famous violinist Camillo Sivori performed Paganini. Margaret Fuller's groundbreaking *Woman in the Nineteenth Century* (1845) was read and discussed. Brisbane, whose Fourierist ideas Ellen also admired, paid frequent visits. He may have brought along Horace Greeley, whose paper, the *New York Daily Tribune*, printed Brisbane's column on the progress of Fourierist Associationism (as the movement came to be called). Not since childhood had Ellen felt this way—full of wonder and hope, her mind brimming with new concepts, new worlds, a new promised land.[9]

A new course of life with its own covenant opened for Ellen. Gove planned to launch a series of classes for women seeking to learn the practice of water-cure therapy. Such work could help redeem what Mary Gove called a "sick and sinful" world.[10] Ellen must enroll. In the midst of this tumult of possibilities, Uncle George came to New York.

New York looks its filthiest in the beastly heat of August. Anxious, damp with perspiration, George Mordecai worked his way through the crowds, finally halting before the brownstone at 201 East Tenth Street near Tompkins Square and fearing the worst. He stepped down to the basement-level door marked "Dr. Marx E. Lazarus," knocked, and entered. Marx rose from his writing table and greeted his uncle with surprise. "Where is Ellen?" George asked worriedly. Marx said she was upstairs and offered to bring her down. Ellen "came in looking as well as I have seen her in a long time," George conceded in a letter home to Raleigh. He nevertheless felt uneasy. Everything about Marx and Ellen's life in New York showed a bewildering "spirit of independence and contempt for the opinions of the world." George handled the situation as delicately as possible. He reminded Ellen that almost a year had passed since she had left Richmond and she owed her family a visit. He assured her that she could return north in the fall if after due consideration with her "friends" at home she still wished to do so.[11]

Ellen loved Uncle George and wanted his approval, so she agreed to his terms. She recognized that hydropathy's followers were viewed as radicals by many. On the other hand, her health bore witness to the efficacy of the water cure. Her family, no matter how strange they might find the ideas of her associates, must recognize her right as an adult to choose them. In this last assumption, Ellen discovered that she was painfully mistaken.[12]

In the weeks that followed, the more George, Aunt Ellen, Uncle Sam, and Aunt Eliza learned of Ellen's life in New York, the more determined they grew to prevent her return to Tenth Street. Aunt Ellen wrote to George that it must under no circumstances be permitted. Nor should their niece be permitted to communicate with her erstwhile acquaintances. Indeed, Ellen Mordecai felt that it would have been better had Ellen "never recovered from small pox" (which she had contracted soon after arriving in New York) than that she "fall a victim to the demoralizing influence of her chosen patroness."[13]

The life Ellen led in New York in 1845–1846 violated the principles of female purity and self-sacrifice that the Mordecais, along with mainstream middle-class Americans, so heartily embraced in the mid-nineteenth century. In such a context, Ellen's willfully placing her own health, pleasure, and career aspirations above the needs and advice of her family was radical and unacceptable. Because Ellen was an orphan, such choices may have seemed to some degree less extreme to her—she was not disobeying her parents—but not so to her Mordecai aunts and uncles, who considered her behavior embarrassing, selfish, and exceedingly naive. Ellen appeared ready to sacrifice her good name to her independence, since living among persons who questioned everything from traditional medicine to capitalism to the sanctity of marriage meant becoming a pariah in polite society—especially polite southern society.[14] Indeed, her case points up all the tensions surrounding not only women's role in the bourgeois cult of true womanhood but also the way women bore a disproportionate burden when it came to the underlying paradox between newer impulses toward the pursuit of individualism and older principles of community cohesion. It was a paradox that had plagued the Mordecais ever since Jacob and Judy moved south.

To Ellen's dismay, her family was prepared to think the most terrible things of her New York acquaintances, people they didn't even know. She found herself continually on the defensive. "I love chastity and virtue," she assured George some weeks after he left her in Richmond. From his siblings, however, George heard another story. Eliza heard Ellen employ "terms familiarly" that revealed "knowledge as no lady ought to know exists." Ellen made the further mistake of confiding to Eliza about Albert Brisbane's amicable separation from his wife after she had fallen in love with another man and how the former couple still "correspond regularly and . . . are the most affectionate friends." The Mordecais tried to restrict their expressions of dismay to their letters. They must not incite what Aunt Ellen called their niece's "indiscreet boldness of disposition" to full rebellion. But more was at work. The Mordecais did not want her distasteful contacts and conduct to become known. Even more important, they were reminded of the pains Rachel had taken in rearing her eldest daughter and could not bear to see her throw herself away. "We will try to make her comfortable and happy here," Ellen Mordecai told George. "If we fail and she be sick and unhappy, she will at least be respectably situated and innocent."[15]

Ellen, for her part, was certain her future happiness lay not in Richmond but in a career as a water-cure physician ministering to women. "For the first time," she realized, "my mind is *calmly, firmly fixed* on a *life* purpose." Echoing Rachel's words when she sought Jacob's assent to her conversion, Ellen Lazarus begged George to have "mercy" on her and give "your sanction and your blessing on my efforts." Like her mother, Ellen tried to place what others viewed as rebellion in the context of God's will. How could George not respect a holy mission to heal others? Would he tell her that she was less "responsible to God" than he? Would he condemn her for seeking what her mentor called an "escape from the inanities and inactivity" that defined the lives of so many women? The answer was an imperative yes. George could see no resemblance between Ellen's bid for freedom of conscience and Rachel's; the mother was, in his eyes, a paragon of piety, reason, and propriety, the daughter a source of shame.[16]

Not a soul in Richmond or Raleigh, it seemed, understood Ellen's heart. Unlike her mother, Ellen was not burdened with family ties; she need not remain in such a place. "In forsaking your guidance," she told Uncle George, "I commend myself to God," and thus she absolved her guardian of responsibility for her actions.[17]

Ellen's determination to commence her medical training under Mary Gove in the fall of 1846 evaporated when she realized the true extent of her relatives' "reprobation." First Uncle Sam wrote directly to Gove, ordering her to cease all attempts to turn Ellen against her "natural and proper protectors." The insinuation of improper pressure insulted Gove, who fired off a reply. This she enclosed with Sam's letter in an envelope addressed to Ellen herself. Gove only wished the best for her patient: If Ellen were happy living with her family, Gove would be happy for her. Should Ellen return to New York, however, she had in Mary Gove another loving tie, someone who would "be a mother to her, so far as I am qualified for that sacred office."[18]

Ellen remained in Richmond; Gove's hydropathic classes for women went on without her. "Stern" opposition from her relatives—and "fear of what they would cause me to suffer" should she ignore that opposition—halted Ellen in her tracks, for even she understood that their and her mother's images of duty were in many senses not so far apart. Relations with her aunts and uncles, predictably, grew stiff. Eventually Ellen's spirit burst forth, and she lashed back. In a "confession . . . wrung from me in anguish," Ellen told her Mordecai family that she had never been happy while under their care. It was perhaps this statement, implied by so much of Marx's and Ellen's behavior but made explicit by their adopting surrogate parents and families, that stung the Mordecai aunts and uncles so sharply. The fabled family cohesion and enlightened domesticity that Rachel's siblings attempted to achieve had grown threadbare and was experienced by Ellen Lazarus as one more example of the rigid hypocrisy that stood in the way of true happiness.[19]

In some measure, these aunts and uncles, not always being so happy under each other's care, must have sympathized. Sam's broken spirits and financial failures prevented his being more than a figurehead of male authority in the nearly all-female Richmond household.[20] Emma found comfort in Judaism and applied her energies to occasional religious writings and communal activities, while the elder Ellen's dedication to benevolent work bespoke her continued Christian zeal.[21] Ellen Mordecai and Emma Mordecai continued their wary sparring, although they stood united when it came to Ellen Lazarus's challenge to middle-class standards. The Mordecais had sweated real sweat and shed real tears and blood to achieve those standards. The height from which they condemned Ellen was hard-earned. Whatever religious differences existed between the sisters, they emphatically shared their identity as respectable members of their class.

28

TOWARD THE KINGDOM OF
GOD ON EARTH

Farther north, on a dark afternoon in January 1847, Marx Edgeworth Lazarus stood in the home of a Boston business-man and joined hands with thirty-two men and women who, according to the meeting's minutes, pledged "to devote their lives to the establishment of the Kingdom of God on Earth." The circle contained veteran supporters and residents of the utopian Brook Farm community, where, since the fall of 1846, Marx had been working for the Associationist newspaper. The group was honored by the presence of Fourierism's American leader, Albert Brisbane, who had traveled from New York to attend the birth of the movement's spiritual arm: the Religious Union of Associationists.[1]

Marx hailed the event in the columns of *The Harbinger*, and it might have surprised his Mordecai relatives, Christian and Jewish alike, to read his announcement that the true purpose of Fourierist communalism was "nothing less than to remould all the outward institutions and relations of society in harmony with the spirit of Christ." Witness to so much religious infighting, Marx reached for a spirituality that transcended debates, an inclusive theology that fed not only transformation of the self but transformation of the world as well. Sects and denominations only hindered man's progress toward the divine. In contrast, the new "Church of Humanity" celebrated the essential "at-one-ment" with God that was called for by the Hebrew prophets and Jesus, as well as by Fourier.[2]

Temporally, however, Brook Farm itself stood at the brink of collapse. A fire in 1846 turned the grand, newly erected Fourierist residential building—the phalanstery—to ashes. The community's already precarious financial condition wavered as enrollment in its school shrank and *The Harbinger* became the chief source of revenue. But the men and women gathered that January night in Boston to resolve a different weakness in the movement: Associationism, they believed, could never thrive until it spoke to the spirit. Fourierism—with its mathematical divisions of labor, laws of human behavior, stages and series, and demanding requirements of 1,620 persons per settlement— could seem dry, intimidating, and alienating. But its adherents, like Marx, perceived Associationism as a social revolution leading to millennial harmony at every level of existence. For them, Fourier united the sundered spheres of religion and science and, as one leader said, "revealed the means of living the law of love." Such a theology deserved its own church to spread the word.[3]

Although the Church of Humanity rejected all priests, it did have a leader. William Henry Channing (a Unitarian minister like his popular uncle, William Ellery Channing) had for years preached a theology of liberation that sought to bring an exploitative capitalist system into alignment with the kingdom of heaven. Under his nurture, the Religious Union of Associationists would offer the American public another expression of—and another conduit to—the promised land of blissful, classless utopia.[4]

Throughout the spring of 1847, as U.S. troops won victory after victory in the nation's controversial war with Mexico, Marx attended the weekly meetings of the Religious Union of Associationists. He participated in discussions of slavery, vegetarianism, and religion. He captivated the group with his life story, read from his own and Fourier's writings, and donated fifty dollars, though he had little cash to spare.

From time to time, he sent Uncle George issues of *The Harbinger*. "As I have no interests apart from Association," Marx noted, the publication would give the family a complete picture of his activities. Predictably, the only relative to sympathize with its contents was his sister Ellen, who remained trapped in Richmond. But these activities proved taxing to Marx. His health worsened. Unable to work, hardly fit even to write, and calling himself "a spirit chained to a corpse," he returned to New York and Mary Gove's maternal and medical care.[5]

Spurred by her brother's illness and her sympathy for the causes he had adopted, twenty-one-year-old Ellen Lazarus asserted her full rights and in June 1847 traveled to New York to meet Marx. She nursed him and accompanied him to Providence for electromagnetic treatments. What of her studies with Mary Gove? Perhaps the lectures did not recommence until the fall. Very likely, Ellen had promised the Mordecais not to place herself under the tutelage of a person to whom they so vehemently objected.[6]

Ellen would not entirely skirt reform and its perceived taint, however. When Marx departed Providence to spend the winter months in the South, she went to Boston and secured lodging at the home of Marx's friends the Southwicks, one of New England's most ardent abolitionist families. Whatever her southern relations may have thought (or known) of this arrangement, Ellen was happy. She met William Henry Channing and other Brook Farmers and reformist leaders and found a spiritual home in the Religious Union of Associationists. On October 10, 1847, she pronounced the Church of Humanity's Statement of Faith, and the circle opened to receive her as a member.[7]

John Allen also joined the Religious Union of Associationists that evening. A Universalist minister whose congregation had balked at his antislavery views, Allen became a member of the Brook Farm community with his young son after the death of his wife. John's lovable character easily overcame his lack of good looks, and he won many friends there. He advocated Brook Farm's adoption of Fourierism, became a traveling lecturer for the cause, and in 1846 served on the executive committee of the American Union of Associationists. The following year he fell in love with Ellen Lazarus.[8]

In a letter to George, Marx carelessly let drop the news that Ellen was engaged. George accused his niece of "immodesty" for taking such a step without consulting her relations back home. Moreover, how could she link herself to someone she knew so slightly, a man George accused of having no respect for civilized institutions, including marriage? Why on earth could she not "live as other people do" and find happiness with her faithful protectors? Again family censure caught Ellen off guard. In her reply Ellen defended her honor and John's. Unthinking prejudice alone could lead George to excoriate the reforms they advocated. And yet Ellen wavered. However unjust her uncle's accusations, she felt incapable of opposing him and broke the engagement even as she regarded doing so as the weakest, least "*noble*" act of her life.[9]

Too hurt to resist striking back, Ellen laid her uncle's lack of understanding at the feet of his apostasy. Perhaps he, as an Episcopalian, could not see "that it is possible or intended that man should cease from sinning." Ellen, as "a Jewess," felt "called to . . . bless 'all the families of the earth' " with Fourier's utopianism. Her faith, she said, was grounded in her Judaism, and she beckoned "all Israel" to join the Church of Humanity. The kingdom of God required of Jews no conversion; all people could share in the glory of the New Jerusalem. But only man could prepare the way.[10]

On this point precisely, Channing's theology, which Marx, Ellen, and John Allen shared, challenged faithful but conservative Americans. Even Aunt Ellen recognized that "extreme benevolence" underlaid Marx's and Ellen's efforts; yet their plan could "never precede the millennium, to promote of which our Creator does not require our aid." Though she pursued a better life on earth by ministering to female convicts and orphans, she accused Rachel's children of arrogance in not trusting mankind to God's greater wisdom. George was still less generous. He ridiculed Marx's writings as arrant foolishness and dismissed Ellen's "mad career."[11]

Neither Marx nor Ellen fit their Christian relatives' idea of piety, for they did not practice Christianity in any recognizable way. Indeed, they never rejected Judaism. Neither of them converted. Certainly, Jesus Christ stood at the spiritual center of Channing's Religious Union of Associationists, but Ellen Lazarus's membership in that group in no way conflicted with her contributions to Boston's fledgling Jewish community life. Several years before Congregation Ohabei Shalom had its own sanctuary, "Miss Ellen Lazarus of Wilmington" organized a Sunday school for Jewish youth—just as Rebecca Gratz and Emma Mordecai had done before her.[12]

What neither the Lazarus children nor their aunts and uncles could grasp in these years was that Marx and Ellen never questioned whether they should be proud of their heritage. That staple of previous generations, the Mordecai family covenant, bulwark against failure and blueprint for success, had worked its magic so well that pride in their accomplished family and security in its social standing were, for Marx and Ellen, a given. Since they had not struggled for stature, they could not quite understand how precarious their relatives felt the family's middle-class respectability was, or why their choices of career and companions were so distressing. At times, and in ways that were not true for earlier generations, Marx's and Ellen's Jewishness mattered rather little: Marx and Ellen didn't see the boundary between Judaism and Christianity as one that required strict monitoring, and their relatives often wished that these wayward children, Jewish or not, would just act respectably.

Certainly, the ecumenical nature of the Church of Humanity was bewildering to the Mordecais, as it was to most people. Ellen and Marx found in Associationism a spiritual cope broad enough to embrace all religions, and yet the spirit was, in this case, dedicated to the eradication of class exploitation and the evils of middle-class marriage and family relations. Thus, the Lazarus siblings skillfully applied Scripture, especially from the New Testament, in ways that astonished and dismayed their relatives. Perhaps invisible to the southern Mordecais was the way Marx's and Ellen's attraction to communal living captured millennial qualities of the bourgeois ideal of reforming society through the family and domestic sphere. Instead, their rejection of the traditional household seemed to defy the springboard of the family's covenant and to toss away the respectability that it had helped them gain.

Yet Marx and Ellen demonstrated a level of commitment that earned the tolerance if not the respect of some Mordecai family members. For instance, when, six months after calling off her engagement, Ellen informed them that she and John Allen would marry after all, Emma waved off her siblings' criticisms. Ellen Lazarus was, Emma judged, "as happy, as quietly deeply and serenely happy as a bride should be." "As to the groom, that is her affair and not ours, and since she loves him and he is now a lawful protector to her," they ought to see that marriage to John Allen was "far better than" the independent and unladylike life she had pursued since first visiting the North.[13]

Emma, one of the few Mordecais of her generation to practice her father's religion, had reason to be pleased with her niece. Ellen Lazarus's eclectic ideas allowed her to marry a preacher of Christ's and Fourier's gospels but first insist that he accept Judaism as she accepted Christianity. "Marriage," Ellen explained to Uncle George, "is not *holy*, is not true, certainly is not *complete*, where there is not *perfect* material, intellectual, and *spiritual* atonement." Whatever this meant, John Allen seemed to agree, and before the wedding he established his commitment to Jewish law and entered into Abraham's covenant with God by undergoing circumcision. The traditional marriage was then conducted by the hazan of Boston's Congregation Ohabei Shalom.[14]

In one respect at least, George Mordecai approved of Ellen's marriage. Gravely suspicious of Allen himself, George was relieved when, well in advance of the wedding, Ellen asked his legal advice on how to retain control of her inheritance. The first woman's rights convention, at Seneca Falls, New York, that same year, underscored the limits on women's freedom and urged passage of laws protecting married women's property. But without special provisions, Ellen's assets under current law would revert entirely to her husband's control. George hardly supported the feminist cause; as the trustee of a well-off young woman, however, he gladly drew up a statement of Ellen's separate property and sent it to Boston with a marriage settlement prepared for their signatures. He told her not to neglect to have the signing witnessed.[15]

Soon after the wedding, at which Marx was Ellen's only family member in attendance, the couple embarked for the West. John's travels had convinced him that the "rich, luxuriant garden" of Ohio and Illinois, with their freshly settled and fast-growing communities, was "the best prepared field for" Fourier's ideas. After several months of John's itinerant lecturing, Ellen wrote to George asking for three thousand dollars. She did not tell him that she was pregnant but explained that she and John had located a pretty farm in Patriot, Indiana, overlooking the Ohio River as it coursed from Cincinnati to Louisville. They would start a vineyard, and their purpose, as Ellen said, was "to *make money.*" George did not dissuade them from this uncharacteristically enterprising venture; perhaps, he mused, the agricultural life would "drive Fourierism out of their hearts."[16]

29

CRUCIFIXIONS

If George expected the West to temper enthusiasms, he likely felt
certain the North contributed to Marx's continual passions. At
age thirty, Marx stood at the height of his celebrity—a social
critic bold enough to call for the abolition of marriage, a man whose
ideas were generating ardent debates in the pages of the respected *New
York Daily Tribune*. Nevertheless, his long struggle to locate the divine
in himself and humanity and to live purely by its dictates brought him
neither health nor happiness. Indeed, at times he barely clung to his
sanity. An abiding faith in the power of ideas and the potential for social reform led Marx to commit all his available resources to the
"promulgation of truths vital to society." The ten books he wrote and
paid to publish in 1851 and 1852 were intended to move the "mountains
of moral rubbish" blocking the realization of the kingdom of God on
earth. Love, liberated from all constraints, formed the centerpiece of
Marx's philosophy, a combination of Fourier's communalism,
Emanuel Swedenborg's mysticism, and American transcendentalism.
"For in heaven they neither marry nor are given in marriage," Marx

wrote, citing the Apostles, "but are as the angels of God."[1] Such a convergence of ideas placed Marx squarely at the forefront of new approaches to cultural politics, gender roles, and sex.

Marx spent manic periods between 1846 and 1851 composing the volumes that appeared in 1851 and 1852. His ideas poured forth almost uncontrollably, and he scanned the map for outposts where they might be amiably received or put into effect—utopian communities, religious groups, alternative newspapers, nontraditional sites of healing. The search was, of course, really for himself. He blamed his upbringing and the surrounding society for his difficulties, for, as he wrote, "the absurdities of a civilized, scholastic, and moral education" such as he had received "overruled with an iron hand every natural instinct, and crushed or perverted one's impulses."[2]

It was an upbringing, of course, that could not have been more carefully thought-out. Marx's anger was not directed, however, at Rachel, who had implemented her ideals of enlightened domesticity to the best of her ability, hoping to achieve the kind of domestic happiness and accomplished family the 1796 covenant promised. He denounced not her intention but her methods—the unceasing demands to strive for perfection, to subordinate oneself to the good of the group, and to display unexceptionably respectable behavior. When reason and duty left Rachel still yearning for meaning, she had, in her own way, defied propriety and the patriarchs in her life. Indeed, Marx could feel that his rebellion against conventional marriage and his battle for individual sovereignty carried his mother's battle forward. Alienation permeated Marx's rhetoric; yet alienation was but the reverse side of exalted expectations of belonging. Whereas Rachel and her siblings carved out a world of their own where they could belong, Marx worked to change the world so he could happily belong in it.[3]

His alienation made him especially sensitive to hypocrisy. It distressed Marx that even the most committed Associationists would not openly discuss relations between the sexes. The leaders of the Fourierist movement focused on the general harmony and prosperity that life in the phalanstery would bring and shied away from the master's ecstatic visions of free love. Putting to use the French that Rachel had taught him, Marx read Fourier's "secret doctrines" (as Emerson called them) in the original and pressed the leadership of the American Union of Associationists to disclose the whole truth of the promised land of Fourierist harmony. Writing to the secretary of Boston's Religious Union of Associationists, Marx complained, "Mr. Channing has preached nearly six months without unfolding the laws of the passional series without which life and the world, humanity heaven and God himself, would for us be one great lie."[4]

Marx found an opportunity to share his views when illness prevented William Henry Channing from officiating at a meeting of the Religious Union of Associationists. He initiated a discussion of the erotic freedom that would characterize the state of harmony, referring to Fourier's four sexual types, with the monogamous "Vestals" at one end of the spectrum and the free-loving "Bayaderes" at the other. According to the minutes, an "animated" debate followed. The Religious Union of Associationists agreed to examine the topic more closely.[5]

Marx's cause received welcome support from the wealthy New York intellectual Henry James Sr., who had published an anonymous translation of a racy French work, *Love in the Phalanstery* (1848). Meanwhile, some of Marx's friends put these ideas into practice. He applauded the free-love wedding that summer of his friend Mary Gove to the journalist and reformer Thomas Low Nichols. Mary promised fidelity not to the groom but to "the deepest love of my heart," wherever it might lead.[6]

Marx Edgeworth Lazarus's critique of conventional marriage placed him at the vanguard of the free-love movement, which developed largely alongside, but with little encouragement from, the Fourierist American Union of Associationists. His writings identified the social structures that perverted male-female relationships and conveyed his frustration at the timidity of those who agreed with him but shrank from the social opprobrium their views would provoke. The most daring among the Associationists were willing to say that materialism and competitive individualism infected marriage. Marx, however, went further. Building on his readings of Fourier and his own painful memories and observations while growing up in a middle-class household, he drew attention to the "terrible position in which women were placed."[7]

In truth, Marx argued, men and women were not very different. Intellectually the sexes were equal. Any man or woman might exhibit traits associated more with one or the other sex, and indeed Marx thought men would gain if they adopted more feminine elements. Separate spheres—public for men, private for women, or work for men, home for women—only alienated the sexes from each other while justifying the special subordination of the females of all classes. Poor women, who had to work, received miserable wages even as they were scorned for not adopting middle-class standards of domesticity and child rearing. Marx also described the "anguish" better-off women suffered because they were told that the roles of "Wife and Mother" supplied the "*only* prospect for joy and peace in the world." So limited was their ability to travel, learn, teach, and labor outside their "isolated households" that the altar became the only choice. For many women, Marx believed, it was a fate no better than the "tomb." Once they were married, middle- and upper-class women were harnessed to housekeeping duties, which he decried as "systematic slavery, an immolation of one's personal predilections and pursuits on the altar of . . . domestic comfort."[8]

How to liberate the captives? Reform must begin by eradicating economic dependence. All women should work, and both parents should contribute, through either cash earnings or fairly valued domestic labor or some combination thereof, to the support of their children. Children themselves should spend part of their time performing practical labor from an early age in order to earn part of their keep. The individual household, in his plan, would gradually become extinct, replaced by cooperative dwellings where economies of scale could be applied to the work of cooking, laundry, cleaning, and child care. How many times Marx had "observed the loveliest beings, of a nature remarkably self-poised, and superior in their spiritual powers, become the victims of puppies, whose sense of their wife's superiority only intensified the tyranny." Did Marx write consciously of his own parents? Probably not, for such a reading would have reflected too painfully on his childhood; but Rachel must have inspired his sympathy with the female sex and specifically with "Mothers, whose love toward their offspring," he declared, "comes nearest to divine."[9]

Though discussion among Associationists of humankind's erotic destiny was kindled in 1848, the flame was guttering by 1850, and Marx had resolved to reignite debate in such a manner that the movement would be forced to incorporate the issue in all future plans. He passed the early months of 1851 under Uncle Sol's roof in Mobile, Alabama, and there, "amid the amenities of this southern home, of this dear family," he applied the finishing touches to *Love vs. Marriage*, the work he hoped would revolutionize social and sexual relations.[10]

How could Marx's readers ameliorate what, in a direct reference to chattel slavery, he called "that peculiar institution," the marital tie? The most prosaic course of action was to liberalize divorce laws. No union should continue unless both parties desired it. He hailed the man or woman "who fearlessly and spontaneously exhibits his or her type of passional [or sexual] character" and followed where it led. On the other hand, Marx conceded that free-love experimentation within current social arrangements would mean infamy for those involved. He could not recommend it. The real solution rested, he felt, in the speediest possible establishment of a true Fourierist phalanx, one extensive and courageous enough to incorporate the philosopher's plans for *all* aspects of social life. Members of the phalanx would be freed from the artificial, often devastating constraints of middle-class sexual and marital mores. A few colonists might choose celibacy or monogamy, but Marx believed that God instilled in human beings a pure and natural promiscuity: in the proper setting, he predicted, most residents would pursue "numerous and varied love relations" full of "vigor" and "charm." Marriage would vanish (indeed, would be outlawed in the phalanx). Women would be liberated from the oppressions of the isolated household, and all children would attend a community nursery. The result would be dramatic: "the family, as it now exists," Marx wrote, was "destined . . . to pass into the state of myth," to be viewed by later generations as a "monstrosity."[11]

Marx had entered dangerous territory. He expected the gentlest of his critics to call him ahead of his time or perhaps "forlorn and Quixotic." But harsher ones thrashed him in the press for "impious in solence," and others viewed his dream as "disgusting and detestable." Marx had written that civilization regularly enacted the "crucifixion of genius," and he was willing to risk even this for the good of the revolution. He understood the revolution in terms of an earlier revolt about which his grandfather Jacob Mordecai had told him many stories. At that time, "political liberty was the subject of a life-struggle for the American people," Marx explained in *Love vs. Marriage*. "Now comes . . . another declaration of independence," of sexual and social freedom, and Marx was proud to be among humanity's patriots.[12]

The book was an act of courage, its author publicly announcing his opposition to bedrock sexual mores, and it fell like a cannonball onto a rickety Associationist movement. *The Harbinger* had folded for lack of funds, and only one of the movement's twenty-five communal experiments was still active. Brisbane had sailed for Europe, hoping to persuade Fourier's leading French disciple, Victor Considérant, to concentrate the international movement's efforts on a colony in North America. Into such circumstances came *Love vs. Marriage*, which found its way to Henry James Sr. for review in Greeley's *New York Daily Tribune*. The ensuing debate continued for months.[13]

To help his readers more fully understand the utopian principles of free love, Marx appended to *Love vs. Marriage* a selected bibliography. In that list forty-year-old Henry James Sr., a married man with five small children, found several of his own works. If his fellow Associationists would not own up to their aims, Marx would do it for them. "I take pleasure," Marx impishly announced, "in acknowledging the substantial integrity of the writings of Henry James . . . [and] of Albert Brisbane . . . among our American friends" of free love even if "considerations entirely personal may prevent them from taking openly the same ground as myself."[14]

Owing to just the kind of personal considerations Marx alluded to, James set out in his review of *Love vs. Marriage* to make *Tribune* readers believe that he had no regard for a book he called a "needless affront to public decorum." James strained to distinguish between the intellectual exploration of passional liberties that might reign in some hazy future era and Marx's demand that the work of sexual revolution begin. A steamy debate followed, in which several free-love leaders took up for Marx. Their exchanges with James consumed a great deal of *Tribune* ink. By the time James closed the subject, he had renounced his hopes for a purer sexual union (even in the future) and claimed that conventional marriage served the vital purpose of taming man's wayward and sinful sexual tendencies. He had also placed the author of *Love vs. Marriage* at the level of the "insatiable ape."[15]

During the same period, Marx suffered intermittently from mental illness. Fellow radicals like Mary Gove, his sister Ellen, and her Fourierist husband, John Allen, expressed concern for his stability, whereas more conventional friends and relatives viewed his bizarre ideas as part and parcel of his derangement. Everyone had an opinion about what caused his sickness, and Marx continually found himself prodded and pleaded with by those who claimed to have his best interest at heart. From time to time he admitted that he needed help. On the whole, however, he spent the years from 1847 to 1854 battling critics of reform with one hand and "internal tortures" with the other.[16] In the end, he found comfort in, of all things, a wife.

For several years Marx had been unable to tell which of his impulses were true and which the products of an affliction that threatened to overwhelm his will, his mind, and his body. Marx pointed to his flawed education as a source of his physical weakness and overintellectualizing tendencies.[17] But only in the wake of his final confrontation with Uncle George over access to the moneys needed to publish *Love vs. Marriage*—a contest George lost—did the family learn the depth of Marx's struggle for sanity and gain a fuller understanding of why free love meant so much to him.[18]

Nobody guessed that Marx was beset with a most distressing condition: he could hardly allow himself to sleep for fear of waking to find his sheet or nightshirt sticky with semen. The man who challenged everything from marriage to the market economy apparently did not question the wisdom of the day when it came to "involuntary seminal losses" or their more sinister sibling, masturbation. Even his fellow sex radicals agreed that these acts had grave consequences—wholesale moral, mental, and physical degeneration.[19]

His brother-in-law John Allen took it upon himself to reveal the nature of Marx's affliction to George Mordecai. Like the rest of the family, John and Ellen feared for Marx's future when he demanded the sum value of his estate to publish his writings. John explained to Uncle George that Marx's friends had begged him to preserve "his patrimony," but Marx refused to listen. John believed Marx beyond reason because of what he considered Marx's disease. Then John gave the strange history of the case as he knew it.[20]

Blaming the onset of the wet dreams on a snake or reptile bite in the genital area some years earlier, John described Marx as reduced "to the weakness of a child." Either the repeated orgasms or the nightly vigilance Marx maintained to prevent them rendered him insomniac and depressed and, according to John, "driven to desperation." By 1848, unable to withstand what he called the "agony from the collapsed heart of the victim of seminal losses," Marx had committed himself to electromagnetic treatments in Providence. He believed that the electric charges to his brain and nerves restored some of the energies depleted by his nocturnal emissions. The therapy also filled him with "happy thoughts," which were in stark contrast to his bouts of paranoia, fretfulness, and introversion. He experienced more regular sleep patterns and a "comparative suspension" of wet dreams, yet he resented the way the magnetic treatments disabled him for "much exertion either physical or mental." His physician proceeded on the hypothesis that by keeping Marx quiet and passive "for several months . . . [in] a sort of chrysalis state," she could effect "organic changes" in his neurological system. But four months after the treatments began, he was "miserable" again, "extremely so," and spent each day writing manically at Harvard's library.[21]

Marx devoted a portion of his time to researching and writing about his own condition. *Involuntary Seminal Losses: Their Causes, Effects, and Cure* (1852) offered his observations as a homeopathic practitioner and, though he did not say as much, as a sufferer from spermatorrhea. Marx argued that involuntary seminal loss explained many patients' general "nervous prostration." The condition, he believed, could develop from habitual masturbation, or, as it was then called, "self-abuse." The book offered tips on diagnosis and treatment.

As to the latter, Marx recommended the regimen he himself had followed: cold-water bathing (à la Mary Gove), electromagnetism, travel, and homeopathic remedies for insomnia. Genital "cauterization, catheritism, acupuncture, galvanism [electric shock], [and] circumcision" were more invasive medical options; it is unclear whether Marx himself submitted to any of these.[22]

The book's most affecting passages involve two poignant letters, supposedly from a young male patient in Philadelphia whose "spiritual struggles and tortures" closely resemble those of Marx Edgeworth Lazarus. The sufferer took homeopathic drugs and interrupted his sleep each night with a cold bath, according to Dr. Lazarus's prescriptions. For a month his symptoms receded. Accumulated physical exhaustion brought a return of the nocturnal emissions, however, and his mental agony amplified until he experienced "a painful void as though the soul were baffled." Was it possible, the letter writer asked, that his virginity—sexual "continence unnaturally protracted to this my twenty-fifth year"—caused a degree of sensual pressure that could only find release in involuntary ejaculations? If so, he would be lost, for how could he find an honorable marital outlet for his desire as long as he remained so ill?[23]

Marx confirmed his patient's dispiriting line of thought. Sexual inactivity, sedentary occupations, and early mental overstimulation all contributed to spermatorrhea, in the doctor's opinion. Marx cited a French clinician's view that "moderate" sexual activity "not only determines attraction to the opposite sex, but renders all affections more tender." Abstinence upset this harmonious heterosexual balance. According to this thesis, to abide by the bourgeois male morality of the day—to study hard at school, to achieve stature within a profession, to suppress sexual passion until marriage—amounted to a prescription for mental instability, impotence, and even sterility. Public health joined the list of benefits Fourierist free love would bring.[24]

Perhaps at some point Marx set out to follow his own prescriptions. Three years after his volume on seminal losses was published, he fell in love. When he married nineteen-year-old Mary Laurie of Indiana, whose father Marx knew through Fourierist circles, some free lovers called him a traitor. Mary Gove Nichols defended her old friend, explaining that Marx had "submitted to the legal handcuffing process, by an Indiana Justice of the Peace," only to avoid "being sent to State prison" for having unlawful sexual relations. Just as "the slave must show his pass," she wrote, "the civilizee" must render up "his marriage certificate." If free-love advocates accused him of hypocrisy and desertion, Marx's family gasped at the idea of his undertaking the responsibilities of a husband. Marx as provider, as parent! But George, himself recently and happily married after many years of bachelorhood, must have smiled a little at Marx's warm testimony that his life had been "deeply and very gratefully changed."[25]

If George Mordecai's election to the presidency of the Bank of North Carolina in 1849 did not seal his position as a preeminent and fully accepted citizen, his marriage in 1853 to Margaret Cameron, the daughter of the bank's previous president, did. Jacob Mordecai's legacy of business failures and worries about fitting in as a Jew in the South were distant shadows when Sam applauded the news that George, at the age of fifty-two, was to "abandon celibacy and its gloomy perspective." In a quiet Episcopal ceremony George wedded one of North Carolina's wealthiest women, and if any of the Mordecais doubted Margaret Cameron's qualifications to join their family, they kept it to themselves. By all accounts, the forty-two-year-old Margaret was generous and nurturing, a pillar of strength within her clan. She also held title to vast tracts of land and more than one hundred slaves. Over the years George had given generously of his time to his family, investing his sisters' savings, managing trusts, plantations, and investments for eight nieces and nephews, and serving as man of the house to Moses's widow, Nancy. Now he could give even more generously.[26]

30

DARK DAYS

George Mordecai had given generously to his relatives for years, and over the course of his early career George's younger brother Alfred regretted his inability to assist. Living on his military pay required strict economies, and his growing family consumed all his meager resources. For both pecuniary and political reasons, Alfred occasionally questioned his service to the nation. Like most of his family, he was no fan of Andrew Jackson or his party and often wrote grimly of the low caliber of leadership in military affairs. In 1837, a year after he married Sara Hays in Philadelphia, he sought a civil engineering job in the private sector that would have doubled his pay. But economic times called for a cautious approach, and the vicissitudes of the marketplace, indelibly impressed on all of Jacob's children, encouraged Alfred to keep to his army commission. Rather than pursue a civilian career, he applied himself diligently to his work in the War Department's ordnance bureau, which he found in a state of disarray. Alfred's labors did not go unrecognized by his superiors. In 1840 the secretary of war handpicked for him the coveted assignment of inspecting foundries of the European powers and observing methods of heavy-weapon production.[1]

Top missions and promotions came regularly to Alfred. Author of manuals on ordnance and artillery, an expert in ballistics, a chief designer of the first integrated munitions system (including guns, howitzers, and mortars) for the U.S. Army, and an officer whose professional accomplishments won wide esteem, Alfred understandably became a symbol of family pride. By the time his military career came to a close, no Jew had ascended to higher rank and position of authority in the U.S. Army than Alfred Mordecai.[2]

Yet not all went smoothly in Alfred's life. Two of his and Sara's children died young. And his siblings did not admire the way in which he and Sara were rearing the remaining children, who by 1849 numbered six. During a visit to the Washington Arsenal, Emma complained that the little Mordecais were "slaves to their humours and their parents are slaves to them." In the all-important realm of enlightened domesticity, Alfred was found wanting. The Mordecais, protective of their own, laid the blame largely on Sara, who, aside from her eight pregnancies, was often unwell and suffered her husband's many absences badly. On visits to Richmond to see Alfred's mother and other family, Sara felt unappreciated by her in-laws. And perhaps he failed to defend her as she might have wished or expected, for Alfred and Sara often did not see eye to eye, especially on religion and politics. The domestic arrangements enshrined by Judy and Rachel, values Alfred had always shared, proved hard if not impossible for him to replicate—or so it seemed to his siblings. As Sam remarked to Ellen in 1849 after a visit to the arsenal, "Poor Alfred's domestic happiness is dreadfully marred."[3]

During her years in Washington, Sara missed not only her family in Philadelphia but the religious community that went with it. (The capital had no synagogue and just a handful of Jewish residents.) Alfred, who did not share his wife's longings, resisted her persistent attempts to bring him closer to the faith of their ancestors. With regard to religious practices within the home and the rearing of the children, Sara had a free hand. But Alfred stood apart. "My wife is of a strict Jewish family," he informed Maria Edgeworth shortly after Rachel's death. Their children would "be instructed accordingly" until they reached the age at which they would decide for themselves. And yet, to Sara's dismay, Alfred insisted that his sons not be circumcised.[4]

Sara, whose father had emancipated his slaves well before her birth, also disliked the fact that chattel slavery flourished in Washington throughout the antebellum period. Although Alfred expressed no serious reservations about the "peculiar institution," he apparently purchased only one slave in his lifetime. Alfred employed a free black and his wife, Eugenia, once the property of Thomas Jefferson, as domestic servants. When Eugenia's owner announced plans to leave the city, the couple faced forced separation and Alfred the loss of a good servant. In an act of compassionate self-interest, Alfred purchased Eugenia and permitted her to buy her freedom by working off her purchase price. Yet he defended slavery on moral and constitutional grounds. In general, slaves in the United States were better-off, he believed, than what he called the "savages in Africa, or . . . freemen." Since his days at West Point, Alfred had gravitated largely toward southerners; when considering a move to civilian work, he had expressed his desire to live in the South. He abhorred abolitionism and decried any effort to interfere with the institution of slavery or its expansion, although he recognized and lamented the political threat the chattel system had become. Alfred's and Sara's differences on these points were stark indeed and may have contributed to her uneasiness during visits to Richmond, where slaveholding was part of daily life for the Mordecais.[5]

Yet Sara remained firm in her beliefs, religious and political. Her commitment to Alfred was also steady, even if their correspondence sometimes betrays a degree of tension. In December 1855, having recently returned from six months overseas observing the military conflict in the Crimea, Alfred left his family to visit the Mordecais for Christmas. Sara recalled to her absent husband Christmases spent together in Washington, wrapping gifts and filling their children's stockings; he must always remember the loving hearts at his "own fireside." Alfred, too, seems to have grown in his appreciation for Sara, and when George told his brother of his upcoming nuptials, Alfred replied that he could only hope George would be as happy after seventeen years of marriage as he was with Sara.[6]

By the time George Mordecai and Marx Edgeworth Lazarus began married life, Ellen Lazarus Allen had borne three children. In the winter of 1849 she had paced the floors of her Indiana farmhouse trying to shush her first child, a colicky baby named for a Fourierist leader. She felt a sudden desire to have something of her own mother's close at hand and wrote to George asking him to send Rachel's copies of Maria Edgeworth's collected works. Isolated from intelligent companionship—John was away for weeks at a time lecturing on Associationism, and the neighbors offered scant relief—Ellen at times experienced a domestic alienation far greater than Rachel's in Wilmington. Ellen, who had paid so dearly in family ties when she found her own sympathetic community, clearly considered the Indiana bluffs trying. She also confronted conditions Rachel never had: managing a household and a farm without slaves.

Wage laborers were scarce along the thinly settled banks of the Ohio River; hired domestic help was almost nonexistent. For the first time in her life, Ellen faced laundry, cooking, cleaning, nursing children, gardening, fieldwork, and animal husbandry. Fortunately, she had married a man who was "somewhat of a factotum," for she knew less than nothing about managing a household in a Free State. John spent Sundays preaching to a Universalist congregation. Monday mornings he resumed his labors in the vineyards at Moss-Side, their farm in Patriot, "leading," Ellen Mordecai concluded unflatteringly, "a real old Negro preacher's life."[7]

The foray into agriculture did not make any money. Ill luck dogged Ellen and John from the start: hogs destroyed their first garden; drought withered the young vines; and, as she told Uncle George in a letter to Raleigh, the "corn lay in the ground without sprouting." If the locals worked together to build an irrigation system, such disasters could be averted, but, Ellen noted sharply, they seemed "to prefer to suffer alone rather than incur the risk of aiding a neighbor." In 1851 a late frost and locusts damaged the grape harvest, and the next year blackbirds attacked the fruit and "had to be shot by the hundred." In 1853, with help from an experienced French vigneron, Moss-Side yielded nearly a thousand gallons of wine, and Ellen, elated, wrote to George that they expected to erase their debts and clear the way for a steady income in the future. Then, with the rise of the temperance movement in Cincinnati, where most of their product went, the bottom dropped out of the wine market and the Allens had to wait for a rise in prices. The bad luck returned in 1856 when someone—perhaps the Dutch tenant with whom they had a legal dispute, perhaps local residents hoping to flush radicals from their midst—torched their hay barn. The Allens had labored eight years, draining Ellen's inheritance and never recording a profit.[8]

Setbacks and undiminished millennial expectations proved taxing. John spent much of 1853 and 1854 establishing a Fourierist community in Texas, which proved a spectacular failure. In 1856 he began to fear for Ellen's sanity. There were breakdowns, periods, he told Uncle George, in which she lost her "memory and even the power to think or act." John concluded that they could not remain at Moss-Side. In the spring of 1857 the Allens and their three children arrived at Berlin Heights, some forty-five miles west of Cleveland. In writing to George, Ellen chose not to mention that Berlin Heights was a hotbed of free-love advocates, instead emphasizing the town's excellent school, in which the elder Allen children were enrolled.[9]

No doubt her relatives would have sympathized with local reactions. Soon after the Allens settled in, the townspeople banned the free lovers' children from the school. Officials arrested radical leaders on charges of immorality and confiscated the group's real estate, while vigilantes burned their printing press.[10]

Amid the turmoil, Ellen gave birth to a fourth child. Soon thereafter, she and John fled. In New York, while John threw himself into establishing a reformist newspaper, Ellen and the children joined the Long Island free-love community, Modern Times. Perhaps the Allens' marriage faltered; certainly many hopes had been dashed. When John returned to Indiana in the summer of 1858 to check on Moss-Side, he was brokenhearted. His spirits slid further when he found the property mired in the usual difficulties—discontented tenants and poor crops.

Before he could make much headway, he fell victim to "congestive fever" and died without seeing his wife or children again. A widow with four dependent children, an object of her family's worry, Ellen found herself in the throes of an increasingly ostracized and waning social reform effort. Rather than arguing about any emerging utopia, the nation's eyes were on Bleeding Kansas, where battles between settlers over whether to permit slavery illustrated the rising tensions between the North and the South. Even Marx, with whom she had commenced her journey into radicalism, offered no comfort; the siblings fell to bickering over old debts in the wake of John Allen's death.[11]

As Ellen Lazarus Allen drifted, her aunt Ellen Mordecai sealed a new covenant with Sol, the polestar of her universe whose attraction never lost its potency. Marriage and life in Mobile had meant thirty years' separation from his family, including Ellen. But in 1853 Sol wrote asking her pardon for his long silence. He needed her sympathy. "Within the last year," he explained, "my sight has failed so much that I read with difficulty either print or [manuscript]." Medical science could supply no remedy. Sol spent a portion of his dark days instructing his younger children in Latin and French. Most of his hours, however, were passed in solitude. His sister Caroline Plunkett, who had settled near him in Mobile, considered it barbarous that Sol's wife and children did so little to alleviate his sad spirits. "May God forgive her wickedness," Caroline prayed.[12]

Then, wonder of wonders, Ellen received an invitation to Mobile—from Sol's wife herself. Ellen Mordecai was nearly seventy years old when the riverboat descended the Alabama River into Mobile late in 1858. Her dearest hopes were realized almost before she knew it. One morning less than a fortnight after her arrival, Ellen, not wanting to disturb Sol's rest, sat alone reading from the Book of Common Prayer. He called her to read to him at his bedside, for severe arthritis as well as complete blindness now confined him. "I am at my morning prayers," Ellen replied, and when he said nothing, she asked whether "he could join me through our Saviour Jesus Christ." Sol said he would. They repeated the Lord's Prayer, she told George's wife, Margaret, and for the next several visits they discussed the New Testament, working, as Sol said, "to clear away the doubts" implanted by his Jewish origin. Each time she visited, they repeated the morning prayer service, studied religious books, and discussed literature in theological terms. As the sun went down, Ellen knelt by Sol's bed to read evening prayers. He held her hand and pressed it, she said, "where the words are most expressive of our beloved Redeemer." They were as one. To Emma she wrote that "every moment spent" with her brother was "a mental, moral, and a religious treasure."[13]

When Ellen returned to Richmond from Mobile in 1859, she found Sam so infirm he could hardly make his daily trip to the post office. His mood, too, often approached despair. Given his state of mind and her own recent triumph, Ellen worked to bring Sam into "the fold."[14]

Sam did not follow in Sol's footsteps. Other issues concerned him more, and indeed the times were growing fearful. A veteran Whig activist on the state level, Sam had watched his party crumble as the nation polarized over slavery's extension into western territories. Sam held abolitionists and "traitorous politicians" responsible for the peril the country now faced, and he frowned to think of Moses's son Henry taking a seat in the North Carolina legislature. In such times "the post of honor" lay, Sam said, in private life. Thus, while Ellen spoke to him of "the true light," Sam fumed over the latest national outrage. John Brown, who three years earlier had hacked to death a group of pro-slavery settlers in Kansas, reappeared in Virginia in 1859 and, hoping to incite a slave rebellion, seized the federal arsenal at Harpers Ferry. On his walk to the gallows, Brown produced a note predicting that "the crimes of this guilty land: will never be purged *away*: but with Blood." Sam shuddered to think that some in the North hailed John Brown as a martyr. He clipped story after story from the local papers to send to Alfred in New York, so that he could better view the events from the southern perspective.[15]

Alfred read the clippings with a heavy heart. For more than two years he had filled the top station in the army's Ordnance Department, command of Watervliet Arsenal, across the Hudson from Troy, New York. His service and researches into artillery and munitions had yielded promotion to major. Alfred watched anxiously as political tensions rose, and with talk of secession and war growing louder all the time, he was forced to contemplate what he, as an officer in the U.S. Army, could be called upon to do. Politicians floated compromises aimed at preserving the Union. But as Abraham Lincoln prepared to take office, the nation seemed liable to split at the seams. George questioned Alfred closely on his "position"—what steps he would take should political conciliation fail. Alfred refused to speculate. For a ranking member of the military to declare his personal sentiments could, Alfred believed, only add fuel to the fire of disunion. He planned to pursue calmly his "duty" as a commissioned officer, hoping thus to do his part to "discourage the mad proceedings of fanatics North and South." Three days later, a unanimous South Carolina convention voted to secede. Thereafter, duty would prove difficult for Alfred to discern.[16]

Conventions in one lower South state after another followed suit. Increasingly distressed and, in New York, isolated from the immediate course of events, Alfred wrote confidingly to George. Each state's secession, Alfred said, alienated more moderate northerners. Yet he believed the Constitution protected slavery, and he understood why southerners were aggrieved at the restrictions being placed on their property. The brothers saw that a "revolution" was under way, and each yearned for a peaceful resolution, even if it meant that the United States of America split in two.[17]

Alfred's private political beliefs didn't immediately dictate his public reaction to the crisis. The strain on him rose a notch when, in January 1861, North Carolina's governor urged him to resign his post and come to his native state to prepare it for war. The proposal offended Major Mordecai; North Carolina had not even seceded, and would not for several months. In February 1861, the former Mississippi senator and secretary of war Jefferson Davis, who knew Alfred well, assumed the presidency of the newly baptized Confederate States of America. As Lincoln was inaugurated in Washington and vowed that the Union would not initiate military conflict with the Confederacy, Davis offered

Alfred the command of the Confederate Corps of Artillery. Alfred demurred—at least for the present. He prosecuted his duties at the arsenal, where orders for munitions poured in daily from the War Office. Workers at the local foundries where the orders were being filled questioned Alfred's loyalties, and some rumored that the weapons they were making were destined to be wielded by Confederate soldiers. More rumors circulated when Alfred traveled to Virginia to witness with other ordnance officers a test of coastal guns and took Sara and one of his daughters with him. Would he seize the opportunity to throw himself behind the Confederacy? While at Point Comfort, the fort he had helped construct at the outset of his military career, Alfred learned of Lincoln's order to resupply the Federal troops holding Fort Sumter in Charleston harbor. He now saw war as inevitable. Ordered back to Watervliet, Alfred hastened with his family to his post as Sumter was bombarded and fell to South Carolina's forces. Alfred could delay no longer. He must decide his course.[18]

Three days after the surrender of Fort Sumter, delegates to Virginia's secession convention, meeting just a few blocks from the Mordecais' house in Richmond, voted to join the Confederacy.

When a boy in 1797, Sam had participated in the "funeral pageant" honoring George Washington as it wound through the streets of Richmond. On the night Virginia withdrew from the Union, Sam sat alone in his room. Thousands of enthusiastic supporters of secession formed "a massive torchlight procession, with bands playing, crowds singing, southern flags flying, and Roman candles and rockets blazing in the night sky." Sam watched and listened from afar. "I cannot express the misery that overcomes me at the thought of secession, however necessary," he told George, "when I think of the . . . desecration of a glorious government formed when I was an infant by a band of sages, patriots, and honest men." The deed was done, however, and Mordecai after Mordecai fell into line behind the Confederacy.[19]

One issue remained. Now that war had come, Alfred, who had long regretted his inability to help his relatives financially during his years in the U.S. Army, had it in his power to do what no other Mordecai—

and few southerners—could. At the birth of the new nation, the Confederacy, Alfred could in one gesture render the Mordecai name glorious, a synonym for southern patriotism. "How I wish he would join the Southern army," Emma breathlessly wrote a few days after Virginia's secession, and George expected any day to receive word of Alfred's arrival in Dixie.[20]

31

WAR

In the wake of Fort Sumter's fall to South Carolina forces, Lincoln declared a state of insurrection and called up troops to put it down. Nascent battle lines hardened as the Union faced a fledgling and still evolving Confederacy. The Union began enlisting soldiers, while Confederate volunteers massed in Richmond and throughout the South; in Richmond what Emma called the "serious, anxious, determined" spirit of mobilization overtook the Mordecai household.[1]

National strife became cause for familial reconciliation. Ellen and Eliza sewed shirts for soldiers' uniforms, overcoming the coolness that resulted from Ellen's attempts to proselytize among the Mordecais. Jacob's widow, Becky, now blind, scraped lint from the cotton that Caroline Plunkett wound into bandages. Only a few months earlier, Caroline, long at one remove from her Virginia and North Carolina kin, had answered her stepmother's summons to "come to your paternal home and to our hearts."[2]

Not since leaving Spring Farm to marry Achilles Plunkett had Caroline felt truly welcome in that "paternal home." But at sixty-six, she sold her house in Mobile and packed her belongings. Caroline's home-coming, occasioned by the impending crisis, coincided with the eman-cipation of her three slaves, who, with her financial support, settled in the North. Before Sumter, Caroline had opposed the "warped . . . sec-tional feeling" threatening to split "*my country.*" Now that Virginia had seceded, she entered a period of fasting and mourning from which she emerged, as Emma said, "a strong warm southern rights woman."[3]

Sixteen-year-old Caroline Myers, Eliza's daughter, became an en-thusiastic secessionist, too. Grandsons of Jacob's set off to join the Confederate forces. George converted large sums into war bonds. De-spite regrets at the sundering of the Union, the Mordecais closed ranks.[4]

Still no word came from Alfred. George softened the almost un-bearable silence from Watervliet with the suggestion that letters to or from Alfred were very possibly being intercepted. He pointed out that due to the suspicions about Alfred among Troy's citizens, many of whom worked at the arsenal, their brother would need to step cau-tiously in order to transport his large family safely out of hostile terri-tory and cross with them into the Confederacy. Day after agonizing day passed as Lincoln ordered the entire southern coastline blockaded and Richmond became the capital of the new Confederate States of America. Jefferson Davis appointed an officer decidedly Alfred's infe-rior in experience and capability to head the ordnance division of the Confederate army, and family members, stopped on the streets and asked what Alfred's plans were, had to admit that they did not know. To Ellen, Alfred seemed "further off than when he was in Moscow." Fi-nally, notwithstanding Ellen's prayer that the now divided nation be preserved from what she called "the sin of Civil War," representatives of the seceded states formally declared war on the United States of America.[5]

In the months following Fort Sumter, sectional opinion hardened. Lincoln appealed to northerners, originally staking the Union's claim to just cause on the argument that secession was illegal, tantamount to treason. To permit the rebelling states to leave peacefully would make the political system the hostage of any one state's demands. Southerners, on the other hand, rallied to states' rights and the revolutionary spirit of opposing oppression. The Union was predicated on the consent of the states under its government, they argued. Thus armed with powerful sentiments, both sides set about positioning their forces and assembling the tools for war, while slavery—the war's root cause—went largely unmentioned.

Alfred returned to New York after the surrender of Fort Sumter having decided one thing at least. He wrote to his superiors asking to be relieved of his command at the arsenal and posted to some out-of-the-way place, perhaps California, where, he hoped, the war would not reach. As he waited for a response, Alfred oversaw the manufacture of six-pounder cannon carriages with caissons for immediate delivery to Washington, D.C.—weapons intended to batter the Confederacy into submission.[6]

George was correct in supposing that local circumstances complicated Alfred's position. The newspaper in Troy called for his arrest to prevent what many considered his imminent departure to join the Confederacy. Meanwhile, pressing letters arrived from Richmond and Raleigh. George bewailed the "want of system and organisation" in North Carolina, which resulted in throngs of newly enlisted men waiting idly for supplies. Experienced military men like Alfred were desperately needed. "All eyes . . . are turned towards you," Ellen wrote. George reminded Alfred that he was a southerner and now great "honor and distinction" awaited his service to his homeland. Sara's family would surely understand. Sara herself and Alfred's children, George assured him, would meet the warmest welcome in his own beautiful and spacious Raleigh home. If, on the other hand, Alfred refused to fight and remained in the North, George threatened, his honor would be besmirched both in the family's eyes and among his own neighbors. "You will be regarded with jealousy and superstition," marooned "among a people with whom you can have no sympathy."[7]

After two dreadful weeks Alfred received the Ordnance Office's reply to his request for transfer. It was denied. His services at Watervliet could not be spared, and the office was confident of Alfred's "integrity and fidelity" despite accusations of treason issuing from locals in Troy.

Three days later Alfred resigned from the U.S. Army. On May 24, hours after Federal troops first entered Virginia, Alfred, Sara, and five of their children left the Watervliet Arsenal under cover of darkness.[8]

News of the resignation spread quickly. But weeks passed before it became clear to his southern relations that Alfred would not, as Ellen and many other southerners hoped, "come and help." Instead, he would live with his family in Philadelphia, among Sara's relations. There he would remain for as long as what he called "this horrible strife" continued.[9]

So egregious did Alfred's passivity in the face of duty appear—and so mortifyingly shameful to his southern relatives—that some questioned his manhood. It was far easier to conclude that Alfred had submitted to his wife's demands, trading patriotism and honor on the national stage for his own domestic peace, than to believe him unwilling to side with his southern homeland. Ellen let her brother know that Rachel, dead now twenty-three years, would be ashamed of him. "And thus," Sam and George told Alfred, "you sink into obscurity instead of attaining the position and honors to which you are entitled."[10]

So it was that the Mordecais entered the Civil War with their southern patriotism tarnished instead of gleaming, feeling robbed of their rightful place in the region Jacob and Judy had adopted three-quarters of a century before. Since his days as a cadet, Alfred had symbolized the family's patriotism as well as their faith that their own talents and diligence would secure success and honor in America's highest places. They had applauded each commission, each promotion, and each international mission. Yet when their loyalty shifted to the Confederacy, the Mordecais were shocked to find Alfred out of step. Jefferson Davis himself one day stopped Sam to inquire after Alfred, and it was "most painful" to be able only to repeat what he read in the papers: that the former major Mordecai intended to retreat to private life.[11]

Little wonder, given the symbolic burden Alfred carried for his family, that his decision struck them so hard. Certainly, the Confederacy suffered from Alfred's decision; but the old Mordecai covenant, already tattered, sustained a near-mortal blow. In shirking what his siblings considered duty to country and kin, Alfred in an important sense abandoned the covenant that had defined the family in Warrenton and beyond. Setting themselves apart and above in their struggle to find a place as respected citizens, the Mordecais were to "foster and protect" one another. That meant sustaining each other through failure and sharing in the glow of victory and success when it came. Such mutuality was always as much an ideal as a reality, and as Marx and Ellen Lazarus's radical quests made clear, the covenant broke down in the face of dreams or accomplishments that fell outside the bounds of bourgeois respectability. The great paradox was that Alfred's uneasy position was born of his own success, his ascension among the middle-class and national elite. In casting his family's fate with the North, Alfred forsook a crucial part of the strenuous ideal that took him through his studies, to the top of his class at West Point, and up the ranks of the military in an era when promotions were rare to a position of such importance that what he did actually mattered.[12] Rather than fulfill the covenant by securing glory for his father's name by performing the one act that would establish a family of outsiders as indisputable insiders at last, Alfred acted on his own account.

Having grown up under the dark cloud of Jacob's early failures, having woven the magic of their covenant to assuage and overcome their sense of exclusion, and now straining to preserve what they could of the ideas that bound them together, Alfred's siblings could not comprehend the irony that success, not some failure of character, produced his decision. For Alfred did not define himself by the myth. He had made his own decisions about what was appropriate behavior. That he considered his actions appropriate bewildered the family in part because this time the explicit choice that challenged their covenant did not, as had most often been the case, concern religious identity or violations of bourgeois rectitude. Alfred's decision was about politics (heretofore a source of broad agreement) and about family—but his and Sara's rather than the "band" of Warrenton days. The Virginia and North Carolina branches, perhaps by dint of having remained so near the site of their covenant's founding and so near one another, could not quite imagine what it meant *not* to be driven by the need to assimilate upward. Their brother's highly personal choice arose from the fact

that he was already there and that in getting there he had placed himself at a greater distance from his southern family than they (and even
Alfred) knew.

Alfred did not, as the Mordecais told themselves, merely succumb
to "petticoat appeals" from his northern wife. He did, however, place
the feelings of his immediate family high in his agonizing calculations
of 1860 and 1861. He and Sara had six children, all of whom had grown
up in the North. As the war began, their eldest son, Alfred junior, graduated near the top of his class at West Point. The younger Alfred
Mordecai harbored no doubts as to his loyalties and soon enlisted in
the Union army. For the father to cast his lot with the South would
have meant fighting against his own son, and dropping Sara and the
other children into a world, as Alfred told Ellen, "which should be
painful to them and not of their own choosing." Adding to his reservations were his nearly forty years of service in the U.S. Army. He well
knew the South's inferiority when it came to arms and supplies. No
skill on an officer's part could make up for such deficiency. Of course,
his decision made no one happy; he was criticized by family members
in both sections and pilloried in the press, North and South, as an un-
principled coward and traitor. But he had chosen, he said, to "suffer
any extremity myself in order to spare the feelings of those immediately dependent on me." Perhaps, as he insisted to his siblings to the
south, Sara had not asked him to take this step; very possibly, her pref-
erences needed no articulation. In any case, Alfred defended his conclusion to resign from the army as his own. His letters south did not
describe how it comforted him that his decision won warm support
from Sara and his daughters. With his military commission, however,
went his income, and in the fall of 1861 Alfred's daughters set about doing what Mordecais always did when times got hard: they opened a
school.[13]

A letter from his eighty-five-year-old mother ensured that the anguish surrounding Alfred's decision would persist well beyond 1861. As
the war began, Alfred turned to his mother for consolation. Becky's reply began warmly enough. Never had the son who had long been the
apple of her eye given her "one moment's cause of sorrow or regret"—
"Until now." Alfred must find his solace elsewhere—perhaps from

God, to whom she knew Alfred rarely looked. In her eyes, Alfred had become unworthy to carry Jacob Mordecai's name. "Consider your father's course in the different epochs of his life," she wrote, "when he had so many sorrows to encounter, so many difficulties to sustain." Jacob, she emphasized, "*never succumbed to the trials* wh[ich] others would have sunk under." Stingingly, Becky reminded Alfred that his father "had not your resources, the resources which the education he procured for you have given you." In an irony beyond Becky's ability to comprehend, these were the very resources that made Alfred's relationship to his family and the Confederacy so tenuous. During the Revolution, Jacob did what he had to do, even if it meant taking a dubiously patriotic job with a dubious patriot. Jacob started life with so little; at the time of Alfred's birth he was still scrambling upward in Warrenton. Unlike his father, Alfred had arrived. At the same time, he found himself disowned.[14]

His mother, brothers, sisters, nieces, and nephews thought they knew what Alfred was denying them. His principled stand meant that the single greatest opportunity for the ascension of the Mordecai name to the ranks of the regionally, even nationally famous was lost. Not only his own efforts but, they felt, the family's dedication to the tenets of the covenant had placed Alfred in the position to bring honor and glory on them all. The covenant originally espoused by Judy Mordecai, and further burnished by the now nearly sainted Rachel, set Alfred in a position in society where he could afford to make that principled choice. That his choice seemed an abdication of those ideals meant that, to his southern family, his was the most egregious act of apostasy yet. His southern relatives understood his value—to them and to the southern nation. Had he elected to side with the South, Alfred might today stand memorialized on Monument Avenue, Richmond's grand nod to the heroes of the Confederacy.

July 1861 brought the first major clash between the armies of the North and the South. At Bull Run in Virginia, Stonewall Jackson earned his nickname for sticking his ground, and eventually the Union troops retreated, driving sightseers from Washington before them. Casualties were high, and Richmond received many of the wounded. With the hospitals overflowing, several soldiers were nursed at the

Mordecai house. Neither side staged any large offensives in the following months as both focused on preparing for a longer conflict than
first anticipated. The family's first casualties came not on the battle-
field but within the household as the women's constant war work and
the confined quarters in Richmond took their toll. Caroline Mordecai
Plunkett succumbed to insanity, and George, over protests from his
sister Eliza, removed her to an asylum in Raleigh. "What an intellect to
be thus wrecked," lamented Sol upon learning of Caroline's illness.
Only a few months later, the accomplished but often anxious Eliza
broke under the strain as well; as the Civil War entered its first winter,
she died at the age of fifty-two, leaving her daughter, Caroline Myers,
an orphan.[15]

For a time after Eliza's death, Caroline Myers remained in the
mournful Richmond house with her grandmother Becky, aunts Emma
and Ellen, and uncle Sam. The spring of 1862 brought the Battle of
Shiloh in Tennessee, where both armies suffered frightful casualties
without gaining any significant military objective. By summer the
mood in Richmond had turned grim as captured Union soldiers and
wounded Confederates swelled the population. Meanwhile, the prosperous plantation-based life of the North Carolina branch of the family went on more or less as usual. There Eliza's orphaned daughter,
Caroline, in the bloom of early womanhood, was sent, but she remained somewhat aloof from her prominent or, as she would later call
them, her "pre-eminent" relations. She was serious, educated at home
by Eliza, as Eliza had been by Rachel. These studies she capped with
three years of private schooling in Richmond. Caroline Myers loved
books and music; in the crucible of the Confederacy, she learned to
love even more her heritage, Jewish and southern alike.[16]

In this she took her model from the devoted Jewish women and
zealous Confederates who had surrounded her in Richmond—including Emma and her grandmother Becky. Emma, with full responsibility
for both the house and the ailing Becky, felt "very much confined."
Nevertheless, she seemed curiously satisfied. Struggling for the words
to describe her state of mind, she said that when the fighting broke
out, the "morbid weakness or misery or whatever the wretchedness
may be called that has been the bane of my inner life for so long" dissi-

pated. Becky was an inspiration. While composing a family memoir half a century later, Caroline vividly recalled her grandmother "quoting with gusto after a Confederate victory in the winter of 1861–1862: 'Now is the Winter of our discontent / Made Glorious Summer by *these Sons* of York.' "[17]

After the siege of Richmond that began in the spring of 1862, there were precious few occasions when Becky could repeat her twist on Shakespeare's lines. A surprise attack on General Ulysses S. Grant's forces at Shiloh in Tennessee resulted in nearly ten thousand Confederate casualties. On all sides the Federals were closing in. Like many southerners, Sam Mordecai castigated the Confederacy for glorifying its forces' minor victories and shrugging off the enemy's constantly replenished strength. He described drunkenness and prostitution flourishing in the capital city and tarnishing the Confederacy.[18]

It was at this point that Sam asked George to sell fifteen hundred dollars' worth of Confederate war bonds so he could invest the money in cotton. In a failure of planning for which the Confederacy would pay dearly, southern farmers, rather than growing the foodstuffs required for the war effort, continued to plant cotton even as European textile manufacturers found alternate suppliers in India and Egypt. Cotton prices fell to the lowest point in years. Even necessary items like salt to cure meat grew scarce early in the war, and all over the South high prices for food intensified disaffection among the people. Want on the home front accompanied the bloody toll at the battlefront. Writing to George in the summer of 1862, with battles raging within earshot of Richmond, Sam sighed, "Such fields of slaughter as the country around us contains are inconceivable."[19]

Becky grew weaker. Near the end she ate nothing but eggs, drank only brandy, and recited Joseph Addison's rendering of Cato's soliloquy. Cato prepared to end his own life rather than submit to the despotic reign of Caesar, for whom Becky substituted Abraham Lincoln. In July 1863 Robert E. Lee suffered defeat at Gettysburg, Pennsylvania, and retreated deep into Virginia. Perhaps Becky was spared the news of the first Mordecai casualty at Chickamauga the following month, when Sol's son Waller, aged twenty-two, fell. A week later, eighty-seven-year-old Becky departed peacefully for what Emma called "the abodes of the blest," certain, with Cato, that her soul would "flourish . . . / Unhurt amidst the War of Elements / The Wreck of Matter, and the crush of Worlds." Her body was laid in the Hebrew Cemetery beside Jacob's.[20]

The passing of the last member of the first generation of southern Mordecais provoked reflection among younger family members. Alfred mourned with his own "peculiar grief." He had given his mother "pain . . . in her declining years, and," he feared, "deprived myself even of her dying benediction." Months later, Emma, turning an old dress of her mother's into a skirt for herself, contemplated "the beauty of her character, of which, I fear, I do not inherit one trait." Even her stepchildren, who had once disparaged Becky's intellectual and managerial abilities and blamed her for her pregnancies, honored her in death. Sol could not "recall a harsh word or an unkind look" in all his childhood, "merited though they must often have been." With Becky gone, the remnants of the covenant that once united the Mordecai family—already worn thin—unraveled. The surviving Mordecais—spread across many states, on both sides of the Civil War, Christian and Jewish, practicing and nonpracticing alike—were free as never before to go their separate ways.[21]

For a time the Richmond household, like the assaulted Confederacy, clung together. One day in January 1864 Sam made three trips to the market. Each time he found it "almost abandoned," with only four of the usual forty stalls conducting any business; the effort required merely to supply the table, he told George, "breaks me down." How, Sam wondered, did the poor survive? Increasingly, the Mordecais' staples—hominy, bacon, cornmeal, vegetables—came at high cost on boxcars from Raleigh. When Sam thanked George's wife, Margaret, for the new suit she had sewn for him, he implored her to overlook his infirm script: "Excuse blunders and bad writing. My nerves are not always steady tho my love is."[22]

The time had come to pack and leave. Sam found a government official to rent the house for a year for four thousand dollars in inflated (and soon to be worthless) Confederate currency. He shipped his good bedroom furnishings to Raleigh; the rest of the furniture he sold off. A world of family objects had to be divided or discarded, and Ellen and

Emma spent their days packing books and papers. Attentive to the memory of her sister, Ellen carefully wrapped and labeled the china bowl used at Rachel's baptism. As the armies of Grant and Lee massed north of the city for the gory Wilderness Campaign (Lee's Army of Northern Virginia alone sustained more than thirty thousand casualties), the family prepared its own retreat to Raleigh.[23]

Emma remained behind, throwing in her lot with Richmond, with her Jewish community, and with her orphaned niece Caroline Myers, who had returned from North Carolina. She took refuge with Rosina Mordecai, Augustus's widow, who had three sons fighting with the Richmond Howitzers and a daughter, Augusta, at home on the outskirts of the city, just a short walk from Spring Farm, the old Mordecai place. There Emma began keeping a journal. One day she recorded attending the funeral in Richmond of Private Isaac Levy, who died defending Petersburg. He had obeyed Jewish dietary laws throughout his service, and Emma hailed him as "an example to all young men of any faith—to those of our own most especially . . . a soldier of the Lord and a soldier of the South." She observed religious holidays in Richmond with Caroline and other Myers relatives, and young Caroline paid frequent visits to her Mordecai aunts and cousins on the farm. As a matter of personal heroism, Emma wanted to ensure the war disrupted neither her religious nor her day-to-day life. A few weeks after Ellen and Sam's departure, she strolled through the woods to the old millpond, her basket full of blue lupine, cannons thundering all the while.[24]

Raleigh at least was quieter. Ellen moved into the spacious Cameron house with George and Margaret—"you and Lady Bountiful," as the family called them. Indeed, the couple's devotion to all their relatives overcame the awkwardness their wealth might have caused. They paid sad visits to Caroline Plunkett at the asylum and when she died carried her remains to Warrenton for burial alongside Achilles and their three boys in the fenced plot Caroline had maintained for almost half a century. George offered Sol and his large family a home in Raleigh when Mobile came under threat from Union forces, but Sol remained to face whatever came. "George and Margaret carry out one of the precepts of the communion," Ellen told a niece: "Let your light so shine before men that they may see your good works and glorify your Father in Heaven."[25]

As president of two state banks, George played a leading role in financing the war in North Carolina, buying and selling Confederate bonds on the state's behalf. He met with politicians all the way up to Jefferson Davis and generally had his hands full. He could muster little patience or time for Marx, who proved as flighty in wartime as in peace. Marx began conventionally enough, joining the City Light Guards of Columbus, Georgia, where he was living with Lazarus relations when war broke out in 1861, and by June he had reportedly become the physician for his hometown company, the Wilmington Artillery in North Carolina. Marx quickly returned to civilian life, however, appearing in Richmond, where he stayed mostly with Rosina, wrote articles for the *Enquirer*, and offered homeopathic treatments to sick and wounded soldiers. He considered going off to fight with a company of Confederate Marylanders and served briefly as a brigadier general's private doctor before his younger sister Julia convinced him to stop his wanderings, join her in Asheville, North Carolina, and concentrate on his medical practice.[26]

Ellen Lazarus Allen weathered the war in the barrens of central Long Island at the utopian colony of Modern Times. She continued to search for "a life . . . far superior" to the one that the middle-class conventions of work, marriage, faith, and family could afford, though she sometimes doubted whether her ideals could be achieved "in my day."[27]

Her doubts notwithstanding, Ellen continued to experiment. She and her four children shared the household of the positivist exponent Henry Edger and his wife, with Mrs. Edger managing domestic affairs and Ellen teaching the couple's children. The arrangements between Ellen and Mr. Edger are not clear but were likely not of a nature to write home about. The world soon caught up with Ellen, however. On a visit to Manhattan in April 1861, she was swept up by the crowd greeting Major Robert Anderson and his men, who had surrendered Fort Sumter in South Carolina. Tears came to her eyes as she met, she said, "soldiers at every step, brave youth preparing for a terrible family feud." For the next four years, Ellen received neither letters nor money from the South. A second marriage, more children, and very straitened circumstances led her to violate the central tenet of Jacob and Judy's covenant—to keep family intact in the face of difficulty—by giving her two eldest children over to the Shakers of New Lebanon, New York.[28]

Sam spent the Civil War's final year in the home of a widowed niece, his brother Moses's eldest daughter, Ellen, with whom he had for years enjoyed an affectionate relationship. Ellen recalled that despite his frailty, Sam retained his lovable traits, "his quickness at repartee, and the keen but good-natured satire which was never used to wound." He was less unhappy than in past times. These forty years, his ill-fated investment of the family's earnings from the Warrenton school had burdened Sam, and late in life he wished he had followed his love of literature and become a bookseller rather than an unsuccessful merchant unable to fulfill his duty to his beloved kin. But in 1865, as William Tecumseh Sherman left Atlanta burning behind him and marched across Georgia and north into the Carolinas, Sam had reason to hope that he could cancel the debt that had weighed on him so long. The cotton he had purchased in 1862 at eight cents would in March 1865 fetch between seventy and eighty-nine cents a bale. With a single brilliant bet, Sam could repay the losses of the panic of 1819.[29]

A somber spirit prevailed among the Confederacy's supporters. Wherever Union troops held ground, slaves were emancipated. The South's forces were vastly outnumbered. Lincoln, reelected on a platform that would concede no negotiated end to the war, vowed to see the South succumb and the Union restored. People began to talk about what would happen after the war. While the Confederacy entered its death throes, Sam came down with a severe infection. His niece nursed him as Federal troops occupied Richmond and Davis and his cabinet abandoned the city.

Sam's many years as a nonpracticing Jew make it seem unlikely that he adopted the doctrines of the Christian faith in his last days. Nevertheless, his Raleigh relatives arranged his funeral at Christ Church and his burial in Oakwood Cemetery's Mordecai plot. As the priest uttered the final words of the service, an announcement rang through the sanctuary: Lee had surrendered to Grant at Appomattox, and General Sherman's troops were expected in Raleigh at any moment. The mourners hastened home to hide their valuables and store away food, for the advancing army might seize all. Most likely, Sam never learned that as Union forces marched through South Carolina that spring, the cotton he had cached there and planned soon to sell had gone up in flames. He and the southern nation expired together, but Sam died happy, believing he had at last made good on the family covenant. It was fate's courtesy to let him die ignorant.[30]

In occupied Richmond, Emma knew nothing of her brother's death. The week between April 2 and April 9 had been the most harrowing of her life. She was at Rosina's with Caroline Myers when Lieutenant R. J. Moses, a Jewish officer from Georgia, came to the farm with the news that the Confederates were evacuating the capital. He escorted Caroline into the town; the remaining women spent an uneasy night in the farmhouse while Richmond burned. The building shook when arsenals were set afire and Confederate gunboats exploded on the river. The following day Emma set off for the city, hoping to store belongings safely and retrieve valuables being held in a bank, but the smoke and flames that rose over the town and the news that Federals were soon expected turned her back. The very next day brought plunder. A black soldier stole the family's last horse and saddle. Plucky as always, Emma, determined to get them back, marched again toward town to "see what could be done."[31]

The city itself was changed beyond recognition. Union officers galloped through the streets. Emancipated slaves celebrated noisily. Emma found one block "ankle deep with fragments of Confederate printed blanks & other papers." When a great volley of gunfire rang through the air, she was told it meant President Lincoln had landed on the banks of the James. Not wanting to remain in the same locale as the enemy leader, Emma turned toward home. Passing a soldier she described as "a Black ruffian," she cursed his race and Lincoln, too, as "ill-bred." The man aimed his rifle at her. "You haven't got things here no longer as you *have* had them," he said. "Don't you know that? Don't you know that?"[32]

In the days that followed, former slaves departed, some without a word. On Sunday, April 9, Emma, Rosina, and Augusta huddled together and listened to "volleys of artillery all night long . . . in celebration," they later realized, of Lee's surrender and the demise of the Confederacy. Emma wished "the earth might open and swallow us all up." Soon afterward, she sat writing a letter to George at a little table in the Yankee quartermaster's office while she waited to register a claim for the stolen horse. A world had ended, but Emma found herself strengthened by faith. "I never felt such an entire and comforting reliance upon the great Disposer of events," she told her brother, "as I have done since the capture of Richmond." Caroline Myers echoed her beloved aunt's sentiments. Passover was upon them, and Caroline declared it truly a time of "humiliation, fasting, and prayer."[33]

The Mordecais had impressed themselves indelibly on Eliza's daughter, Caroline Myers. By the time of her birth in 1844, the mythical Mordecai unity had already suffered many blows. Yet the covenant, belief in which had dominated her mother's childhood, remained strong enough to attract young Caroline's notice, and from both Eliza and Emma, who became a surrogate parent when Caroline was orphaned in 1861, the young woman caught a sense of the magic the family had wrapped around its difference as its members sought meaning, success, and security. As she grew older, Caroline found the Mordecais' struggles to overcome adversity absorbing, their intellectual bent admirable, their "morbid capacity for suffering" interesting, and their religious falling away as Jews poignant and instructive.[34]

In early 1862, seventeen-year-old Caroline had crossed paths with twenty-eight-year-old Edward B. Cohen. Cohen belonged to a large and established Jewish family in Baltimore, and, disappointed that his native state had remained in the Union, he had arrived in Richmond to fight for the South. Emma called him "clever and gentlemanly" and admired his sacrifice in throwing his lot with the Confederacy. Due to his poor health, Edward spent two years aiding the Confederate home front, first in South Carolina and then in Richmond, where he and the much older Emma Mordecai became warm friends. In 1864, as he began to court Caroline Myers, he joined the Virginia infantry as a lieutenant, serving under General Joseph E. Johnston until the surrender. Edward returned to Caroline in the spring of 1865. Though he was penniless, they became engaged, and he went to work as a stockbroker. In December 1865, as the Thirteenth Amendment to the Constitution formally abolishing slavery was about to go into effect, Edward and twenty-one-year-old Caroline married in a Jewish ceremony in Richmond.[35]

Alfred Mordecai did not attend his niece's wedding and may well have heard of it only after the fact, his relations with his southern family never fully recovering from his failure to join the Confederacy. In the immediate aftermath of his decision to retire from the army and remain in the North, he had arrived in Philadelphia scarred by the isolation his resignation brought on him. Early in the conflict he sought his southern siblings' forgiveness for his decision, telling them how grateful he was for their love and the sacrifices they had made on his behalf. Not everyone received such expressions warmly, but Sam and Ellen sent comforting words his way, which he read with "almost blinding tears."[36]

Throughout the war Alfred needed work, though he refused to do anything that might be construed as relating to the military. While he fell back on teaching mathematics, the bulk of the household's income derived from his daughters' school. His earnings would never recover from what he called "this great reverse of fortune" that came "in the evening of life."[37]

The "philosophical patience" with which Alfred bore his own sacrifice, so little valued by nearly all branches of his family, nevertheless strengthened his ability to exist apart—from the trappings of success, from the opinions of others, from his family of birth, and at times from his wife and children as well. He even found small triumphs in doing so. At the end of the war Alfred accepted an offer to work as an engineer for the Imperial Mexican Railway, in the process making clear that his unwillingness to fight for the South hardly reflected any identification with the cause of blacks or the politics of Radical Reconstruction that followed the cessation of hostilities. His conservative views, which during the next few years showed in his outrage at the steps being taken to grant freedom and political equality to ex-slaves, were warmly welcomed by the former Confederate officers with whom he spent leisure hours discussing the possibility of a slaveholding colony in Mexico. For a time he even considered moving the family there from Philadelphia, but after sixteen months the railway position evaporated as the French-installed emperor Maximilian, soon to be executed, lost his grip on the nation. Alfred headed north, again out of a job.[38]

Before returning to Philadelphia, he stopped briefly in Raleigh to see George. One niece, Margaret Mordecai Devereux, complained of having to welcome someone who had "tacitly encouraged the devastation of my country and the murder of my friends." Nevertheless, George brought Alfred to call on her, in what must have been a difficult meeting for all. With his sister Ellen, Alfred then departed Raleigh for Washington, D.C., where they attended the wedding of his son, Lieutenant Colonel Alfred Mordecai Jr., another ordnance man, to Sally Maynadier, a Christian whose father penned the letter from the Ordnance Office refusing Alfred's 1861 request for transfer from Watervliet. Sara and the girls, however, "unwilling to see Alfred [junior] married in church," would not be present at the ceremony. In attending his son's wedding, Alfred staked out his own ground. To him, perhaps, it was about choosing rather than being chosen. In any case, accepting intermarriage—or, construed differently, countenancing the marriages of Mordecai men to respectable Gentile women—had a long history in his family.[39]

Alfred and Sara celebrated another wedding in 1886—their own. Whatever the couple's differences, their sometimes difficult cross-sectional marriage had nevertheless endured half a century. They sent six hundred notices to family, friends, and colleagues around the country. On June 1, they and their children received well-wishers at home on Delancy Place. Tellingly, only one relative came from the South. Perhaps equally telling, Alfred seemed not to mind.[40]

In 1886 Caroline Myers Cohen and her husband were playing a prominent role in Richmond's reviving civic, social, and religious life. Edward, having long since moved from his one-man stockbrokerage into banking, served as president of the city's most exclusive men's club, helped organize one bank and became president of another, contributed to the fire department, and assumed positions of leadership in Congregation Beth Shalome.[41]

Two years later Edward Cohen died of heart disease. Caroline was forty-four and childless. She had always kept her mother's letters and remained in contact with her cousin Ellen Mordecai Mordecai of Raleigh, Moses's daughter, who held many more old documents. As Caroline began to read the family papers, the trials and sorrows and triumphs of three generations of Mordecais sprang to life. In 1913 she privately published a family history of her Myers, Hays, and Mordecai ancestors, having realized that among the three families "only five persons professing the Jewish faith" remained. Even these would soon pass away, taking with them, she feared, "all understanding" of their Jewish heritage.[42]

But in the end her narrative rotated not on religion but on character and the circumstances of the Mordecais' struggle to define themselves as successful Americans. The manuscript version of the volume contained a passage cut from the final published book in which Caroline expressed the key to what made the Mordecais the most fascinating of her forebears:

> So remarkable a family were they that I would their chronicle might be written in fuller fashion than I have ventured to do in this slight sketch, wherein I have endeavored to show the difficulties which beset [Jacob Mordecai's] life, how these were conquered by energy and industry, how self training took . . .[43]

There she broke off and this narrative begins.

AFTERWORD

In her "slight sketch" of the Mordecais, Jacob Mordecai's southern Jewish granddaughter grasped the essential striving and creative energy that lent the family its mythic quality. She was also acutely conscious that the covenant that had carried them through so many early "difficulties" had yielded neither unity (for she mourned the dilution of Jewish identity) nor its opposite. Even after Christian Mordecais sprang from the conversions and intermarriages of the second generation, and even though the migrations that began in the 1790s when Jacob and Judy left New York for the South continued in the years after the Civil War, relations between the branches of the long-lived third Mordecai generation remained strong into the twentieth century, an echo of the covenant that had bound their parents and grandparents a hundred years before.[1]

Consciously or unconsciously, Caroline Myers Cohen and her cousins apprehended the irony of their family history. Beginning in the 1790s as triple outsiders by virtue of being newcomers to the South, being Jewish, and being Jews unsuccessful in business, the Mordecais potently expressed the pride, aspirations, and tensions that have marked countless families hoping to secure advancement and a respectable place in America.

The covenant bade each Mordecai to foster in his or her own way an enlightened home, a happy sphere of reason, faith, and love, whose inhabitants pursued the highest standards of rectitude and cultivation of the heart and head. This was possible for Jews in a land where religious liberty and tolerance were woven into the founding creed. The Mordecais thus declared their chosen-ness, their difference, and their commitment to character, which they believed would sustain them in the American wilderness. Granting sacred status to their own bonds, they would become, as Ellen had once said, a "little faithful band of love and duty." Within their home they created a realm where religion was taken to be a matter of individual conscience and where rational sensibility and familial harmony were meant to reign supreme. Such a household could appear almost a world unto itself, at once a shelter from and a model for reforming an often uncertain and sometimes hurtful outside world.

Such an overarching dream of unity and safety could not, of course, be achieved in reality. Sometimes this was due to external forces. The Second Great Awakening and the evangelical efforts it spawned weakened the Revolutionary era's celebration of religious tolerance and diversity. Economic depressions repeatedly tore wealth and comfort from the Mordecais just as they seemed within grasp. Radical reform movements threatened the second generation's hard-won respectability. And the Civil War uprooted the Mordecais' sense of themselves as American patriots and forced them to recast their identities along painfully divided sectional lines.

Difficulties arose from internal sources as well. Over and over the Mordecais encountered and struggled to conceal or reconcile the confusing and sometimes distressing contradictions within their covenant.

To begin with, virtuous reason, so vaunted in the family ideal and so central to the expectation of tolerance, sometimes proved insufficient to explain or defend strongly felt religious faith. As Rachel and Jacob's conflict most vividly illustrates, reason and faith often keep uncomfortable company.

The love, respect, and domestic harmony between parents, children, and siblings that were to supply self-worth to the Mordecais as they took steps to advance themselves in the eyes of the wider world were not easily sustained. This was particularly the case when reason and faith parted company. But happy relations were also upset when romance led to outside attachments, for Mordecai family members rarely saw their own virtues replicated in their in-laws and marriages were experienced, to varying degrees, as violations of the covenant.

Tensions flared and were damped down at considerable cost to the myth when the patriarch exerted authority with commands that violated the respect that ideally subsisted between parent and child. The Enlightenment ideals to which Judy subscribed suggested that logic, persuasion, and mutual affection would render a child obedient to parental wishes. When Jacob failed to follow this model—or when it failed to produce the results he wanted—it became clear how vulnerable women were despite the promises of mutuality inherent in the covenant. Liberation and oppression existed in tandem as women empowered by enlightened domesticity played leading roles creating and sustaining family myths even as they were kept emotionally and economically dependent on men in the family.

The covenant rested on the belief that self-worth was more important than wealth. Indeed, virtuous reason pursued within a harmonious and loving home would produce the self-worth that in time would realize wealth and position. But once attained, wealth and position did not guarantee that the principles of domestic intellectual refinement and mutual support would be maintained. Moreover, wealth attained didn't always mean feelings of self-worth. Marx and Ellen Lazarus, who could easily have supported themselves in comfort and ease, wandered the world laboring passionately for greater freedom and justice and suffered some of the greatest doubts as to their own worth.

If the peculiarly strenuous record of their hopes and the demands they made on themselves seems to set the Mordecais apart, the content of their covenant sets them squarely in the path of one of the nineteenth century's great social projects: the economic and cultural shaping of an American middle class. Of course, Jacob, Judy, Becky, Moses,

Sam, Rachel, Ellen, Solomon, Caroline, George, Alfred, Eliza, and Emma couldn't have viewed themselves that way. Deeply invested in the idea of their chosen-ness, their superiority of mind and talent, they often could not see how tightly their covenant merged with the broader American dream. They were hardly alone, however, in taking seriously the infant nation's Revolutionary declarations of equality and liberation from injustice, its promise that power should derive not from royal or inherited authority but from reason and virtue. America itself was a promised land, and in Warrenton the Mordecais set out to prove their fitness—first as citizens who happened to be Jewish and later as both Jews and Christians—for a place of honor among their neighbors.

Thanks to thousands of letters and other writings, the Mordecais can be seen transmitting, reaffirming, and adapting the ideal to their shifting circumstances until each individual found for him or herself the security, success, and sense of belonging it had promised in the first place. But that security usually came as much or more from outside as from within the family circle. While the qualities the covenant demanded and celebrated still shaped the identities of many of Jacob's grandchildren, they were no longer members of the "little faithful band of love and duty" unified by domestic enlightenment and intimacy. The price of success and belonging—whether as self-conscious southern Jews, as deposed members of the plantation aristocracy, as pious Christians, as assimilated members of the armed forces, as free-love dreamers, as Shakers, or as anarchists—was that the covenant that made their actions and relationships to one another so intense and freighted with meaning became not a pattern to live by but a matter of family lore and memory.[2]

So it is that their story reveals the human drama of a family forging a myth—beset from the beginning by contradictions and tensions and buffeted by changing circumstances—as it was asserted, challenged, violated, and, over time, found inadequate to the needs of the people who helped create it. Their project was in many ways that of the striving nation's writ small.

In 1817 Ellen Mordecai declared, "There never was a family more united or whose happiness was so individually dependent on the welfare and happiness of the whole than ours." A generation later, in 1845, when the conflict over religious identity among Jacob's descendants was at its apex, Eliza Kennon Mordecai Myers complained of what had been lost. Christian zeal among the Mordecais, she claimed, had spoiled the dream. She wrote bitterly, "Our family has never been the same in point of union, happiness, and I will even add, respectability, since the spirit of proselytism entered it."[3] But just as it would be too simple to view the Mordecai record in terms of Jewish assimilation or declension, it was too easy for Eliza to lay at the feet of religious conflict the burden of destroying a glorious and powerful but always flawed family myth that never was and never could be truly realized.

ABBREVIATIONS

SELECTED NAMES

AL	Aaron Lazarus
AM	Alfred Mordecai
CDR	Catherine DeRosset
CM, CMP	Caroline Mordecai, CMP after 1821 marriage to Achilles Plunkett
CMC	Caroline Myers Cohen
EL	Ellen Lazarus
Eliza	Eliza Kennon Mordecai Myers
EM	Ellen Mordecai
EM II	Ellen Mordecai Mordecai
Emma	Emma Mordecai
GM	George Mordecai
JL	Julia Lazarus
JM	Jacob Mordecai
JMM	Judith Myers Mordecai
Julia	Julia Mordecai
Laura	Laura Mordecai
MAC	Moses Ashley Curtis
MCL	Mary Catherine Lazarus
MCM	Margaret Cameron Mordecai

ME	Maria Edgeworth
MEL	Marx Edgeworth Lazarus
MM	Moses Mordecai (1785–1824)
MMD	Margaret Mordecai Devereux
RM, RML	Rachel Mordecai, RML after 1821 marriage to Aaron Lazarus
RMM	Rebecca Myers Mordecai
SM	Samuel Mordecai
Sol	Solomon Mordecai

SELECTED UNPUBLISHED SOURCES

AJA	Jacob Rader Marcus Center of the American Jewish Archives, Cincinnati
AMP	Alfred Mordecai Papers, Manuscript Division, Library of Congress
BAA	Beth Ahabah Archives, Richmond
CFP	Cameron Family Papers, Southern Historical Collection, University of North Carolina–Chapel Hill
DFP	Devereux Family Papers, Rare Books, Manuscripts, and Special Collections Library, Duke University
DRFP	DeRosset Family Papers, Southern Historical Collection, University of North Carolina–Chapel Hill
EMP	Ellen Mordecai Papers, Virginia State Archives, Library of Virginia, Richmond
GFP	Gratz Family Papers, American Philosophical Society, Philadelphia
GMP	George Mordecai Papers, Southern Historical Collection, University of North Carolina–Chapel Hill
HFP	Hays Family Papers, American Jewish Historical Society, Center for Jewish History, New York
ILP	Isaac Leeser Papers, American Jewish Historical Society, Center for Jewish History, New York
JMP	Jacob Mordecai Papers, Rare Books, Manuscripts, and Special Collections Library, Duke University
JTFP	James T. Fisher Papers, Massachusetts Historical Society, Boston
KFP	Kennon Family Papers, Virginia Historical Society, Richmond
LFP	Lazarus Family Papers, American Jewish Historical Society, Center for Jewish History, New York
LMFP	Little-Mordecai Family Papers, North Carolina Division of Archives and History, Raleigh
LV	Library of Virginia, Richmond
MACP	Moses Ashley Curtis Papers, Southern Historical Collection, University of North Carolina–Chapel Hill

MFP	Mordecai Family Papers, Southern Historical Collection, University of North Carolina–Chapel Hill
MFP-AJHS	Mordecai Family Papers, American Jewish Historical Society, Center for Jewish History, New York
MYFP	Myers Family Papers, Virginia Historical Society, Richmond
NCDAH	North Carolina Division of Archives and History, Raleigh
PMP	Pattie Mordecai Papers, North Carolina Division of Archives and History, Raleigh
RGP	Rebecca Gratz Papers, Jacob Rader Marcus Center of the American Jewish Archives, Cincinnati
RUAR	Religious Union of Associationists Records, Massachusetts Historical Society, Boston
SCDAH	South Carolina Department of Archives and History, Columbia
TIPP	Penny Leigh Richards, " 'A Thousand Images, Painfully Pleasing': Complicating Histories of the Mordecai School, Warrenton, North Carolina, 1809–1818." Ph.D. dissertation, University of North Carolina–Chapel Hill, 1996.
WLDP	William Lord DeRosset Papers, Rare Books, Manuscripts, and Special Collections Library, Duke University

SELECTED PUBLISHED SOURCES

COW	Manly Wade Wellman. *The County of Warren, North Carolina, 1586–1917.* Chapel Hill: University of North Carolina Press, 1959.
DNCB	William Stevens Powell. *Dictionary of North Carolina Biography.* 6 vols. Chapel Hill: University of North Carolina Press, 1979–1996.
EAJ	Jacob Rader Marcus. *Early American Jewry.* 2 vols. Philadelphia: Jewish Publication Society of America, 1951–1953.
EJ	Cecil Roth, ed. *Encyclopedia Judaica.* New York: Macmillan, 1971–1972.
EOTH	Edgar E. MacDonald, ed. *The Education of the Heart: The Correspondence of Rachel Mordecai Lazarus and Maria Edgeworth.* Chapel Hill: University of North Carolina Press, 1977.
HJP	Edwin Wolf II and Maxwell Whiteman. *The History of the Jews of Philadelphia from Colonial Times to the Age of Jackson.* Philadelphia: Jewish Publication Society of America, 1956.
HJR	Herbert T. Ezekiel and Gaston Lichtenstein. *The History of the Jews of Richmond from 1769 to 1917.* Richmond: Herbert T. Ezekiel, 1917.
MHMF	Caroline Myers Cohen. *Record of the Myers, Hays, and Mordecai Families from 1707 to 1913.* Privately printed. Washington, D.C., 1913.
RJ	Myron Berman. *Richmond's Jewry, 1769–1976: Shabbat in Shockoe.* Charlottesville: University Press of Virginia, 1979.

SOW   Lizzie Wilson Montgomery. *Sketches of Old Warrenton*. Raleigh, N.C.: Edwards and Broughton Printing Co., 1924.

WOW   Jean E. Friedman. *Ways of Wisdom: Moral Education in the Early National Period, Including the Diary of Rachel Mordecai Lazarus.* Athens: University of Georgia Press, 2001.

NOTES

INTRODUCTION

1. [Mary Gove Nichols], *Mary Lyndon; or, Revelations of a Life, an Autobiography* (New York: Stringer and Townsend, 1855), pp. 303–6.

2. For the false dichotomies that often plague writing about Jewish assimilation, see Amos Funkenstein, "The Dialectics of Assimilation," *Jewish Social Studies* 1 (1995), p. 4; and Werner Sollors, *Beyond Ethnicity: Consent and Descent in American Culture* (New York: Oxford University Press, 1986).

3. JM to MM et al., July 20, 1796, MYFP.

4. RM to ME, Aug. 7, 1815, *EOTH*, p. 6. "All religions are equally good," one of the Mordecai children wrote of the family creed, "and . . . a strict adherence to what our consciences tell us is right, is the conduct most acceptable to our maker" (EM to Sol, Sept. 19, 1821, JMP).

5. RM to ME, Aug. 7, 1815, *EOTH*, p. 6.

6. [EM], "Past Days, a Simple Story for Children," MYFP.

7. Enlightened domesticity has much in common with other ideological models that have received attention from historians of American women. It bears important similarities as well to the ideal of *Bildung* (or enlightened self-culture) that characterized German thought during the same period. The literature on both is immense; I have outlined the most salient works in the Notes on Sources.

8. Hannah More, "Sensibility" (1782), as copied by RM, EM scrapbook, LMFP.

9. Richard S. Tedlow quoting Pierce Butler's 1907 biography of Judah P. Benjamin, in "Judah P. Benjamin," in Nathan M. Kaganoff and Melvin I. Urofsky, eds., *"Turn to the South": Essays on Southern Jewry* (Charlottesville: University Press of Virginia for the American Jewish Historical Society, 1979), pp. 24, 176 n. 2.

10. RM to SM, March 20, 1814, PMP.

11. Ibid.

1. ROOTS

1. JM to JMM, Oct. 25, 1783, MFP; JM to SM, March 4, 1816, MFP; *HJR*, pp. 15, 17–18; *RJ*, pp. 1–2, 4–6.

2. JM to JMM, Oct. 25, 1783, MFP; JM to MM et al., July 20, 1796, MFP.

3. *EJ*, vol. 11, p. 1039.

4. JM to SM, March 4, 1816, MFP.

5. Eli Faber, *A Time for Planting: The First Migration, 1654–1820* (Baltimore: Johns Hopkins University Press, 1992), p. 107.

6. JM to SM, March 4, 1816, MFP.

7. Sephardic Jews had roots in the Iberian Peninsula (Spain and Portugal), from which they fled during the Inquisition, spreading both to the East and westward toward the Americas. They, along with central and eastern European (or Ashkenazic) Jews, migrated to colonial America, and, though the two groups observed somewhat different rituals, they cooperated in the establishment of Jewish communities. The liturgy at most early American synagogues was Sephardic—often called Portuguese— even though Ashkenazic Jews usually dominated the membership (Faber, *Time for Planting*, pp. 53–66). Shaye J. D. Cohen, *The Beginnings of Jewishness: Boundaries, Varieties, Uncertainties* (Berkeley: University of California Press, 1999), pp. 198–238; and "Proselytes," *EJ*, vol. 13, pp. 1183–86.

8. Nothing in the Mordecais' papers discusses Moses Mordecai's life before 1761, when he and Esther arrived in Philadelphia. Strong circumstantial evidence points to a criminal background. See Peter Wilson Coldham, *Home Counties, 1655–1775*, vol. 4 of *Bonded Passengers to America* (Baltimore: Genealogical Publishing Co., 1983), p. 51; Eric L. Goldstein, *Traders and Transports: The Jews of Colonial Maryland* (Baltimore: Jewish Historical Society of Maryland, 1993), pp. 3, 21, 28–29, 35, 39, 49, 61; and Todd Endelman, *The Jews of Georgian England, 1714–1830* (Philadelphia: Jewish Publication Society of America, 1979), pp. 173, 177.

9. *HJP*, pp. 50, 394 n. 68; Goldstein, *Traders and Transports*, p. 24.

10. "Addenda to Watson's Annals of Philadelphia: Notes by Jacob Mordecai, 1836," edited by Whitfield J. Bell Jr., *Pennsylvania Magazine of History and Biography* 98 (1974), pp. 154, 162. Non-transportation Agreement, Philadelphia, Oct. 25, 1765, AJA. On Franks, see *EAJ*, vol. 2, pp. 90–94; and *HJP*, pp. 84–86.

11. Abraham J. Karp, ed., *The Jewish Experience in America: Selected Studies from the Publications of the American Jewish Historical Society* (Waltham, Mass.: American Jewish Historical Society, 1969), vol. 1, pp. 323–29; *HJP*, pp. 89–91.

12. Inventory of Moses Mordecai estate, June 26, 1781, and "Account of Elizabeth [Esther] Mordecai Administratrix . . . of Moses Mordecai," May 27, 1782, MFP-AJHS; JMM to JM, March 11, 1784, LMFP; JM to MM et al., July 20, 1796, MYFP; [EM], "Past Days, a Simple Story for Children," p. 82, MYFP.

13. *EAJ*, vol. 2, p. 185; *HJP*, p. 126. Philadelphia tax lists for 1780 assessed Moses at seventy-seven hundred pounds. In 1781, Esther's holdings were assessed at "no value." In 1782, she was assessed at twelve pounds.

14. *HJP*, p. 126; *HJR*, pp. 17–18; *RJ*, pp. 5–6.

15. In 1918, an American rabbi looked to the Bible to support his arguments about intermarriage, distinguishing between the illegitimacy of Abraham's son Ishmael, whose mother was not born a Jew, and his son Isaac, "the son of a Hebrew wife" (Rabbi David de Sola Pool, quoted in Anne C. Rose, *Beloved Strangers: Interfaith Families in Nineteenth-Century America* [Cambridge, Mass.: Harvard University Press, 2001], p. 125). Account for the building of the new synagogue, 1781–1782, kept by Simon Nathan, treasurer, Myer Myers File, AJA; Minute book of Mikveh Israel, quoted in *HJP*, p. 126.

16. See Jacob I. Cohen ketubah (1782), AJA; Ann Lynn Lipton, "Anywhere, So Long As It Be Free: A Study of the Cohen Family of Richmond and Baltimore, 1773–1826" (master's thesis, College of William and Mary, 1973), pp. 13–14; *RJ*, p. 6; *EAJ*, vol. 2, pp. 185–86.

17. Account for the Building of the New Synagogue 1781–1782, kept by Simon Nathan, AJA.

18. On Myers's career and reputation, see David L. Barquist, *Myer Myers: Jewish Silversmith in Colonial New York* (New Haven, Conn.: Yale University Press, 2001); Jane Bortman Larus, *Myer Myers, Silversmith, 1723–1795* (Washington, D.C.: B'nai B'rith, 1960); Alfred Werner, "Myer Myers, Silversmith of Distinction," *American Art and Antiques* 2 (May–June 1979), pp. 50–57.

19. "Address of Israelites to Governor Clinton [of New York]," Myer Myers File, AJA; Affidavit by Myer Myers and Peter Betts against Ralph Isaacs, suspected Loyalist, Norwalk, Conn., Oct. 6, 1776; and Account book of Nehemiah Curtis of Stratford, Conn., 1781 and 1783, both in Myer Myers File, AJA; JMM to Joyce Mears Myers and Myer Myers, Aug. 26, 1782, MFP; JM to MM et al., July 20, 1796, MFP; *HJP*, p. 98.

20. Of the four members of the *adjunta*, one was a friend and client of Myer Myers's and another was his brother-in-law. See *EAJ*, vol. 2, pp. 185–86; "Address of Israelites to Governor Clinton."

21. Karp, *Jewish Experience in America*, vol. 1, p. 308.

2. THEIR OWN VINE AND FIG TREE

1. Lance J. Sussman, "Our Little World: The Early Years in Warrenton" (paper submitted to Dr. Jacob Rader Marcus, Hebrew Union College, AJA).

2. *HJP*, pp. 106–8, 109.

3. *HJP*, p. 412 n. 63.

4. Undated copy or draft of letter from JM to [Moses] Myers, [after 1791], JMP.

5. John J. McCusker and Russell R. Menard, *The Economy of British America, 1607–1789* (Chapel Hill: University of North Carolina Press, 1985), pp. 368–73.

6. JM to Esther Cohen, July 26, 1786, MFP.

7. Moses Myers and Samuel Myers account book, box 2, Sept. 14, 1786, and March 19, 1797, Myers Family [Norfolk] Papers, AJA.

8. Moses Myers [no relation] to Samuel [Samy] Myers, June 9, 1786, quoted in *EAJ*, vol. 2, pp. 202–3; *EAJ*, vol. 2, pp. 208–9, 212; JM to MM et al., July 20, 1796, MFP; Malcolm S. Stern, "Moses Myers and the Early Jewish Community of Norfolk," *Journal of the Southern Jewish Historical Society* 1 (Nov. 1958), pp. 5, 6; Moses Myers and Samuel [Samy] Myers account book, box 2, Feb. 26, 1787; Myers Family Papers (Norfolk), AJA; and *EAJ*, vol. 2, p. 214.

9. Not only Samy did well. The Richmond business of Jacob's stepfather, Cohen, was booming, as was that of his friend Marcus Elcan. See Ann Lynn Lipton, "Anywhere, So Long As It Be Free: A Study of the Cohen Family of Richmond and Baltimore, 1773–1826" (master's thesis, College of William and Mary, 1973); and Carl Coleman Rosen Sr., *244 Years of Elcan Family History* (Westminster, Md., 1994), pp. 1–3.

10. Operating a store, as opposed to managing wholesale imports or transactions, placed Jacob "on the lower rung of the mercantile ladder," according to Edwin J. Perkins, in *The Economy of Colonial America*, 2nd ed. (New York: Columbia University Press, 1988), p. 128. On the family's isolation, see JM to MM et al., July 20, 1796, MFP; "Notes on Family History," MYFP.

11. Richmond City personal property tax list, 1791.

12. The ascription of Jacob's business troubles to his "Gentile blood" appears in print in Alexander Wilbourne Weddell, "Samuel Mordecai: Chronicler of Richmond, 1786–1865," *Virginia Historical Magazine* 53 (1945), p. 272. See also Jacob Rader Marcus, *United States Jewry, 1776–1985* (Detroit: Wayne State University Press, 1989), vol. 1, p. 99; *EAJ*, vol. 2, p. 191; and *RJ*, p. 2.

13. JMM to Joyce Mears Myers, Feb. 1794, MFP; "Samuel Myers," *EJ*, vol. 12, p. 726; Stern, "Moses Myers and the Early Jewish Community of Norfolk," p. 3. "Notes on Family History," n.d., MYFP.

14. JMM to Rebecca Mears Myers [Becky], Dec. 3, 1792, MFP; JMM to Joyce Mears Myers and Myer Myers, Dec. 5, 1792, MFP; JM to MM et al., July 20, 1796, MFP.

15. JMM to Joyce Mears Myers and Myer Myers, Dec. 5, 1792, MFP; JMM to JM, Feb. 11, 1793, MFP.

16. *MHMF*, p. 28; for "connexions," see JMM to Joyce Mears Myers, Dec. 19, 1792, MFP.

17. *SOW*, pp. 7–8, 10–11, 114, 166; *COW*, pp. 73, 80–81; JM to JMM, Feb. 28, 1793, MFP; Guion Griffis Johnson, *Ante-bellum North Carolina: A Social History* (Chapel Hill: University of North Carolina Press, 1937), pp. 17, 148–49; Lewis E. Atherton, *The Southern Country Store, 1800–1860* (1949; New York: Greenwood Press, 1968), pp. 42–48; Joseph Clarke Robert, *The Tobacco Kingdom: Plantation, Market, and Fac-*

tory in Virginia and North Carolina, 1800–1860 (Durham, N.C.: Duke University Press, 1938).

18. On the location of the store and house, see "The Life of Alfred Mordecai: As Related by Himself," edited by James A. Padgett, *North Carolina Historical Review* 22 (1945), p. 65; and "Map of Warrenton, N.C., about 1800," courtesy Richard Hunter, Warrenton, N.C. For Jacob's preparations, see JMM to JM, Feb. 17, 1793, MFP; and JM to JMM, Feb. 28, 1793, MFP.

19. JM to JMM, Feb. 11, 1793, MFP; JMM to Joyce Mears Myers, Feb. 1794, MFP.

20. On Judy's contentment, see JMM to Myer Myers and Joyce Mears Myers, April 24, 1793, MFP. On her siblings, see JMM to Joyce Mears Myers, Feb. 1, 1794, MFP; JMM and JM to Moses Myers [of Norfolk], n.d., Myers Family Papers (Norfolk), AJA; JMM to Rebecca Mears Myers, Dec. 3, 1792, MFP; JMM to JM, March 1, 1794, LMFP.

21. JMM to Joyce Mears Myers, Feb. 1, 1794, MFP. On Marx, see "Notes by one of Moses Mordecai's granddaughters from conversation with EM on family history," n.d., MYFP; JMM to Myer Myers and Joyce Mears Myers, April 24, 1793, MFP; JMM to Joyce Mears Myers, Aug. 27, 1793, MFP, quoted in *RJ*, pp. 70 n. 12, 359; *HJR*, pp. 47–50; JMM to Joyce Mears Myers, Feb. 1794, MFP.

22. JM to MM et al., July 20, 1796, MFP.

23. JM to Esther Cohen, April 7, 1796, MFP. In 1795 Jacob Mordecai was assessed for one "lott" and three slaves (Warren County list of taxables, NCDAH). *COW*, pp. 80–81, 87; Samuel Oppenheim, "The Jews and Masonry in the United States before 1810," *Publications of the American Jewish Historical Society* 19 (1910), pp. 2–3, 74.

24. Garden, JMM to Myer Myers and Joyce Mears Myers, April 24, 1793, MFP. JM to MM et al., July 20, 1796, MFP. See [EM], "Past Days, a Simple Story for Children," p. 48, MYFP.

25. JM to MM et al., July 20, 1796, MFP; JM to Esther Cohen, April 7, 1796, MFP.

26. JM to MM et al., July 20, 1796, MFP.

27. JM to the warden and brethren of Johnston Caswell Lodge, Jan. 27, 1796, PMP; JM to Esther Cohen, April 7, 1796, MFP.

28. JM to MM et al., July 20, 1796, MFP.

29. Ibid.

3. CAST DOWN AT THE FEET OF FORTUNE

1. On the relocations, see *MHMF*, p. 29; and JM to Esther Cohen, April 7, 1796, MFP. On Hodgson's School, see RM to SM, Aug. 19, 1809, MFP; and Margaret Meagher, *History of Education in Richmond* (Richmond, 1939), p. 36. On the girls' homesickness, see [EM], "Past Days, a Simple Story for Children" (1840–1841), pp. 43–44, MYFP; and JM to RM and EM, Dec. 10, 1796, JMP.

2. JM to RM, Jan. 10, 1797, MFP; JM to RM and EM, Dec. 10, 1796, JMP, quoted in Lance J. Sussman, "Our Little World: The Early Years in Warrenton" (paper submitted to Dr. Jacob Rader Marcus, Hebrew Union College, AJA); "Past Days," pp. 82–83, MYFP. JM to RM, Sept. 4, 1797, JMP; JM to EM and RM, March 18, 1799, MFP.

3. *MHMF*, p. 30.

4. JM to EM and RM, March 17, 1799, MFP; JM to RM, May 14, 1799, MFP; and SM to MM, July 18, 1799, MFP.

5. SM, addition to "Retrospect of 1857," JMP.

6. *SOW*, pp. 129–31; and CMP to EM, Jan. 13, 1838, MFP.

7. SM to RM, Sept. 6, 1800, MFP.

8. SM, "Retrospect of 1811" and addition to "Retrospect of 1811," JMP. Samson Myers (1772–1803) scandalized his family by marrying a Christian woman about this time.

9. On Jacob Mordecai's debts, see Warren County will book 10, Nov. 21, 1799, p. 164; Warren County will book 12, Aug. 1, 1804, and Aug. 1804, pp. 262, 284. The girls supervised the babies (Joyce Mears Myers to RMM, Dec. 13, 1804, JMP) and sewed countless shirts for Jacob and their brothers (RM to SM, Feb. 9, 1805, and Dec. 1, 1807, JMP; and SM to RM, Feb. 9, 1808). On the boys' business, see MM to SM, Sept. 6 and July 25, 1805, JMP.

10. For the holiday dates, see SM to RM, Sept. 16, 1805, JMP. On the lax religious observance in Richmond, see *RJ*, pp. 38–40. Jacob Mordecai was appointed justice of the peace in 1798 and served at least seven years (Governor's Office, List of Justices of the Peace and Militia Officers, 1784–1806, p. 208, NCDAH; and Warren County Court minutes, 1805–1807, NCDAH).

11. RM to SM, Oct. 15, 1805, JMP; and Dana Evan Kaplan, "The Determination of Jewish Identity below the Mason-Dixon Line: Crossing the Boundary from Gentile to Jew in the Nineteenth-Century South" (paper in possession of the author), pp. 15–16, 17–18.

12. *COW*, pp. 61, 68, 258. On the new store and the lawsuit, see "Map of Warrenton, N.C., about 1800," courtesy Richard Hunter, Warrenton; Warren County Court minutes, May 1806, p. 43, NCDAH; MM to SM, Sept. 6, 1805, JMP; "Notes on Family History," MYFP; RM to SM, Sept. 30, 1807, JMP.

13. JM to RM, Nov. 19, 1805, JMP; RMM to JM, March 28, 1806, MFP; RM, "Memories," MYFP. "Notes on Family History" suggests that Jacob eventually got a favorable judgment and significant damages in his case with Johnson, but this could not be confirmed from surviving court records or contemporary family correspondence.

14. RM, "Memories."

15. *COW*, p. 81; RM, "Memories," MYFP; RM to SM, Feb. 9, 1805, JMP.

16. RM to SM, Jan. 3, 1808, JMP; SM to RM, Jan. 20, 1808, MFP.

17. On the Kennons, see John McGill, *The Beverley Family of Virginia: Descendants of Major Robert Beverley, 1641–1687, and Allied Families* (Columbia, S.C.: R. L. Bryan Co., 1956), p. 616; RM to SM, Nov. 17, 1806, JMP; Elizabeth B. Kennon to RM, Dec. 21, 1820, KFP; and Beverley Kennon to EM, Dec. 25, 1829, KFP.

18. RM to SM, Jan. 6, 1807, JMP.

19. William E. Craig, "The Mysterious Frenchman: Alexander Calizance Miller in America, 1797–1831," *Bulletin of the Lower Cape Fear Historical Society* 29 (Oct. 1985),

p. 1; RM to SM, Feb. 9, 1806, JMP; EM to Sol, Aug. 28, 1811, LMFP (inserted in EM scrapbook I).

20. RM to SM, Feb. 9 and Jan. 6, 1807, JMP.

21. RM to SM, Sept. 7, 1806, JMP; MM to SM, Oct. 4, 1807, JMP. Moses was apparently the first Jewish-born lawyer in North Carolina. On Jewish lawyers, see Jacob Rader Marcus, *United States Jewry, 1776–1985* (Detroit: Wayne State University Press, 1989), vol. 1, pp. 197–200.

22. Sol to SM, Oct. 31, 1806, JMP; RM to SM, May 28, 1809, MFP; *SOW*, pp. 117, 122.

23. JMM to JM, March 11, 1784, LMFP; JMM to JM, April 23, [1784], MFP; [EM], "Past Days," pp. 82–83.

24. RM to SM, Jan. 3, 1808, JMP.

25. SM to RM, April 7, 1811, MFP; SM to EM, May 6, 1815, MFP.

26. EM to SM, March 21, 1808, MFP.

27. [EM], "Fading Scenes Recalled," quoted in *SOW*, p. 116; RM to SM, Dec. 1, 1807, JMP.

28. Jacob supplemented his 1808 income by recording the county tax rolls. RM to SM, Jan. 3, 1808, and Dec. 1, 1807, JMP; RM to SM, Feb. 12, 1808, MFP; Warren County miscellaneous tax records, 1808, NCDAH.

29. RM to SM, July 13, 1808, JMP; RM, "Memories." Also see the discussion of myths surrounding the founding of the Mordecai School in TIPP, pp. 16–32.

30. RM to SM, July 13, 1808, JMP; [EM], "Past Days," p. 63; advertisement, "Female Education in Warrenton," Aug. 18, 1808, MFP.

31. RM to SM, Nov. 17, 1806, and March 1, 1808, JMP; RM to SM, Nov. 15, 1818, MFP.

4. KEEPING SCHOOL

1. RM to SM, Aug. 2, 1808, JMP; RM to EM, Sept. 1, 1808, MFP. For Rachel's attributes, see [EM], "Past Days, a Simple Story for Children," pp. 48–49, MYFP; and SM to RM, April 7, 1811, JMP.

2. RM to SM, Jan. 1, 1809, MFP; RM to SM, Oct. 15, 1805, JMP, cited in Lance J. Sussman, "Our Little World: The Early Years in Warrenton" (paper submitted to Dr. Jacob Rader Marcus, Hebrew Union College, AJA); RM, "Memories," MYFP; [EM], "Past Days," p. 52.

3. The context of Rachel's teaching work is examined at length in "The Female Academy and Beyond: Three Mordecai Sisters at Work in the Old South," in Susanna Delfino and Michele Gillespie, eds., *Neither Lady nor Slave: Working Women of the Old South* (Chapel Hill: University of North Carolina Press, 2002), pp. 174–97. The tension between learning and femininity is apparent in RM to SM, Feb. 27, 1814, PMP; RM to MM, Oct. 4, 1817, MFP; and EM to Sol, Feb. 12, 1818, JMP.

4. [EM], "Past Days," p. 77. The dream reflects her preoccupation with the figure of the aged schoolmistress in a William Shenstone poem: "In every village mark'd with

a little spire / Embowered in trees and hardly known to fame, / There dwells, in lowly shed and mean attire, / A matron old, whom we schoolmistress name" (Shenstone, "The Schoolmistress," 2:1–4, in *The Poetical Works of William Shenstone, with Life, Critical Dissertation, and Explanatory Notes by George Gilfillan* [1854; New York: Greenwood Press, 1968], p. 262).

5. RM, "Memories."

6. RM to SM, Jan. 1, 1809, MFP; RM, "Memories."

7. Mary P[ugh Jones] Govan to EM, Oct. 29, 1864, EMP; RM, "Memories"; RM to SM, July 5, 1809, MFP.

8. For Jacob's role, see SOW, pp. 133–41; EM to Sol, Dec. 10, 1827, JMP; EM to CMP, Jan. 27, 1828, JMP. For the authority Rachel wielded, see [EM], "Past Days," pp. 92, 90–91.

9. EM to SM, Feb. 22, [1810?], JMP.

10. Advertisement, "Female Education in Warrenton," Aug. 18, 1808, MFP; RM to SM, July 13, 1808, JMP, quoted in Sussman, "Our Little World," p. 19.

11. RM, "Memories"; EM to SM, Sept. 12, 1808, MFP.

12. Total enrollment varied from 70 to 110 between 1809 and 1818. The proportion of day students in the first year could not be determined. In the school's second year, two out of three pupils boarded—a proportion applied above to year one. See TIPP, pp. 44, 46. On Becky, see EM journal, Oct. 21, 1815, LMFP.

13. EM and RM to SM, Jan. 25, 1809, MFP.

14. TIPP, pp. 67–71; [EM], "Past Days," p. 74; EM to SM, June 25, 1815, MFP; RMM to EM, Oct. 8, 1817, MFP.

15. [EM], "Past Days," p. 95; RM to SM, Aug. 19, 1809, MFP; SM to RM, Aug. 10, 1810, JMP; EM to CMP, Jan. 24, 1857, JMP; RM to SM, Feb. 12, 1809, PMP.

16. RM to SM, May 28, 1809, MFP; Sol to EM, n.d., LMFP.

17. On the school's enrollment, see RM to SM, May 28, 1809, MFP; on Sol's counsel, see SM to RM, June 4, 1809, MFP (in 1811 a music teacher was offered twelve hundred dollars; see RM to SM, Jan. 27, 1811, MFP); on teaching as a detour in Sol's career, see TIPP, p. 143; on Sol as a partner, see RM to SM, July 5, 1809, MFP; RM, "Memories."

18. RM, "Memories"; TIPP, pp. 86–87, 93, 70; EM to SM, Feb. 4, 1811, MFP.

19. MM to SM, June 22, 1814, and Aug. 29, 1816, JMP; AM to EM, Dec. 26, 1821, AMP. On men teaching, see Bingham and Richards, "The Female Academy and Beyond," pp. 178–79.

20. RM to SM, May 28, 1809, MFP; "Goods and services purchased during school years (1811–1818)," in TIPP, p. 66; RM to SM, July 27, 1810, and July 3, 1811, MFP.

21. RM to SM, Jan. 1, 1809, MFP.

22. RM, "Memories" JM to SM, Nov. 28, 1817, JMP.

23. SM to RM, Dec. 30, 1810, MFP; RM to SM, July 10, 1811, MFP.

24. RM, "Memories," MYFP; RM to SM, Aug. 2, 1811, MFP; Sol and RM to SM, March 8, 1812, MFP. For the state currencies that made trade difficult in this period, see

Lewis E. Atherton, *The Southern Country Store, 1800–1860* (1949; New York: Green-wood Press, 1968), p. 178.

5. A SERIOUS DEPORTMENT

1. TIPP, pp. 100–5. In an undated note (EM to Sol, PMP), Jacob urged his children to "fix up when people come because they like us the better for it."

2. Sol to EM, n.d., EM scrapbook, LMFP.

3. RM journal, Feb. 15, 1818, WOW, pp. 200–1.

4. RM to SM, Feb. 11, 1810, PMP; SM to EM, Feb. 25, 1810, JMP.

5. Advertisement by Myer Myers for the runaway slave Daphne, *New York Mercury*, May 11, 1763, AJA; Warren County, N.C., list of taxables for 1795, 1797, 1800, 1808, NCDAH; Henrico County, Va., personal property tax list, 1820, LV.

6. Keith C. Barton, " 'Good Cooks and Washers': Slave Hiring, Domestic Labor, and the Market in Bourbon County, Kentucky," *Journal of American History* 84 (1997), pp. 436–60.

7. EM to SM, Sept. 7, 1810, MFP; JM to SM, Nov. 29, 1810, MFP; SOW, pp. 170–71, 40. Bible study was typical of many schools' curricula (TIPP, p. 77). On Jacob's tolerance, see JM to SM, Nov. 29, 1810, MFP; JM to MM et al., July 20, 1796, MFP.

8. EM to SM, Sept. 7, 1810, MFP.

9. RM to SM, Sept. 24, 1810, PMP; SM to RM, Oct. 3, 1810, JMP; RM to SM, July 28, 1807, JMP.

10. On Richmond Jews and religious practice, see *RJ*, pp. 38–40. For mentions of Passover, see EM to SM, March 21, 1808, MFP; RM to SM, April 29, 1807, MFP; RM to SM, April 21, 1807, JMP. In 1812 in Warrenton, the family made do with unleavened hoecake (cornmeal batter cooked in a skillet), while Sam complained of having to eat matzo (SM to EM, March 29, 1812, JMP). For the difficulty in obtaining matzo, see RM to SM, April 29, 1807, MFP; RM to SM, March 4, 1816, PMP.

11. SM to MM, Sept. 19, 1817, MFP; note from JM in Julia to Sol, Aug. 10, 1817, MFP.

12. Sol to EM, Feb. 14, 1814, LMFP. Synagogues loosened sanctions regarding Sabbath observance during this period, signaling reduced orthodoxy among many American Jews (Eli Faber, *A Time for Planting: The First Migration, 1654–1820* [Baltimore: Johns Hopkins University Press, 1992], p. 123). But variations existed. Ellen, visiting her Myers cousins, hurried to finish a letter before sundown one Friday, a restriction not enforced in Warrenton (EM to Sol, March 4, 1814, JMP; and Sol to EM, Feb. 26, 1814, LMFP). Other Richmond cousins, the Marxes, attended school on Saturdays, having been given the choice of keeping Sabbath either on Saturday or on Sunday (EM to Sol, Dec. 15, 1813, JMP). On Sabbath at the Mordecai School, see TIPP, p. 71; RM to SM, May 8, 1814, MFP.

13. JM, "Introduction to the New Testament," n.d., AJA; JM to SM, Nov. 29, 1810, MFP.

14. SM to Sol, Dec. 17, 1810, JMP; JM to SM, Nov. 29, 1810, MFP.

15. EM to SM, Feb. 22 [c. 1810], misfiled 1816, JMP.

16. Anne C. Rose, in *Beloved Strangers: Interfaith Families in Nineteenth-Century America* (Cambridge, Mass.: Harvard University Press, 2001), distinguishes neatly between the ideology of religious Enlightenment of the late eighteenth and the early nineteenth century and the centrality of religious concerns of mid-nineteenth-century America. The Mordecais' awareness of the importance of demonstrating religious affiliation seems to have begun with Jacob's entanglement with the revival of 1810.

17. SM to RM, Nov. 21, 1813, JMP; RM to EM, Jan. 30 and March 20, 1814, MFP; EM to Sol, Feb. 15, 1818, JMP; RM to EM, June 22, 1823, MFP. Empie helped organize the Diocese of North Carolina in 1817 (Guion Griffis Johnson, *Ante-bellum North Carolina: A Social History* [Chapel Hill: University of North Carolina Press, 1937], p. 335).

18. On Jacob's books, see Sol to SM, Nov. 8, 1811, MFP; SM to RM, Nov. 21, 1813, JMP; Sol to EM, Dec. 26, 1813, LMFP; SM to EM, May 28, 1814, JMP. On educating his children and others against "anti-semites and missionaries," see RM to Sol, July 27, 1817, MFP; RM to SM, July 27, 1817, JMP; RM to SM, April 24, 1814, MFP; EM to Sol, Feb. 15, 1818, JMP.

6. SMALL SLIGHTS AND CONTEMPT

1. *RJ*, p. 65; *MHMF*, p. 18; SM, "Retrospect of 1811," JMP.

2. SM, "Retrospect of 1811."

3. Ibid.

4. RM, "Memories," MYFP; SM, "Retrospect of 1811"; *Wilmington Advertiser*, May 7, 1811, Mordecai School File, MFP.

5. SM, "Retrospect of 1811."

6. Thomas Syndham describing gout (1850), quoted in *Professional Guide to Diseases*, 5th ed. (Springhouse, Pa.: Springhouse, 1995), p. 556.

7. SM, "Retrospect of 1811"; SM to RM, Aug. 17 and Aug. 28, 1811, MFP.

8. SM to Sol, May 17, 1812, JMP; SM to RM, Dec. 15, 1811, MFP; SM, addition to "Retrospect of 1811," JMP.

9. SM, addition to "Retrospect of 1811"; SM to Sol, March 13, 1813, MFP.

10. RM to SM, Sept. 3, 1813, MFP.

11. Judith Hays Myers and Samuel Myers to Judah Hays, Sept. 13, 1813, MYFP; JM to SM, Sept. 2, 1813, MFP; EM to Sol, Jan. 2, 1814, and Dec. 26, 1813, JMP; RM to EM, Feb. 26, 1814, MFP; JM, RM, et al. to EM, Dec. 20, 1813, JMP; EM to Sol, Feb. 18, 1814, JMP; RM to EM, Dec. 12, 1813, MFP.

12. EM to SM, Aug. 27, 1814, JMP.

13. EM to SM, Sept. 12, 1814, PMP; Sol to SM, Sept. 26, 1814, MFP; RM to SM, Sept. 19, 1814, PMP.

14. SM, addition to "Retrospect of 1811"; SM to Sol, Sept. 15, 1814, JMP; SM to RM, Sept. 2 and Sept. 11, 1814, MFP; SM to EM, Sept. 22, 1814, JMP; Donald R. Hickey, *The War of 1812: A Forgotten Conflict* (Chicago: University of Illinois Press, 1989), pp. 221, 301.

15. RM to Sol, July 12, 1820, JMP; RM to SM, May 4, 1817, JMP.

16. SM to EM, April 17, 1816, JMP; RM to SM, Jan. 23, 1816, MFP.

17. For their use of humor regarding the name of Mordecai, see RM to EM, Jan. 30, 1814, MFP. They sometimes exchanged the name for "Moran," perhaps a reference to their occupation, since *moran* in Hebrew means "teacher" (Sol to SM, Aug. 27, 1815, MFP; Sol to EM, Feb. 14, 1814, EM scrapbook, LMFP; EM journal, Sept. 17, 1815, LMFP).

18. SM to EM, April 17, 1816, JMP; SM to EM, May 16, 1815, MFP; Sol to RM, n.d., miscellaneous file, JMP; Julia to RM, n.d., miscellaneous file, JMP; RM to SM, Aug. 19, 1809, MFP.

19. RM to SM, April 16, 1816, JMP; RM to SM, Aug. 19, 1809, MFP; RM to EM, Aug. 7, 1821, MFP; RM to SM, Jan. 23, 1816, MFP.

20. RM to SM, April 16, 1816, JMP; RM, essay on "fits," among papers accompanying JM to MM et al., July 20, 1796, MFP; SM to EM, May 6, 1814, JMP. The affair with Louisa Marx unfolds in a series of letters, including EM and RM to SM, April 21, 1816, MFP; EM to SM, Feb. 19, 1816, JMP; EM journal, Jan. 20, 1816, LMFP; SM to EM, May 15, 1815, MFP; SM to EM, April 17, 1816, JMP.

21. RM to SM, March 5, 1815, PMP. The term "friend" carried a peculiar weight in the Mordecais' lexicon—bearing not only on matters of affective relations but also on business and morality. "Friends" were those who looked after one's best interest. For the reference to their religion as a "persuasion," see RM to Sol, July 27, 1816, MFP.

22. EM journal, Oct. 1, 1815, LMFP; TIPP, pp. 137, 116; RM to SM, May 1, 1810, PMP; RM to SM, July 17, 1814, MFP.

23. RM to SM, March 20, 1814, PMP; EM to Sol, Dec. 26, 1813, PMP. "The most profound pitch of my possible degradation," Rachel announced, would be to be severed from her family (RM to SM, April 19, 1818, JMP).

7. REASON COMBINED WITH VIRTUE AND NOURISHED BY EDUCATION

1. RM journal, Feb. 23, 1817, *WOW*, p. 177.

2. RM to SM, Aug. 19, 1809, MFP.

3. RM to ME, Aug. 4, 1816, *EOTH*, p. 11. Rachel especially valued the work of Maria Edgeworth (1767–1849), Anna Letitia Barbauld (1743–1825), Marie de Sévigné (1626–1696), and Stéphanie-Félicité de Genlis (1746–1830).

4. On Eliza's lessons, see RM to EM, Jan. 30, 1814, MFP; and RM journal, Sept. 13, 1816, *WOW*, p. 164. For the quotation, see RM to SM, Feb. 25, 1816, MFP. For an example of Rachel's faulting parents for her pupils' deficiencies, see RM to SM, May 25, 1817, JMP.

5. RM journal, May 19, 1816, Jan. 11, 1818, July 14, 1816, *WOW*, pp. 157, 196, 159. The idealism of this strict patrolling of a child's environment is addressed in Carol Strauss-Sotiropoulos, "Where Words Fail: Rational Education Unravels in Maria Edgeworth's *The Good French Governess*," University of Connecticut, on-line at http://web. nwe.ufl.edu/los/csotiropoulos.html; and Tony Lyons, "Play and Toys in the Educa-

tional Work of Richard Lovell Edgeworth (1744–1817)," *History of Education and Childhood* (2001), on-line at http://www.socsci.kun.nl/ped/whp/histeduc/edgeworth.html.

6. RM journal, May 19, 1816, *WOW*, p. 158.

7. RM journal, Aug. 30, 1816, *WOW*, p. 159.

8. RM journal, Feb. 9, 1817, *WOW*, p. 173.

9. RM journal, Feb. 9, 1817, *WOW*, pp. 173–74. Even this punishment was lifted from Maria Edgeworth. See "The Good French Governess" (1801), in *Tales and Novels of Maria Edgeworth* (London: Baldwin and Craddock, 1832), vol. 3, pp. 174–75. Such "small errors" were worth serious attention, as Mitzi Myers has shown in "Deromanticizing the Subject: Maria Edgeworth's 'The Bracelets,' Mythologies of Origin, and the Daughter's Coming to Writing," in Paula R. Feldman and Theresa M. Kelley, eds., *Romantic Women Writers: Voices and Countervoices* (Detroit: Wayne State University Press, 1994), p. 92.

10. RM journal, Feb. 23, 1817, *WOW*, pp. 176–77.

11. RM to SM, Feb. 25, 1816, MFP; RM to ME, Aug. 7, 1815, *EOTH*, p. 4.

12. Maria Edgeworth, *Memoirs of Richard Lovell Edgeworth*, 2nd ed. (London: R. Hunter, 1821), vol. 1, pp. 253–54; Marilyn Butler, *Maria Edgeworth: A Literary Biography* (Oxford: Clarendon Press, 1972), pp. 35, 64, 1–2; Mitzi Myers, "Reading Rosamund Reading: Maria Edgeworth's 'Wee-Wee Stories' Interrogate the Canon," in Elizabeth Goodenough et al., eds., *Infant Tongues: The Voice of the Child in Literature* (Detroit: Wayne State University Press, 1994), pp. 57–58.

13. RM to ME, Sept. 16, 1821, *EOTH*, p. 25.

14. RM to ME, Aug. 7, 1815, *EOTH*, p. 3. Also see RM to SM, Feb. 25, 1816, MFP; and RM to ME, Sept. 25, 1816, *EOTH*, pp. 11–12.

15. SM to RM, Jan. 19, 1817, JMP.

16. Maria Edgeworth, *The Absentee* (1812), in *Tales and Novels*, vol. 9, p. 10.

17. RM to ME, Aug. 7, 1815, *EOTH*, p. 3; also see RM to ME, Sept. 16, 1821, *EOTH*, p. 28.

18. RM to ME, Aug. 7, 1815, *EOTH*, p. 6.

19. Ibid.

20. RM to SM, April 7, 1816, MFP.

8. MORDECAI A HANDSOME NAME?

1. RM to SM, Sept. 26, 1816, MFP; RM journal, Sept. 25, 1816, *WOW*, p. 166; RM to ME, Sept. 25, 1816, *EOTH*, p. 9.

2. Richard Lovell Edgeworth to RM, Aug. 4, 1816, *EOTH*, pp. 7–8.

3. ME to RM, n.d., *EOTH*, p. 8.

4. Sol to SM, Sept. 17, 1817, JMP; Richard Lovell Edgeworth, preface to Maria Edgeworth, *Harrington* (1817), in *Tales and Novels of Maria Edgeworth* (London: Baldwin and Craddock, 1833), vol. 17, p. v.

5. Edgeworth, *Harrington*, p. 13.

6. Sol to EM, Sept. 18, 1817, MFP; Edgeworth, *Harrington*, pp. 97, 46–49. On *Har-*

rington's influence in England, see Michael Ragussis, *Figures of Conversion: "The Jewish Question" and English National Identity* (Durham, N.C.: Duke University Press, 1995), pp. 56–58.

7. SM to RM, Sept. 27, 1817, JMP; Sol to SM, Sept. 17, 1817, JMP. For the reactions from Jews, see Sol to SM, Sept. 23, 1817, JMP; and Jacob Rader Marcus, *United States Jewry, 1776–1985* (Detroit: Wayne State University Press, 1989), vol. 4, p. 197. On what Ellen referred to as Rachel's "feminine delicacy," see RM to EM, Sept. 28, 1817, MFP; RM to SM, Sept. 26 and Oct. 6, 1816, MFP; EM journal, Oct. 9, 1817, MFP; RM journal, Sept. 25, 1816, WOW, pp. 165–66; Mary Kelley, *Private Woman, Public Stage: Literary Domesticity in Nineteenth-Century America* (New York: Oxford University Press, 1984). On the respect gained by Rachel, see Sara Hays to RML, Sept. 12, 1833, AMP.

8. SM to Sol, Sept. 29, 1817, JMP; Edgeworth, *Harrington*, pp. 253, 293–96.

9. Jacob Mordecai's reading of *Harrington* is conveyed in RM to ME, Oct. 28, 1817, EOTH, p. 16, but echoes the approach to religion in JM to MM et al., July 20, 1796, MYFP. For critical readings, see Ragussis, *Figures of Conversion*, pp. 77–79; and Judith W. Page, "Maria Edgeworth's *Harrington*: From Shylock to Shadowy Peddlers," *Wordsworth Circle* 32 (2001), pp. 9–13.

10. RM to ME, Oct. 28, 1817, EOTH, p. 16; for this view of Jacob Mordecai, see [EM], "Fading Scenes Recalled," MFP.

11. See SM to RM, Nov. 19, 1816, MFP; MM to JM, Dec. 17, 1821, JMP; RM to SM, Nov. 16, 1806, JMP; EM journal, July 6, 1815, LMFP; JM et al. to SM, Oct. 19, 1812, MFP; RM to SM, July 10, 1811, MFP; EM to SM, Jan. 3, 1823, MFP; RM to SM, Feb. 11, 1815, MFP.

12. RM to SM, July 5, 1809, MFP. The full amount of the Mordecais' holdings is difficult to ascertain. The calculations are based on letters and account books, though other investments (and debts) may not have been recorded or records of them not preserved. See SM, addition to "Retrospect of 1811," JMP; RM to SM, Aug. 25, 1813, MFP; JM cashbook, 1811–1818, JMP; RM to EM, Feb. 6, 1814, JMP; RM to SM, Feb. 11, 1815, MFP.

13. EM journal, July 14, 1816, LMFP; EM to SM, June 25, 1815, MFP.

14. RM and CM to EM, Sept. 29, 1817, JMP.

15. On Sol, see EM journal, March 16, 1817, LMFP; RM to SM, March 23, 1817, JMP; EM journal, May 17, 1817, LMFP; Sol to EM, July 20, 1817, MFP; Sol to CM, Aug. 10, 1817, MFP. On Ellen, see EM journal, Sept. 25, 1815, Aug. 3, 1816, Aug. 10, Aug. 30, Sept. 7, 1817, all LMFP; and Dec. 9, 1817, MFP. On gender difference in the treatment of TB, see Sheila M. Rothman, *Living in the Shadow of Death: Tuberculosis and the Social Experience of Illness in American History* (New York: Basic Books, 1994), pp. 1–9 and chap. 2.

16. On the idea that being sedentary contributed to consumption, see Rothman, *Living in the Shadow of Death*, p. 4. SM to RM, March 9, 1817, MFP; RM to SM, March 23, 1817, JMP; GM to SM, June 6, 1817, JMP; Sol to EM, Oct. 14, 1817, MFP; EM to SM, Aug. 28, 1817, JMP.

17. RM to SM, Nov. 1, 1818, JMP; RM to SM, Nov. 15, 1818, MFP. The school's buyers, with Plunkett, were Joseph Andrews and his son-in-law, Thomas P. Jones. See JM to SM, Sept. 17, 1818, JMP; RM and Sol to SM, Aug. 5, 1818, PMP; *SOW*, pp. 142–43; "The Life of Alfred Mordecai: As Related by Himself," edited by James A. Padgett, *North Carolina Historical Review* 22 (1945), p. 73.

9. RELIGIOUS SCRUPLES ASIDE

1. MM to SM, Aug. 29, 1816, JMP; MM to Sol, Feb. 9, 1817, JMP; MM to JM, Jan. 22 and Jan. 31, 1815, JMP; MM to EM, Jan. 19, 1813, PMP; MM to SM, June 22, 1814, JMP. Moses's "lucrative" practice and reputation for genius were remembered long after his death, and an early local historian suggested that Moses would have merited a seat on the North Carolina Supreme Court. See John Hill Wheeler, *Historical Sketches of North Carolina from 1584 to 1851* (1851; Baltimore: Regional Publishing Co., 1974), p. 418.

2. RM to Sol, Sept. 23, 1817, JMP; MM to SM, Aug. 29, 1816, JMP.

3. EM to SM, April 21, 1816, MFP; SM to EM, Sept. 8, 1816, MFP; EM journal, Dec. 31, 1816, LMFP; MM quoted in RM to SM, March 30, 1817, JMP.

4. Margaret's father, Henry, died intestate in 1811, orphaning four daughters. On their family history and financial legacy, see "Joel Lane," *DNCB*, vol. 4, p. 12; Marshall De Lancey Haywood, *Joel Lane: Pioneer and Patriot* (Raleigh: Alford, Bynum, and Christopher, 1900); Wake County wills 1771–1966, NCDAH. For the quotation from Moses, see MM to SM, Sept. 27, 1817, JMP; for Jacob's reaction, see EM journal, Oct. 9, 1817, MFP. For a survey of the furnishings, see Kenneth Joel Zogry, " 'Plain and Handsome': Documented Furnishings at the Mordecai House, 1780–1830," *Journal of Early Southern Decorative Arts* 15 (1989), pp. 93–115.

5. RM to SM, Oct. 1, 1817, JMP; EM journal, Oct. 9, 1817, MFP.

6. RM to MM, Oct. 4, 1816, MFP.

7. Sol to EM, Oct. 22, 1817, MFP.

8. Sol to EM, Oct. 14, 1817, MFP. Also see Moses quoted in RM to MM, Oct. 4, 1817, MFP; RM to SM, Oct. 19, 1817, JMP; Sol to EM, Oct. 22, 1817, MFP. For Moses's lack of interest in religion (Jewish or otherwise), see EM to Sol, Feb. 15, 1818, JMP; and SM to RM, July 2, 1811, MFP.

9. EM journal, March 16, 1817, LMFP.

10. EM journal, July 6, 1817, LMFP; EM to Sol, July 27, 1817, MFP. (In this letter, Ellen compared herself to the biblical Naomi—"where thou goest, will I go.")

11. Sol to EM, Oct. 1, 1817, MFP; EM journal, Oct. 9, 1817, MFP; EM journal, July 6 and March 7, 1817, LMFP. Also see SM to RM, Nov. 18, 1817, MFP; and CM to RM, Nov. 24, 1817, JMP.

12. See RM to EM, Nov. 14, 1813, JMP; EM journal, July 6 and Feb. 9, 1817, LMFP; Sol to EM, n.d., LMFP. For more on such sibling relationships, see James B. Twitchell, *Forbidden Partners: The Incest Taboo in Modern Culture* (New York: Columbia University Press, 1987), pp. 12–14, 25.

13. Sol to EM, undated note describing his gift to her of a knife, LMFP; EM to Sol,

Dec. 26, 1813, JMP. The siblings' undated notes (carefully preserved by Ellen) began around 1809, as the school opened.

14. RM to SM, March 17, 1809, MFP; EM scrapbook, EMP; RM to EM, Dec. 11, 1810, PMP; RM to CM, Dec. 1, 1810, MFP; and Sol to SM, Dec. 8, 1810, PMP. For flirtations between male teachers and students, see TIPP, pp. 107–9.

15. Miller married Mary Brown. See RM to SM, Jan. 27, 1811, MFP; William E. Craig, "The Mysterious Frenchman: Alexander Calizance Miller in America, 1797–1831," *Bulletin of the Lower Cape Fear Historical Society* 29 (Oct. 1985), pp. 1–4; "Thomas Brown," *DNCB*, vol. 1, p. 249.

16. Sol to EM, Aug. 28, 1811, LMFP.

17. Ibid.; RM to SM, Sept. 9, 1813, KFP; Sol to EM, Feb. 1, 1814, LMFP.

18. SM to EM, July 2, 1814, JMP; Sol to SM, Aug. 21, 1814, MFP; Sol to EM, Oct. 22, 1817, MFP; EM to Sol, July 24, 1817, MFP; EM to Sol, April 30, 1824, JMP; SM to EM, July 2, 1814, JMP; Sol to EM, Dec. 26, 1813, LMFP; Sol to EM, Dec. 5, 1813, LMFP; EM to Maria R. Brownloo, May 14, 1878, MFP-AJHS; EM to Sol, March 2, 1823, JMP. Madame de Genlis's *Les Fleurs; ou, les artistes* (1810) previsioned the fad for flower language of the 1820s and 1830s (see Beverley Seaton, *The Language of Flowers: A History* [Charlottesville: University Press of Virginia, 1995]).

19. RM to SM, July 7, 1814, MFP; Sol to EM, n.d., PMP; EM to MCL, Jan. 22, 1849, MFP.

20. SM to Sol, Dec. 8, 1814, JMP; EM to Sol, Dec. 12, 1814, LMFP; Sol to EM, n.d. [Dec. 12, 1814], LMFP.

21. EM to Sol, Dec. 12, 1814, LMFP.

22. Sol to EM, n.d. [Dec. 12, 1814], LMFP.

23. EM journal, Oct. 1, 1815, LMFP.

24. RM to EM, April 18, 1812, MFP.

10. THE CHILDREN OF DISAPPOINTMENT

1. RM to SM, Nov. 1, 1818, JMP.

2. JM to SM, Dec. 7, 1817, JMP; SM to RM, March 9, 1817, MFP; GM to SM, Nov. 3, 1818, JMP.

3. JM to General Joseph Gardner Swift, Jan. 13, 1818, AJA; "The Life of Alfred Mordecai: As Related by Himself," edited by James A. Padgett, *North Carolina Historical Review* 22 (1945), p. 73; and copy of the acceptance letter from the General Service Administration Records, March 24, 1819, AJA.

4. The average marriage age ranged between nineteen and twenty-three years old. See Jack Larkin, *The Reshaping of Everyday Life, 1790–1840* (New York: Harper Perennial, 1988), p. 63; and Jane Turner Censer, *North Carolina Planters and Their Children, 1800–1860* (Baton Rouge: Louisiana State University Press, 1984), pp. 91–92.

5. For cash payments from the school's buyers, see RM to SM, Jan. 4, 1818, MFP. For savings and investments, see Sol to EM, Feb. 16, 1818, MFP; SM to RM, March 29, 1818, JMP.

6. On property hunting, see RMM to JM, March 6, 1819, MFP; and SM to RM, March 6, 1819, JMP. On the quality of the soil, see JM to SM, Jan. 13, 1819, JMP. For the cost of the land, see John Brooke Mordecai, "Family Notes," BAA.

7. EM journal, Dec. 13, 1818, MFP. For the effect on the slaves, see SM to RM, Jan. 3, 1819, JMP; SM to RM, March 6, 1819, MFP; JM and Sol to SM, Dec. 18, 1818, JMP. For the list of items for sale, see Mordecai School Folder, March 1, 1819, MFP.

8. Sol to RM and EM, April 21, 1819, JMP; EM journal, June 11, 1819, MFP; EM II, *Gleanings from Long Ago* (1933; Raleigh, N.C.: Capital Area Preservation Inc., 1974), pp. 43–48.

9. Julia quoted in EM journal, n.d. [early summer 1819], MFP. RM to CM, Aug. 22, 1819, JMP; EM to CM, Aug. 1, 1819, JMP; and RM to CM, Aug. 9, 1819, JMP. Julia appears to have been treated with an electromagnetic device.

10. EM journal, [June 11?] 1819, and April 15, 1820, MFP; and EM to CM, Nov. 5, 1819, MFP.

11. CM to Sol, July 9, 1820, JMP; RM to SM, Dec. 6, 1819, JMP; Sol to EM, June 4, 1820, MFP; RM to Sol, Nov. 18, 1819, JMP; EM to Sol, April 27, 1821, JMP; JM and EM to Sol, Feb. 17, 1820, JMP.

12. SM to RM, March 23, 1819, JMP; GM to SM, Nov. 15, 1818, JMP; SM to RM, July 26, 1818, JMP; "Samuel Mordecai account with Jacob Mordecai," Oct. 1, 1819, JMP.

13. On the economic conditions during this catastrophic time, see Samuel Rezneck, *Business Depressions and Financial Panics: Essays in American Business and Economic History* (New York: Greenwood Publishing, 1968), pp. 51–72. On the panic, see SM to JM, April 5, 1819, JMP; on land purchases, see SM to RM, July 26, 1818, JMP; on paying the debt to Marx, see SM to Sol, June 8, 1820, JMP, and RM to Sol, Jan. 11, 1821, JMP. For the quotation, see SM to EM, n.d. [c. 1819–1820], JMP. Sam managed to cut his debt to his family by eleven thousand dollars in 1820, but the balance due was still more than twenty-five thousand dollars.

14. EM journal, June 11, 1819, MFP; RM to SM, Dec. 28, 1818, JMP; EM journal, May 6, 1820, MFP; EM to Sol, Feb. 15, 1829, JMP.

15. CM to Sol, May 18, 1820, JMP; Henrico County personal property tax, 1820; EM journal, May 6, 1820, MFP.

16. EM journal, July 31 and May 6, 1820, MFP.

17. See Emily Bingham and Penny Leigh Richards, "The Female Academy and Beyond: Three Mordecai Sisters at Work in the Old South," in Susanna Delfino and Michele Gillespie, eds., *Neither Lady nor Slave: Working Women in the Old South* (Chapel Hill: University of North Carolina Press, 2002), pp. 181–82.

11. TWO WEDDINGS

1. On Plunkett's background, see TIPP, pp. 137–38; EM to Sol, Nov. 25, 1825, MFP; and GM to EM, Oct. 19, 1826, MFP. On the affair, see Sol to EM, Nov. 11, 1813, MFP; Sol to EM, Feb. 14, 1814, LMFP; Sol to EM, Nov. 11, 1813, MFP; Sol to SM, Dec. 2, 1812, MFP; RM to SM, Feb. 27, 1814, PMP. For the quotation, see RM to SM, Sept. 19, 1814, PMP.

2. RM and JM to CM, Aug. 22, 1819, JMP; EM journal, July 18, 1819, and Jan. 15, 1820, MFP.

3. The scene is recounted in EM journal, Sept. 20, 1820, MFP. On Jacob's decision, see EM to Sol, Sept. 3, 1820, JMP; and RM to Sol, Sept. 7, 1820, JMP.

4. EM journal, May 10, 1820, MFP; RM to Sol, Sept. 7, 1820, JMP; JM to Achilles Plunkett, Sept. 26, 1820, MFP.

5. Caroline blamed Margaret Lane Mordecai for calling off the wedding in Raleigh simply because Achilles "was not rich. This with [the Lanes] is you know enough," she later told Ellen. She would never forgive Margaret or Moses for their "cruelty" (CMP to EM, Oct. 20, 1826, JMP). On the reversals, see RM to Sol, Dec. 14, 1820, JMP. On the marriage ceremony in Warrenton, see CMP to RM, Dec. 28, 1820, JMP.

6. RM to Sol, Sept. 7, 1820, JMP.

7. RM to Sol, Feb. 22, 1821, JMP; EM to CMP, March 30, 1821, MFP.

8. For the physical description of Aaron Lazarus, see Elizabeth McKoy, *Early Wilmington Block by Block, from 1733 On* (Wilmington, N.C., 1967), p. 106. On Esther's father, Gershon Cohen, see James William Hagy, *This Happy Land: The Jews of Colonial and Antebellum Charleston* (Tuscaloosa: University of Alabama Press, 1993), pp. 221, 165, 42, 66, 73. On Marks Lazarus, Aaron's father, see Charleston city directory for 1803, Charleston Library Society; and the Kahal Kadosh Beth Elohim ledgers (1799–1818) and offering books (1805–1815), Special Collections, College of Charleston. On Aaron's time in Wilmington, see *Wilmington Gazette*, Dec. 16, 1802, March 17, 1803, Jan. 3, 1809. For the record of AL's purchase of the lot for his house, see Lazarus-Divine House file, Historic Wilmington Foundation, Lower Cape Fear Historical Society Archives.

9. RM to Sol, July 27, 1817, MFP. Two of Aaron's younger sisters also attended the Mordecai School (TIPP, p. 218).

10. Rachel did think Aaron might seek Ellen's hand. See RM to EM, March 1, 1818, MFP; EM to Sol, March 11, 1818, JMP; Sol to EM, March 8, 1818, MFP.

11. RM and Sol to SM, Jan. 2, 1819, JMP.

12. EM journal, Aug. 13, 1820, MFP.

13. RM to Sol, Oct. 19 and Aug. 23, 1820, JMP.

14. RM to Sol, Oct. 19, 1820, JMP.

12. RELIGION, FAMILY, FORTUNE

1. Sol to EM, April 15, 1821, MFP; EM to Sol, April 19, 1821, JMP; William Barlow and David O. Powell, "A Dedicated Medical Student: Solomon Mordecai, 1819–1822," *Journal of the Early Republic* 7 (Winter 1987), pp. 385–93; Sol to EM, May 24, and June 6, 1821, MFP.

2. Dr. Joseph Parrish to JM, June 15, 1821, MFP; Sol to JM, June 27, 1821, MFP; Sol to EM, July 21, 1821, MFP; Sol to EM, July 28, 1821, JMP.

3. Sol to EM, July 28, 1821, JMP.

4. Sol to EM, Aug. 5, 1821, MFP; Anna Tennant to EM, Sept. 19 and Nov. 12, 1821, MFP.

5. Sol to SM, Sept. 1, 1821, MFP.

6. EM to Sol, Sept. 19, 1821, JMP. One European rabbi of the time, with whose work the Mordecais may have been familiar, stated bluntly that such conversions as the one Sol offered were inspired by "sordid interest" (Shalom ben Jacob Cohen, *Elements of Jewish Faith* [Philadelphia, 1820], p. 6).

7. Sol to EM, Oct. 17, 1821, MFP; Anna Tennant to EM, Jan. 20, 1822, MFP; Sol to EM, Sept. 24, 1821, JMP.

8. Anna Tennant to EM, Jan. 20, 1822, and Nov. 12, 1821, MFP; Sol to EM, Sept. 24, 1821, JMP.

9. Sol to EM, March 22, 1822, JMP; Sol to JM, March 8, 1822, JMP; EM to Sol, April 10, 1822, JMP.

10. John Harley Warner, "Medical Sectarianism, Therapeutic Conflict, and the Shaping of Orthodox Professional Identity in Antebellum American Medicine," in W. F. Bynum and Roy Porter, eds., *Medical Fringe and Medical Orthodoxy, 1750–1850* (London: Croom, Helm, 1987), pp. 239, 256 n. 17; GM to EM, March 18, 1824, MFP.

11. EM to Sol, Feb. 13, 1823, MFP. Daniel Haskel and J. Calvin Smith, *A Complete Descriptive and Statistical Gazetteer of the United States of America* (New York: Sherman & Smith, 1843), pp. 419, 568.

12. Clipping of wedding announcement in Monroe County, Ala., April 22, 1824, loose materials, EM journal, 1819–1820, MFP; Sol to SM, March 29, 1824, MFP; Sol to EM, March 26, 1824, JMP; Sol to EM, June 15, 1824, MFP.

13. Sol to EM, Jan. 14, 1821, and March 11 and March 3, 1823, MFP; EM to Sol, May 16, 1824, JMP, and May 7, 1824, MFP.

14. RM to SM, July 26, 1818, JMP; RML to CMP, Nov. 4, 1823, JMP; TIPP, pp. 108, 137 n. 72; EM to Sol, May 4, 1823, JMP; EM to Sol, Aug. 7, and May 14, 1823, MFP.

15. EM to Sol, May 14, 1823, MFP; Sol to EM, July 3, 1823, JMP; EM to Sol, July 3, 1823, JMP. After years of late payments to Jacob, Plunkett's partners, Andrews and Jones, fled Warrenton. Plunkett bought them out in the fall of 1822, but payments to the Mordecais remained in dispute.

16. Sol to EM, July 19, 1823, MFP; EM to Sol, July 24, 1823, JMP.

17. Sol to SM, March 29, 1824, JMP; EM to Sol, May 23, 1824, JMP; Sol to SM, June 15, 1824, MFP; Sol to JM, June 21, 1825, JMP.

18. Sol to EM, June 15, 1824, MFP.

19. RML to EM, May 20, 1824, MFP; EM to Sol, June 20, 1824, MFP; Sol to JM, July 15, 1824, MFP.

20. Sol to EM, June 15, 1824, MFP. Moses's wealth had entered realms that seemed stratospheric to other Mordecais. In 1820, as Sam faced a mountain of debt, Moses earned ten thousand dollars from his practice alone. To his income Moses could add the value of thousands of acres of land and dozens of slaves. In 1822, a client bequeathed to him eighty-five shares of U.S. Bank stock (worth about eighty-five hundred dollars), lands in Tennessee, and her interest in her brother's estate. On Moses, see EM to Sol, June 27, 1824, MFP.

21. Moses to JM, May 26, 1824, LMFP; Joseph Marx to SM, Sept. 9, 1824, JMP. On malaria's long-term effects, see K. David Patterson, "Disease Environments of the Antebellum South," in Ronald L. Numbers and Todd L. Savitt, eds., *Science and Medicine in the Old South* (Baton Rouge: Louisiana State University Press, 1989), pp. 160–61.

22. JM, "Discourse Delivered at the Consecration of the Hebrew Congregation Beth Shalome," last day of Elul 5582 [Sept. 15, 1821], MFP-AJHS, pp. 18–19, 31, 13, 6–7; *RJ*, pp. 36–37.

13. SOUTH AND NORTH

1. EM almanacs, 1823, 1825, 1826, 1828, LMFP; RML to EM, Jan. 23, 1825, MFP; EM to Sol, June 13, 1824, JMP; Sol to EM, July 26, 1828, June 15, 1824, and Nov. 9, 1826, MFP; EM to Sol, July 16, 1827, May 25, 1829, and July 4, 1830, JMP.

2. EM to Sol, July 16, 1827, and March 21, 1830, JMP; Sol to EM, Feb. 4, 1830, MFP; EM to Sol, Feb. 19, 1831, JMP. The length of Ellen's residence in Mobile was not determined at the time of her departure (see SM to EM, March 11, 1832, JMP).

3. EM to Sol, Feb. 21, 1830, JMP.

4. EM to Sol, Feb. 21 and July 4, 1830, JMP.

5. Penny L(eigh) Richards, " 'Could I But Mark Out My Own Map of Life': Educated Women Embracing Cartography in the Nineteenth-Century South," *Cartographica* (forthcoming); EM to Sol, April 5, 1831, JMP.

6. Extracts from Ellen in Julia to RML, May 9, 1831, MFP; and EM to Sol, March 21, 1831, JMP.

7. AM to EM, July 27, 1831, AMP. George Bancroft (1800–1891) and Joseph G. Cogswell (1786–1871) opened the school, modeled on the German gymnasium, in 1823. It closed in 1834. See James McLachlan, *American Boarding Schools: A Historical Study* (New York: Scribner, 1970), pp. 71–101.

8. EM II, *Gleanings from Long Ago* (1933; Raleigh, N.C.: Capital Area Preservation Inc., 1974), pp. 1–18, 62–63; CMP to EM, June 16, 1828, LMFP; CMP to EM, March 21, 1830, JMP; EM to SM, April 3, 1818, MFP.

9. AM to EM, Feb. 4, 1828, and May 16, 1831, AMP.

10. MMD [?], "A Tribute to the Memory of Uncle George," DFP; GM to EM, April 27, 1830, MFP; GM to Sol, Jan. 31, 1832, MFP.

11. "The Life of Alfred Mordecai: As Related by Himself," edited by James A. Padgett, *North Carolina Historical Review* 22 (1945), pp. 59–60, 73–89; AM to EM, Jan. 10, 1824, AMP; AM to [?], May 21, 1825, JMP; AM to RML, May 30, 1827; AM to EM, March 4, and Dec. 1, 1830, AMP.

12. "Life of Alfred Mordecai," p. 90; AM to EM, July 27, 1831, AMP.

13. "Life of Alfred Mordecai," p. 91; Walter H. Merrill, *Against Wind and Tide: A Biography of William Lloyd Garrison* (Cambridge, Mass.: Harvard University Press, 1963), pp. 41, 45, 48–49; Walter H. Merrill, ed., *I Will Be Heard, 1822–1835*, vol. 1 of *The Letters of William Lloyd Garrison* (Cambridge, Mass.: Harvard University Press, 1971), pp. 119–23. On Henry's slaves, see settlement, Jan. 15, 1841, GMP.

14. Merrill, *Against Wind and Tide*, p. 50; GM to JM, Sept. 2, 1831, GMP; SM to EM, Aug. 29, 1831, JMP.

15. RML to GM, Oct. 6, 1831, LMFP; also see RML to EM, Oct. 9, 1831, MFP.

16. *Cape Fear Recorder* report, in *Raleigh Register*, Sept. 29, 1831. MAC journal, Sept. 10, 1831, MACP. Also see Charles Edward Morris, "Panic and Reprisal: Reaction in North Carolina to the Nat Turner Insurrection, 1831," *North Carolina Historical Review* 62 (1985), pp. 38–41, 43–44; James Sprunt, *Tales and Traditions of the Lower Cape Fear, 1661–1896* (1896; Spartanburg, S.C.: Reprint Co., 1973), pp. 20–21; Lawrence Lee, *New Hanover County: A Brief History* (Raleigh, N.C.: State Department of Archives and History, 1971), pp. 55–56.

17. RML to EM, Oct. 9, 1831, MFP; MAC journal, Dec. 3, 1831, MACP; RML to JM, Nov. 13, 1831, JMP.

18. Eliza to EM, Oct. 18, 1831, MYFP.

14. RECEIVED LIKE A PROPHET IN ISRAEL

1. JM to RML, Oct. 30, 1831, JMP; GM to EM, Sept. 15, 1828, MFP; GM to EM, Dec. 12, 1829, MFP; EM to CMP, July 14, 1829, JMP; EM to Sol, July 5, 1829, JMP.

2. Newspaper clipping of advertisement for auction, June 10, 1831, JMP. GM to JM, July 24, 1831, GMP; Julia to EM, Aug. 14, 1831, MFP.

3. JM to RML, Oct. 30, 1831, JMP; Lance J. Sussman, *Isaac Leeser and the Making of American Judaism* (Detroit: Wayne State University Press, 1995), pp. 53, 55; *HJP*, pp. 118–21, 360–71; *RJ*, p. 49.

4. [?] to [Aunt Maria?], Oct. 23, 1831, RGP; JM to RML, Sept. 27, 1824, MFP.

5. AM to EM, Nov. 3, 1831, AMP. Jacob kept and used as a means of guiding doubting Jews his correspondence with the Episcopal priest Adam Empie, although it has not been located in the archives (RML to EM, Oct. 5, and Nov. 16, 1823, MFP; Benjamin Mears Myers to JM, Aug. 22, and Sept. 14, 1826, JMP). In the preface to his work *The Jews and the Mosaic Law* (1833; Philadelphia, 1834), p. v, Leeser expressed thanks to Jacob. For other written work, see JM, "Apologetics for [also referred to as "Remarks on"] the Old Testament," 2 vols., AJA; A Congregationalist of Richmond Virginia [JM], "Remarks on Harby's Discourse Delivered in Charleston (S.C.) on the 21st of November 1825 before the Reformed Society of Israelites on Their First Anniversary" (Jan. 1826), typescript, AJA; JM, "Remarks on Miss Martineau's Tract entitled Providence as manifested through Israel and on the Writings of the Reverend Alexander Keith entitled Evidence of the truth of the Christian Religion, derived from the literal Fulfilment of Prophecy, particularly as illustrated by the History of the Jews and by discoveries of recent travelers" (1836), AJA; [JM?], "On the Festivals, Games, and Amusements of the American Jews," copied by Emma or Julia Mordecai, n.d. Referred to in Mordecai correspondence but not found in the archives was JM's "Discourse" on creation and "the approaching day of atonement," delivered at Beth Shalome, c. 1824 (see JM to RML, Sept. 27, 1824, MFP).

6. JM to RML, Oct. 30, 1831, JMP. Barnard Jacobs's book, with Jacob's notes, is reprinted in Malcolm Stern, "Two Jewish Functionaries in Colonial Pennsylvania," *American Jewish Historical Quarterly* 57 (1967), pp. 24–51. Rebecca Gratz to Maria Gist Gratz, Feb. 16, 1832, HFP. On Jacob's private reasons for conducting his religious studies, see RMM to RML, Feb. 2, 1824, MFP.

7. JM to Raphael de Cordova, June 10, 1824, quoted in Sussman, *Isaac Leeser*, p. 49. Sussman claims Leeser as "the outstanding Jewish religious leader" of the antebellum era (*Isaac Leeser*, p. 12). For Jacob's relationship with the new immigrant, see Sussman, *Isaac Leeser*, pp. 40, 42–43; and *RJ*, pp. 49–53. Joseph Wolff, "On the Present State of the Jews," *London Quarterly Review* 8 (1828), p. 138. For Leeser's response, see *Constitutional Whig* (Richmond), Jan. 9, 1829, also reprinted in Leeser, *Jews and the Mosaic Law*. Also see Leeser's draft preface to *Jews and the Mosaic Law*, Monday 3 Nisan [April 6, 1829], with note addressed to JM, ILP.

8. Sussman, *Isaac Leeser*, pp. 55–71.

9. Thomas Lawson to JM, Sept. 30, 1831, JMP; Julia to EM, Oct. 16, 1831, MFP; AM to EM, Nov. 3, 1831, AMP; GM to JM, Nov. 15, 1829, CFP; RML to EM, Aug. 3, 1831, MFP; Sussman, *Isaac Leeser*, p. 40; RML to JM, Oct. 4, 1826, MFP; EM to Sol, Oct. 17, 1830, JMP; Julia to EM, July 22, 1824, MFP; JM to RML, Aug. 22, 1832, JMP; Julia to EM, Dec. 18, 1831, MFP; EM to RML, Aug. 19, 1831, JMP.

10. CMP to EM, June 30, 1824, JMP; AM to EM, April 24, 1824, AMP; RMM to RML, Jan. 16, 1825, MFP; RMM to CMP, Jan. 9, 1825, MFP.

11. On Caroline's stepchildren, see CMP to EM, Dec. 27, 1827, JMP. On Louisa, see CMP to EM, Jan. 20, 1828, JMP. For the struggling school, see CMP to EM, Aug. 10, 1829, JMP; and EM to CMP, Nov. 3, 1829, JMP. On Warrenton's economy, see CMP to EM, Nov. 21, 1828, JMP. On the neighbors' migration, see CMP to EM, Aug. 20, 1830, JMP. For George's tally of her accounts, see CMP to EM, Oct. 2, 1830, JMP. For her sense of the family's attitude, see CMP to EM, Feb. 21, 1830, JMP; EM to CMP, Feb. 14, 1830, JMP; and CMP to EM, Feb. 7, 1830, JMP.

12. Advertisement, *Cape Fear Recorder*, Jan. 18, 1832; GM to JM, April 16, 1832, GMP; RML to Lucy Ann Lippitt, June 2, 1832, LFP; RML to EM, June 27, 1832, MFP.

13. JM to CMP, June 17, 1834, MFP; CMP to EM, June 20, 1832, JMP. There is a gap in family correspondence in the early summer of 1832, suggesting that letters surrounding the tempest over Caroline's conversion were separated and/or destroyed. A year and a half later, Ellen asked Sol to destroy a letter she had written him describing the situation (Sol to EM, Dec. 8, 1833, JMP).

14. CMP to EM, June 20 and July 30, 1832, and July 20, 1833, JMP; Julia to EM, Dec. 9, 1832, JMP; CMP to EM, Feb. 10, 1843, LMFP; RML to EM, April 14, 1834, JMP. On Curtis, see Edmund Berkeley and Dorothy Smith Berkeley, *A Yankee Botanist in the Carolinas: The Reverend Moses Ashley Curtis, D.D. (1808–1872)* (Berlin: J. Cramer, 1986), pp. 37, 39, 45, 48.

15. RML to EM, April 14, 1834, JMP; Berkeley and Berkeley, *Yankee Botanist*, p. 39;

CMP to EM, July 30, 1833, JMP; GM to SM, Oct. 2, 1833, MFP. She was not at ease with anyone in the family (Emma to EM, Sept. 24, 1833, MFP; SM to GM, April 26, 1834, GMP; CMP to EM, April 1, 1834, JMP).

16. JM and RMM to CMP, June 17, 1834, MFP; *EJ*, vol. 12, pp. 485–92; Celia Moss, "The Two Pictures: Sketches of a Domestic Life," *Occident* 4 (1846), pp. 386, 435; GM to EM, June 12, 1833, MFP.

17. Baptisms of Ellen, Jacob, and Margaret Mordecai, May 5, 1833, parish register, Christ Church, Raleigh, N.C., NCDAH; GM to EM, June 12, 1833, MFP.

18. GM to EM, June 12, 1833, MFP.

19. AM to EM, April 7, 1832, AMP; CMP to EM, April 8, 1832, JMP; RML to EM, April 13, 1832, MFP; Emma to CMP, June 25, 1832, JMP; Henry and GM to EM II, Nov. 30, 1834, PMP; Henry to EM, Nov. 13, 1834, LMFP; AM to EM, Jan. 3, 1833, AMP; EM to Lelia Skipwith, Feb. 10, 1833, Skipwith Family Papers, Virginia Historical Society; GM to EM, April 25, 1833, MFP; EM to RML, Oct. 8, 1832, JMP. The Mordecais consulted the Philadelphia physician Dr. Philip Syng Physick (1768–1837), noted for his treatment of juvenile arthritis ("hip joint disease") by traction (*Dictionary of American Biography* [New York: Scribner, 1934], vol. 7, pp. 554–55).

15. RECONCILIATION

1. Mordecai and McKimmon advertisement, *Register and North Carolina Gazette* (Raleigh), May 14, 1833; GM to SM, Jan. 27, 1833, MFP; Augustus to SM, March 30, 1833, MFP. On Augustus's horse business, see Julia to EM, April 30, 1832, MFP; and Augustus to JM, Dec. 19, 1832, JMP. On Augustus's character, see Emma to EM, Dec. 2, 1833, MFP. On Emma's expectation of a social life, see Emma to EM, Sept. 24, 1833, MFP. On her character, see RML to EM, March 11, 1831, PMP. For the quotations, see Julia to Emma, Feb. 25, 1834, MFP; and MAC journal, Jan. 14, 1831, MACP.

2. Emma to EM, Sept. 24, 1833, MFP; Emma to EM, Jan. 5, 1834, PMP; Isaac Leeser, *The Jews and the Mosaic Law* (1833; Philadelphia, 1834), pp. v, x, 212.

3. RML to Eliza, Dec. 22, 1833, MFP; Emma to EM, March 21, 1834, PMP; RML to EM, April 25, 1831, JMP; Emma to EM, Oct. 1, 1834, PMP; William Grimes advertisement, *Star and North Carolina Gazette* (Raleigh), Nov. 15, 1833, and *Register and North Carolina Gazette* (Raleigh), Jan. 7, 1834; GM to SM, Jan. 15, 1834, MFP; Emma to EM, Jan. 26, 1834, MFP; GM to SM, Jan. 30, 1834, MFP; Sol to EM, Dec. 8, 1833, MFP; RML to EM, Feb. 2, 1832, MFP.

4. EM to Sol, July 27, 1828, JMP; Augustus to Emma, Feb. 27, 1834, MFP.

5. EM to Sol, May 8, 1823, JMP.

6. GM to SM, Jan. 15, 1834, MFP.

7. GM to JM, April 20, 1834, CFP.

8. SM to GM, April 26, 1834, GMP; EM to GM, Sept. 7, 1834, LMFP; Emma to EM, Oct. 1, 1834, PMP; Emma to EM, Aug. 19, 1836, MFP. Her niece Caroline Myers Cohen later judged that it may have been better that Emma remained single (*MHMF*, p. 53).

9. AM to CMP, Aug. 21, 1825, JMP; "The Life of Alfred Mordecai: As Related by

Himself," edited by James A. Padgett, *North Carolina Historical Review* 22 (1945), pp. 92–93; AM to EM, Aug. 15 and Oct. 2, 1832, AMP.

10. Alfred to EM, June 27, 1830, AMP. On the Thruston family and anti–Jackson and Van Buren politics, see J. Buckner Thruston to Robert Thruston Hubbard, April 8, 1840 (typescript copy), Filson Historical Society, Thruston Family File.

11. AM to EM, Nov. 13, 1832, AMP; Eliza to RML, Dec. 10, 1832, JMP. Alfred later said the judge never knew of his addresses to Jeannette because, conscious of his temper and affection for Alfred, Jeannette's mother feared he would be angry at Jeannette if he learned of the rejection (AM to EM, Feb. 6, 1833, AMP).

12. AM to EM, June 27 and March 17, 1830, AMP. Alfred had been ready to give "up all doubts and fears for the future in the fullness of a love which I have never yet permitted myself to indulge to the degree that I believe myself capable of" (AM to EM, Aug. 15, 1832, AMP; also see AM to EM, March 3, 1832, AMP).

13. AM to EM, Jan. 3, Feb. 22, and May 5, 1833, AMP. In 1832 Alfred had published a handbook on military law.

14. SM to EM, Oct. 6, 1833, March 22 and June 23, 1834, and Nov. 20, 1833, JMP.

15. SM to Sol, Aug. 13, 1821, JMP; SM to EM, May 6, 1814, JMP; CM to SM, Nov. 9, 1815, MFP; EM journal, Nov. 19, 1815, LMFP; SM to EM, Aug. 1, 1809, MFP. EM journal, Jan. 20, 1816, LMFP; RM to SM, Jan. 23, 1816, MFP; SM to EM, March 1, 1816, MFP; SM to RM, Sept. 27, 1818, JMP; EM journal, Dec. 31, 1816, LMFP; MM to SM, Feb. 9, 1817, JMP; RM to SM, Feb. 2, 1817, JMP; EM II to E. V. Valentine, April 6, 1909, E. V. Valentine Papers, Valentine Richmond History Center.

16. RML to EM, April 14, 1834, JMP; JM to CMP, June 17, 1834, MFP.

17. CMP to EM, April 1 and Aug. 12, 1834, JMP.

18. RML to EM, June 3, 1834, MFP.

16. SO MUCH TO ADMIRE AND TO LOVE

1. William H. Pease and Jane H. Pease, *The Web of Progress: Private Values and Public Styles in Boston and Charleston* (New York: Oxford University Press, 1985), pp. 122–25, 17–20, 221.

2. EM to Sol, Nov. 23, 1820, JMP; RM to ME, Aug. 7, 1815, *EOTH*, p. 6; Karen Lystra, *Searching the Heart: Women, Men, and Romantic Love in Nineteenth-Century America* (New York: Oxford University Press, 1989), p. 123.

3. James Sprunt, *Tales and Traditions of the Lower Cape Fear, 1661–1896* (1896; Spartanburg, S.C.: Reprint Co., 1973), pp. 13–14; Alan D. Watson, *Wilmington: Port of North Carolina* (Columbia: University of South Carolina Press, 1992), pp. 68, 453–54; Lawrence Lee, *New Hanover County: A Brief History* (Raleigh, N.C.: State Department of Archives and History, 1971), pp. 34, 37–38; Lazarus-Divine House file, Historic Wilmington Foundation, Lower Cape Fear Historical Society; Elizabeth McKoy, *Early Wilmington Block by Block, from 1733 On* (Wilmington, N.C., 1967), p. 106; MAC journal, Oct. 23 and 24, 1830, MACP; JM to RML, April 26, 1821, MFP; *Cape Fear Recorder* (Wilmington), April 14, 1821; RML to EM, Nov. 8, 1821, MFP.

4. RML to EM, June 13, 1823, MFP; SM to Sol, Dec. 16, 1821, MFP; JM to RML, June 6, 1821, MFP; EM to Sol, Nov. 8, 1821, JMP; RML to EM, Nov. 22, 1821, MFP; *Cape Fear Recorder*, Dec. 8, 1821. Unfortunately, Aaron's mercantile correspondence with his brothers-in-law Sam and George Mordecai has not remained in the family collections, although it is referred to (for example, in SM to EM, Jan. 21, 1824, JMP; and RML to EM, July 16, 1824, MFP). Aaron had considered leaving Wilmington in 1818 (advertisement for rental of house and warehouses, *Cape Fear Recorder*, Sept. 19–Nov. 21, 1818). Prices were dropping for the goods Aaron shipped (market quotations, *Cape Fear Recorder*, Nov. 28, 1818, and April 14, 1821).

Aaron's arrival in Wilmington is dated between 1795 and 1802, while he was in his twenties (David J. Goldberg, "An Historical Community Study of Wilmington Jewry, 1738–1925" [paper, University of North Carolina–Chapel Hill, 1976], p. 9; Lazarus-Divine House file, Historic Wilmington Foundation); "New Hanover County, North Carolina, Tax Lists, 1815 & 1845," NCDAH, p. 6; *Cape Fear Recorder*, Sept. 19, 1818; Raymond Parker Fouts, "Abstracts from Newspapers of Wilmington, North Carolina, 1801–1803," vol. 3, p. 74, NCDAH; Raymond Parker Fouts, "Abstracts from Newspapers of Wilmington, North Carolina, 1807–1810 . . . ," vol. 5, pp. 19, 53, 62, 66, 67, NCDAH. On the lumber and naval-stores industry, see Watson, *Wilmington*, pp. 12–13; and Robert B. Outland III, "Suicidal Harvest: The Self-Destruction of North Carolina's Naval Stores Industry," *North Carolina Historical Review* 78 (2001), pp. 309–34. On Aaron's recovery of his fortune, see EM to Sol, Sept. 4, 1823, JMP; *Cape Fear Recorder*, April 13, 1825; RML to EM, Jan. 3 and Aug. 16, 1826, MFP.

5. RML to EM, May 21 and Oct. 14, 1821, MFP; RML and Eliza to EM, June 10, 1821, MFP; RML to EM, Aug. 1 and June 6, 1821, MFP; RML to EM, May 25, 1823, JMP; Sol to EM, May 10, 1825, MFP; RML to EM, Nov. 8, 1821, MFP.

6. Lazarus-Divine House file, Historic Wilmington Foundation; Tony P. Wrenn, *Wilmington, North Carolina: An Architectural and Historical Portrait* (Charlottesville: University Press of Virginia and the Junior League of Wilmington, 1984), pp. 170–71; Eliza to EM, Nov. 3, 1822, MFP; RML to CMP, Oct. 7, 1821, JMP; and RML to EM, April 20, 1823, MFP.

7. RML to EM, Oct. 14, 1821, MFP; also see RML to EM, June 24, 1821, MFP.

8. RML to EM, June 24, 1821, MFP; RML to Sol, June 28, 1821, PMP; RML to EM, Aug. 1, May 21, and May 28, 1821, MFP; RML to ME, Sept. 16, 1821, *EOTH*, p. 27; RML to EM, Oct. 3, 1824, JMP.

9. AL to Sol, Oct. 3, 1821, JMP.

10. RML to EM, Oct. 14, 1821, MFP. Also see RML to EM, Oct. 6, 1822, Aug. 1, 1821, and Dec. 17, 1827, MFP. Richard C. Wade, *Slavery in the Cities, 1820–1860* (New York: Oxford University Press, 1964), pp. 28–42.

11. RML to EM, June 23, 1822, MFP.

12. RML to EM, n.d. [c. fall 1821], MFP; RML to Lucy Ann Lippitt, Oct. 26, 1828, MFP.

13. RML to EM, Feb. 3, 1822, MFP; AL to Sol, Feb. 6, 1822, JMP; Julia to CMP, June 3, 1822, JMP.

14. RML to CMP, Feb. 24 and March 24, 1822, JMP; AL to JM, July 28, 1822, JMP.

17. A PEW AT ST. JAMES

1. E. B. Kennon to RML, fragment, n.d. [c. 1822], and fragment, Aug. 16, 1823, KFP; RML to CMP, May 16, 1821, MFP; RML to EM, May 4, 1823, MFP.

2. Richard Rankin, *Ambivalent Churchmen and Evangelical Churchwomen: The Religion of the Episcopal Elite in North Carolina, 1800–1860* (Columbia: University of South Carolina Press, 1993), pp. 57–59; Joseph Blount Cheshire, "Decay or Revival," in *Sketches of Church History in North Carolina* (Wilmington, N.C.: William Lord DeRossett, 1892), pp. 243–78.

3. EM to Sol, Feb. 12, 1818, JMP; Julia to EM, Feb. 22, 1818, MPF; EM to SM, Feb. 25, 1818, JMP; RML to EM, May 4, 1823, MFP.

4. Rankin, *Ambivalent Churchmen*, p. 55; Leora Hiatt McEachern, *History of St. James Parish, 1729–1979* (Wilmington, N.C., 1983), p. 70; Ida Brooks Kellam and Elizabeth Frances McKoy, *St. James Church Historical Records* (Wilmington, N.C., 1965), vol. 1, pp. 35–36; AL to the Reverend Richard C. Moore, July 1, 1823, JMP.

5. Tony P. Wrenn, *Wilmington, North Carolina: An Architectural and Historical Portrait* (Charlottesville: University Press of Virginia and the Junior League of Wilmington, 1984), p. 171; David J. Goldberg, "An Historical Community Study of Wilmington Jewry, 1738–1925" (paper, University of North Carolina–Chapel Hill, 1976), p. 13; RML to EM, June 29, 1823, MFP; RML to EM, Oct. 7, 1821, JMP; Jacob Rader Marcus, *United States Jewry, 1776–1985* (Detroit: Wayne State University Press, 1989), vol. 4, p. 618; RML to EM, April 26, 1823, MFP.

Aaron's lax fulfillment of domestic religious rituals was not unusual; indeed, it indicates a shift in Jewish history in which responsibility for religious practices increasingly fell to women. See Dianne Ashton, "Rebecca Gratz and the Domestication of American Judaism" (Ph.D. diss., Temple University, 1986), pp. 59–61; and, for women's roles in a different setting, Marion A. Kaplan, "Priestess and Housefrau: Women and Tradition in the German-Jewish Family," in Paula Hyman and David Cohen, eds., *The Jewish Family: Myths and Reality* (New York: Holmes and Meier, 1986), pp. 62–93.

6. RML to EM, June 29, 1823, and Nov. 22, 1821, MFP.

7. RML to EM, Dec. 1, 1822, and Jan. 5, 1823, MFP. The correspondence between Empie and Jacob was not found in the family papers. References to it are in SM to RM, Nov. 21, 1813, JMP; RM to EM, March 20, 1814, MFP; RM to SM, April 24, 1814, MFP.

8. RML to JM, March 24, 1823, JMP; William S. Simpson to Mrs. T. Scales, March 11, 1823, William S. Simpson Papers, LV; *Israel's Advocate* 1 (March 1823), p. 48, and 1 (July 1823), p. 114; Jonathan D. Sarna, "The American Jewish Response to Nineteenth-Century Christian Missions," *Journal of American History* 68 (1981), p. 37; Todd Endelman, *Radical Assimilation in English Jewish History, 1695–1945* (Blooming-

ton: Indiana University Press, 1990), p. 148; Lee M. Friedman, *Early American Jews* (Cambridge, Mass.: Harvard University Press, 1934), pp. 96–112, esp. p. 107; Mark Eisen, "Christian Missions to the Jews in North America and Great Britain," *Jewish Social Studies* 10 (1948), p. 65; Mel Scult, *Millennial Expectations and Jewish Liberties: A Study of the Effort to Convert the Jews in Britain, up to the Mid-nineteenth Century* (Leiden: E. J. Brill, 1978), p. 38.

9. RML to EM, May 25, 1823, JMP.

10. RML to EM, May 9 and January 5, 1823, MFP; RML to EM, May 25, 1823, JMP.

11. RML to EM, May 25, 1823, JMP; Rankin, *Ambivalent Churchmen*, p. 56.

12. RML to EM, May 25, 1823, JMP; AL to the Right Reverend Richard C. Moore, bishop of the Episcopal Church of Virginia, July 1, 1823, JMP.

13. Ibid.

14. AL to the Right Reverend Richard C. Moore, bishop of the Episcopal Church of Virginia, July 1, 1823, JMP; EM to Sol, July 24, 1823, JMP; Gershon Lazarus to Phila Calder, Nov. 15, 1846, Lazarus-Calder Records, Lower Cape Fear Historical Society.

18. NOT EXACTLY AS SHE MOST WISHED

1. RML to EM, Nov. 16, 1823, MFP. St. James's surviving records are incomplete, but Aaron Lazarus does not appear in those that remain for the period after 1823.

2. RML to ME, June 6, 1825, *EOTH*, p. 83; RML to EM, April 16, 1827, MFP.

3. RML to EM, Aug. 3 and April 26, 1823, MFP. For criticism of other mothers, see RML to EM, Sept. 14 and April 20, 1823, MFP; RML to RMM, Dec. 4, 1824, JMP.

4. See, for instance, Leo Baeck, *The Essence of Judaism* (New York: Schocken Books, 1948), pp. 37, 205, 265; and Dianne Ashton, *Rebecca Gratz: Women and Judaism in Antebellum America* (Detroit: Wayne State University Press, 1997), p. 91. While such Jewish traditions were a part of Rachel's ethical and religious upbringing, she and many of her siblings typically did not experience them as explicitly Jewish. A different emphasis can be seen in *WOW*, p. xv, which places Rachel's writing in the tradition of orthodox "wisdom literature."

5. The impact of the Enlightenment on gender relations and women deserves greater exploration. Key texts for beginning such an exploration include Dorinda Outram, *The Enlightenment* (New York: Cambridge University Press, 1995); Henry F. May, *The Enlightenment in America* (New York: Oxford University Press, 1976); Peter Gay, *The Rise of Modern Paganism*, vol. 1 of *The Enlightenment: An Interpretation* (New York: Knopf, 1967); Donald Meyer, *The Instructed Conscience: The Shaping of the American National Ethic* (Philadelphia: University of Pennsylvania Press, 1972); and Mary Wollstonecraft, *A Vindication of the Rights of Woman* (1792; New York: Norton, 1975).

6. See, for instance, the discussion of false associations in Carol Strauss-Sotiropoulos, "Where Words Fail: Rational Education Unravels in Maria Edgeworth's *The Good French Governess*," University of Connecticut, on-line at http://web.nwe. ufl.edu/los/csotiropoulos.html.

7. Barbara M. Solomon, *In the Company of Educated Women: A History of Women in Higher Education in America* (Boston: Houghton-Mifflin, 1979), pp. 14–16.

8. In terms of women's potential role in the middle-class family's goals of intimacy, virtuous behavior, and respectability, enlightened domesticity is related to but considerably broader than Republican Motherhood and Moral Motherhood, the two predominant ideological models historians have advanced to describe late-eighteenth- and early-nineteenth-century middle-class and elite American women's roles. The ideal the Mordecais and Rachel embraced reflected the movement toward companionate marriage that gained popularity throughout the nineteenth century. "Republican Motherhood" is Linda Kerber's term for the set of ideas that gave women a vicarious, semipolitical identity in the early Republic by making the education of virtuous American citizens a patriotic vocation for mothers. Ruth Bloch's construct of Moral Motherhood combines evangelical notions of essential female morality, which sanctioned sentiment and piety, with women's expanded roles as educators of children. Moral Motherhood describes an interesting link between new notions of women's moral virtue, child rearing, and an emergent sentimental Victorian domesticity. Whereas Bloch argued that Moral Motherhood challenged patriarchal intellectual and rational authority, Kerber credits republican ideology with improvements in female education, which women could not, however, readily translate into political gains. Enlightened domesticity fuses the rationalism and intellectual roots of Republican Motherhood with Bloch's concept that in assuming responsibility for children's education, women redefined domestic roles—all during a period in which Enlightenment concepts of cognitive development made nurture and education central cultural concerns. I suggest that Kerber's and Bloch's constructs depend on an underlying ideal of enlightened domesticity, which established women's intellectual authority yet cast its operation within the domestic sphere. Broader than the politically focused Republican Motherhood, and more intellectually oriented than Moral Motherhood or later constructs such as True Womanhood and the Cult of Domesticity, domestic enlightenment envisioned a less gendered world in which feeling and intellect could meet in the home to create true community. In addition, enlightened domesticity is more weighted toward reason and the concerns of this world than the nineteenth-century evangelical domesticity popularized by Hannah More and highly sentimentalized in popular books and magazines by mid-century. Enlightened domesticity was limited as a strategy for women's authority because women lacked effective birth control and because it relied on patriarchal benevolence, shortcomings that emerge in the story of the Mordecai family and from other families where the ideal is in evidence.

In the Mordecais' case, the clearest model for enlightened domesticity came from the landed family of Maria Edgeworth as reflected in their writings. See Marilyn Butler, *Maria Edgeworth: A Literary Biography* (Oxford: Clarendon Press, 1972). For evidence of the appeal of enlightened domesticity elsewhere, see, for instance, Mary Kelley, "Reading Women/Women Reading: The Making of Learned Women in

Antebellum America," *Journal of American History* 183 (1996), pp. 401–24; Lucia Mc-Mahon and Deborah Schriver, eds., *To Read My Heart: The Journal of Rachel Van Dyke, 1810–1811* (Philadelphia: University of Pennsylvania Press, 2000); Anya Jabour, " 'Grown Girls, Highly Cultivated': Female Education in an Antebellum Southern Family," *Journal of Southern History* 64 (1998), pp. 23–64; Anya Jabour, *Marriage in the Early Republic: Elizabeth and William Wirt and the Companionate Ideal* (Baltimore: Johns Hopkins University Press, 1998); Edith B. Gelles, *Portia: The World of Abigail Adams* (Bloomington: Indiana University Press, 1992); Mary Kelley, ed., *The Power of Her Sympathy: The Autobiography and Journals of Catharine Maria Sedgwick* (Boston: Massachusetts Historical Society, 1993); Marilyn S. Blackwell, "The Republican Vision of Mary Palmer Tyler," *Journal of the Early Republic* 12 (1992), pp. 11–35; Marie Marmo Mullaney, "Feminism, Utopianism, and Domesticity: The Career of Rebecca Buffum Spring, 1811–1911," *New Jersey History* 104 (1986), pp. 1–21; Patricia Ann Carlson, "Sarah Alden Ripley, Emerson's *Other* Aunt," *American Transcendental Quarterly* 40 (1978), pp. 309–21; Frances W. Knickerbocker, "New England Seeker: Sarah Bradford Ripley," *New England Quarterly* 30 (1957), pp. 3–22.

9. Rachel's ideology pushed her role as an educator within the family considerably beyond the nineteenth-century stereotype of the pious mother inculcating morals in her children. For an interesting glimpse of how and why such teaching may be overlooked in the historical literature, see Jan Lewis, "Mothers as Teachers: Reconceptualizing the Role of the Family as Educator," in William J. Weston, ed., *Education and the American Family: A Research Synthesis* (New York: New York University Press, 1989), pp. 122–37.

10. RML to ME, Dec. 20, 1823, *EOTH*, p. 106; RML to CMP, April 6, 1823, JMP.

11. RML to EM, April 29, 1823, MFP; RML to EM, Sept. 7, 1823, JMP; RML to CM, Nov. 11, 1822, MFP.

12. RML to CMP, Nov. 11, 1822, MFP. Rachel nursed Marx longer than Aaron wanted her to, perhaps because she hoped that breast-feeding would prevent another pregnancy (RML to EM, Dec. 15, 1822, MFP). On her intellectual frustration, see RML to EM, Oct. 5, Nov. 22, and Dec. 13, 1823, MFP. The broad range of her reading is evident throughout the family papers and receives special notice in her correspondence with Maria Edgeworth.

13. RML to EM, Feb. 3 and Feb. 27, 1825, JMP; Julia to GM, Aug. 4, 1823, LMFP.

14. Lawrence Lee, *New Hanover County: A Brief History* (Raleigh, N.C.: State Department of Archives and History, 1971), p. 57; RML to EM, May 4, 1823, MFP; Lawrence Lee, *The History of Brunswick County, North Carolina* (Bolivia, N.C.: Brunswick Co., 1980).

15. EM to Sol, April 27, May 8, July 12, July 24, Aug. 8, and Sept. 28, 1825, JMP; RML to ME, Oct. 4, 1825, *EOTH*, p. 92.

16. RML to EM, April 17, 1826, MFP; AL and RML to JM, Sept. 24, 1826, JMP; RML to ME, June 24, 1827, *EOTH*, p. 133; RML to EM, Nov. 22 and April 2, 1826, MFP. Also see RML to EM, April 16, 1827, MFP.

17. RML to ME, June 24, 1827, *EOTH*, p. 133.

18. Ibid., p. 132.

19. ME to RML, April 9, 1824, and May 2, 1825, *EOTH*, pp. 59, 72; RML to ME, July 17, 1824, *EOTH*, p. 63.

20. RML to ME, July 29, 1822, *EOTH*, p. 32; ME to RML, Sept. 30, 1823, and April 9, 1824, *EOTH*, pp. 40, 51; RML to ME, July 17, 1824, *EOTH*, p. 61.

21. RML to ME, July 20, 1826, *EOTH*, pp. 105–6; Maria Edgeworth, *Harry and Lucy Concluded* (London: Baldwin, Cradock, and Joy, 1825), vol. 3, pp. 287–99.

19. OUR RELIGIOUS EXERCISES

1. RML to EM, Aug. 16 and June 18, 1826, MFP. Elisabeth Donaghy Garrett, *At Home: The American Family, 1750–1870* (New York: Harry N. Abrams, 1990), pp. 35, 74–75, 114–16, 138.

2. The family was pleased by the "likeness" of John Wesley Jarvis's production (EM to Sol, May 21, 1826, MFP; and RML to JM, July 10, 1826, MFP).

3. RML to JM, July 10, 1826, MFP.

4. James William Hagy, *This Happy Land: The Jews of Colonial and Antebellum Charleston* (Tuscaloosa: University of Alabama Press, 1993), pp. 129–30, 134; Gary Philip Zola, *Isaac Harby of Charleston, 1788–1828: Jewish Reformer and Intellectual* (Tuscaloosa: University of Alabama Press, 1994), pp. 124–25.

5. The Jewish response to the American model of public and benevolent displays of piety is evident from the life of Rebecca Gratz and the involvement of Jewish women in the life of the synagogue in the later nineteenth and the twentieth century (Dianne Ashton, *Rebecca Gratz: Women and Judaism in Antebellum America* [Detroit: Wayne State University Press, 1997]; and Karla Goldman, *Beyond the Synagogue Gallery: Finding a Place for Women in American Judaism* [Cambridge, Mass.: Harvard University Press, 2000]).

6. AM to RML, Sept. 14, 1823, AMP.

7. AL to the Right Reverend Richard C. Moore, July 1, 1823, JMP; RML to EM, Sept. 14, 1823, MFP.

8. RML to EM, Nov. 8, 1823, JMP; RML to EM, Nov. 22, 1823, MFP; RML to JM, Oct. 10, 1824, MFP. She cited Psalm 42:1–2, King James Version.

9. RML to JM, Oct. 10, 1824, MFP.

10. Sol to EM, Sept. 24, 1820, MFP. Even sober Julia (her mental instability had eased considerably by 1824) admitted her distaste for the strange rituals observed at her Myers grandmother's death (Julia to EM, July 22, 1824, MFP). Whether and how Reform Judaism affected Jewish assimilation has stirred much debate. See Jacob Rader Marcus, *United States Jewry, 1776–1985* (Detroit: Wayne State University Press, 1989), vol. 1, pp. 614–37; Todd Endelman, *The Jews of Georgian England, 1714–1830* (Philadelphia: Jewish Publication Society of America, 1979), pp. 160–65; Todd Endelman, *Radical Assimilation in English Jewish History, 1695–1945* (Bloomington: Indiana University Press, 1990), pp. 52–54; and David Sorkin, *The Transformation of German Jewry, 1780–1840* (New York: Oxford University Press, 1987), p. 160.

11. "Memorial [Petition] to the President and members of the Adjunta of Kahal Kadosh Beth Elohim of Charleston, South Carolina [Dec. 1824]," quoted in Hagy, *This Happy Land*, pp. 129, 131; Isaac Harby, "A Discourse delivered in Charleston (S.C.) on the 21st of November 1825 . . . ," quoted in Zola, *Isaac Harby*, pp. 125, 113; "Memorial," quoted in Samuel Gilman, "Harby's Discourse on the Jewish Synagogue," *North American Review* 23 (1826), pp. 71, 69. The full "Memorial" (1824) is reprinted in Barnett A. Elzas, *The Reformed Society of Israelites of Charleston, S.C.,* . . . (New York: Bloch Publishing, 1916).

12. RML to JM, Dec. 19, 1824, JMP; [JM], "Remarks on Harby's Discourse Delivered in Charleston (S.C.) on the 21st of November 1825 before the Reformed Society of Israelites on Their First Anniversary" (Jan. 1826), typescript, AJA.

13. Hagy, *This Happy Land*, pp. 132, 154; AL and RML to JM, Dec. 25, 1826, JMP; Zola, *Isaac Harby*, p. 124; Gilman, "Harby's Discourse," p. 68; [JM], "Remarks on Harby's Discourse," pp. 1, 7; JM to RML, July 2, 1826, MFP.

14. Gilman, "Harby's Discourse," pp. 67–68; Hagy, *This Happy Land*, pp. 152, 154; Zola, *Isaac Harby*, p. 136.

15. RM to ME, Aug. 7, 1815, *EOTH*, p. 4; [JM], "Remarks on Harby's Discourse," pp. 2, 15, 13; AL and RML to JM, Sept. 24, 1826, JMP; RML to JM, Oct. 4, 1826, MFP. Also see Benjamin Mears Myers to JM, Aug. 22 and Sept. 14, 1826, JMP. Jacob's discourse was probably never published. Further consultation by Aaron and Rachel with Jews in Charleston led them to strongly recommend "a more limited circulation" on the grounds that publication would "rather gratify" the reformers. Rachel added that if it were to be printed, all negative comments about Christianity or the American government should be excised (AL and RML to JM, Jan. 8, 1827, private collection of Dr. Richard Weiner, Durham, N.C.).

20. CHRISTIAN FRIENDSHIP

1. AL to SM, Dec. 16, 1826, MFP; RML to EM, May 2, 1829, and July 30, 1828, MFP. The subject of Judaism had dropped almost completely from Rachel and Maria's correspondence by the mid-1820s (RML to EM, Jan. 18, 1824, and Nov. 16 and Oct. 5, 1823, MFP). The interweaving of religious and social life in Wilmington is evident from such letters as RML to EM, April 17, 1826, and Jan. 9, 1828, MFP.

2. Daniel Beckwith, *The Lippitt Family of Rhode Island* (Providence, 1873), p. 3; James N. Arnold, *Vital Records of Rhode Island, 1636–1850* (Providence: Narragansett Historical Publishing Co., 1891), pp. 78, 232; RML to EM, March 26, 1827, JMP; RML to EM, April 16, 1827, MFP.

3. "St. James Church History," pp. 2–3, DRFP; Leora Hiatt McEachern, *History of St. James Parish, 1729–1979* (Wilmington, N.C., 1983), p. 41; Ann Hill to Catherine "Kitty" DeRosset, Aug. 6, 1817, DRFP.

4. Two of the chief influences in Rachel's religious life in the late 1820s and early 1830s were Jane Dickinson and Catherine DeRosset. For a sense of their spiritual tracks, see RML to EM, May 7, 1828, MFP; CDR to Elizabeth Fullerton, July 28, 1820,

WLDP; CDR diary, June 18–Sept. 10, 1798, DRFP; CDR to John DeRosset, Jan. 1, 1823, DRFP. Joseph Crool, *The Restoration of Israel* (London: B. R. Goakman, 1814); RML to EM, April 16, 1827, MFP.

5. RML to EM, April 16, 1827, MFP. On Crool, see Todd Endelman, *The Jews of Georgian England, 1714–1830* (Philadelphia: Jewish Publication Society of America, 1979), p. 280. Alfred Mordecai read Scott's "Notes on the Bible" (Thomas Scott, *The Holy Bible, containing the Old and New Testaments, with original notes . . .* [1804–1809]) at West Point, having found his knowledge of Scripture embarrassingly inadequate (AM to EM, Oct. 24, 1823, AMP). Scott's sermon "The Jews a blessing to the nations, and Christians bound to seek their conversion to the Saviour" had appeared in 1810.

6. RML to EM, Feb. 11, 1828, and Nov. 26, 1827, MFP; RML to EM, March 3, 1828, JMP; "The Life of Alfred Mordecai: As Related by Himself," edited by James A. Padgett, *North Carolina Historical Review* 22 (1945), p. 86.

7. JM, miscellaneous apologetics, AJA; Alexander V. Griswold to Lucy Ann Lippitt, March 19, 1828, MFP. The disputed passage was Zech. 8:23.

8. TIPP, pp. 210–11; James Sprunt, *Tales and Traditions of the Lower Cape Fear, 1661–1896* (1896; Spartanburg, S.C.: Reprint Co., 1973), app. 3; RM to Sol, Nov. 1, 1820, JMP; RML to CMP, May 17, 1821, MFP; RML to RMM, Jan. 13, 1822, JMP; Phila Lazarus to EM, July 14, 1822, MFP; RML to CMP, Nov. 4, 1823, JMP; RML to EM, March 19, 1826, MFP; RML to EM, March 3 and April 13, 1828, JMP; RML to EM, May 7, 1828, MFP.

9. RML to EM, May 7, 1828, MFP; Harold Newman, *An Illustrated Dictionary of Jewelry* (London: Thames and Hudson, 1981), p. 208; Martha Pike, "In Memory Of: Artifacts Relating to Mourning in Nineteenth Century America," in Ray B. Browne, ed., *Rituals and Ceremonies in Popular Culture* (Bowling Green, Ohio: Bowling Green University Popular Press, 1980).

10. RM to EM, May 7, 1828, MFP. Rachel was then five months pregnant. Deathbed scenes became a highly stylized aspect of Victorian-era Christianity, integrating evangelical concerns about salvation into a sentimental culture where death came often and early.

21. THE VALLEY OF THE SHADOW OF DEATH

1. Eliza to CMP, May 30, 1828, JMP; RML to EM, June 9, 1828, MFP; GM to RM, June 1, 1828, JMP; RML to EM, Aug. 13, 1828, MFP.

2. RML to EM, June 9, 1828, MFP; Mary Orme (for RML) to EM, Sept. 26, 1828, MFP; RML to EM, Oct. 13, 1828, JMP.

3. AL to JM, Sept. 12, 1828, MFP; Anna Lazarus to EM, Sept. 24, 1828, MFP; Anna Lazarus to EM, Sept. 21, 1828, JMP; RML to EM, Oct. 13, 1818, JMP. See Sally McMillan, *Motherhood in the Old South: Pregnancy, Childbirth, and Infant Rearing* (Baton Rouge: Louisiana State University Press, 1990), pp. 48–50 119–20, 125–26; Judith Walker Leavitt, *Brought to Bed: Childbearing in America, 1750–1950* (New York: Oxford University Press, 1986); and Richard W. Wertz and Dorothy C. Wertz, *Lying In: A History of Childbirth in America* (New York: Free Press, 1977).

4. RML to EM, Oct. 13, 1828, JMP; AL to EM, Oct. 10, 1828, MFP. Rachel's disease closely followed the typical malarial cycle: onset of symptoms in the first week, a degree of improvement in the second week, and a "crisis" in the third week.

5. RML to EM, Oct. 13, 1828, JMP; Mary Orme (for RML) to EM, Sept. 26, 1828, MFP; CDR daybook, May 31, 1817, MACP.

6. RML to EM, Oct. 13, 1828, JMP. On Catherine's piety, see Richard Rankin, *Ambivalent Churchmen and Evangelical Churchwomen: The Religion of the Episcopal Elite in North Carolina, 1800–1860* (Columbia: University of South Carolina Press, 1993), pp. 42–43, 45, 102; CDR to Elizabeth Fullerton, July 28, 1820, WLDP; obituary, *Wilmington Advertiser*, March 17, 1837; CDR commonplace book, 1819, MACP.

7. RML to Lucy Ann Lippitt, Oct. 26, 1828, MFP. On the bonds formed between women during childbirth, see Leavitt, *Brought to Bed*, pp. 95–98.

8. RML to ME, June 24, 1827, *EOTH*, p. 132; Eliza Hassell to CDR, Aug. 26, 1826, DRFP.

9. "The Morning Star," poem from or by Lucy Ann Lippitt, Eliza Ann DeRosset notebook, DRFP; RML to Lucy Ann Lippitt, Oct. 26, 1828, MFP.

10. AL to EM, Oct. 10, 1828, MFP; AL to EM, Oct. 13, 1828, JMP; RML to EM, Oct. 20 and Nov. 6, 1828, MFP; Mary Orme (for RML) to EM, Sept. 26, 1828, MFP.

11. RML to SM, Sept. 7, 1822, JMP; RML to GM, Oct. 6, 1831, PMP; editorial, *Cape Fear Recorder*, April 11, 1827; Lazarus and Whitmarsh advertisement, *Cape Fear Recorder*, July 22, 1829, and July 21, 1830; editorial, *People's Press and Wilmington Advertiser*, Nov. 11, 1834; RML to EM, Nov. 16, 1834, MFP; Harry L. Watson, *Jacksonian Politics and Community Conflict: The Emergence of the Second American Party System in Cumberland County, North Carolina* (Baton Rouge: Louisiana State University Press, 1981), pp. 45–48. For Aaron's real estate holdings, see New Hanover County tax lists, 1817, 1836, NCDAH.

12. RML to EM, May 2, 1829, and Nov. 6, 1828, MFP; Almira Lazarus to EM, Dec. 13, 1829, JMP; RML to EM, July 8, Dec. 23, and Nov. 23, 1829, MFP.

13. Until the 1860s, medical experts believed that a woman's fertile period occurred just before and just after menstruation (McMillan, *Motherhood in the Old South*, p. 31). Birth-control products and abortifacients began to be marketed in the 1830s. Coitus interruptus was probably the most common means of controlling fertility in Rachel's time. See Janet Farrell Brodie, *Contraception and Abortion in Nineteenth-Century America* (Ithaca, N.Y.: Cornell University Press, 1994), pp. 28, 35–37, 44. Eliza to CMP, March 21, 1830, JMP; RML to CMP, March 21, 1830, JMP. On Myers, see *MHMF*, p. 46; and Slowey Hays to Rebecca Gratz, Aug. 19, 1813, GFP.

14. RML to SM, July 1, 1832, JMP; RML to EM, Feb. 13, 1830, July 21, 1832, and April 4, March 24, and July 13, 1830, MFP. Marx's reference was to Maria Elizabeth Budden, *A Key to Knowledge; or, Things in Common Use Simply and Shortly Explained in a Series of Dialogues* (1814), a book Rachel used in her teaching.

15. RML to EM, Nov. 26, 1828, Feb. 15, 1830, and Oct. 29, 1826, MFP; SM to EM,

June 15, 1830, JMP; RML to EM, July 12, 1830, MFP; EM to CMP, July 14, 1830, JMP; RML to EM, Oct. 4, 1830, MFP.

16. RML to EM, Oct. 4, 1830, MFP; EM to RML, Aug. 19, 1831, JMP; RML to EM, Sept. 11 and Oct. 9, 1831, MFP.

17. Julia to EM, Nov. 25, 1832, PMP.

18. RML to EM, Jan. 10, 1833, MFP. Five steam-driven lumber mills were already operating in Wilmington (editorial, *People's Press and Wilmington Advertiser,* June 18, 1834).

22. DEVOURING FLAMES

1. AM to EM, May 24, 1833, AMP.

2. AM to EM, June 7, 1833, AMP; RML to EM, June 5, 1833, JMP.

3. RML to EM, June 5, 1833, JMP. Jonathan D. Sarna, "Seating and the American Synagogue," in Philip R. Vandermeer and Robert P. Swierenga, eds., *Belief and Behavior: Essays in the New Religious History* (New Brunswick, N.J.: Rutgers University Press, 1991), p. 192.

4. RML to EM, June 5 and July 4, 1833, JMP; RML to EM, Aug. 20, July 17, and Oct. 6, 1833, MFP; ME to RML, June 27, 1833, *EOTH,* pp. 245–46; RML to ME, July 18, 1833, *EOTH,* pp. 248–50. On the Flushing Institute, see James McLachlan, *American Boarding Schools: A Historical Study* (New York: Scribner, 1970), pp. 105–35.

5. Sara Ann Hays to RML, Sept. 12, 1833, AMP. Sara's aunt Rachel Gratz was a bridesmaid at Rachel's parents' wedding in 1784, so Sara had heard stories of Rachel's mother (SM to RM, Sept. 1, 1812, MFP; and JM to RML, Oct. 30, 1831, JMP).

6. AM to EM, March 29, 1835, AMP; AM to RML, Nov. 19, 1828, AMP; RML to EM, Nov. 26, 1828, MFP; AM to EM, Jan. 26, 1830, AMP; AL to EM, March 17, 1830, AMP.

7. On Samuel Hays, see *HJP,* pp. 144, 173, 183, 207, 259, 340, 363; and Samuel Hays to AM, April 18, 1836, AMP.

8. Laura to CMP, May 1, 1836, JMP; Emma to Laura, May 13, 1836, MFP; SM to EM, June 2, 1836, JMP; Julia to CMP, June 16, 1836, MFP; GM to EM, May 29, 1836, MFP; GM to RML, June 5, 1836, CFP.

9. Editorial, *Raleigh Register,* May 5, 1835; advertisement for Paul Sabbaton, *People's Press and Wilmington Advertiser,* Oct. 1, 1834; GM to SM, Jan. 30, 1834, MFP. One of Aaron's major exports, turpentine, rose in price from $2.15 to $2.75 per barrel between early 1833 and early 1834 (price lists, *People's Press and Wilmington Advertiser,* Feb. 5, 1834, and Jan. 9, 1833). Whitmarsh advertisement, *People's Press and Wilmington Advertiser,* May 7, 1834. Whiteville, Waccamaw, and Cape Fear Canal or Railroad Company stock subscription announcement, *People's Press and Wilmington Advertiser,* June 4, 1834.

10. RML to EM, May 18 and June 3, 1834, MFP. Rachel's misgivings proved prescient when a few weeks later a rumor circulated that Wilmington lumber was substandard. Soon thereafter the turpentine market crashed in confusion over quality

controls (editorials, *People's Press and Wilmington Advertiser*, June 18 and Aug. 6, 1834; advertisement signed by Aaron Lazarus and other naval-stores merchants, *People's Press and Wilmington Advertiser*, Aug. 6, 1834).

11. RML to EM, June 3, July 27, and May 18, 1834, MFP.

12. RML to EM, May 18, 1834, MFP. Blackwell P. Robinson, "The Episcopate of Levi Silliman Ives," in *The Episcopal Church of North Carolina* (Raleigh: Episcopal Diocese of North Carolina, 1987), pp. 176–78; Richard Rankin, *Ambivalent Churchmen and Evangelical Churchwomen: The Religion of the Episcopal Elite in North Carolina, 1800–1860* (Columbia: University of South Carolina Press, 1993), pp. 90–92; McLachlan, *American Boarding Schools*, p. 100; Robert Emmett Curran, *From Academy to University, 1789–1889*, vol. 1 of *Bicentennial History of Georgetown University* (Washington, D.C.: Georgetown University Press, 1993), pp. 108–14, 412. Marx's cousin Jacob Mordecai II, Moses's son, also enrolled there (in 1833), but the promise of an Episcopal school near home led his relatives to recall him to Raleigh in 1834.

13. RML to EM, Sept. 6 and June 3, 1834, MFP; RML to CMP, Sept. 14, 1834, MFP.

14. Elisheva Carlebach, *Divided Souls: Converts from Judaism in Germany, 1500–1750* (New Haven, Conn.: Yale University Press, 2001); James William Hagy, *This Happy Land: The Jews of Colonial and Antebellum Charleston* (Tuscaloosa: University of Alabama Press, 1993), pp. 69, 83–85; Barnett A. Elzas, *The Reformed Society of Israelites of Charleston, S.C.,* . . . (New York: Bloch Publishing, 1916), pp. 8–16; Harriet Martineau, *Providence as Manifested through Israel: An Address to the Descendants of Abraham* (Boston: L. C. Bowles, 1833), pp. 110, 73; JM, "Remarks on Miss Martineau's Tract entitled Providence as manifested through Israel and on the Writings of the Reverend Alexander Keith entitled Evidence of the truth of the Christian Religion, derived from the literal Fulfilment of Prophecy, particularly as illustrated by the History of the Jews and by discoveries of recent travelers" (1836), AJA; RML to EM, May 9, 1827, MFP; RML to EM, April 13, 1828, JMP; MEL, "Autobiography" (n.d., c. 1885), Labadie Collection, Special Collections Library, University of Michigan.

15. The Lazarus girls did not attend school in the fall of 1834 or the spring of 1835 (RML to EM, Nov. 30, 1834, MFP); RML to EM, March 9, 1835, MFP.

16. RML to EM, Aug. 21, 1836, MFP; EM to Sol and CMP, July 3, 1838, MFP; RML to EM, July 29, 1835, MFP.

17. RML to EM, March 9 and April 9, 1835, MFP; RML to EM, April 26, 1835, JMP.

18. Editorial, *People's Press and Wilmington Advertiser*, May 6, 1835; advertisement, *People's Press and Wilmington Advertiser*, May 6, 1835; editorial, *Raleigh Register*, May 5, 1835; AL to SM, May 3, 1835, JMP.

19. AL and RML to SM, May 3, 1835, JMP; AL to EM, May 8, 1835, MFP; RMM note on AL to JM, May 24, 1835, JMP; GM to SM, June 4, 1835, MFP.

20. Sketches of Mordecai plantation, courtesy Mordecai Historic Park, and interview with Sally Poland, director, Mordecai Historic Park, Raleigh, N.C., 1994. GM to SM, June 14, 1835, MFP.

21. EM, "History of a Heart," p. 3, MFP; GM to SM, June 4, 1835, MFP; Julia to EM, June 1, 1835, MFP; AL to JM, May 24, 1835, JMP.

22. RML to EM, July 5, 1835, MFP; RML to EM, June 26, 1835, PMP; mill advertisement, *People's Press and Wilmington Advertiser*, July 1, 1835.

23. RML to RMM, July 12, 1835, JMP.

24. RML to CDR, Aug. 1, 1835, DRFP.

25. Henry Mordecai and RML to EM, July 29, 1835, MFP; RML to CDR, Aug. 1, 1835, DRFP.

26. Henry Mordecai and RML to EM, July 29, 1835, MFP; RML to CDR, Aug. 1, 1835, DRFP; RML to JM, Aug. 19, 1835, MFP.

27. The letter Rachel wrote to Jacob circa July 31, 1835, and her own copy were probably both destroyed; hers to Aaron has not survived, either. However, both are referred to in other correspondence: Henry Mordecai and RML to EM, July 29, 1835, MFP; RML to CDR, Aug. 1, 1835, DRFP; RML to EM, Sept. 18, 1836, MFP; EM to Sol and CMP, July 3, 1838, MFP.

28. RML to CDR, Aug. 1, 1835, DRFP; RML to EM, Sept. 18, 1836, MFP.

29. Henry and RML to EM, July 29, 1835, MFP; EM to Sol and CMP, July 3, 1838, MFP; RML to EM, June 26, 1836, MFP.

30. RML to JM, Aug. 19, 1835, MFP.

31. RML to EM, Sept. 18 and Aug. 21, 1836, MFP; JM to Sol, March 29, 1829, JMP; RML to RMM, Aug. 26, 1835, JMP.

32. RML to EM, Aug. 21, 1836, MFP; RML to RMM, Aug. 26, 1835, JMP; RML to JM, Aug. 19, 1835, MFP; RML to EM, Sept. 18, 1836, and Sept. 6, 1835, MFP.

23. DUPLICITY

1. RML to EM, June 26, 1836, and Sept. 6 and Sept. 24, 1835, MFP.

2. RML to ME, Jan. 10, 1836, *EOTH*, p. 273; RML to EM, Oct. 30, 1835, MFP; AM to RML, Dec. 19, 1835, AMP; RML to EM, Dec. 28, 1836, MFP; Mary DeRosset Curtis to Magdelen DeRosset, Sept. 4, 1835, MACP.

3. Emma to RML, Dec. 21, 1835, JMP; Leora Hiatt McEachern, *History of St. James Parish, 1729–1979* (Wilmington, N.C., 1983), p. 41; *People's Press and Wilmington Advertiser*, Dec. 4 and Dec. 18, 1835; St. James Church Materials, DRFP. On the tradition of such fairs, see Suzanne Lebsock, *The Free Women of Petersburg: Status and Culture in a Southern Town, 1784–1860* (New York: Norton, 1984), pp. 211, 218–20. For the shipping report, see *People's Press and Wilmington Advertiser*, Oct. 30, 1835.

4. On internal improvements and railroad development, see editorials, *People's Press and Wilmington Advertiser*, Dec. 4 and Dec. 23, 1835; editorial, *Wilmington Advertiser*, April 15, 1836. On the Wilmington and Raleigh Railroad Company, see James Sprunt, *Tales and Traditions of the Lower Cape Fear, 1661–1896* (1896; Spartanburg; S.C.: Reprint Co., 1973), pp. 132–34. On political party realignments and railroad issues in North Carolina, see Harry L. Watson, *Jacksonian Politics and Community Conflict: The*

Emergence of the Second American Party System in Cumberland County, North Carolina (Baton Rouge: Louisiana State University Press, 1981), pp. 49–56, 151–97; Marc W. Kruman, *Parties and Politics in North Carolina, 1836–1865* (Baton Rouge: Louisiana State University Press, 1983), pp. 8–9, 16–26; Charles G. Sellers Jr., "Who Were the Southern Whigs?" *American Historical Review* 59 (1953–1954), pp. 335–46. On railroad development, see James A. Ward, "A New Look at Antebellum Southern Railroad Development," *Journal of Southern History* 39 (1973), pp. 409–20; and Thomas E. Jeffrey, "Internal Improvements and Political Parties in Antebellum North Carolina, 1836–1860," *North Carolina Historical Review* 55 (1978), pp. 111–56.

5. *People's Press and Wilmington Advertiser*, Jan. 1, 1836; *Wilmington Advertiser*, Jan. 8, Jan. 15, Jan. 22, 1836; RML to Emma, Oct. 30, 1835, MFP; RML to EM, Dec. 28, 1835, and April 2, 1836, MFP.

6. According to Andrew J. Howell, in *The Book of Wilmington* (Wilmington, N.C., 1930), pp. 87–88, the town's ebullient citizens actually invested more in the railroad than the total value of Wilmington's real estate. GM to SM, Aug. 12, 1835, MFP; Elizabeth Reid Murray, *Wake: Capital County of North Carolina* (Raleigh, N.C.: Capital County Publishing, 1983), vol. 1, p. 246; Nancy Lane Mordecai to EM, Jan. 11, 1836, MFP; GM to SM, April 10, 1836, JMP; RML to EM, Feb. 2, 1836, MFP; Julia to EM, March 29, 1836, MFP; *Wilmington Advertiser*, March 18, 1836; GM to EM, Feb. 21, 1836, LMFP; RML to EM, April 2 and June 14, 1836, MFP.

7. Prov. 27:1; RML to EM, Dec. 28, 1835, and Aug. 21, 1836, MFP; *Wilmington Advertiser*, April 22, 1836; EM, "History of a Heart," p. 4, MFP.

8. RML to EM, June 14, Feb. 2, and June 26, 1836, MFP; EM, "History of a Heart," pp. 4, 6.

9. RML to EM, June 26, 1836, MFP; EM, "History of a Heart," pp. 4, 6; Matt. 10:37.

10. RML to EM, Sept. 18, Aug. 21, and Oct. 23, 1836, MFP.

11. RML to EM, Sept. 18, 1836, MFP.

12. RML to EM, Aug. 21, 1836, MFP.

13. RML to EM, June 26, Sept. 18, and Aug. 21, 1836, and Feb. 16, 1837, MFP.

14. RML to EM, Sept. 18 and Oct. 23, 1836, MFP.

15. RML to EM, Dec. 28, 1836, MFP; Julia to EM, Jan. 17, 1837, MFP; RML to EM, Feb. 5, 1837, MFP; Laura to EM II, Feb. 26, 1837, MFP; Julia to CMP, April 2, 1836, JMP; RML to EM, May 21, 1837, JMP; Laura to RMM, March 28, 1837, JMP; GM to CMP, May 14, 1837, JMP.

16. Advertisement, *Wilmington Advertiser*, April 7, 1837; editorial, *Wilmington Advertiser*, April 14, 1837; advertisement, *Wilmington Advertiser*, May 5, 1837; Watson, *Jacksonian Politics*, pp. 247–48; advertisement, *Wilmington Advertiser*, July 7, 1837. RML to JM, April 23, 1837; Julia to CMP, May 7, 1837, JMP; EM II to RMM, March 20, 1837, JMP. Marx's school was operated by my ancestor; see Robert I. Curtis, "The Bingham School and Classical Education in North Carolina, 1793–1873," *North Carolina Historical Review* 73 (1996), pp. 328–77.

17. On the panic of 1837, see Samuel Rezneck, *Business Depressions and Financial*

Panics: Essays in American Business and Economic History (New York: Greenwood Publishing, 1968), pp. 75–100; Watson, *Jacksonian Politics*, p. 246; *Wilmington Advertiser*, May 5, May 19, May 26, 1837, and June 9, 1837.

18. RML to JM, April 23, 1837, JMP; RML to EM, May 21, 1837, JMP; JM and Emma to CMP, June 30, 1837, JMP; Emma to RML, Dec. 21, 1835, JMP; Sol to JM, Jan. 16, 1836; Julia to CMP, Jan. 22 and May 7, 1837, JMP.

19. SM to CMP, Oct. 2, 1837, JMP; RML to EM, Aug. 23 and Sept. 3, 1837, MFP.

24. THE POWER OF THE GRAVE

1. RML to EM, Dec. 17, 1837, JMP; EM to Sol and CMP, July 3, 1838, MFP; RML to EM, April 16, 1838, MFP.

2. RML to EM, April 16, 1838, MFP; RML to Emma, June 11, 1838, MFP; Laura to EM II, June 13, 1838, MFP; AL to EM, July 4, 1838, JMP; EM to Sol and CMP, July 3, 1838, MFP.

3. SM to CMP and Sol, June 24, 1838, JMP; Emma journal, June 23 and May 7, 1838, MFP; EM to Sol and CMP, July 3, 1838, MFP.

4. EM to Sol and CMP, July 3, 1838, MFP; the Reverend [Hobart] Bartlett to EL, July 23, 1838, MFP; *The Book of Common Prayer* . . . (New York: Protestant Episcopal Press, 1833); EM to MCM, March 28, 1864, CFP.

5. EM to ME, Oct. 17, 1838 (copy), JMP; SM to AL, June 24, 1838, JMP. The cause of Rachel's death is not clear but may have been blackwater fever, a fatal strain of the malaria that in milder form appears to have plagued her since around 1828. Other possibilities include a bacterial infection, appendicitis, and intestinal obstruction ending in peritonitis. See K. David Patterson, "Disease Environments of the Antebellum South," in Ronald L. Numbers and Todd L. Savitt, eds., *Science and Medicine in the Old South* (Baton Rouge: Louisiana State University Press, 1989), pp. 160–61.

6. AL to SM, July 2, 1838, JMP.

7. AL to EM, July 2, 1838, JMP; Emma journal, July 15, 1838, MFP.

8. Emma journal, June 26, June 30, Aug. 11, and Aug. 22, 1838, MFP; AL to EM, July 22, 1838, MFP; Stanley L. Falk, "Artillery for the Land Service: The Development of a System," *Military Affairs* 28 (1965), pp. 102–3; AM to RMM, Sept. 8, 1838, MFP; AL to EM, Sept. 7, 1838, JMP.

9. Werner Sollors, *Beyond Ethnicity: Consent and Descent in American Culture* (New York: Oxford University Press, 1986), pp. 203, 221.

10. The original inscription on Jacob's tombstone is recorded in the Mordecai family Bible, which remains in the Mordecai House, Raleigh, North Carolina. The words may be taken from Hos. 13:14. AL to EM, Sept. 4 and Sept. 7, 1838, JMP; AL to EM, Oct. 9, 1838, MFP; EM, "History of a Heart," p. 13, MFP.

25. SOULS

1. EM to GM, Jan. 10, 1839, MFP; EM to Sol, Dec. 31, 1838, MFP; EM, "History of a Heart," pp. 10, 13–14, MFP.

2. JM to JMM, Feb. 28, 1793, MFP; EM to GM, Jan. 10, 1839, MFP.

3. EM fragment, June 23, 1839, in EM journal, 1819–1820, MFP; GM to EM, June 27, 1839, MFP; Christ Church, Raleigh, Miscellaneous Records, 1823–1898, NCDAH.

4. At the time of her death Laura was engaged to John Brooke Young, the younger brother of Augustus Mordecai's Gentile wife, Rosina. Emma to EM II, July 4, 1839, MFP; *MHMF*, pp. 50–51; obituary, *Richmond Enquirer*, July 9, 1839; Caroline Hays Myers to CMP, July 7, 1839, MFP; Eliza and Rebecca Hays Myers, July 16, 1839; Emma to CMP, Aug. 15, 1839, JMP; EM to CMP, March 9, 1840, MFP.

5. Eliza to CMP, June 21, 1839, PMP; RML to EM, Dec. 28, 1836, MFP; Laura to Emma, May 6, 1839, MFP; Eliza to CMP, Oct. 1, 1839, PMP; Eliza to GM, July 1, 1842, GMP; SM to EM, Oct. 16, 1842, JMP; Eliza and Samuel Hays Myers to SM, Jan. 28, 1844, JMP.

6. Eliza to EM, Aug. 25, 1839, MYFP; Eliza to CMP, Oct. 1, 1839, PMP.

7. RMM to Emma, Jan. 16, 1839, MFP.

8. Emma to CMP, March 31, 1839, MFP; Eliza DeRosset to Mary DeRosset Curtis, July 9, 1838, and Jan. 28, 1839, MACP.

9. Emma to EM, Aug. 4, 1839, MFP; William Beveridge, *Private Thoughts upon Religion* (1709); Eliza to Rebecca Hays Myers, July 16, 1839, MYFP; Emma to EM, Sept. 22, 1839, JMP.

10. Emma to EM, Sept. 22, 1839, JMP; [Emma] to editor (Isaac Leeser), *Occident* 2 (Jan. 1845), p. 487; Eliza to CMP, Oct. 1, 1839, PMP. The reference to "household" apparently derives from Matt. 10:36.

11. On Samuel, see EM to GM, Jan. 10, 1839, MFP. On Alfred, see Jacob Rader Marcus, *United States Jewry, 1776–1985* (Detroit: Wayne State University Press, 1989), vol. 1, p. 102; AM to SM, Feb. 12, 1846, MFP; "The Life of Alfred Mordecai: As Related by Himself," edited by James A. Padgett, *North Carolina Historical Review* 22 (1945), p. 83. On Sol, see CMP and Sol to EM, Feb. 19, 1838, MFP; and EM to Sol, Dec. 31, 1838, MFP.

12. AL to EM, Oct. 9 and Oct. 25, 1838, MFP; Suzanne Lebsock, *The Free Women of Petersburg: Status and Culture in a Southern Town, 1784–1860* (New York: Norton, 1984), pp. 173–74, 191. Gratz recommended the same school, operated by the wife of a French refugee whose father had served as king of Naples under Napoleon, to her brother and sister-in-law (Rebecca Gratz to Maria Gist Gratz, Sept. 22, 1839, HFP). Rebecca Gratz to Miriam Gratz Moses, Sept. 10, 1838, RGP; AL to EM, Sept. 7, 1838, JMP; Emma to EM II, Nov. 12, 1838, MFP; AL to EM, Oct. 25, 1838, MFP; RMM to AL, Nov. 16, 1838, MFP.

13. EM to Sol, Dec. 31, 1838, MFP; EM to GM, Jan. 10, 1839, MFP.

14. MCL and Laura to CMP, March 5, 1839, JMP; Eliza to CMP, May 13, 1839, PMP; advertisements, *Cape Fear Recorder*, May 11, 1831, and Jan. 18, 1832; RML to EM, Dec. 23, 1832, MFP; AL to EM, Oct. 25, 1838, MFP; Emma to CMP, March 31, 1839, MFP.

15. *Wilmington Advertiser*, Nov. 30, 1838, Feb. 18, 1841, June 7, 1839; AL to John Huske and Son, Nov. 30, 1839, AJA; James Sprunt, *Tales and Traditions of the Lower Cape Fear, 1661–1896* (1896; Spartanburg, S.C.: Reprint Co., 1973), p. 134; Marc W. Kru-

man, *Parties and Politics in North Carolina, 1836–1865* (Baton Rouge: Louisiana State University Press, 1983), pp. 23–24; Harry L. Watson, *Jacksonian Politics and Community Conflict: The Emergence of the Second American Party System in Cumberland County, North Carolina* (Baton Rouge: Louisiana State University Press, 1981), pp. 280, 309.

16. AL to EM, Oct. 29, 1839, MFP; MCL and Emma to CMP, Nov. 3, 1839, JMP; Emma to EM, Oct. 4, 1841, MFP.

17. MEL, *Love vs. Marriage* (New York: Fowlers and Wells, 1852), pp. 182, 191; MEL, "Autobiography," Special Collections Library, University of Michigan.

18. Balance sheets for JM's estate, Sept. 5, 1838, and Oct. 1, 1841, JMP. GM to EM, Jan. 21, 1841, MFP; EM to GM, Feb. 5, 1843, GMP; EM to EM II, Feb. 6, 1843, MFP; Emma to EM, Oct. 31, 1841, JMP.

19. EM, April 18, 1842, 1842 almanac, LMFP; Eliza to CMP, Feb. 3, 1842, MFP; AM to EM, Oct. 10, 1841, AMP. From August 1842 until about March 1843, Ellen was employed by Dr. John Wakefield Francis, a widower with three small boys. See Julia Ward Howe, *Reminiscences, 1819–1899* (Boston: Houghton, Mifflin, and Co., 1899), pp. 12, 36, 38, 44–49, 61, 88; John Wakefield Francis, *Old New York* (New York: W. J. Middleton, 1865), pp. lxxiv, xciii, lxxxviii. EM, July 29, 1842, 1842 almanac, LMFP; Emma to EM, Jan. 7, 1843, MFP; CMP to EM, Feb. 10, 1843, LMFP; SM to GM, Dec. 14, 1842, GMP; SM to EM, Oct. 16, 1842, JMP; EM to Francis Lister Hawks, Oct. 5, 1844, Francis Lister Hawks Papers, New-York Historical Society.

20. EM to EM II, Feb. 6, 1843, MFP; SM to GM, May 5, 1843, GMP; EM to ME, Oct. 17, 1838, JMP; MEL to GM, May 4, 1842, GMP; AM to SM, July 30, 1843, JMP; MCL to EM II, May 14, 1845, JMP; Isabella Donaldson to EM, July 8, 1842, JMP.

21. EM to GM, March 30, 1844, GMP; EM and MCL to EM II, June 10, 1844, MFP.

22. Emma to Eliza, Aug. 30, 1844, MFP; Emma to SM, Sept. 5, 1845, JMP; EM, Aug. 26, 1844, 1844 almanac, LMFP; EM to SM, Sept. 30, 1844, MFP; EM to GM, Oct. 21, 1844, GMP.

23. MCL to EM, Nov. 11, 1844, JMP; MCL to Isabella [Donaldson], Nov. 20, 1844 (copy), JMP. On the house, Will's Forest, see Catherine W. Bishir, *North Carolina Architecture* (Chapel Hill: University of North Carolina Press, 1990), p. 195.

24. Emma to GM, Nov. 18, 1844, GMP.

25. MCL to EM, Sept. 8, 1844, JMP; EM to SM, Jan. 16, 1845, JMP; Julia to CMP, Dec. 5, 1844, MFP.

26. EM to GM, Oct. 21, 1844, GMP.

27. EM to GM, March 13 and May 19, 1845, GMP; EM to EM II, Aug. 12, 1845, MFP; MCL to EM II, May 14, 1845, JMP.

28. EM to MCL, Sept. 27, 1845, JMP.

29. Esther Whitlock [EM], *Past Days: A Story for Children* (New York: D. Appleton, 1841). Ellen's clippings of reviews of *Past Days* are held in LMFP (see inventory, 21–22); CMP to EM, July 6, 1842, LMFP. On Ellen's literary work, see Lucy Ann Lippitt to EM, Aug. 5 and Nov. 26, 1840, MFP; EM to Joseph G. Cogswell, Dec. 1, 1840 (copy), MFP; Joseph G. Cogswell to EM, Dec. 12, 1840, MFP; Lucy Ann Lippitt to EM, Dec. 29,

1840, MFP; EM note in Eliza to CMP, Feb. 3, 1842, MFP; H. A. M. Murray to W. S. Simpson, March 8, 1842 (copy), MFP; and sales accounts by Simpson in EM financial papers, MFP.

30. *RJ*, pp. 56–57; Emma to EM II, July 2, 1842, MFP; Emma, Dec. 25, 1842, 1842 journal fragments, MFP. Gratz's Hebrew Sunday school opened in Philadelphia in 1838 (Dianne Ashton, *Rebecca Gratz: Women and Judaism in Antebellum America* [Detroit: Wayne State University Press, 1997], pp. 140–48). On Leeser's *Occident and American Jewish Advocate*, see Lance J. Sussman, *Isaac Leeser and the Making of American Judaism* (Detroit: Wayne State University Press, 1995), pp. 131–54. *The Teachers' and Parents' Assistant* (Philadelphia: C. Sherman, 1845) is filed under Gratz's name in the Library of Congress Catalog. Its author was still unknown when it was reprinted by the Jewish Publication Society of America in 1975. The text's style reflects the influence of the Edgeworths and of Thomas Gallaudet's *The Child's Book on the Soul* (1830), which Rachel had sent to Maria in 1835 (RML to ME, Jan. 1, 1835, *EOTH*, p. 268). For Alfred's mother-in-law's recommendation of the book, sec Richea Gratz Hays to Sara Hays Mordecai, May 16, 1845, AMP.

31. [EM], "History of a Heart," pp. 1, 15–16, 2, 3, 5, 14, MFP. Ellen rallied support from her Christian acquaintance and among societies to convert Jews in England and America. As Jonathan D. Sarna points out, Leeser's *Occident* and other publishing enterprises became critical outlets for Jewish frustration in the face of proselytizing (Jonathan D. Sarna, "The American Jewish Response to Nineteenth-Century Christian Missions," *Journal of American History* 68 [1981], pp. 35–51). Also see Sussman, *Isaac Leeser*, p. 106; and Lorman Ratner, "Conversion of the Jews in Pre–Civil War Reform," *American Quarterly* 13 (Spring 1961), pp. 49, 51. Ellen's awareness of the movement's transatlantic nature is also evident from her reference to the duchess of Kent, whose husband was an influential supporter of the London Society for Promoting Christianity among the Jews (Michael Ragussis, *Figures of Conversion: "The Jewish Question" and English National Identity* [Durham, N.C.: Duke University Press, 1995], pp. 15, 50). For Ellen's efforts to promote her book, see Elizabeth Scott to EM, Oct. 21, 1845, MFP; John Johns [assistant to the Episcopal bishop of Virginia] to EM, Jan. 2, 1846, MFP; Catherine Hale to EM, June 15, 1846, MFP; R. Elton to EM, Oct. 22, 1846, LMFP; EM to Duncan Cameron, Nov. 18, 1845, CFP. For sales of the book, see H. D. Turner and Co. to W. S. Simpson, April 5, 1847, MFP.

32. RMM to RML, Feb. 23, 1824, MFP. When exactly Ellen became Abby's owner has not been determined, though she had full title in 1842, when Abby was sold.

33. EM, April 5, 1839, 1839 almanac, LMFP; EM to CMP, March 9, 1840, MFP; Julia to EM, May 14, 1837, MFP; Eliza to CMP, April 29, 1840, MFP. Sam eventually secured from the former clerk, William Beasley, the promise of five hundred dollars, half of which was not paid until 1856. On Beasley and the agreement, see SM to EM, Sept. 16, 1836, and Nov. 24, 1842, JMP; EM, Nov. 25, 1856, 1855 almanac, LMFP. By 1860, Beasley, forty-six, had married and acquired a tobacco-stemming factory. When he fathered

Abby's child, he was about twenty-four years old and had little property (Petersburg City land taxes, 1838; Dinwiddie County, Va., Census 1860, p. 444).

34. Ellen's almanac of 1840 records correspondence with "Miss Ware" (June 9, July, August, 1840, LMFP).

35. P. M. S. [?] to EM, Aug. 7, 1842, MFP; Eliza to CMP, Feb. 3, 1842, MFP.

36. Isabella Donaldson to EM, July 8, 1842, JMP; address for "Catherine W. Morris . . . Manager of the Shelter for Colored Children," EM, 1842 almanac, LMFP; and Rachel Hays Myers to EM, July 25, 1842, MFP.

37. Ellis P. Oberholtzer, *Philadelphia: A History of the City and Its People* (Philadelphia: S. J. Clarke, n.d.), p. 288; W. E. B. DuBois, *The Philadelphia Negro: A Social Study* (1899; New York: Benjamin Bloom, 1967), pp. 29–30; SM to EM, Aug. 7, 1842, JMP; Emma to EM, Sept. 6, 1842, MFP.

38. EM to EM II, Feb. 6, 1843, MFP; Emma to EM, Sept. 6, 1842, MFP. For rules and the girls' behavior, see Emma to EM, Jan. 7, 1843, MFP; EM to MCL, Dec. 1, 1845, JMP; Emma to EM, June 20, 1847, and Feb. 13, 1848, MFP.

39. Emma to EM, July 8, 1846, MFP; EM to SM, Oct. 17, 1844, JMP.

26. ESCAPE FROM CONSTRAINT

1. The 1840s and 1850s marked an era of radical middle-class reform that bears comparison to the 1960s for its overt questioning of authority—particularly in the realms of family, religion, sex, race, and class. John C. Spurlock, *Free Love: Marriage and Middle-Class Radicalism in America, 1825–1860* (New York: New York University Press, 1988).

2. Alexander Anderson to GM, Feb. 18, 1842, AL Estate Papers, GMP; New Hanover County estate records, 1741–1939, NCDAH; MEL to GM, March 23, 1842, GMP; the lots held in trust appear in an abstracted, indexed volume, *New Hanover County, North Carolina, 1815 and 1845 Tax Lists*, NCDAH.

3. Emma to SM, May 10, 1845, JMP; "Record of Proceedings of the [Boston] Religious Union of Associationists" ("RUA Proceedings"), March 7, 1847, RUAR. For a brief sketch of Fourier's vision, which included residential phalanxes occupied by 1,620 individuals, see Guarneri, *The Utopian Alternative: Fourierism in Nineteenth-Century America* (Ithaca, N.Y.: Cornell University Press, 1991), pp. 15–20. MEL to GM, March 24, 1846, JMP.

4. "RUA Proceedings," March 7, 1847; MEL to GM, Dec. 30, 1846, GMP; MEL to GM, March 24, 1846, JMP; SM to GM, April 14, 1846, GMP.

5. MCL to EM II, May 14, 1845, JMP; SM to GM, March 10, 1846, GMP, and account, March 1, 1846, Lazarus estate records, GMP; EL to GM, May 17, 1846, GMP; [Mary Gove Nichols], *Mary Lyndon; or, Revelations of a Life, an Autobiography* (New York: Stringer and Townsend, 1855), p. 306; Emma to SM, Sept. 5, 1845, JMP; EM to GM, Sept. 16, 1845, GMP.

6. SM to GM, Oct. 17, 1845, GMP; EL to GM, Nov. 30, 1845, GMP. Ellen's physician,

Abraham Howard Okie, published *Homeopathy: with Particular Reference to a Lecture by O. W. Holmes* (Boston: Otis Clapp, 1842) after Oliver Wendell Holmes attacked homeopathy in *Homeopathy, and Its Kindred Delusions* (Boston, 1842). Also see William Harvey King, ed., *History of Homeopathy and Its Institutions in America* (New York: Lewis Publishing Co., 1905), vol. 1, pp. 275–76. EL to GM, Nov. 11 and Nov. 30, 1845, GMP; MCL to GM, March 6, 1846, GMP; EM to GM, Dec. 9, 1845, GMP.

7. Mary Gove to Eliza, April 29, 1846, GMP.

8. On the Shews and their Grahamite regimen, see Stephen Nissenbaum, *Sex, Diet, and Debility in Jacksonian America: Sylvester Graham and Health Reform* (Westport, Conn.: Greenwood Press, 1980), pp. 40, 149, 156 n. 21. The Shews' Bond Street establishment is also featured in Harry B. Weiss and Howard R. Kemble, *The Great American Water Cure Craze: A History of Hydropathy in the United States* (Trenton, N.J.: Past Times Press, 1967), p. 69. On the gender implications of water cure, see Ann Douglas Wood, " 'The Fashionable Diseases': Women's Complaints and Their Treatment in Nineteenth-Century America," *Journal of Interdisciplinary History* 4 (1973), pp. 25–32, 40. For a discussion of the way hydrotherapy engaged with female sexuality, see Rachel P. Maines, *The Technology of Orgasm: "Hysteria," the Vibrator, and Women's Sexual Satisfaction* (Baltimore: Johns Hopkins University Press, 1998), pp. 72–82; and Kathryn Kish Sklar, "All Hail to Pure Cold Water," in Judith Walzer Leavitt, ed., *Women and Health in America: Historical Readings* (Madison: University of Wisconsin Press, 1984), p. 252. A fine historical overview of hydropathy in the United States that takes gender into account is Susan E. Cayleff's, *Wash and Be Healed: The Water-Cure Movement and Women's Health* (Philadelphia: Temple University Press, 1987).

9. [Nichols], *Mary Lyndon*, pp. 284–85. Mary Gove married Thomas Low Nichols in 1848; I refer to her as Gove because that was her name when Marx and Ellen met her.

10. EM to GM, Aug. 21, 1846, GMP; [Nichols], *Mary Lyndon*, p. 295; Edgar Allan Poe, quoted in Guarneri, *Utopian Alternative*, p. 356; Gove, quoted in Janet Noever, "Passionate Rebel: The Life of Mary Gove Nichols, 1810–1884" (Ph.D. diss., University of Oklahoma, 1993), p. 99. Also see Jean Silver-Isenstadt's full-length biography *Shameless: The Visionary Life of Mary Gove Nichols* (Baltimore: Johns Hopkins University Press, 2002).

11. [Nichols], *Mary Lyndon*, pp. 305–6.

27. A HOUSE ON TENTH STREET

1. [Mary Gove Nichols], *Mary Lyndon; or, Revelations of a Life, an Autobiography* (New York: Stringer and Townsend, 1855), p. 303; MEL to GM, March 24, 1846, JMP.

2. MEL to GM, March 24, 1846, JMP; Susan E. Cayleff, *Wash and Be Healed: The Water-Cure Movement and Women's Health* (Philadelphia: Temple University Press, 1987), p. 54.

3. MEL to GM, March 24, 1846, JMP; EM to GM, Aug. 21, 1846, GMP; EL to GM, Sept. 25, 1846, GMP.

4. SM to GM, May 2, 1846, GMP; EL to GM, May 17, 1846, GMP, EL to GM, June 26, 1846, GMP.

5. On Gove's marriage and early career, see Jean Silver-Isenstadt, *Shameless: The Visionary Life of Mary Gove Nichols* (Baltimore: Johns Hopkins University Press, 2002), pp. 26–71; John C. Spurlock, *Free Love: Marriage and Middle-Class Radicalism in America, 1825–1860* (New York: New York University Press, 1988), pp. 184–92.

6. Gove, quoted in Spurlock, *Free Love*, p. 190; Mary S. N. Gove to J[ames] Russell Lowell, June 30, 1843, James Russell Lowell Papers, Houghton Library, Harvard University.

7. EL to GM, May 17, 1846, GMP; GM to Nancy Lane Mordecai, Aug. 8, 1846, MFP.

8. MEL, quoted in [Nichols], *Mary Lyndon*, p. 303; Carl J. Guarneri, *The Utopian Alternative: Fourierism in Nineteenth-Century America* (Ithaca, N.Y.: Cornell University Press, 1991), pp. 407–10. GM to Nancy Lane Mordecai, Aug. 8, 1846, MFP; EL to GM, June 26, 1846, GMP; [MEL], "Society—an Aspiration—or, the Actual and the Possible," *Harbinger* 3 (Oct. 29, 1846), pp. 305–8.

9. On the Saturday evenings and intellectual life, see [Nichols], *Mary Lyndon*, pp. 323–24, 361; Noever, "Passionate Rebel," pp. 143–44; Guarneri, *Utopian Alternative*, p. 356. Sivori (1815–1894) trained under Paganini and began touring at the age of twelve. For Poe's connections, see Dwight Thomas and David K. Jackson, *The Poe Log: A Documentary Life of Edgar Allan Poe, 1809–1849* (Boston: G. K. Hall, 1987), pp. 669–70, 683–87. For Ellen's response, see EL to GM, Sept. 25, 1846, GMP.

10. [Nichols], *Mary Lyndon*, p. 320.

11. GM to Nancy Lane Mordecai, Aug. 8, 1846, GMP.

12. EL to GM, June 26, 1846, GMP; [Nichols], *Mary Lyndon*, p. 323; EL to GM, Oct. 12, 1846, GMP.

13. EM to SM, Aug. 30, 1846, JMP; EM to GM, Sept. 25, 1846, GMP; EM to SM, Oct. 7, 1846, JMP.

14. Sam rather gently observed "how tender is a female's character and that the world has little mercy on those who have the temerity to brave its opinion" (SM to EM, Oct. 12, 1846, JMP).

15. EL to GM, Sept. 2 and Aug. 21, 1846, GMP. For more on Brisbane, see Guarneri, *Utopian Alternative*, p. 361.

16. EL to GM, Sept. 10, 1846, GMP; Gove to SM, Oct. 1, 1846, JMP.

17. EL to GM, Sept. 25, 1846, GMP.

18. SM to Gove, Sept. 29, 1846, GMP; Gove to SM, Oct. 1, 1846, JMP. Also see [Nichols], *Mary Lyndon*, p. 306.

19. John B. Blake, "Mary Gove Nichols, Prophetess of Health," in Judith Walzer Leavitt, ed., *Women and Health in America* (Madison: University of Wisconsin Press, 1984), p. 364; EL to GM, Oct. 12, 1846, and May 31, 1847, GMP.

20. See SM to GM, April 14, 1847, and Jan. 15, 1846, GMP; SM to EM II, Oct. 15, 1848, MFP; SM to GM, Aug. 2, 1848, GMP; notation, Oct. 1848, Virginia, vol. 6, R. G. Dun and Co. Collection, Baker Library, Harvard University Graduate School of Business Administration.

21. Emma served on committees raising money for the Hebrew Sunday school and contributed to the Jewish press. Emma to SM, July 3, 1846, JMP; Emma to Sara Hays Mordecai, Sept. 17, 1846, AMP; "Hebrew School Fund Ball, at Richmond, Va.," *Occident* 5 (1847), pp. 47–48; Emma to EM, Feb. 13, 1848, MFP; *RJ*, p. 56; Emma to EM II, May 1, 1846, MFP; American Jewess [Emma], "Essay," *Occident* 5 (July 1847), pp. 188–99. Ellen served as "directress" of the mission to female convicts in Richmond's penitentiary (see EM to GM, July 23, 1845, GMP; EM to MCL, Sept. 27, 1845, JMP).

28. TOWARD THE KINGDOM OF GOD ON EARTH

1. Minutes from Jan. 3, 1847, meeting, RUAR and JTFP. For an annotated version of the Religious Union of Associationists' records, see Sterling F. Delano, "A Calendar of Meetings of the 'Boston Religious Union of Associationists,' 1847–1850," in Joel Myerson, ed., *Studies in the American Renaissance* (Boston: Twayne, 1985), pp. 187–267.

2. Marx's preview of the RUA appeared anonymously in *The Harbinger* 3 (Nov. 21, 1846), pp. 381–83, as "Union of Associationists in the Church of Humanity."

3. On Brook Farm and Fourierism, see Carl J. Guarneri, *The Utopian Alternative: Fourierism in Nineteenth-Century America* (Ithaca, N.Y.: Cornell University Press, 1991), pp. 44–59; Henry W. Sams, ed., *Autobiography of Brook Farm* (Englewood Cliffs, N.J.: Prentice-Hall, 1958), esp. pp. 101–206; Zoltan Haraszti, *The Idyll at Brook Farm* (Boston: Trustees of the Public Library, 1937), pp. 27–45; Anne C. Rose, *Transcendentalism as a Social Movement* (New Haven, Conn.: Yale University Press, 1981). On the Brook Farm school, see Katherine Burton, *Paradise Planters: The Story of Brook Farm* (New York: Longmans, Green and Co., 1939), p. 210. For the quotation, see William Henry Channing, quoted in Haraszti, *Idyll at Brook Farm*, p. 27.

4. David Robinson, "The Political Odyssey of William Henry Channing," *American Quarterly* 34 (1982), pp. 167–78.

5. Marx's participation in discussions at the RUA meetings is noted for Jan. 3, 24, 31, Feb. 7, 14, 28, March 7 and 28, and April 11, 1847 (Delano, "Calendar of Meetings," pp. 195–205). He most likely left Boston in May to attend the New York convention of the American Union of Associationists. On his donation, see Delano, "Calendar of Meetings," p. 192; and MEL to James T. Fisher, June 19, 1847, JTFP. For his cash situation, see MEL to GM, Feb. 25, 1847, GMP. On the Mordecais and *The Harbinger*, see MEL to GM, Nov. 26, 1846, GMP; SM to GM, Nov. 26, 1846, GMP; MEL to GM, Dec. 30, 1846, GMP; MCL to CMP, Jan. 26, 1847, JMP. On Marx's health, see MEL to GM, June 1, 1847, GMP; Emma to EM, June 20, 1847, MFP.

6. SM to EM, June 7, 1847, MFP; SM to GM, July 5, 1847, GMP; Emma to EM, June 20, 1847.

7. EL to GM, Sept. 19, 1847, GMP; Emma to EM, Dec. 28, 1847, MFP; Delano, "Calendar of Meetings," pp. 215, 256.

8. Delano, "Calendar of Meetings," p. 215; Rose, *Transcendentalism as a Social Movement*, p. 154; John Allen to Mehitable Eastman, Oct. 1, 1845, Abernathy Library of American Literature, Middlebury College; George Ripley, "Brook Farm Lecturers,"

Harbinger 2 (Feb. 21, 1846), p. 175; John Allen, president of the Old Colony (Plymouth County) Anti-slavery Society, to the Reverend A. Phelps of the American Anti-slavery Society, Oct. 2, 1834, Boston Public Library; John Thomas Codman, *Brook Farm: Historic and Personal Memoirs* (Boston: Arena, 1894), p. 123; Guarneri, *Utopian Alternative*, pp. 238–44; Marianne Dwight to Anna Parsons, Dec. 12, 1845, in *Autobiography of Brook Farm*, p. 157.

9. EL to GM, Dec. 13, 1847, GMP.

10. Ibid.

11. EM to MCL, June 22, 1848, MFP; GM to EM, Feb. 14, 1848, MFP.

12. Albert Ehrenfried, *A Chronicle of Boston Jewry: From the Colonial Settlement to 1900* (Privately printed, 1963), pp. 340–42. For an assessment of Marx's employment of Christian language and symbolism, see John C. Spurlock, *Free Love: Marriage and Middle-Class Radicalism in America, 1825–1860* (New York: New York University Press, 1988), pp. 170–71.

13. Emma to EM, Oct. 9, 1848, MFP. Also see SM to EM, March 21, 1848, JMP; and Emma to Julia, March 8, 1848, JMP.

14. EL to GM, Dec. 13, 1847, GMP; Eliza to CMP, July 30, 1848, PMP; Emma to EM, Oct. 9, 1848, MFP; Ehrenfried, *Chronicle of Boston Jewry*, pp. 339–41.

15. EL to GM, July 19 and Aug. 21, 1848, GMP.

16. EL to GM, Sept. 17, 1848, GMP; John Allen to John Sullivan Dwight, April 27, 1848, Special Collections, Boston Public Library; EL to GM, Feb. 15 and Oct. 19, 1849, GMP; GM to EM, May 15, 1849, MFP.

29. CRUCIFIXIONS

1. MEL to GM, Nov. 8, 1850, GMP; MEL, *Love vs. Marriage* (New York: Fowlers and Wells, 1852), pp. 44, 143. The biblical references are drawn from Matt. 22:30, Mark 12:25, and Luke 20:35. Marx's publications included: *Love vs. Marriage*; *Involuntary Seminal Losses: Their Causes, Effects, and Cure* (1852); *Comparative Psychology and Universal Analogy* (1851); *Passional Hygiene and Natural Medicine* (1852); *Homeopathy* (1851); *The Zend-Avesta, and Solar Religions* (1852); *The Trinity, in Its Theological, Scientific, and Practical Aspects* (1851); *The Incarnation* (1851); *The Human Trinity; or, Three Aspects of Life: The Passional, the Intellectual, the Practical Sphere* (1851); translation of Alphonse Toussenel, *Passional Zoology; or, Spirit of the Beasts of France* (1852).

2. MEL, *Love vs. Marriage*, p. 115.

3. John C. Spurlock, *Free Love: Marriage and Middle-Class Radicalism in America, 1825–1860* (New York: New York University Press, 1988), p. 175.

4. Ralph Waldo Emerson, quoted in Alfred Habegger, *The Father: A Life of Henry James, Sr.* (New York: Farrar, Straus and Giroux, 1994), p. 278; MEL to James T. Fisher, June 19, 1847, JTFP.

5. Sterling F. Delano, "A Calendar of Meetings of the 'Boston Religious Union of Associationists,' 1847–1850," in Joel Myerson, ed., *Studies in the American Renaissance* (Boston: Twayne, 1985), pp. 228–29.

6. [Mary Gove Nichols], *Mary Lyndon; or, Revelations of a Life, an Autobiography* (New York: Stringer and Townsend, 1855), p. 385; John B. Blake, "Mary Gove Nichols, Prophetess of Health," in Judith Walzer Leavitt, ed., *Women and Health in America* (Madison: University of Wisconsin Press, 1984), p. 365.

7. MEL, quoted in Delano, "Calendar of Meetings," March 7, 1847, p. 202.

8. Ibid.; MEL, *Love vs. Marriage*, pp. 68, 26, 109.

9. MEL, *Love vs. Marriage*, pp. 235–37; Spurlock, *Free Love*, p. 120; MEL, *Love vs. Marriage*, p. 121; MEL to GM, April 26, 1848, GMP.

10. MEL, *Love vs. Marriage*, pp. 170–71.

11. MEL, quoted in Spurlock, *Free Love*, pp. 119, 120; MEL, quoted in Carl J. Guarneri, *The Utopian Alternative: Fourierism in Nineteenth-Century America* (Ithaca, N.Y.: Cornell University Press, 1991), p. 358; MEL, quoted in Habegger, *Father*, p. 331; MEL, *Love vs. Marriage*, p. 237.

12. MEL, *Love vs. Marriage*, pp. 118, 45, 44; "Origin, Progress, and Position of the Anti-marriage Movement," *New York Daily Times*, reprinted in *New Jerusalem Magazine* 28 (1855), pp. 237–38.

13. Habegger, *Father*, p. 329; Guarneri, *Utopian Alternative*, pp. 407–8.

14. MEL, *Love vs. Marriage*, p. 250.

15. For James's long flirtation with Fourierism and his reversal under pressure from Marx Lazarus, see Habegger, *Father*, pp. 246–342; Henry James Sr., review of *Love vs. Marriage*, *New York Daily Tribune*, Sept. 18, 1852, p. 6.

16. For views of Marx's mental instability, see, for instance, [Nichols], *Mary Lyndon*, pp. 284–86, 300; EM to GM, Oct. 12, 1846, and April 10, 1848, GMP; GM to EM, Nov. 14, 1848, JMP; JL to GM, March 15, 1851, GMP.

17. See for his articulation of this theme, MEL to GM, Jan. 20, 1849, GMP; and MEL, *Involuntary Seminal Losses*, p. 63.

18. On the financial dispute, see, for instance, MEL to GM, Oct. 6 and Nov. 8, 1850, GMP; SM to GM, Jan. 16, 1851, GMP; GM to EM, Jan. 20, 1851, JMP.

19. MEL, *Involuntary Seminal Losses*, pp. iv, 11.

20. John Allen to GM, March 17, 1851, GMP.

21. Ibid.; MEL, *Involuntary Seminal Losses*, p. 29; MEL, *Love vs. Marriage*, pp. 298–300; EL to GM, Sept. 17, 1848, GMP.

22. MEL, *Involuntary Seminal Losses*, pp. 12, 14, 46–47, iii–iv, 29–37, 77.

23. Ibid., pp. 21–25.

24. Ibid., pp. 63, 17–19, 48, 66–67, 18; MEL, *Love vs. Marriage*, p. 299. Marx quoted from François Lallemand's *A Practical Treatise on the Causes, Symptoms, and Treatment of Spermatorrhoea* (Philadelphia, 1839).

25. JL to GM, Nov. 4, 1854, GMP; EM to Eliza, Nov. 15, 1854, MFP; MEL to GM, March 11, 1855, GMP. For accusations against Marx and Nichols's defense, see Taylor Stoehr, ed., *Free Love in America: A Documentary History* (New York: AMS Press, 1979), pp. 272–76.

26. In 1858 a credit agency reported that George's "situation is that of a rich man" (R. G. Dun and Co., June 22, 1858, North Carolina, vol. 1, p. 326, Baker Library, Harvard University Graduate School of Business Administration). George and Margaret had planned an earlier wedding but waited until after the death of her father, who opposed the union (Emma to EM II, June 21, 1852, DFP; and Nancy Lane Mordecai to MMD, Feb. 8, 1852, DFP). For the quotation, see SM to GM, May 19, 1853, GMP. On Margaret's holdings, see Jean Bradley Anderson, *Piedmont Plantation: The Bennahan-Cameron Family and Lands in North Carolina* (Durham, N.C.: Historical Preservation Society of Durham, 1985), pp. 45–46, 95, 129. Margaret soon became pregnant, but the infant was stillborn in 1854 (Eliza to GM, May 18, 1854, GMP). She and George never had another child.

30. DARK DAYS

1. AM to SM, June 13, 1835, AMP; AM to RML, Dec. 19, 1835, and May 26, 1829, AMP; AM to SM, May 13, 1837, JMP; SM to CMP, Aug. 22, 1837, JMP; AM to SM, Jan. 7, 1845, JMP; AM to SM, Feb. 12, 1846, MFP; AM to GM, March 31, 1855, GMP; Eliza to CMP, May 13, 1839, PMP; AM to SM, March 6, 1840, AMP; "The Life of Alfred Mordecai: As Related by Himself," edited by James A. Padgett, *North Carolina Historical Review* 22 (1945), pp. 98–99.

2. On the family's high regard for Alfred, see, for instance, "Life of Alfred Mordecai," p. 99, and Stanley L. Falk, "Divided Loyalties in 1861: The Decision of Major Alfred Mordecai," *Publications of the American Jewish Historical Society* 48 (1959), p. 163. The highest-ranking Jew in the U.S. military was Commodore Uriah P. Levy of the Navy (private e-mail correspondence with Bob Marcus, Feb. 26, 2002).

3. AM to SM, Feb. 12, 1846, MFP; Emma to EM II, March 15, 1846, MFP; Sara Hays Mordecai to AM, Nov. 6, 1855, AMP; SM to EM, March 13, 1849, JMP.

4. Myron Berman, *The Last of the Jews?* (Lanham, Md.: University Press of America, 1998), pp. 88–89; AM to ME, Oct. 7, 1838, quoted in Berman, *Last of the Jews?*, p. 91; Jacob Rader Marcus, *United States Jewry, 1776–1985* (Detroit: Wayne State University Press, 1989), vol. 1, p. 713 n. 34.

5. *HJP*, pp. 191, 437 n. 25; AM to EM, Aug. 7, 1833, AMP; Falk, "Divided Loyalties in 1861," pp. 149–50; AM to EM, March 4, 1830, AMP; AM to SM, Feb. 22, 1837, JMP.

6. Sara Hays Mordecai to AM, Dec. 20, 1855, AMP; AM to GM, May 22, 1853, GMP.

7. EL to GM, Dec. 4, 1849, GMP; JL to GM, March 10, 1850, GMP; MEL to GM, Oct. 6, 1850, GMP; EL to GM, Nov. 22, 1850, and Jan. 7, 1851, GMP; EM to GM, June 26, 1849, GMP.

8. EL to GM, July 1, 1849, June 27, 1850, Oct. 5, 1851, Dec. 1, 1852, and Aug. 15, 1853, GMP; JL to GM, Sept. 25, 1853, GMP; EL to GM, Jan. 9 and Feb. 3, 1854, and Oct. 15, 1856, GMP.

9. SM to GM, April 16, 1853, GMP; EL to GM, Jan. 17, 1855, GMP; JL to GM, Aug. 27, 1855, GMP; Rondel V. Davidson, "Victor Considerant and the Failure of La

Réunion," *Southwestern Historical Quarterly* 76 (1973), pp. 277–96; EL to GM, Oct. 15, 1856, GMP; John Allen to GM, Jan. 29, 1857, GMP; EL to GM, March 22, July 2, Aug. 21, and Oct. 12, 1857, GMP.

10. John C. Spurlock sketches the history of the Berlin Heights community in *Free Love: Marriage and Middle-Class Radicalism in America, 1825–1860* (New York: New York University Press, 1988), pp. 157–62.

11. EL to GM, July 19, Sept. 5, Oct. 13, and Oct. 18, 1858, GMP.

12. Sol to EM, [fall 1853], GMP; CMP to EM, Sept. 9, 1854, LMFP; EM to Eliza, Nov. 15, 1854, MFP; CMP to EM, Feb. 17, 1855, and n.d. [1854–1855], LMFP.

13. CMP to EM, Oct. 7, 1858, GMP; EM to MCM, Jan. 8, 1859, CFP; EM to EM II, Jan. 17 and Jan. 24, 1859, MFP; EM to Emma, May 5, 1859, MFP.

14. SM to GM, June 17, 1859, GMP; SM to EM, March 4, 1860, JMP; SM to GM, Sept. 23, 1859, GMP; EM to EM II, June 2, 1859, MFP; EM II to EM, n.d. [spring 1859], JMP.

15. Eliza to EM, April 21, 1844, MFP; Sara Hays Mordecai and AM to EM, Feb. 10, 1841, AMP; EM to SM, Nov. 8, 1848, JMP; SM to GM, Nov. 20, 1844, GMP; SM to EM, Jan. 29 [1859], JMP; SM to GM, June 17, 1860, GMP; EM II to EM, n.d. [spring 1859], JMP; John M. Blum et al., *The National Experience: A History of the United States*, 5th ed. (New York: Harcourt, Brace, Jovanovich, 1981), p. 338; AM to EM, Nov. 29, 1859, AMP.

16. AM to EM, Nov. 29, 1859, AMP; Marcus, *United States Jewry*, vol. 1, p. 102. AM to EM, June 16, 1861, AMP; and AM to GM, Dec. 17, 1860, GMP.

17. AM to GM, Jan. 20, 1861, GMP; GM to AM, Jan. 17, 1861, AMP; GM to AM, Feb. 28, 1861, JMP; AM to SM, March 17, 1861, AMP.

18. For Governor Ellis's offer, see AM to GM, Jan. 20, 1861, GMP. For Davis's offer, see Stanley L. Falk, "Jefferson Davis and Josiah Gorgas, an Appointment of Necessity," *Journal of Southern History* 28 (1962), pp. 84–86; and AM to GM, March 10, 1861, GMP. Jefferson Davis was a plebe at West Point when Alfred taught there (Falk, "Jefferson Davis," p. 84). In her memoir of her husband, Davis's wife, Varina, described Alfred flatteringly as a man whose "habits of thought were . . . so perfectly systematized as to make everything evolved from his fecund mind available for the use of mankind. His moral nature was as well disciplined as his mental . . . ; he was an 'Israelite without guile' " (Varina Davis, *Jefferson Davis, Ex-President of the Confederate States of America: A Memoir by His Wife* [New York: Belford Co., 1890], vol. 1, pp. 535–36). On the workers' questioning Alfred, see AM to Colonel H. R. Craig, April 15, 1861, AMP; and Falk, "Divided Loyalties in 1861," p. 154. On Alfred's journey south, see AM to SM, April 2, 1861, JMP; and "Life of Alfred Mordecai," p. 105.

19. SM, *Richmond in By-Gone Days* (1860; Richmond: Dietz Press, 1946), p. 144; Marie Tyler-McGraw, *At the Falls: Richmond, Virginia, and Its People* (Chapel Hill: University of North Carolina Press, 1994), p. 135; SM to GM, April 18, 1861, GMP; Emma to EM II, April 21, 1861, MFP.

20. Emma to EM II, April 21, 1861, MFP; GM to SM, April 21, 1861, JMP.

31. WAR

1. Emma to EM II, April 21, 1861, MFP.

2. Emma to EM II, April 26, 1861, MFP; RMM to CMP, Oct. 21, 1860, MFP.

3. EM almanac, Oct. 21, 1860, LMFP; EL to GM, Nov. 26, 1860, GMP; CMP to AM, March 11, 1861, AMP; Emma to EM II, April 21, 1861, MFP.

4. Emma to EM II, April 26, 1861, MFP; EM to GM, May 6, 1861, GMP.

5. GM to SM, April 21, 1861, JMP; E. B. Long with Barbara Long, *The Civil War Day by Day: An Almanac, 1861–1865* (1971; New York: Da Capo Press, 1985), pp. 61–62, 70, 76; Stanley L. Falk, "Jefferson Davis and Josiah Gorgas, an Appointment of Necessity," *Journal of Southern History* 28 (1962), pp. 84–86; Emma to Sara Hays Mordecai, April 21, 1861, AMP; EM to GM, May 6, 1861, GMP.

6. AM to Colonel H. R. Craig, April 15, 1861, AMP; J. W. Ripley to AM, April 29, 1861, reprinted in clipping, AMP; Stanley L. Falk, "Divided Loyalties in 1861: The Decision of Major Alfred Mordecai," *Publications of the American Jewish Historical Society* 48 (1959), p. 160.

7. *Troy Daily Times*, May 8, 1861, AMP; Falk, "Divided Loyalties in 1861," p. 166; GM to SM, May 5, 1861, JMP; EM to AM, May 28, 1861, AMP; GM to AM, April 16, 1861, AMP.

8. J. W. Ripley to AM, April 29, 1861, quoted in Falk, "Divided Loyalties in 1861," pp. 163, 166; AM obituary, miscellaneous papers, MFP.

9. AM to SM, June 2, 1861, AMP; EM to AM, June 6, 1861, EMP; AM to EM, June 16, 1861, AMP. Among the letters Falk cites are two from other southern Jews urging Alfred to come over to the Confederate side ("Divided Loyalties in 1861," pp. 166–67 n. 81).

10. EM to AM, May 18, 1861, AMP; GM and SM to AM, June 26, 1861, AMP; SM to GM, June 9, 1861, AMP; EM to GM, May 6, 1861, GMP.

11. SM to GM, June 9, 1861, GMP.

12. William B. Skelton, *An American Profession of Arms: The Army Officer Corps, 1784–1861* (Lawrence: University Press of Kansas, 1992), p. 194.

13. EM to GM, May 6, 1861, GMP; SM to GM, June 9, 1861, GMP; AM to EM, June 16, 1861, AMP; Emma to EM II, Jan. 5, 1862, MFP; SM to GM, Sept. 16, 1861, GMP; "Major Alfred Mordecai," *Jewish Exponent*, Nov. 25, 1887; AM to SM, June 2, 1861, AMP; AM to EM, Aug. 9, 1861, AMP.

14. RMM to AM, Aug. 25, 1861 (copy), GMP.

15. The Confederates counted 387 killed and 1,582 wounded (Long, *Civil War Day by Day*, p. 99). EM to MCM, May 19, 1861, CFP; EM to AM, June 6, 1861, GMP; SM to GM, Aug. 8, 1861, GMP; Sol to EM, Sept. 26, 1861, MFP; Emma to GM, Nov. 4, 1861, GMP; EM to MCM and Mildred Cameron, Oct. 15, 1861, GMP; GM to MCM, Aug. 17, 1861, CFP; Sol to EM, Nov. 23, 1861, MFP; *MHMF*, p. 52.

16. GM to SM, Oct. 24, 1860, JMP; EM to GM, Aug. 15, 1862, and EM almanac, March 31, 1864, LMFP; *MHMF*, pp. 42, 52. Also see SM to GM, March 29, 1849, GMP; and Emma journal, July 21, 1864, MFP.

17. SM to GM, July 28, 1862, GMP; Emma to GM, March 10 and March 15, 1863, GMP; Emma to EM II, Aug. 18, 1862, MFP; *MHMF*, p. 57. Becky's enthusiasm for the war is echoed in Emma's Civil War diary (MFP) and Caroline Myers Cohen's *MHMF*.

18. SM to GM, March 1, 1862, GMP.

19. SM to GM, April 13, 1862, GMP; Richard N. Current, ed., *Encyclopedia of the Confederacy* (New York: Simon and Schuster, 1993), vol. 1, pp. 419–20; SM to GM, June 1 and July 11, 1862, GMP.

20. *MHMF*, p. 40; Sol to EM, Oct. 11, 1863, MFP; Long, *Civil War Day by Day*, pp. 411–12; Emma to GM, Sept. 14 and March 15, 1863, GMP; EM to GM, March 10, 1863, GMP. Soliloquy from Joseph Addison, *Cato* (1787), V, i.

21. AM to EM, Oct. 16, 1863, AMP; Emma journal, June 23, 1864, MFP; RMM to CMP, Oct. 21, 1860, MFP; EM to Eliza, Nov. 15, 1854, MFP; Sol to EM, Oct. 11, 1863, MFP.

22. SM to GM, Nov. 21, 1863, and Jan. 15, 1864, GMP; Emma to MCM, Feb. 25, 1864, CFP; SM to MCM, Jan. 22, 1864, CFP.

23. SM to GM, March 16 and March 18, 1864, GMP; EM to MCM, March 28, 1864, CFP.

24. CMC, "MHMF Draft," p. 50, MYFP; Emma journal, May 10, Aug. 24, Oct. 1, Oct. 10, Oct. 14, 1864, MFP.

25. SM to GM, March 29, 1863, GMP; GM to [?], April 17, 1862, CFP; EM, April 22, 1862, LMFP; Elizabeth Reid Murray, *Wake: Capital County of North Carolina* (Raleigh, N.C.: Capital County Publishing, 1983), vol. 1, p. 427; SM to GM, March 16, 1864, GMP; EM to EM II, April 28, 1862, MFP. Also see MMD, "A Tribute to the Memory of Uncle George," DFP.

26. Obituary, March 9, 1871, MYFP; "George Mordecai," *DNCB*, vol. 4, pp. 315–16; EM almanac, Feb. 13, 1864, LMFP; JL to GM, April 21, 1861, GMP; GM to SM, June 13, 1861, JMP; SM to GM, Aug. 8, 1861, GMP; GM to MCM and Mildred Cameron, Aug. 17, 1861, CFP; SM to GM, Sept. 16, 1861, GMP; EM to MCM and Mildred Cameron, Oct. 15, 1861, GMP; Emma to EM II, Aug. 18, 1862, MFP.

27. Roger Wunderlich, *Low Living and High Thinking at Modern Times, New York* (Syracuse, N.Y.: Syracuse University Press, 1992); John C. Spurlock, *Free Love: Marriage and Middle-Class Radicalism in America, 1825–1860* (New York: New York University Press, 1988), pp. 107–38; Sidney Ditzion, *Marriage, Morals, and Sex in America: A History of Ideas* (1953; exp. ed., New York: Octagon Books, 1969), pp. 159–63; Madeleine B. Stern, *The Pantarch: A Biography of Stephen Pearl Andrews* (Austin: University of Texas Press, 1968), pp. 73–86; Verne Dyson, *A Century of Brentwood* (Brentwood, N.Y.: Brentwood Village Press, 1959), p. 38; EL to GM, Oct. 28, 1858, GMP.

28. EL to GM, July 29 and Sept. 28, 1859, May 17, 1861, and [no day] Oct. 1866, GMP.

29. EM II to E. V. Valentine, April 6, 1909, E. V. Valentine Papers, Valentine Rich-

mond History Center; SM, addition to "Retrospect of 1811" (Jan. 24, 1857), JMP; SM to GM, April 13 and April 4, 1862, and March 16, 1864, GMP; *Herald of the Union* (Wilmington, N.C.), March 2, 1865.

30. EM II to E. V. Valentine, April 6, 1909, E. V. Valentine Papers, Valentine Richmond History Center.

31. Robert N. Rosen, *The Jewish Confederates* (Columbia: University of South Carolina Press, 2000), pp. 142, 326; Emma to Edward B. Cohen, April 5, 1865, included in typescript copy of Emma diary, pp. 115–21, MFP.

32. Emma to Edward B. Cohen, April 5, 1865, included in typescript copy of Emma diary, pp. 122–29, MFP.

33. Emma journal, April 15, 1865, SHC; Emma to GM, April 21, 1865, GMP; CMC, quoted in Emma to Edward B. Cohen, April 5, 1865, included in typescript copy of Emma diary, pp. 115, 127, MFP.

34. *MHMF*, p. 53.

35. Emma journal, Jan. 5, 1862, and Oct. 10, 1864, MFP; *RJ*, p. 238; Aaron Baroway, "The Cohens of Maryland," *Maryland Historical Magazine* 19 (1924) p. 66; genealogical notes in Julia scrapbook, Virginia Historical Society; Solomon Cohen to [Emma?], July 21, 1865, JMP.

36. AM to "My dear brother and sister," Aug. 9, 1861, AMP, quoted in Falk, "Divided Loyalties in 1861," p. 168.

37. "The Life of Alfred Mordecai: As Related by Himself," edited by James A. Padgett, *North Carolina Historical Review* 22 (1945), p. 107; Sara Hays Mordecai to EM, Aug. 9, 1861, AMP.

38. Late in the war, Alfred received an anonymous gift of one thousand dollars. He tried to return the money, only to be told that the deposit was irreversible (A. J. Drexel to AM, Sept. 9 and Sept. 12, 1864, AMP). Also see "Life of Alfred Mordecai," pp. 105–6, 107; AM to GM, Aug. 9 and Aug. 20, 1865, and March 30, 1868, GMP; James A. Padgett, ed., "Life of Alfred Mordecai in Mexico in 1865–1866 as Told in His Letters to His Family," *North Carolina Historical Review* 22 (1945), pp. 218, 221, 224, 355, 374.

39. "Life of Alfred Mordecai," pp. 106, 62; MMD to GM, Oct. 15, 1866, GMP; AM to GM, Nov. 2, 1866, GMP; Falk, "Divided Loyalties in 1861," p. 161.

40. "Life of Alfred Mordecai," p. 108. The visitors included "Miss Martha Mordecai" (nicknamed Patty), Jacob's great-granddaughter and Moses's granddaughter, who was then seventeen years old. "List of Visitors on the Fiftieth Anniversary, June 1 1886," AMP.

41. Baroway, "Cohens of Maryland," p. 67; Myron Berman, *The Last of the Jews?* (Lanham, Md.: University Press of America, 1998), p. 86.

42. "Edward Cohen" biographical sketch, in Julia scrapbook, p. 71, Virginia Historical Society; *MHMF*, p. 3. Caroline Myers Cohen expressed her commitment to her family and to Jewish causes in her will. Bequests went to the Orphan's Home of the Independent Order of B'nai B'rith in Atlanta, the Zionist women's organization Hadas-

sah, the Jewish National Fund, and the Richmond Hospital, as well as to relatives, Christian and Jewish alike (Berman, *Last of the Jews?*, p. 83).

43. CMC, "Draft of MHMF," p. 39, MYFP.

AFTERWORD

1. See, for instance, Mrs. J. G. Brunner (née Almira Emma Lazarus, Marx's half sister) to William Calder, May 28 [1895], Calder Family Papers, Lower Cape Fear Historical Society; "Notes on Family History," MYFP; E. T. D. Myers (Eliza's son) to Emma, Oct. 9, 1901, MYFP; EM II to E. V. Valentine, April 6, 1909, E. V. Valentine Papers, Valentine Richmond History Center; CMC to E. V. Valentine, April 30, 1909, E. V. Valentine Papers, Valentine Richmond History Center; EM II, *Gleanings from Long Ago* (1933; Raleigh, N.C.: Capital Area Preservation Inc., 1974); John Brooke Mordecai (Jacob's great-grandson and Augustus's grandson), "Family Notes," Dec. 1951, BAA. On geographic migrations, see, for instance, George Washington Mordecai Jr. (son of Augustus) to [?], March 29, 1871, in *The Mordecai Papers: Correspondence of a Madera County Pioneer from the Fresno Plains, 1868–1876* (Madera, Calif.: Madera County Centennial Press, 1992), p. 94.

2. Moses's daughter Margaret Mordecai Devereux published her memoir of the happy pre–Civil War slavery days, *Plantation Sketches* (1906). Marx Edgeworth Lazarus died in 1895 in Guntersville, Alabama, having spent many years writing on social, political, and economic issues for the radical press. On Marx's later career, see James J. Martin, *Men against the State: The Expositors of Individualist Anarchism in America, 1827–1908* (New York: Libertarian Book Club, 1957), pp. 241, 245–56; MEL, Autobiography (n.d.), Labadie Collection, Special Collections Library, University of Michigan; Katherine McKinstry Duncan and Larry Joe Smith, *The History of Marshall County, Alabama* (Albertville, Ala.: Thompson Printing, 1969), vol. 1, p. 58. Ellen Lazarus Allen's daughter Mary Catherine remained with the Shakers until her death. She was a leader at New Lebanon and espoused radical social reforms (see Stephen J. Stein, *The Shaker Experience in America: A History of the United Society of Believers* [New Haven, Conn.: Yale University Press, 1992], pp. 308–12).

3. EM journal, May 17, 1817, LMFP; Eliza to CMP, Aug. 3, 1845, PMP.

NOTES ON SOURCES

Because the Mordecai story touches on many aspects of life in the early United States, the research for this book led into several historical specializations as I sought to contextualize the flood of manuscript information from the Mordecais and associated families or individuals. What follows is a selective listing of the works that were most useful to understanding the cultural, religious, economic, and social forces and conditions under which the Mordecais lived and strove to fulfill the promise of their covenant.

GENERAL WORKS

This study would have been extremely difficult without the tremendous amount of data contained in Malcolm S. Stern, *First American Jewish Families: 600 Genealogies, 1654–1988* (Baltimore: Ottenheimer Publishers, 1988). For a general sense of material conditions and middle-class values as they appeared in daily life, I have relied on Jack Larkin, *The Reshaping of Everyday Life, 1790–1840* (New York: Harper Perennial, 1988), and Richard L. Bushman, *The Refinement of America: Persons, Houses, Cities* (New York: Vintage Books, 1992).

JEWISH HISTORY

The Mordecais demonstrate how complex and varied Jewish identity could be in this period. Especially helpful surveys of Jews in the pre–Civil War United States include: Jacob Rader Marcus, *Early American Jewry,* 2 vols. (Philadelphia: Jewish Publication Society of America, 1951–1953); Eli Faber, *A Time for Planting: The First Migration, 1654–1820* (Baltimore: Johns Hopkins University Press, 1992); Hasia R. Diner, *A Time for Gathering: The Second Migration, 1820–1880* (Baltimore: Johns Hopkins University Press, 1992). Myron Berman's *Richmond's Jewry, 1769–1976: Shabbat in Shockoe* (Charlottesville: University Press of Virginia, 1979) was a critical community study for this project. Also useful have been two biographies of leading American Jewish figures in the early nineteenth century: Lance J. Sussman, *Isaac Leeser and the Making of American Judaism* (Detroit: Wayne State University Press, 1995), and Gary Philip Zola, *Isaac Harby of Charleston, 1788–1828: Jewish Reformer and Intellectual* (Tuscaloosa: University of Alabama Press, 1994). Reform Judaism was in its infant stages during the period this story covers, but the Mordecais took a keen interest—and played a role—in its formation. For a broad study of the movement, see Michael A. Meyer, *Response to Modernity: A History of the Reform Movement in Judaism* (New York: Oxford University Press, 1988).

Because there were so few Jews in the United States during the eighteenth and early nineteenth centuries, English and European Jewry have received greater attention from scholars exploring questions of assimilation and acculturation. See Elisheva Carlebach, *Divided Souls: Converts from Judaism in Germany, 1500–1750* (New Haven, Conn.: Yale University Press, 2001); David Sorkin, *The Transformation of German Jewry, 1780–1840* (New York: Oxford University Press, 1987); Todd Endelman, *The Jews of Georgian England, 1714–1830* (Philadelphia: Jewish Publication Society of America, 1979); Todd Endelman, *Radical Assimilation in English Jewish History, 1695–1945* (Bloomington: Indiana University Press, 1990); Todd Endelman, ed., *Jewish Apostasy in the Modern World* (New York: Holmes and Meier, 1987). Maria Edgeworth's novel *Harrington* is one of the texts Michael Ragussis examines in his cultural study *Figures of Conversion: "The Jewish Question" and English National Identity* (Durham, N.C.: Duke University Press, 1995). On assimilation generally, see Werner Sollors, *Beyond Ethnicity: Consent and Descent in American Culture* (New York: Oxford University Press, 1986), and Amos Funkenstein, "The Dialectics of Assimilation," *Jewish Social Studies* 1 (1995), pp. 1–14.

For the roles women played in nineteenth-century American and European Jewish life, see Karla Goldman, *Beyond the Synagogue Gallery: Finding a Place for Women in American Judaism* (Cambridge, Mass.: Harvard University Press, 2000); Dianne Ashton, *Rebecca Gratz: Women and Judaism in Antebellum America* (Detroit: Wayne State University Press, 1997); Marion A. Kaplan, *The Making of the Jewish Middle Class: Women, Family, and Identity in Imperial Germany* (New York: Oxford University Press, 1991); Marion A. Kaplan, "Priestess and Housefrau: Women and Tradition in the

German-Jewish Family," in Paula Hyman and David Cohen, eds., *The Jewish Family: Myths and Reality* (New York: Holmes and Meier, 1986), pp. 62–93; Paula Hyman, *Gender and Assimilation in Modern Jewish History: The Roles and Representation of Women* (Seattle: University of Washington Press, 1995); Ellen M. Umansky, "Spiritual Expressions: Jewish Women's Religious Lives in the United States in the Nineteenth and Twentieth Centuries," in Judith R. Baskin, ed., *Jewish Women in Historical Perspective* (Detroit: Wayne State University Press, 1998), pp. 337–63. For Jewish women and conversion in an earlier period, see Deborah Hertz, "Women at the Edge of Judaism: Female Converts in Germany, 1600–1750," in Menahem Mor, ed., *Jewish Assimilation, Acculturation, and Accommodation: Past Traditions, Current Issues, and Future Prospects* (Lanham, Md.: University Press of America, 1992), pp. 87–109.

Jews in the South have begun to receive greater notice, but most of that is for the period after the Civil War. Eli N. Evans's biography, *Judah P. Benjamin: The Jewish Confederate* (New York: Free Press, 1988), stands as an exception. On the Jews' racial identification in a somewhat later period, see Leonard Rogoff, "Is the Jew White? The Racial Place of the Southern Jew," *American Jewish History* 85 (1997), pp. 195–230. Stephen J. Whitfield's review essay "In the High Cotton," *Southern Jewish History* 4 (2001), pp. 123–44, conveys the state of the field and its chief themes of Jewish acculturation, assimilation, and regional distinctiveness.

RELIGION IN THE EARLY UNITED STATES

The Revolutionary era's influential strain of religious tolerance and liberalism inspired minorities like the Mordecais. For a concise reading of that spirit, see Chris Beneke, "From Many, One: The Religious Origins of American Identity," available on-line from "The American Religious Experience" at http://are.as.wvu.edu.

But in the early nineteenth century, American Jews faced a culture dominated by Protestants and intensely concerned with religious matters, including evangelical awakenings, fast-growing denominations, and religiously inspired reform movements. Jonathan D. Sarna's "The American Jewish Response to Nineteenth-Century Christian Missions," *Journal of American History* 68 (1981), pp. 35–51, and Lance J. Sussman's "Isaac Leeser and the Protestantization of American Judaism," *American Jewish Archives* 38 (1986), pp. 1–21, illuminate the intersections of such developments with American Judaism. For more on the impact of Evangelicalism, see Donald G. Mathews, *Religion in the Old South* (Chicago: University of Chicago Press, 1977), and Christine Leigh Heyrman, *Southern Cross: The Beginnings of the Bible Belt* (Chapel Hill: University of North Carolina Press, 1997). Much evidence suggests the centrality of religion to women's identity during this period. The work of Joanna Bowen Gillespie speaks directly to some experiences in the family; see *The Life and Times of Martha Laurens Ramsay, 1759–1811* (Columbia: University of South Carolina Press, 2001) and "'The Clear Leadings of Providence': Pious Memoirs and the Problems of Self-Realization for Women in the Early Nineteenth Century," *Journal of the Early Repub-*

lic 5 (1985), pp. 197–221. Richard Rankin's *Ambivalent Churchmen and Evangelical Churchwomen: The Religion of the Episcopal Elite in North Carolina, 1800–1860* (Columbia: University of South Carolina Press, 1993) examines the tensions between the pious Christian men and women Rachel and Aaron Lazarus knew well. R. Laurence Moore describes the way religion suffused ideas and learning in his essay "What Children Did Not Learn in School: The Intellectual Quickening of Young Americans in the Nineteenth Century," *Church History* 68 (1999), pp. 42–61.

EARLY AMERICAN FAMILIES, CLASS, AND DOMESTIC LIFE

The intersection of religion and family in the Mordecais' period is compellingly conveyed in Anne C. Rose's *Beloved Strangers: Interfaith Families in Nineteenth-Century America* (Cambridge, Mass.: Harvard University Press, 2001), which features several of the Mordecais' intermarriages. Rose's essay "Religious Individualism in Nineteenth-Century American Families," in Peter W. Williams, ed., *Perspectives on American Religion and Culture* (Malden, Mass.: Blackwell, 1999), pp. 319–30, focuses on a widespread tension the Mordecais manifested with special clarity.

On the formation of middle-class families, values, and material culture, see Mary P. Ryan, *Cradle of the Middle Class: The Family in Oneida County, New York, 1790–1865* (New York: Cambridge University Press, 1981); Steven Mintz, *A Prison of Expectations: The Family in Victorian Culture* (New York: New York University Press, 1983); Elisabeth Donaghy Garrett, *At Home: The American Family, 1750–1870* (New York: Harry N. Abrams, 1990). The ideology of the burgeoning middle class developed on both sides of the Atlantic, and European scholars have explored it deeply. See especially Leonore Davidoff and Catherine Hall, *Family Fortunes: Men and Women of the English Middle Class, 1780–1850* (Chicago: University of Chicago Press, 1987), and John Tosh, *A Man's Place: Masculinity and the Middle-Class Home in Victorian England* (New Haven, Conn.: Yale University Press, 1999).

Scholars have shown an interest in tensions within families arising from Revolutionary-era concepts of equality. See, for instance, Jay Fliegelman, *Prodigals and Pilgrims: The American Revolution against Patriarchal Authority* (New York: Cambridge University Press, 1985), and Jan Lewis, *The Pursuit of Happiness: Family and Values in Jefferson's Virginia* (New York: Cambridge University Press, 1983).

While my arguments tend to run against the idea of highly differentiated regional cultures during this period, Jane Turner Censer's *North Carolina Planters and Their Children, 1800–1860* (Baton Rouge: Louisiana State University Press, 1984) and Anya Jabour's *Marriage in the Early Republic: Elizabeth and William Wirt and the Companionate Ideal* (Baltimore: Johns Hopkins University Press, 1998) illuminate family patterns among better-off Americans in the upper South.

As the Mordecais attest, siblings played substantial roles in the large families of the nineteenth century. For the impact of this family structure, see Lorri Glover, *All Our Relations: Blood Ties and Emotional Bonds among the Early South Carolina Gentry* (Baltimore: Johns Hopkins University Press, 2000), and Arnette Atkins, *We Grew Up To-gether: Brothers and Sisters in Nineteenth-Century America* (Urbana: University of Illinois Press, 2001).

On courtship, marriage, sex, and reproduction in this period, see Karen Lystra, *Searching the Heart: Women, Men, and Romantic Love in Nineteenth-Century America* (New York: Oxford University Press, 1989); Lee Chambers-Schiller, *Liberty, a Better Husband: Single Women in America: The Generations of 1780–1840* (New Haven, Conn.: Yale University Press, 1984); John D'Emilio and Estelle B. Freedman, *Intimate Matters: A History of Sexuality in America* (New York: Harper and Row, 1988); Janet Farrell Brodie, *Contraception and Abortion in Nineteenth-Century America* (Ithaca, N.Y.: Cornell University Press, 1994); Sally McMillan, *Motherhood in the Old South: Pregnancy, Childbirth, and Infant Rearing* (Baton Rouge: Louisiana State University Press, 1990); Judith Walker Leavitt, *Brought to Bed: Childbearing in America, 1750–1950* (New York: Oxford University Press, 1986); Richard W. Wertz and Dorothy C. Wertz, *Lying In: A History of Childbirth in America* (New York: Free Press, 1977).

For legal constraints on family members, see Peter Bardaglio, *Reconstructing the Household: Families, Sex, and the Law in the Nineteenth-Century South* (Chapel Hill: University of North Carolina Press, 1995); Jane Turner Censer, " 'Smiling through Her Tears': Antebellum Southern Women and Divorce," *American Journal of Legal History* 25 (1981), pp. 24–47; Michael Grossberg, *Governing the Hearth: Law and Family in Nineteenth-Century America* (Chapel Hill: University of North Carolina Press, 1985).

Throughout this project, I have stressed that family, complete with its power relations and domestic conflicts, is something men, women, parents, siblings, and children construct together and experience as individuals in relationship with one another. For an analysis of the importance of bringing a gendered perspective to family history, see Judith E. Smith, "Family History and Feminist History," *Feminist Studies* 17 (1991), pp. 349–64.

MEN, WOMEN, AND THE ECONOMY IN EARLY AMERICA

Late-eighteenth- and early-nineteenth-century economic conditions and the ideology surrounding the economic roles of men and women were crucial to understanding the Mordecai story. For a sense of the market turbulence Americans experienced, see Samuel Rezneck, *Business Depressions and Financial Panics: Essays in American Business and Economic History* (New York: Greenwood Publishing, 1968). Toby L. Ditz's "Shipwrecked; or, Masculinity Imperiled: Mercantile Representations of Failure and the Gendered Self in Eighteenth-Century Philadelphia," *Journal of American History* 81 (1994), pp. 51–80, and Thomas M. Doerflinger's *A Vigorous Spirit of Enterprise: Merchants and Economic Development in Revolutionary Philadelphia* (Chapel Hill: University of North Carolina Press, 1986) explore the experience and identity of men in eighteenth-century business. Women's economic functions within the household and urbanizing economy are analyzed in Jeanne Boydston's *Home and Work: Housework,*

Wages, and the Ideology of Labor in the Early Republic (New York: Oxford University Press, 1990), which argues that women's social status was damaged by the growing division between paid and unpaid work. Also see Emily Bingham and Penny Leigh Richards, "The Female Academy and Beyond: Three Mordecai Sisters at Work in the Old South," in Susanna Delfino and Michele Gillespie, eds., *Neither Lady nor Slave: Working Women in the Old South* (Chapel Hill: University of North Carolina Press, 2002); Christine Stansell, *City of Women: Sex and Class in New York, 1789–1860* (1982; Urbana: University of Illinois Press, 1987); Suzanne Lebsock, *The Free Women of Petersburg: Status and Culture in a Southern Town, 1784–1860* (New York: Norton, 1984); Elizabeth Fox-Genovese, *Within the Plantation Household: Black and White Women of the Old South* (Chapel Hill: University of North Carolina Press, 1988); Catherine Clinton, *The Plantation Mistress: Woman's World in the Old South* (New York: Pantheon, 1982).

Keith C. Barton's article " 'Good Cooks and Washers': Slave Hiring, Domestic Labor, and the Market in Bourbon County, Kentucky," *Journal of American History* 84 (1997), pp. 436–60, focuses on the way the slave system adapted to middle-class ideals of women's work and domesticity that are typically identified with the antebellum North but in fact bore heavily on southern social structures as well. For the integration of slavery in the urban South, see Richard C. Wade, *Slavery in the Cities, 1820–1860* (New York: Oxford University Press, 1964).

GENDER IDEOLOGY, WOMEN'S ROLES, AND INTELLECTUAL LIFE

The Mordecai women were central to creating a covenant of domestic enlightenment that determined and sustained family identity even as it staked women's claim for cultural and familial authority. On the ideological and practical opportunities for (and limits on) women's power, see Linda K. Kerber, *Women of the Republic: Intellect and Ideology in Revolutionary America* (Chapel Hill: University of North Carolina Press, 1980); Ruth Bloch, "The Gendered Meaning of Virtue in Revolutionary America," *Signs* 13 (1987), pp. 237–52; Ruth Bloch, "American Feminine Ideals in Transition: The Rise of the Moral Mother, 1785–1815," *Feminist Studies* 4 (1978), pp. 102–26; Nancy Cott, *The Bonds of Womanhood: "Woman's Sphere" in New England, 1780–1860* (New Haven, Conn.: Yale University Press, 1977); Dorinda Outram, *The Enlightenment* (New York: Cambridge University Press, 1995); Elizabeth Kowaleski-Wallace, *Their Fathers' Daughters: Hannah More, Maria Edgeworth, and Patriarchal Complicity* (New York: Oxford University Press, 1991); Mitzi Myers, "Deromanticizing the Subject: Maria Edgeworth's 'The Bracelets,' Mythologies of Origin, and the Daughter's Coming to Writing," in Paula R. Feldman and Theresa M. Kelley, eds., *Romantic Women Writers: Voices and Countervoices* (Detroit: Wayne State University Press, 1994); Mitzi Myers, "Reform or Ruin: A Revolution in Female Manners," in Harry C. Payne, ed., *Studies in Eighteenth-Century Culture* (Madison: University of Wisconsin Press, 1982), pp. 199–216; Mary Kelley, *Private Woman, Public Stage: Literary Domesticity in Nineteenth-Century America* (New York: Oxford University Press, 1984); Mary Kelley, "Reading Women/Women

Reading: The Making of Learned Women in Antebellum America," *Journal of American History* 183 (1996), pp. 401–24.

The particular nature of female education in the South receives attention in Anya Jabour's " 'Grown Girls, Highly Cultivated': Female Education in an Antebellum Southern Family," *Journal of Southern History* 64 (1998), pp. 23–64, and Steven Stowe's "The Not-So-Cloistered Academy: Elite Women's Education and Family Feeling in the Old South," in Walter J. Fraser Jr. et al., eds., *The Web of Southern Social Relations: Women, Family, and Education* (Athens: University of Georgia Press, 1985).

As the nineteenth century progressed, the benevolent labor Emma and Ellen Mordecai and so many middle- and upper-class American women took part in became a vital feature of public life and, in some places, a vehicle for women's public influence. See especially Lori D. Ginzburg, *Women and the Work of Benevolence: Morality, Politics, and Class in the Nineteenth-Century United States* (New Haven, Conn.: Yale University Press, 1990), and Barbara Berg, *The Remembered Gate: Origins of American Feminism: The Woman and the City, 1800–1860* (New York: Oxford University Press, 1978).

RADICAL REFORM IN THE NINETEENTH-CENTURY UNITED STATES

On moral reform and benevolent work aimed at uplift and order—religious, social, and cultural—see Paul Boyer, *Urban Masses and Moral Order in America, 1820–1920* (Cambridge, Mass.: Harvard University Press, 1978). But Ellen and Marx Lazarus joined a movement that sought to rescue American society by reorganizing fundamental social and economic structures. The often-religious origins and tone of the radical reformers emerge nicely from David Robinson's "The Political Odyssey of William Henry Channing," *American Quarterly* 34 (1982), pp. 165–84. Various expressions of the movement central to the Mordecai story are found in Anne C. Rose, *Transcendentalism as a Social Movement* (New Haven, Conn.: Yale University Press, 1981); John C. Spurlock, *Free Love: Marriage and Middle-Class Radicalism in America, 1825–1860* (New York: New York University Press, 1988); and Carl J. Guarneri, *The Utopian Alternative: Fourierism in Nineteenth-Century America* (Ithaca, N.Y.: Cornell University Press, 1991). Women's roles within the radical vanguard receive attention from Ellen Dubois, "Feminism and Free Love" (2001), available on-line at H-Women discussion list http://www2.h-net.msu.edu/~woman/papers/freelove.html; Dolores Hayden, *Seven American Utopias: The Architecture of Communitarian Socialism* (Cambridge, Mass.: MIT Press, 1976); and Jean Silver-Isenstadt, *Shameless: The Visionary Life of Mary Gove Nichols* (Baltimore: Johns Hopkins University Press, 2002).

SELECTED SOURCES ON THE MORDECAI FAMILY

The Mordecais were not a famous family; nevertheless, because many of them published writings and because they preserved their letters to the benefit of later historians, they can boast an extensive bibliography. On Jacob's childhood in Philadelphia, see "Addenda to Watson's Annals of Philadelphia: Notes by Jacob Mordecai, 1836," edited by Whitfield J. Bell Jr., *Pennsylvania Magazine of History and Biography* 98 (1974), pp. 131–70.

On members of the second generation, see Samuel Mordecai, *Richmond in By-Gone Days* (1856; reprint, Richmond: Dietz Press, 1946); Alexander Wilbourne Weddell, "Samuel Mordecai: Chronicler of Richmond, 1786–1865," *Virginia Historical Magazine* 53 (1945), pp. 265–87; William Barlow and David O. Powell, "A Dedicated Medical Student: Solomon Mordecai, 1819–1822," *Journal of the Early Republic* 7 (Winter 1987), pp. 377–97; Alfred Mordecai, "The Life of Alfred Mordecai: As Related by Himself," edited by James A. Padgett, *North Carolina Historical Review* 22 (1945), pp. 58–108; and Stanley L. Falk, "Divided Loyalties in 1861: The Decision of Major Alfred Mordecai," *Publications of the American Jewish Historical Society* 48 (1959), pp. 147–69. Central to the portrayal of Rachel was Edgar E. MacDonald, ed., *The Education of the Heart: The Correspondence of Rachel Mordecai Lazarus and Maria Edgeworth* (Chapel Hill: University of North Carolina Press, 1977).

Both Ellen and Emma Mordecai published religious writings under pseudonyms. See Esther Whitlock [Ellen Mordecai], *Past Days: A Story for Children* (New York: D. Appleton, 1841); [Ellen Mordecai], *The History of a Heart* (Philadelphia: Stavely and M'Calla, 1845); [Emma Mordecai], *The Teachers' and Parents' Assistant* (Philadelphia: C. Sherman, 1845); American Jewess [Emma Mordecai], "The Duty of Israel," *Occident and American Jewish Advocate* 2 (Jan. 1845); and American Jewess [Emma Mordecai], "An Essay," *Occident and American Jewish Advocate* 5 (July 1847), available on-line at http://www.jewish-history.com/Occident.

Among the third generation of Mordecais, several wrote works that added significantly to my understanding of the family: Marx Edgeworth Lazarus, *Love vs. Marriage* (New York: Fowlers and Wells, 1852); Caroline Myers Cohen, *Record of the Myers, Hays, and Mordecai Families from 1707 to 1913* (Washington, D.C., 1913); Ellen Mordecai Mordecai, *Gleanings from Long Ago* (1933; Raleigh, N.C.: Capital Area Preservation Inc., 1974).

Finally, three scholars have written about important aspects of the Mordecai family's experiences during the period this book covers. The school years and the nature of the family's enterprise in Warrenton emerge from Penny Leigh Richards, " 'A Thousand Images, Painfully Pleasing': Complicating Histories of the Mordecai School, Warrenton, North Carolina, 1809–1818" (Ph.D. diss., University of North Carolina–Chapel Hill, 1996). Jean E. Friedman published Rachel's journal of educating her sister Eliza and locates the Mordecai family in relation to Jewish tradition in *Ways of Wisdom: Moral Education in the Early National Period, Including the Diary of Rachel Mordecai Lazarus* (Athens: University of Georgia Press, 2001). Myron Berman, whose study of Jews in Richmond sheds much light on the Mordecais, revisited the family as a case study in assimilation in *The Last of the Jews?* (Lanham, Md.: University Press of America, 1998).

ACKNOWLEDGMENTS

Over the years, teachers, colleagues, family members, friends, archivists, and others have aided and enriched my inquiry into the Mordecais. I will spend many more years fully thanking them. Yet the Mordecais themselves have been among the greatest of my tutors, and some of my most compelling companions. Fascinating, flawed, idealistic, tender, ambitious, and proud, these people from long ago wrote with open hearts, and miraculously kept much of what they wrote. I have always admired them and have never tired of them.

While in graduate school, I was fortunate in having a deep bench of instructors, advisors, and fellow students who expressed excitement about the Mordecais while finding ways to sharpen my conceptualization of the project. Some read the manuscript at multiple stages, offering criticism and suggestions that I have incorporated into this work. I hope someday to be able to support other scholars as Charles Capper, Leah Hagedorn, Joy Kasson, Suzanne Lebsock, Michael O'Brien, Penny Richards, Jonathan Sarna, and the phenomenal Peter Walker have supported me. Don Mathews midwifed my Mordecai dissertation at the

University of North Carolina at Chapel Hill and affirmed my ambition to write a story full of the human drama that comes with faith, hope, and love. His grace touched me and my understanding of the Mordecais at many, many turns.

Archivists and librarians, some of whom I have called on repeatedly for assistance and clarification, supplied access to the tiny threads that eventually became the fabric of this story. For their patience and professionalism I owe particularly large debts to John White and the staff of the Southern Historical Collection; Jane Morris and Eleanor Mills of the Duke University Rare Books, Manuscript, and Special Collections Library; Eileen Parris of the Virginia Historical Society; Pen Bogert of the Filson Historical Society; and Kevin Proffitt of the Jacob Rader Marcus Center of the American Jewish Archives. Special thanks to Tom Owen, who secured privileges for me at a full research library, thus opening up a world of critical secondary materials.

My obsession with the Mordecais was validated and my heart touched when Clara Bingham, Molly Bingham, Mary Moss Greenebaum, Anna Hamburger, Molly Reily, Keith Runyon, the Reverend Alfred E. Shands, and Alice Gray Stites—nonhistorians all—read about the Mordecais and inquired, year after year, how my book was coming along.

Were it not for Catherine Clinton's generous mentoring and determination to find a happy home for this manuscript, I might not have met with Thomas LeBien. His editing strikes me as pure art. I could not be more grateful for his commitment to me and the Mordecais. Sincere thanks also to Kristina McGowan, Ingrid Sterner, Abby Kagan, and all those at Hill and Wang and Farrar, Straus and Giroux who helped make *Mordecai*.

While piecing together this tale of three generations of Mordecais—a tale of how creative and affectionate, yet also how devastating family relations can be—I negotiated my own generational transition to marriage and parenthood. Loving thanks to my parents, Edie and Barry Bingham, Jr., for a lifetime of unstinting support and for the confidence they have always placed in me. My beloved and affectionate children, Cason and Henrietta Reily, bring magic and wonder to my days. Debby Hurst's gifted child-care work kept my head clear enough to push this project through to the finish. Finally, no words can thank my husband, Stephen, for his devotion, year in, year out. A counselor in perplexity, a blessing in sorrow and joy, he is my boon companion—dearest of the dear—in the creation of another American family, our own, to which *Mordecai* is dedicated.

Emily Bingham
Louisville, Kentucky
November 2002

INDEX

Mordecai, Laura, 116, 119, 182, 185; death of, 192

Mordecai, Margaret, 105

Mordecai, Margaret Cameron, 234, 241, 254, 255

Mordecai, Margaret Lane, 76–78, 99

Mordecai, Moses (elder), 13, 14

Mordecai, Moses (younger), 79, 97, 119, 265; birth of, 19; business ventures of, 29; childhood of, 21, 23, 28; death of, 99–100; legal career of, 34, 41, 42, 75; and marriages of family members, 90, 98–99; and relationships with family members, 76–78, 99; romantic relationships of, 75–76; weddings of, 76–78, 99

Mordecai, Rachel (later Lazarus), 32, 34, 40, 41, 44–45, 47, 52, 53, 79, 81, 84, 85, 103, 110, 113, 118, 120, 123, 178–79, 201, 266; and Alfred, 106; birth of, 20; and Caroline, 89, 90–91; childhood of, 24, 28, 29, 30; children born to, 131, 142, 159–60, 164; Christian involvement of, 132–34, 154–58, 161–62, 164–65, 166–68, 170–72, 174–79, 181–82, 185–86; conversion of, 179–80; death of, 184–88; and death of Jane Dickinson, 157–58; and Eliza, 59–62; and Ellen, 179–80, 185–86; and enlightened domesticity, 140–41; and family solidarity, 57; fear of spinsterhood of, 38; and friendship with Maria Edgeworth, 62–65, 66–69, 143–46; gender consciousness of, 138–40; health problems of, 142, 159–61, 172–74; and Jacob, 37–38, 39, 69, 123, 174, 175–76; Jewish identity of, 147–53, 161, 168, 180–81; and journey north with Aaron, 165, 166–68; and Lucy Ann Lippitt, 154–57; and Marx, 226, 228–29; and Marx's education, 169–70; and marriages by family members, 77, 78, 89, 90; mar-

ried life of, 127–29, 130; mental cultivation of, 34, 141–42, 164–65; and Moses, 77; and Mordecai school, 36, 37–39, 42, 43, 60, 71; as mother, 137–43, 226; pedagogy of, 58–63, 129, 137–42, 143, 171, 173–74, 179; pregnancy-related depression of, 159–60, 163; relations with stepchildren of, 129–30, 135, 163–64; and Samuel, 33; and slave management, 130–31; on slavery, 107; stoicism of, 55–56; wedding of 90–93

Mordecai, Rebecca Myers (Becky), 23, 61, 66, 69, 78, 84, 112, 115, 116, 149, 166, 174, 176, 193, 195, 200, 265; children born to, 29, 39, 59; and Civil War, 245, 250–51, 252–53; death of, 253–54; and Mordecai school, 39–40; and relationships with family members, 29, 31–32, 85, 191, 250–51; wedding of, 29

Mordecai, Rosina Young, 119, 255, 256, 258

Mordecai, Sally Maynadier, 261

Mordecai, Samuel, 30, 40, 41, 45, 47, 48, 52, 60, 63, 64, 67, 68, 70, 71, 76, 80, 107, 110, 112, 119, 120, 121, 147, 168, 172, 173, 179, 182, 183, 197, 202, 203, 207, 217, 236, 260, 266; birth of, 19; business ventures of, 29, 52–53, 83, 86, 122; Cádiz adventure of, 52–53; childhood of, 23, 24, 28; and Civil War, 243, 248, 253, 254, 257; death of, 257–58; and deaths of family members, 185, 186; financial ruin of, 86, 109; Jewish identity of, 31; and marriages of family members, 88, 91, 234; military career of, 54; Mobile visit of, 104; and Mordecai school, 42; politics of, 108; and relationships with family members, 33, 122, 123, 191; and religious conflict within family, 194; romantic relationships of, 122–23; on slavery, 241; and work for Samy Myers, 29, 30, 51–52